Rick Steves®

ICELAND

Rick Steves & Ian Watson
with Cameron Hewitt

D0041848

CONTENTS

Welcome to Rick Steves' Europe

Travel is intensified living—maximum thrills per minute and one of the last great sources of legal adventure. Travel is freedom. It's recess, and we need it.

I discovered a passion for European travel as a teen and have been sharing it ever since—through tours, my public television and radio shows, and travel guidebooks. Over the years, I've taught thousands of travelers how to best enjoy Europe's blockbuster sights—and experience "Back Door" discoveries that most tourists miss.

This book offers a balanced mix of Iceland's glaciers, volcanoes, spectacular scenery, and fjordside villages. And it's selective—rather than listing dozens of thermal swimming pools, I recommend only the best ones. My self-guided drives, town walks, and museum tours give insight into the country's unique geology, vibrant history, and today's living, breathing culture.

I advocate traveling simply and smartly. Take advantage of my money- and time-saving tips on sightseeing, transportation, and more. Try local, characteristic alternatives to expensive hotels and restaurants. In many ways, spending more money only builds a thicker wall between you and what you traveled so far to see.

We visit Iceland to experience it—to become temporary locals. Thoughtful travel engages us with the world, as we learn to appreciate other cultures and new ways to measure quality of life.

Judging from the positive feedback I receive from readers, this book will help you enjoy a fun, affordable, and rewarding vacation—whether it's your first trip or your tenth.

Góða ferð! Happy travels!

ICELAND

Iceland, the land of the midnight sun and the northern lights, is equally famous for its magnificent glaciers and its active volcanoes. Magma bubbling up between tectonic plates formed this rugged island, leaving it stranded halfway between North America and Europe. Until recently a poor, backward corner of Scandinavia, today it's one of Europe's most expensive countries. Over the last few years, Iceland has vaulted from obscurity to become one of the planet's trendiest places—a can't-miss destination for curious travelers.

With its stunning natural wonders, kind and gregarious people, and unique attractions, this little island stubbornly exceeds the lofty expectations of its many visitors. Most people's single biggest regret after visiting Iceland? That they tried to squeeze it into just a day or two, instead of investing the time to see more of its striking landscape.

Iceland floats alone where the North Atlantic and Arctic oceans meet, just a smidge below the Arctic Circle. Its closest neighbors are Greenland, to the west, and the Faroe Islands, to the southeast. The remote island was uninhabited until the ninth century, when, at the height of the Viking Age, it was settled by farmers looking for a good place to graze their sheep. It remained a land of isolated farms for about a millennium. Up until the late 1800s, Iceland had very few towns aside from Reykjavík. If you stay in the countryside today, you can get close to the agrarian Iceland

Fields of lupine in Iceland's south-east corner; a monster truck gets you into the interior Highlands.

that existed for centuries. Some farms have a storied history, going back hundreds of years.

Social movements that sparked upheaval elsewhere—Christianization, Reformation, independence—arrived in Iceland with strangely little fuss. The country's Viking Age roots and its historic connections to Norway and Denmark give it an unmistakably Nordic aura, while the long-time presence of an American naval base developed Iceland's affinity for all things Yankee. Today, Iceland feels like it has one foot in Europe, and the other in America.

About 830 miles across, Iceland is roughly the size of Maine and smaller than the island of Great Britain. More than half of the country is uninhabited tundra (in the interior Highlands). Almost all of its 340,000 residents live near the coastline, and two-thirds of Icelanders reside in the capital region of Reykjavík, on the southwest coast.

For the traveler, Reykjavík is the natural jumping-off point for exploring Iceland's dramatic countryside. It's an easy hop from Reykjavík to the inland Golden Circle route, studded with natural and historic attractions (from geysers to thundering waterfalls), or south to the famous Blue Lagoon thermal baths (on the Reykjanes Peninsula, near

The Land of Fire and Ice

The country's name is "Ice-land," but that's only part of the story. This little island features a stunning diversity of landscapes—from frigid glaciers to boiling geysers, and from towering mountains to dreamy fjords. That's why, for most visitors, Iceland's raw, awe-inspiring nature is its biggest draw.

Iceland, which plugs the gap between the North American and Eurasian tectonic plates, was formed long ago by **volcanoes** (*eldfjöll,* "fire mountains")—and regular eruptions continue. The best known include those at Surtsey (1963), which added a new island off Iceland's South Coast, and on Heimaey (1973), which increased the size of that little island by a square mile. In 2010, the infamous Eyjafjallajökull volcano blew a column of ash four miles into the atmosphere that drifted east to Europe, halting air travel.

Odds are you won't witness an eruption during your visit; Iceland weathers about one every five years. Even so, it's impossible to come to Iceland without experiencing its volcanic landscapes: Keflavík Airport sits on a petrified lava flow. Things just get more interesting from there, from trapped-in-time sheets of lava, to giant burst bubbles of molten rock, to craters holding vibrantly colored (and still steaming) lakes.

Evidence of Iceland's powerful natural forces: exploding geysers, gushing magma, and volcanic craters.

Iceland's highest volcanic peaks are capped by **glaciers** (*jöklar,* singular *jökull*)—frozen seas of ice, flowing at a rate of a few feet each day. About 11 percent of the country is covered by glaciers, mostly along the South Coast and in the unpopulated Highlands in the island's center. At Sólheimajökull, you ▶▶▶

▶▶▶ can walk up and touch a glacier; at Jökulsárlón and Fjallsárlón, you can ride a boat on a glacier lagoon, circling bobbing icebergs calved off from an icy tongue; at various places, you can hike or snowmobile across the top of a glacier, or enter an ice cave within one.

After nearly 1,200 years of taming their volatile island, Icelanders have harnessed geothermal energy in ways both practical (to heat their homes and generate electricity) and hedonistic. To literally immerse yourself in Iceland's volcanic landscape, visit one (or, better yet, several) of its naturally occurring **thermal baths.** Free hot springs and pools dot the island, attracting Icelanders year-round. Some are easy to reach by car, while others require a bit of a hike—but your reward is a long soak in toasty water surrounded by an incredible landscape. For a less rugged experience, visit a municipal swimming pool—with water naturally heated to around 100°F—or go to one of Iceland's well-advertised premium baths (such as the Blue Lagoon).

Iceland's landscape is dramatic, but there are many ways to make it accessible. The Icelandic Experiences chapter is designed to inspire you with ways you can connect to Icelandic nature, then point you to the details elsewhere in this book. Enjoy! ▮

Hike to a glacier's edge; visit a geothermal plant; soak in a thermal bath.

Keflavík Airport). Two hours away, the South Coast offers glaciers, black sand beaches, and a jagged volcanic landscape. And an hour's drive north of Reykjavík is West Iceland, with Settlement Age history and a volcanic tube cave.

But the ultimate Icelandic thrill is an 800-mile road trip, circling the entire island on the Ring Road (highway 1). Give the Ring Road enough time, and it'll give you charming waterfront towns (Borgarnes, Siglufjörður, Húsavík, and Seyðisfjörður), a pint-sized second city (Akureyri), simmering volcanic landscapes (near Mývatn), jagged fjords (the Eastfjords), and glaciers and glacier lagoons (on the southeast coast).

Iceland has a rich folklore and a strong connection between its heritage and its landscape. It seems every rock has a thousand-year-old name and a legend to go with it. With cinematic scenery and abundant opportunities to experience nature in its rawest form, Iceland thrills outdoorsy travelers. Snowmobile across a glacier. Zip over the waves on a rigid inflatable boat while scanning the horizon for breaching whales or breeding puffins. Go for a ride on an Icelandic horse, hoping to feel the rhythm of its elusive "fifth gait." Scuba or snorkel in a tectonic rift flooded with crystal-clear glacial water. Hike from hut to hut, tracing the path of lava from a (currently) dormant volcano.

For a quintessentially Icelandic experience, be sure to soak in one of the country's spring-fed thermal baths. The

Little churches and little horses dot the landscape.

*Midnight sun in Reykjavík;
Iceland's creative food scene.*

spa-like Blue Lagoon—with milky blue water filling a
volcanic reservoir—is the most famous (and most expensive).
But every village has its own municipal swimming pool filled
with piping-hot water. Those who love the out-of-doors
can find free and hidden opportunities for an al fresco soak
throughout the countryside.

Iceland's natural splendors are what attract most visitors, but Icelanders are also worth getting to know. They
have a gentle spirit and a can-do frontier attitude. They're
also whip-smart (Icelandic scholars were the first to write
down the legends and histories of the early Scandinavian
peoples—collectively called the "sagas"). Enjoy meeting the
easygoing Icelanders; in this little country, everyone's on a
first-name basis.

Two often-repeated Icelandic phrases offer insight into
the local psyche: *kærulaus* (loosely, "careless") describes the
flexible, improvisational, sometimes inconsiderate way Icelanders move through life. And an Icelander facing an unexpected challenge might mutter, *"Þetta reddast"* ("It'll work
out")...and in this mellow land, it usually does (with some
major exceptions, like Iceland's economic crash in 2008).

Iceland has a rich cuisine scene. Trendy restaurants are
enthusiastically organic—literally wallpapered with fish skin
and serving gourmet delights on slabs of rock or rustic little

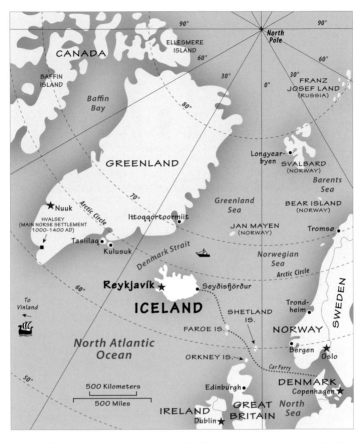

planks. There are few places with fresher seafood—haddock, cod, arctic char, halibut, the controversial minke whale, and the delectable *humar* (langoustine). The rolling, green countryside teems with free-range sheep grazing on grass that seasons a tender and delicious meat. Soup is an Icelandic staple, and every grandma has her own secret recipe for *kjötsúpa* (lamb soup). And Icelandic *skyr*—a yogurt-like, dairy food that's been around since Viking times—is newly trendy in American groceries.

Iceland is also famous for its notorious "hardship foods": an entire boiled sheep's head *(svið),* jerky-like dried cod snacks *(harðfiskur),* and the notorious *hákarl*—gelatinous, unbelievably pungent fermented shark. Locals scarcely eat these anymore, of course, but tourists do...usually on a dare.

Summer or winter, be prepared to bundle up (pack gloves, sturdy boots, and a waterproof jacket). While conditions overall are surprisingly moderate for the latitude, frosty temperatures and bone-chilling wind can happen at any time of year. Icelanders use the term *gluggaveður* ("window weather") to describe weather that's pleasant to look at—from indoors. Blustery days arrive frequently, especially in winter, when strong low-pressure systems roll in regularly, whipping high winds across the whole island. It's not just a little unpleasant to be outside in high winds—you may literally not be able to walk, or open your car door.

Typically, two or three days of cloudy, drizzly skies alternate with two or three days of relatively sunny weather. The cloudy periods lengthen in winter, the sunny periods in summer. It rains often in Reykjavík, but pouring rain is infrequent. Lightning is rare enough to make the evening news.

On the plus side, Iceland is mosquito-free. No one knows exactly why, since the little buggers thrive quite happily in neighboring Greenland. Swarming midges vex visitors to lake Mývatn, but at least they don't bite.

Few places—especially one so remote and cold—have become so popular, so quickly. But Iceland's striking glaciers, craggy peaks, and steamy geysers make this destination increasingly attractive to the inquisitive and the adventurous. Whether or not you can pronounce the names on its map, Iceland is a rewarding place to travel.

Iceland's Top Destinations

There's so much to see in Iceland, and so little time. This overview breaks the country's top destinations into must-see sights (to help first-time travelers plan their trip) and worth-it sights (for those with additional time). I've also suggested a minimum number of days to allow per destination.

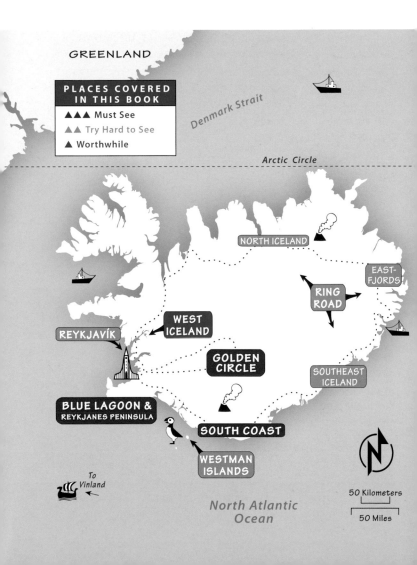

GREENLAND

PLACES COVERED IN THIS BOOK
▲▲▲ Must See
▲▲ Try Hard to See
▲ Worthwhile

Denmark Strait

Arctic Circle

NORTH ICELAND

EAST-FJORDS

RING ROAD

WEST ICELAND

REYKJAVÍK

GOLDEN CIRCLE

SOUTHEAST ICELAND

BLUE LAGOON & REYKJANES PENINSULA

SOUTH COAST

WESTMAN ISLANDS

To Vinland

North Atlantic Ocean

50 Kilometers
50 Miles

MUST-SEE DESTINATIONS

Iceland's capital, Reykjavík, is the natural hub for any visit, with an excellent assortment of accommodations, restaurants, shops, and nightlife. But, while Reykjavík easily has enough sights of its own to fill a day or two, with limited time, I'd spend my evenings in Reykjavík and my days in the countryside—at these top choices:

▲▲▲ Golden Circle (1 day)

Iceland's quintessential day trip is deservedly popular. You'll loop through eye-popping terrain, with stops at Þingvellir (site of Iceland's Viking Age gatherings, situated along a jagged tectonic fissure); Geysir (a steamy field that's home to the world's original "geyser"); and Gullfoss (a thundering waterfall). Along the way, you can tiptoe around the rim of a volcanic crater, visit Iceland's medieval religious center, and take your pick of thermal bath experiences.

▲▲▲ South Coast (1 day)

This dramatic shoreline, shaped by volcanoes and glaciers, rivals the Golden Circle as Reykjavík's top day trip. You'll see spectacular waterfalls tumble over high cliffs, touch the tongue of a glacier, stroll along a black sand beach, and learn about the majestic power of volcanoes. Nearby, avid hikers can make the Þórsmörk nature reserve (nestled between three glaciers) a ▲▲ full day on its own.

▲▲▲ Blue Lagoon (half-day)

This top-end thermal bathing complex, nestled in a volcanic landscape a 45-minute drive south of Reykjavík (and near Keflavík Airport), is relaxing and memorable, and a delightful toe-in-the-water dip into Iceland's thermal bathing culture.

Top and left: Þingvellir and Geysir, on the Golden Circle; above: Þórsmörk, on the South Coast; below: Blue Lagoon

WORTH-IT DESTINATIONS

On a longer visit, these stops—rated ▲ or ▲▲— deserve consideration. All are within easy day-tripping distance of Reykjavík—except the Ring Road, which demands several days.

▲▲ Reykjavík (1-2 days)

An ideal home base for a visit of any length, Reykjavík is a worthwhile sightseeing destination in its own right. Its colorful, pedestrian-friendly downtown has fine museums, a stroll-worthy harbor, and a dozen thermal swimming pools, perfect for a rejuvenating soak among Icelanders. The capital's restaurants are surprisingly good, and its nightlife scene is legendary.

▲▲ Westman Islands (1 day)

While challenging to reach (by weather-dependent boat or flight), this little chain of 15 islands merits the effort. On Heimaey (the only inhabited island), you'll find towering seabird cliffs and the world's largest puffin colony (in summer), an aquarium with a resident puffin, a busy harbor, and two volcanoes (plus an excellent volcano museum).

▲▲ Ring Road (5-10 days)

To really delve into Iceland, circle the island's perimeter on highway 1. It's a demanding drive (the entire circuit is 800 miles), but the scenic payoff is huge: breathtaking waterfalls and fjords, majestic mountains, volcanic cones and craters, otherworldly lava formations, rich birdlife, geothermal springs and geysers, glaciers, black sand beaches, and windswept coastlines. Let the Ring Road tempt you into extending your visit, off the beaten path.

Above: Colorful, quirky Reykjavík; *right:*
enjoy the cuisine scene; *below:* harbor in the
Westman Islands; *bottom:* lunar landscape
near Mývatn, on the Ring Road

▲ West Iceland (1 day)

West Iceland's subtle charms include the dramatically set town of Borgarnes (with a fine exhibition on the Icelandic sagas), the hikable Grábrók volcanic crater, lovely waterfalls, the country's most prolific hot springs, a traditional goat farm, an important religious site, and the chance to walk through an underground lava tube.

*Left and above: Mini icebergs at Jökulsárlón and a boat ride in Fjallsárlón—glacier lagoons on the southeast coast; **below:** exploring a lava tube in West Iceland*

Planning Your Trip

To plan your trip, you'll need to design your itinerary—choosing where and when to go, how you'll travel, and how many days to spend at each destination. For my best advice on sightseeing, accommodations, restaurants, and transportation, see the Practicalities chapter.

DESIGNING AN ITINERARY

As you read this book and learn your options...

Choose your top destinations.

My recommended itineraries in this chapter give you an idea of how to spend your time in Iceland—whether you've got one day or ten. Most visitors focus on the great outdoors: volcanic landscapes, waterfalls, thermal springs, and so on. Reykjavík is the natural home base, and on a very short visit, you can simply overnight there, spending your days side-tripping to attractions near the city (see the Near Reykjavík chapter for advice). Decide early on which special activities you may want to reserve beforehand—such as glacier hikes, volcano tours, or the Blue Lagoon.

Decide when to go.

Your Icelandic experience will vary drastically depending on the time of year in which you visit.

From June through August, summer days in Iceland are long and the weather is at its best. At these northern latitudes, from about June 1 to July 15, the sun only technically sets (staying just below the horizon for only a few hours),

Iceland's Best Short Trips by Car

Iceland rewards a visit of any length. I've outlined two basic itineraries here: a whirlwind 24-hour visit and a more relaxed five-day stay (both can be modified for longer visits). For my suggested Ring Road itineraries, see the next page and the Ring Road chapter. For any itinerary, consider these factors:

Time of Year: My itineraries assume you'll visit in summer, when daylight is virtually endless and roads are clear. In the off-season, you'll want to stay closer to the capital.

Blue Lagoon Scheduling: The Blue Lagoon is located between Reykjavík and Keflavík Airport, so it's easy to combine a soak with your flight. These plans assume you'll arrive in the morning and stop at the Blue Lagoon on your way into town. But it works equally well to visit the Blue Lagoon on your departure day (if you have a late flight). Whenever you go, reserve the Blue Lagoon in advance.

Westman Islands Weather: Connections by air and sea to the Westman Islands are weather-dependent, so have a Plan B ready. If you're home-basing on the South Coast and your island trip is cancelled, do the Golden Circle as a side-trip, or spend more time in Reykjavík. Don't schedule a return from the islands the day before an onward flight from Iceland; give yourself at least a two-night buffer.

Without a Car? Base in Reykjavík and book day-trip excursions to the Golden Circle, South Coast, Blue Lagoon, Westman Islands (by plane from Reykjavík), or Þórsmörk. It's also possible to fly from Reykjavík to Akureyri, a hub for tours in the north (Mývatn, Siglufjörður, whale watching).

Iceland in 24 Hours

If one day is all you have in Iceland, here's how to pack it all in.

Morning:	Arrive, pick up car, head straight to Blue Lagoon and soak.
Midday:	Drive into Reykjavík for lunch and a few hours of browsing, then check into your hotel.
Afternoon:	Set out for Golden Circle loop trip—hitting just the highlights.
Evening:	Dinner in Golden Circle country.
Late:	Collapse at your hotel and sleep for a few hours. Fly out the next morning.

With 48 hours: Add a day trip to the South Coast.
With 72 hours: Spend more time exploring Reykjavík.

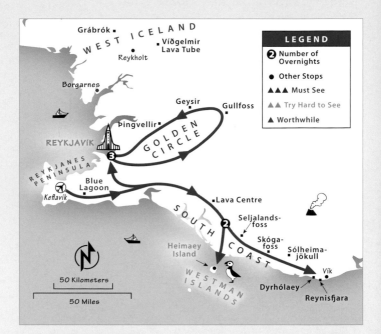

Iceland in 5 Days

Day	Plan	Sleep in
1	Arrive, pick up car, go to Blue Lagoon, then head to South Coast	South Coast
2	Westman Islands day trip	South Coast
3	South Coast sights, to Reykjavík	Reykjavík
4	Golden Circle	Reykjavík
5	Reykjavík (or excursions: whale watching, horseback riding, glacier hikes)	Reykjavík
6	Fly out	

With 4 days: Spend less time in Reykjavík—see it in the two evenings, and on your morning of departure.

With 6 days: See the South Coast on Day 2, then overnight on the Westman Islands (Day 3) before heading to Reykjavík.

7 days: Add another day in Reykjavík (and/or more excursions).

8 days: Day-trip from Reykjavík to West Iceland. With more time, see my 10-day itinerary on the next page.

Iceland's Best 10-Day Road Trip

With enough time, it's possible to see Reykjavík, drive the entire Ring Road route, including the South Coast, side-trip to the Westman Islands, and hit the Golden Circle highlights. The 10-day itinerary outlined here assumes you've rented a car (or campervan) and sets a fast pace, with several long driving days (and one-night stands) in a row. The more time you can devote to the Ring, the more relaxed and rewarding your circuit will be.

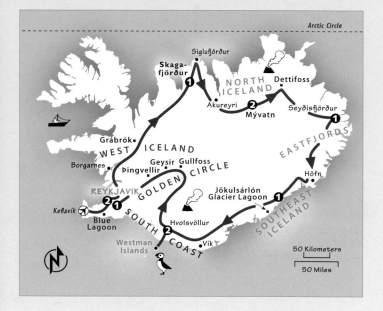

but it never really gets dark. Icelanders take full advantage of these days of "midnight sun," and so should you. July and early August usually bring a few T-shirt days, with temperatures climbing into the 60s and even breaking 70. At this time of year, Iceland can be crowded and more expensive... but it's worth it.

May and September can be a decent compromise in terms of crowds and weather. May is chilly but bright, with the solstice nearing. September brings subtle fall colors to the fields and hillsides, and as evenings darken, the first glimpses of the northern lights. Keep in mind that as late as April or as early as October, snow and extreme weather can disrupt your plans, particularly on higher-elevation roads.

Winter days (mid-Oct to mid-Feb) are short—

Day	Plan	Sleep in
1	Arrive, pick up car, go to Blue Lagoon on the way into Reykjavík	Reykjavík
2	Reykjavík	Reykjavík
3	Begin Ring Road: To Borgarnes, then Skagafjörður	Skagafjörður area
4	Drive the Tröllaskagi Peninsula (stopping in Siglufjörður and Akureyri), evening to Mývatn lake area	Mývatn
5	Mývatn area and Húsavík port town	Mývatn
6	To the Eastfjords (and Dettifoss falls)	Seyðisfjörður
7	Drive the Eastfjords to the southeast (Vatnajökull area)	Höfn, Jökulsárlón, or Skaftafell area
8	South Coast sights	South Coast
9	Westman Islands day trip	South Coast
10	Golden Circle highlights en route to Reykjavík	Reykjavík
11	Drop car and fly out	

With 9 days: Spend only one night in Mývatn (and skip Húsavík).
With 11 days: Add a day in Reykjavík, or overnight in Akureyri.
12 days: Add another day in Reykjavík, and sleep in Akureyri.
13-14 days: Add your choice of excursions (Þórsmörk or Skaftafell hikes, glacier visits, volcano cave tour, whale watching)—and an overnight location to match (either in Reykjavík or on the Ring).

the sun rises after 11:00 all December—and dusk will draw the shades on your sightseeing well before dinner. You can still enjoy a stopover in Reykjavík, though. Christmastime activities (with downtown decorated for shoppers, and bonfires and fireworks on New Year's Eve) offer a warm experience at a frosty time of year. In these months, bus trips to the nearby Golden Circle and South Coast are typically still possible (and leave winter driving to the pros). Driving the Ring Road in winter is inadvisable at best, and impossible at worst.

One benefit of a winter visit is the chance to view the elusive northern lights, though whether you'll actually see them is unpredictable. Weather, location, and luck all play a part (for more on the northern lights, see page 52).

Connect the dots.

Many people drop into Iceland on the way to or from Europe; both Icelandair and the low-cost Wow Air typically allow a layover of up to several days for only a small charge.

Decide if you'll be traveling by car or relying on excursions, or a combination. A car or campervan rental is expensive, but offers maximum flexibility for side-tripping and exploring the countryside (for more on car and campervan rentals, see the Practicalities chapter). Excursion trips make the island accessible to nondrivers, but are pricey, too—skipping the car rental doesn't necessarily save a lot of money.

To determine approximate driving times between destinations, study the driving chart in the Practicalities chapter. Major roads are fairly good, but back roads often have unpaved stretches. Be sure to tune into the peculiarities of Icelandic driving, including how to traverse city roundabouts and one-lane bridges (for Icelandic driving tips, see page 413). Google Maps can help you navigate throughout most of Iceland, but even it has blind spots—be ready to supplement with printed maps if you'll be leaving well-traveled areas.

Write out a day-by-day itinerary.

Figure out how many destinations you can comfortably fit in your time frame. If you're energetic, you can take advantage of long summer days to cram in the maximum.

When planning your trip, give yourself enough time, and don't spend it all in Reykjavík. On a short visit, make Reykjavík your base, then devote your days to the nearby Golden Circle or the South Coast. In summer you'll still have hours of evening sunlight by which to enjoy Reykjavík even after side-tripping (for more on day trips, see the Near Reykjavík chapter).

Decide whether you'll do everything as side trips from Reykjavík or divide your trip into multiple overnights (sleeping on the South Coast mixes in a little variety, and overlaps conveniently with the Golden Circle and Westman Islands). The Ring Road is a long, one-way trip...plan on lots of one-night stays. (To break it up, consider lingering in Mývatn in the north, or in the southeast.)

Check if any holidays or festivals fall during your trip—these attract crowds and can close sights (for the latest, visit www.visiticeland.com). If traveling off-season (Sept-May), be aware of potential weather-related road closures. Many sights and services in the countryside may be closed, and those in Reykjavík have reduced hours.

Give yourself some slack. Every trip—and every traveler—needs downtime for doing laundry, picnic shopping, people-watching, and so on. Pace yourself.

Horns or not—you'll want a warm hat; Icelanders are easygoing and creative.

Above: A two-wheel-drive car is just right for the Ring Road in summer; *right:* Budget accommodations can help your bottom line; *below:* Join an excursion for special activities like a glacier walk; *bottom:* Take advantage of short-hop flights to the Westman Islands or Akureyri.

Trip Costs Per Person

Run a reality check on your dream trip. You'll have major transportation costs in addition to daily expenses.

Flight: A round-trip flight from the US to Iceland's Keflavík Airport costs about $500-2,000, depending on where you fly from and when.

Local Transportation: For a six-day trip using excursion buses and one intra-Iceland flight, allow $800 per person.

Car Rental: Allow roughly $350 per week (more for four-wheel drive), not including tolls, gas, parking, and insurance.

AVERAGE DAILY EXPENSES PER PERSON

$250
Applies to Reykjavík, about 10% less in the countryside

Lodging
Based on two people splitting the cost of a $250 double room.
★★★★★ **$125**

Meals
$25 for lunch, and $50 for dinner
$75

Sights and Entertainment
This daily average works for most people.
$50

Budget Tips

Iceland is one of Europe's most expensive destinations. Here are some strategies for keeping costs down.

Consider Airbnb. Airbnb and similar sites rent properties that are typically far cheaper than hotels. And if you're willing to forego hotel services (like a reception desk and daily cleaning), you'll get more space and amenities for your money. Airbnb can also get you into more local neighborhoods; sleeping in a Reykjavík suburban home is both cheaper and more Icelandic than a touristy downtown hotel.

"Go" down the hall. Iceland's characteristic guesthouses typically offer basic rooms with a shared bathroom, which cost much less than rooms with en-suite bathrooms.

Have a big lunch and a small dinner. Even the fanciest ▶▶▶

▶▶▶ restaurants offer excellent-value lunch specials in the $25 range. Enjoy a high-end, sit-down meal for lunch, then picnic or grab cheap takeout for dinner.

Picnic. Cultivate the art of picnicking in atmospheric settings. Seek out Iceland's discount supermarket chains—Krónan and Bónus—and use them to stock up. Consider bringing a few staples from home: In a place where a basic takeaway coffee costs $5 a cup, packing some single-serving instant coffee lets you caffeinate cheaply.

Know what's included. Icelandic restaurants happily provide diners with a free carafe of tap water—just ask. Don't feel obligated to purchase a drink. If you've paid for unlimited soup and bread, don't be shy about going back for seconds. And if someone offers you free coffee, take it! Since Iceland has no tipping culture and taxes are included, you'll pay exactly the price you see on the menu.

Economize on alcohol. Alcohol is priced at a premium, particularly in bars and restaurants. Stock up at the airport duty-free store on arrival—with the lowest prices in Iceland—or at government-run liquor stores (called Vínbúðin). If you're going to a bar, go during happy hour.

Skip the Blue Lagoon. While famous and a highlight for many visitors, the Blue Lagoon costs ten times as much as Iceland's many thermal swimming pools...which are also a more authentic experience. Reykjavík alone has more than a dozen municipal pools with water just as hot as the Blue Lagoon's. If visiting several pools, invest in a shareable multi-visit card.

Sightsee selectively. Icelandic museums are typically very good...but expensive ($15-20). If you'll be sightseeing a lot in the capital, consider a Reykjavík City Card. Fortunately, many of Iceland's best attractions—its natural wonders—are free.

Splurge where it counts. When you do splurge, choose an experience you'll always remember: If you're a naturalist, invest in a whale-watching tour; if you like to eat, take a culinary walk or dine out at one top-end restaurant; if you're an adventurer, spelunk through a lava cave or hike across a glacier. Minimize souvenir shopping—most shops sell things that are extremely expensive, produced outside Iceland, or both. (Plus, how will you get it all home?) Focus instead on collecting wonderful memories. ▪

BEFORE YOU GO

You'll have a smoother trip if you tackle a few things ahead of time. For more information on these topics, see the Practicalities chapter (and www.ricksteves.com, which has helpful travel talks).

Make sure your passport is valid. If it's due to expire within six months of your ticketed date of return, you need to renew it. Allow up to six weeks to renew or get a passport (www.travel.state.gov).

Arrange your transportation. Book your international flights. If you're planning on renting a car or campervan, do it in advance, and read up on the unique hazards of driving in Iceland.

Book rooms well in advance, especially if your trip falls during peak season (June-Aug, and to a lesser degree May and Sept) or any major holidays or festivals. It's essential to book ahead on the Ring Road at Mývatn and in the southeast.

Book ahead for the Blue Lagoon, which requires reservations (best made at least several days in advance). With the exception of specialized experiences like ice caving or glacier hiking, other excursions can usually be booked a day or two beforehand.

Consider travel insurance. Compare the cost of the insurance to the cost of your potential loss. Check whether your existing insurance (health, homeowners, or renters) covers you and your possessions overseas.

Call your bank. Alert your bank that you'll be using your debit and credit cards in Europe. Ask about transaction fees, and get the PIN number for your credit card. You don't need to bring *króna* for your trip.

Use your smartphone smartly. Sign up for an international service plan to reduce your costs, or rely on Wi-Fi in Iceland instead. Download any apps (or bookmark websites) you'll want to access on the road, such as maps, translations, road conditions, and weather forecasts.

Pack light. I travel for weeks with a single carry-on bag and a daypack. Use the packing checklist in the Appendix so you're sure to include a few important extras for Iceland (such as a small towel for thermal pools; sunglasses for driving with the sun low in the sky; and, in summer, an eye mask to help you sleep when it stays light out). Pack an insect head net if you plan to visit Mývatn (known for its beauty—and its midges). In winter, consider strap-on ice cleats if you plan to do much outdoor walking.

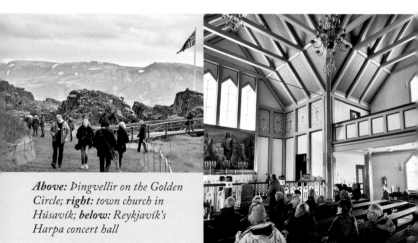

Above: Þingvellir on the Golden Circle; right: town church in Húsavík; below: Reykjavík's Harpa concert hall

Travel Smart

Iceland is famously spectacular, and it's hard to have a bad time here. But it's easy to underestimate the changeable weather, blow through too much money, or waste time by not making a good plan. If you equip yourself with good information (this book) and expect to travel smart, you will.

Read—and reread—this book. To have an "A" trip, be an "A" student. Note opening hours of sights, closed days, crowd-beating tips, and whether reservations are required or advisable. Check the latest at www.ricksteves.com/update.

Be your own tour guide. As you travel, get up-to-date info on sights, reserve tickets and tours, reconfirm hotels and travel arrangements, and check weather forecasts. Upon arrival in a new town, lay the groundwork for a smooth departure; confirm the road conditions and route to your next destination.

Outsmart thieves. While theft is rare in Iceland, some pickpockets are arriving with the tourist crowds. Keep your backup credit cards, passport, and big bills secure in a money belt tucked under your clothes; carry one credit card and a little cash in a wallet in your front pocket. Don't set valuable items down on counters or café tabletops, where they can be quickly stolen or easily forgotten.

Minimize potential loss. Keep expensive gear to a minimum. Bring photocopies or take photos of important documents (passport and cards) to aid in replacement if they're lost or stolen.

Be budget-conscious. Fully experiencing Iceland is worth paying a lot for...but it's not necessary to break the bank. Smart, organized travelers can avoid overpaying. For suggestions, read and heed my "Budget Tips," earlier.

Be flexible. Even with a well-planned itinerary, expect changes, closures, howling winds, sore feet, and so on. Your Plan B could turn out to be even better.

Attempt the language. Most Icelanders—especially in the tourist trade—speak English. But if you learn even just a few Icelandic phrases, you'll get more smiles and make more friends (see the Survival Phrases near the end of this book).

Connect with the culture. Interacting with locals carbonates your experience. Enjoy the friendliness of the Icelandic people. Ask questions; most locals are happy to point you in their idea of the right direction. Set up your own quest for the best fish-of-the-day, volcanic crater, thermal swimming pool, or mountain pass. When an opportunity pops up, make it a habit to say "yes."

Iceland...here you come!

ICELANDIC EXPERIENCES

Gazing into a volcanic crater lake, leaping across a tectonic fissure in the earth's crust, or following a track across a lava field are among the experiences you can have in Iceland. Not to mention descending into the underground magma chamber of an extinct volcano, or boiling an egg in the ashes of a new one. Explore waterfalls, glaciers, geysers, rivers, fjords, and cliffs. The surrounding ocean teems with giant whales and adorable puffins. Or you could luxuriate in an outdoor bath filled with earth-warmed water.

Iceland is a small land that packs in a lot of experiences—and there are things you can do here that you can't do anywhere else (not easily, at least). This chapter is a rundown of some of the quintessential Icelandic experiences, designed to inspire your trip planning and point you to more thorough coverage elsewhere in this book.

Even with a car—and especially without—many of these experiences require going through a tour operator. I've listed some established outfits. But the scene changes frequently, so check online to see if newer variations on these experiences now exist (for instance, the "Things to Do" reviews on TripAdvisor can offer a helpful roundup).

A good one-stop resource is Guide to Iceland, a for-profit consolidator of travel providers that works in partnership with the Reykjavík TI. Guide to Iceland has a desk in Reykjavík's City Hall that can explain the offerings of many different companies—allowing you to comparison-shop easily in person—or you can search their website (www.guidetoiceland.is), which also hosts many evocative blogs. They charge no additional commission and will match a better price if you find one. They work with some, but not all, tour providers in Iceland, so it's smart to also do your own research.

Note that while Reykjavík is usually a good home base, many

The Many Ways Iceland Can Kill You

Several times a year, Iceland is captivated by a full-scale land and helicopter search for travelers sucked out to sea by a wave, separated from their snowmobile tour group, or lost in the wilderness. More so than in any other country in Europe, in Iceland nature can threaten your very existence.

To encourage safe travel, Iceland operates the SafeTravel.is website with detailed advice and up-to-the-minute alerts. Their "112 Iceland" app is free; they also staff a desk at the Reykjavík TI (inside City Hall). There's also a national emergency number with help in English—112.

Travel smart and keep the following risks in mind. For specific driving hazards, see page 417.

Wind: The signature feature of Icelandic weather is wind. For Icelanders, good weather means no wind or a light breeze; bad weather means it's blowing hard. Even in summer, you'll likely encounter winds that are uncomfortable or dangerous to walk or drive in. Check the forecast at the Icelandic weather service's web page (http://en.vedur.is). If it's windy and icy at the same time, use extra care.

Falls: In winter, Reykjavík's sidewalks generally aren't cleared or salted, and are very slippery and icy. Falls are common. Paths in the countryside ice over, too. Cautious travelers visiting from December through February can pack a pair of ice cleats to strap over their shoes.

Exposure and Getting Lost: When traveling in less inhabited parts of the country, be prepared for the unexpected. Your car could break down or run out of gas, or you could take a wrong turn. Travel with extra clothing (even summer days can turn cold and windy, especially at higher elevations) and keep your mobile phone charged (reception is good all around the Ring Road). Carry a paper map as a backup. Before heading into wilderness areas, upload your itinerary to SafeTravel.is.

Sneaker Waves: Iceland's South Coast has some very dangerous beaches with strong waves that regularly pull unsuspecting tourists out to sea. The most notorious are two black sand beaches around Dyrhólaey. One of these, called Kirkjufjara, was chained off for good after a drowning in 2017. The other, at Reynisfjara, is still open, and although picturesque and popular with tourists, it's imperative to obey all signs, stay *much* farther from the water

excursions head to destinations quite far away—which means long hours in a bus and higher prices. Staying closer to your objective and booking a tour that originates nearby may be a better option. For example, if you're interested in glacier activities, consider spending a night or two on the South Coast or in Southeast Iceland.

As you join the hordes of international visitors who treat Ice-

than you think is safe, and never turn your back to the ocean.

Trail Hazards: There are very few ropes, guardrails, or warning signs in Iceland—but if you see any, take them seriously. Step carefully, and watch out for loose stones, crevices, and sharp lava rocks.

Scalding Thermal Water: The water in Iceland's geothermally ac-

tive areas can be boiling hot, and the danger is often unmarked. Every year or two a tourist falls in and gets severely burned, typically in a less-visited geothermal area without ropes or walkways. If you value your fingers, don't use them to test the water.

Avalanches: Icelanders have taken this danger more seriously since 1995, when two avalanches in the Westfjords killed 34 people. Wintertime travelers may encounter avalanche warnings in any settled area close to a steep mountain slope.

Volcanoes: On average, a volcano erupts in Iceland every five years. Some eruptions can be viewed from a safe distance, but others melt glaciers, let loose streams of boiling lava, give off poisonous gases, or spew ash and boulders that will damage you or your car. Volcanic eruptions and their consequences can and regularly do interfere with travel plans. A good place to start following along with eruptions (and earthquakes) is the Icelandic weather service's website.

Earthquakes: Minor earthquakes are frequent in Iceland, but catastrophic earthquakes are rare. In the past century, quakes of about six on the Richter scale have hit different parts of the country every decade or two.

Angry Birds: While not life-threatening, angry birds can be a nuisance. In late spring and early summer, Arctic terns *(kríur)* will dive-bomb your head if you get too close to their breeding grounds. Obey any closure signs near major nesting areas.

land as a newly discovered playground, do so considerately. Respect the land. The nature on display may seem raw and powerful, but it's also extremely fragile. Nobody yet knows precisely what long-term impact the recent influx of tourism will have on this special place. To be part of a sustainable long-term prosperity, treat Iceland as a precious treasure...because that's what it is.

ICELANDIC EXPERIENCES

Glaciers

More than one-tenth of Iceland's surface is covered with glaciers *(jökull)*—mainly along the southern coastline and in the desolate interior. The glaciers are most accessible at so-called tongues, where a slow-motion river of ice flows down a valley.

There are several accessible glacier tongues along Iceland's southern coast, from near Skógar in the west to near Höfn in the east. If traveling on your own, you can **hike close to the tongue of a glacier** in two places: at the Skaftafell wilderness area, where you can walk to a branch of Iceland's largest glacier, Vatnajökull (see page 334); or at Sólheimajökull, along the southern coast closer to Reykjavík (page 216).

There are also two **glacier lagoons**—where a glacier tongue terminates in a beautiful pool of water, and icebergs calve off and float around—a few minutes' drive apart in Southeast Iceland: Jökulsárlón and Fjallsárlón. At either, you can pull over for a good look at the lagoon, or pay to board a boat for an up-close trip between bobbing icebergs. Near Jökulsárlón is another enchanting glacial sight, the so-called **Diamond Beach,** where chunks of shimmering ice from the nearby lagoon wash up on a black sand beach. This is a magical look at the final stage of glacial ice's very long, very slow journey to the open ocean. (For more on all three of these sights, see page 337).

For safety's sake, the activities described above are the only glacier-related ones you should attempt on your own. Properly outfitted and with a guide, you have more options.

Several companies offer **glacier walks.** They'll equip you with cold-weather gear, serious crampons, and ice axes, then tie your group together and carefully amble across the ice. The most popular places for this are Sólheimajökull and Skaftafell in Southeast Iceland. The two big tour companies—Reykjavík Excursions and Gray Line—offer this, as do as a variety of smaller, more specialized operators, including Icelandic Mountain Guides (www.mountainguides.is), Arctic Adventures (www.adventures.is), Troll Expeditions (www.trollaferdir.is), Glacier Guides (www.glacierguides.is), Glacier Journey (www.glacierjourney.is), and Extreme Iceland (www.extremeiceland.is).

For a high-speed trip, consider **glacier snowmobiling.** Mountaineers of Iceland, one of the most established outfits, offers a variety of trips across Langjökull (near the Golden Circle), ranging from $250 to $500 (www.mountaineers.is—also offers ATV and Super Jeep tours; or try Glacier Journey). You can even go on a **dogsled trip** across the glacier (consider Extreme Iceland).

Finally, if you're intrigued by all that ice, you can spelunk through an **ice cave** burrowed into a glacier ($200-300, 3-4-hour experience). There are three ice caves you can visit in Iceland. Into the Glacier takes visitors to an artificial cave in Langjökull in West Iceland; it's the only ice cave open year-round (www.intotheglacier. is; see also page 268). The glacier atop the Katla volcano in southern Iceland has a natural cave that's open from June to December—but it's melting quickly, so could close soon (tours depart from Vík; try Katlatrack, www.katlatrack.is). In the winter (Nov-March), Vatnajökull has a natural cave that you can explore with a tour that departs from the Jökulsárlón glacier lagoon (companies include Arctic Adventures, Extreme Iceland, and Glacier Journey; you'll pay more for pick-up in Reykjavík).

If you won't be venturing beyond Reykjavík, the **Museum of Icelandic Natural Wonders** has a simulated ice cave and glacier, and exhibits that focus on Iceland's glacial geology.

Volcanoes

Travelers come to Iceland hoping for a glimpse of a volcano. When the volcano called Eyjafjallajökull spewed ash into the atmosphere in 2010—bringing European air travel to a halt—it grabbed the imagination of many. While you probably won't see any spewing ash or flowing lava while you're here, there are a variety of volcanic sights where you can learn more about the island's unique geology.

VOLCANIC LANDSCAPES

Much of Iceland is plainly shaped by volcanic activity—you won't have to look hard to find lava landscapes. Here are a few of the most dramatic and accessible.

Westman Islands: This archipelago, just off the South Coast, is the most interesting volcano-related sight in Iceland, and a pilgrimage for those with serious interest. The Westman Islands saw some of Iceland's most spectacular volcanic activity in recent times. First, from 1963 to 1967, the islet of Surtsey literally rose from the Atlantic Ocean; while it can't be visited, on a clear day you can see the islet from the main island, Heimaey. Then, in 1973, the town of Vestmannaeyjar was rudely awoken in the middle of the night by a surprise eruption on the adjacent hillside. The locals were evacuated, and the eastern part of the town was gradually swallowed by flowing lava. Today, streets dead-end at steep walls of volcanic rock, and a few lucky houses are surrounded on three sides by jagged cliffs. The still-warm crater hovers above it all. And the

Iceland's Volcanoes

Iceland is among the most volcanically active places in the world, with roughly one eruption every five years. Aside from liquid lava, Iceland's volcanoes eject gas, ash, cinders, and solid rock (like pumice). The biggest rocks are sometimes called "volcanic bombs." Volcanic eruptions can last from a couple of days to several years.

Grímsvötn, a hard-to-reach volcano under the Vatnajökull glacier (in Southeast Iceland), is currently Iceland's most active; it last erupted in May 2011. Bárðarbunga, another volcano under the same glacier, began rumbling awake as recently as late 2017. The more famous Eyjafjallajökull, on the South Coast, made news in 2010—costing airlines more than $1 billion in disruptions. Other well-known Icelandic volcanoes include Hekla (once nicknamed the "Gateway to Hell"), Krafla, Askja, and Katla, which has the most potential for a damaging eruption (as it could send waves of water washing over coastal hamlets).

Of the roughly 130 volcanoes in Iceland, the most common type is the stratovolcano—the classic cone-shaped peak with explosive eruptions that form a crater in the very top (such as Hekla and Katla). There are also a few dormant shield volcanoes—with low-profile, wide-spreading lava flows (one called Skjaldbreiður is near the Golden Circle). Eruptions from fissure vents (long cracks in the earth's crust) are also common in Iceland, such as the Holuhraun eruption of 2014 or the destructive Laki eruptions in the 1780s.

Iceland's entire surface is made of volcanic rock, most of it basalt—the rock that forms when lava cools. Iceland's towering cliffs and jagged islands and skerries are all made of basalt. When basalt cools in particular ways, it forms the hexagonal rock columns that you see at Reynisfjara (on the South Coast), near Dettifoss (in the north), and other places.

At the lake called Mývatn, in North Iceland, you can see pseudocraters (also called rootless cones), which form after lava flows over a pond or marsh. The water beneath the lava boils and a giant bubble breaks through the lava, leaving a crater-like depression.

New lava is shiny and oily-looking, while old lava loses its gleam. Old lava fields—recognizable by their unique, bumpy appearance—are often covered by a fuzzy layer of Icelandic moss.

Volcano Museum in town is literally built around a house buried by lava—letting you peek into a family home forever trapped in rock. For more on this destination, see the Westman Islands chapter.

Reykjanes Peninsula: Your introduction to Iceland is one of the best looks you'll get at a volcanic landscape, as the area around Keflavík Airport is covered by jagged lava fields. The nearby Blue Lagoon is situated in this same rocky world (see the Blue Lagoon

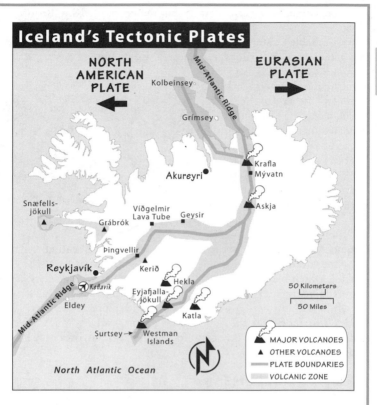

Iceland's Tectonic Plates

NORTH AMERICAN PLATE

EURASIAN PLATE

Mid-Atlantic Ridge

Kolbeinsey

Grímsey

Krafla
Mývatn

Akureyri

Askja

Snæfells-jökull

Viðgelmir Lava Tube

Geysir

Grábrók

Þingvellir

Reykjavík

Kerið

Mid-Atlantic Ridge

Keflavík

Hekla

Eyjafjalla-jökull

Eldey

Katla

Surtsey →

Westman Islands

50 Kilometers

50 Miles

MAJOR VOLCANOES
OTHER VOLCANOES
PLATE BOUNDARIES
VOLCANIC ZONE

North Atlantic Ocean

So why does Iceland have so many volcanoes? The answer lies beneath the surface. Iceland is located on the long, mostly underwater Mid-Atlantic Ridge—the meeting point of the Eurasian and North American tectonic plates. As the two tectonic plates move apart, magma from the earth's mantle rises to the surface (we start calling it "lava" when it erupts). Iceland is located on a mantle plume, where magma is especially close to the surface, which explains why land formed here and not elsewhere along the tectonic ridge.

& Reykjanes Peninsula chapter). Closer to Reykjavík, the suburb of Hafnarfjörður is nicknamed the "Town in the Lava" because it sits on a lava flow.

Mývatn: This North Iceland lake is ringed by a variety of otherworldly features, from the "pseudocraters" at Skútustaðir (where giant bubbles of steam burst through molten rock) to the jagged formations along the lake's eastern shore, at Dimmuborgir, and at the huge, climbable Hverfjall crater. For more, see the Ring Road chapter.

Climbable Craters: Several craters around Iceland invite you to climb up onto their rims for spectacular views. One of the finest examples, **Grábrók,** is alongside the Ring Road in West Iceland, just before the pass to the north. **Kerið,** along the Golden Circle route, requires almost no climbing and has a lovely lake inside. Near Mývatn, in the north, you can hike to the top of **Hverfjall** or drive just over the mountains and up the Katla Valley to reach

Víti ("Hell"), a rugged crater encircling a deep-blue lake.

South Coast: All along the South Coast, you'll see plenty of volcanoes—but you may not realize it, since they're currently dormant and covered with thick glaciers. The most famous is Eyjafjallajökull, which blew its top in 2010. Several other large glaciers, such as Mýrdalsjökull and Vatnajökull, have volcanoes underneath. For a hike with the best possible views of glacier-topped volcanoes, head to **Þórsmörk** (see the South Coast chapter), where a huff up to the Valahnúkur viewpoint affords you panoramas over three different volcanoes.

VOLCANO MUSEUMS

Iceland's best explanation of volcanic activity is at the **Volcano Museum** in the Westman Islands (see page 241). On the South Coast, the high-tech **Lava Centre** in Hvolsvöllur is both entertaining and educational (see page 209). A short drive up the road is the much more modest **Iceland Erupts** exhibit, which focuses on the 2010 Eyjafjallajökull eruption and its ashy impact. Reykjavík's **Volcano House** shows films about the two most famous eruptions, and its **Museum of Icelandic Natural Wonders** (at the Pearl) is developing some volcano exhibits.

VOLCANIC CAVE TOURS

Iceland offers three opportunities to enter dormant volcanic caves. While quite expensive for what you get (especially the first option), they're worthwhile for those interested in an up-close look.

Þríhnjúkagígur (a.k.a. **"Inside the Volcano"**; just southeast of Reykjavík, in the Bláfjöll mountains) offers the chance to descend into the magma chamber of a volcano that erupted about 4,000 years ago. The magma drained out and left a cavity so big that it could contain the Statue of Liberty. The first explorer entered in 1972. Now an elevator is rigged up in the opening every summer, allowing tourists to descend 400 feet into the bottle-shaped chamber, with a floor measuring 160 by 220 feet (the size of three basketball courts). The trip package includes hotel pickup in Reykjavík, the 30-minute bus ride out, a fairly easy 45-minute hike each way from the road to the volcano, the elevator down (5 minutes each way), 30 minutes on the floor of the chamber, and an included lunch. The rock is entirely cool—there's no volcanic activity here anymore. At around $400, it's not cheap, but it's definitely memorable. Book in advance online (42,000 ISK, tours run mid-May–mid-Oct only, tel. 519-5609, www.insidethevolcano.com).

Raufarhólshellir (a.k.a. "**The Lava Tunnel**") is an approximately mile-long, underground lava tube created when a flowing river of molten rock was enclosed, then drained out, leaving behind colorful formations. It's about a 45-minute drive from downtown Reykjavík, roughly on the way to the South Coast. In 2017, the cave was closed to the public and converted into a private attraction—infuriating local spelunkers. Expect uneven footing and chilly temperatures; they'll loan you coveralls and a helmet (6,400 ISK for basic one-hour tour, 9,900 ISK includes Reykjavík bus transfer; 19,900 ISK "extreme" tour lasts 3-4 hours, is more physically demanding, goes deeper into the tunnel, and includes Reykjavík transfer; pre-booking required, www.thelavatunnel.is).

In West Iceland is the similar **Víðgelmir** (a.k.a. "**The Cave**"). This cave is newer (about 1,000 years old rather than 5,000) and more extensive, but also more remote (about a 2-hour drive north of Reykjavík, or an hour east of Borgarnes). With a guide, you can walk about a half-mile into a lava tube (for details, see the West Iceland chapter).

Thermal Waters

Iceland's volcanic activity goes hand-in-hand with naturally heated water—which Icelanders have cleverly harnessed in a number of ways, from thermal baths to sources of electricity and heat.

THERMAL BATHS AND POOLS

Iceland has a wide range of options for enjoying its relaxing (and, yes, slightly stinky) thermal waters. Some bathing experiences cater primarily to tourists, chief among them the heavily advertised "premium baths." The most famous of these is the **Blue Lagoon**

Pool Rules: Visiting an Icelandic Thermal Swimming Pool

Icelanders love going to their local swimming pools, which are heated with natural thermal water. These aren't elaborate water parks, but more like municipal swimming pools back home: functional facilities for taking a dip with family and friends. (Not so long ago, it was common for Icelanders to live in apartments with no shower or bathtub—instead, they had an annual pass for the pool and went daily.)

Of course, the big draw of Icelandic pools is the naturally steamy water, which is pumped right out of the ground. Even the lap pools stay at a warm temperature (around 85°F), while "hot pots" (smaller hot pools) are in the 100°F range. Bigger pools have more facilities, which can be indoors, outdoors, or both. Very windy or cold weather makes indoor bathing attractive. But if it's not too bad out, there's something cozy about submerging yourself in hot water while the wind ruffles your hair and snowflakes settle on your nose.

Iceland's public bathing culture has its own set of customs, which locals take very seriously. You'll quickly get the hang of the system. Here's a step-by-step primer:

1. Bring a swimsuit and towel (rentals are available but expensive). Also bring any other gear you need: bathing cap, goggles, flip-flops (although most Icelanders don't bother with them), or toys for children (you can bring a bag into the pool area and stow it discreetly). There's no need to bring soap or shampoo—there are liquid soap dispensers in the showers.

2. Pay. Most towns have a shareable 10-visit discount card, which can save money with as few as five adult entries. At some pools, you'll be issued a locker key or an electronic wristband that will open a locker; at others, you'll find keys in the locks.

3. Change. Changing rooms are sex-segregated. Young children may go with a parent of either sex. Before entering the locker area, take off your shoes. (Many Icelanders leave them on public shoe racks, but I carry mine along and put them in my locker.)

near Keflavík Airport (see the Blue Lagoon & Reykjanes Peninsula chapter), but a similar (if smaller) version is **Mývatn Nature Baths** in North Iceland—a must for those doing the Ring Road. A less impressive premium bath is **Fontana,** in Laugarvatn and handy to the Golden Circle route. A new facility called **Krauma** has opened at Deildartunguhver in West Iceland. Other tourist-oriented bath-

Find an available locker, disrobe and lock your clothes inside, and carry your swimsuit and towel with you to the shower area.

4. Shower. Store your towel in one of the cubbyholes provided (you'll leave it there until after you've showered on your way out of the pool) and keep your swimsuit handy. Soap down and shower thoroughly. Yes, you're expected to shower naked: Icelanders are relaxed about nudity, and showering is considered a (required) sanitary issue. (Only the Blue Lagoon, where almost all the visitors are tourists, has some frosted-glass stalls for bashful foreigners.) Note: Iceland's water is extremely soft. You don't need very much soap to get clean, and it can take a long time to wash it off.

5. Swim and soak. After showering, slip on your swimsuit and head for the pool area. Typically, people start out in the warm pools (usually a lap pool for swimmers, a shallower pool for recreation, and a wading pool for kids; these are typically around 29°C/85°F). Then they finish off with a soak in the hot tubs (38-40°C/100-104°F) or a visit to the sauna. Each tub is posted with the temperature; anything above 40°C is extremely hot. Stay as long as you want; if you feel dizzy or uncomfortable, take a break outside or in a cooler pool, and take advantage of the water fountain.

6. Finish up. When you're done, return to the shower room, take off your swimsuit, shower again, and retrieve your towel. Towel off *before* returning to the locker area (they like to keep it as dry as possible). Many pools have a centrifuge to wick the water out of your suit. Back at your locker, get dressed, but don't put your shoes on until you exit the locker room. Return any keys or armbands to the counter.

7. Refuel. Most pools have tables and chairs in the entry hall where you can eat a packed lunch or snack. Most also have vending machines, snack counters, or even full-fledged cafés.

Note: At the pool, Icelanders usually just talk to the people they came with and generally leave strangers alone. Everyone is polite and helpful, but don't expect to get into a long conversation. At some times of day, groups of local "regulars" (often senior citizens) may seem to take over one of the hot pots, but you're welcome to squeeze in, too.

ing experiences include the **Secret Lagoon,** a simple but cleverly marketed bath a short drive from the Golden Circle route at Flúðir.

While those baths have big marketing budgets and attract lots of international visitors, they're rarely frequented by Icelanders—who know that you can bathe in equally luxuriant 100°F water for a fraction of the price, albeit in simpler surroundings, at one

of the country's many **thermal swimming pools** *(sundlaug)*. Every community of even a few hundred people seems to have scraped together the funds for their own well-maintained pool complex, often with a (warm) lap pool and at least one or two smaller hot pools (called "hot pots"). Many have a wide variety of different pools, saunas and steam rooms, and colorful waterslides for kids. In addition to being affordable, these provide a pleasantly authentic Icelandic experience, allowing you to rub elbows with locals who come home from work or school, grab a towel, and head to the pool. I've listed several of these in the Reykjavík area, and throughout the country—including in Borg, right along the Golden Circle; in a remote corner of West Iceland, at Húsafell; in tiny Hofsós, just off the Ring Road, with an infinity pool overlooking a fjord; and in Iceland's second city, Akureyri.

Up-to-date opening hours for each pool are on the website of each town, but you usually have to hunt for them a bit amidst the other municipal services. These websites also won't show temporary closures (for special events, maintenance, etc.), so it's wise to confirm opening hours by telephone before making a trek to a distant pool.

Various websites list Iceland's thermal pools (try www.swkmminginiceland.is or www.hotpoticeland.com). The free book-

lets *Áning—Accommodation in Iceland* and *Thermal Bliss* include extensive lists of pools (available at the Reykjavík TI or downloadable at www.icelandreview.com/publications). The *Reykjavík Grapevine* has a great article called "Every Swimming Pool in the Greater Reykjavík Area, Rated" (easily found at www.grapevine.is). Or you can simply keep a look-out for the international "pool" symbol—a swimmer's head poking out above waves—anywhere you go. Even though the clientele is mostly Icelandic, visitors are welcome (just follow the rules—see sidebar).

Finally, Iceland has a few opportunities to (carefully) bathe in **natural thermal springs.** Above the town of Hveragerði, near the end of the Golden Circle route, you can hike an hour to soak in the thermal river of **Reykjadalur** (see page 201). In the Highlands, **Landmannalaugar** ("The People's Pools") has a famous natural thermal area, which takes quite some effort to reach (only with an off-road vehicle, and only in summer); this is best done on a guided excursion (about 20,000 ISK, offered by many companies mid-June–mid-Sept, includes pick-up and drop-off in Reykjavík). It's important to note that tourists routinely wind up in the burn unit of Reykjavík's hospital after being scalded at natural thermal areas. Watch your step, keep on marked trails, bathe only where you see others doing so safely, and remember that a thermal landscape comes with lots of hidden dangers.

THERMAL SIGHTS

Wandering through a steaming, bubbling, colorful, otherworldly thermal landscape is a uniquely Icelandic treat. For such a small island, Iceland has a re-markable variety of these locations. Just watch your step—always stay on marked trails, as a thin crust can cover a boiling-hot reservoir—and be ready for some intense sulfur smells.

The most visited is **Geysir,** on the Golden Circle. But, while it's unique in offering the chance to watch a geyser spurt high into the air, it's crowded. For more interesting and varied thermal landscapes, consider the following options.

Perhaps the best thermal area is at **Námafjall,** just over the hills from Mývatn, in North Iceland. Much closer to Reykjavík, the **Seltún** geothermal area on the Reykjanes Peninsula is quite striking. "Honorable mentions" go to the sputtering shore of **Laugarvatn** lake, along the Golden Circle route; the bubbling spring at **Deildartunguhver,** in West Iceland; and the steaming valley of **Reykjadalur,** above the town of Hveragerði (just off the Golden Circle route). See "Thermal Bath Hikes," later.

To see how Iceland has harnessed the substantial power of its thermal waters, stop by a geothermal plant. **Hellisheiðarvirkjun** sits amidst a lunar land-scape just outside Reyk-javík, on the way to the Golden Circle and South Coast day trips, and boasts Iceland's most extensive visitors center about its geothermal energy indus-try. **Krafla,** with a mod-

est information center, fills a dramatic valley in the north, near Mývatn.

Whales, Birds, and Horses

WHALE WATCHING

Many come to Iceland hoping to catch a glimpse of the elusive whales of the North Atlantic. The waters here are home to 23 different varieties of gentle giants.

On a typical whale-watching trip, you're most likely to see white-beaked dolphins, harbor porpoises, and mid-sized minke whales (the species also listed on local menus). If you have luck, you may spot a breaching humpback whale (most often seen from ports in North Iceland, such as Húsavík and Akureyri) or a black-and-white orca (Keiko, the killer whale of *Free Willy* fame, was captured in Iceland). On very rare occasions, some get a glimpse of one of the two biggest mammals on the planet: the blue whale or the fin whale.

Several companies offer whale-watching boat trips (generally 3-4 hours for about 11,000 ISK). These once were concentrated in North Iceland: in the tiny town of Húsavík, and Iceland's second city of Akureyri (see listings for both in the Ring Road chapter). The same trips (and many of the same companies) are now also well-established in Reykjavík, making it easier to whale watch without a long trek north. See the Reykjavík chapter for a rundown of your options.

Ideally, don't book your whale-watching trip too far in advance. Follow the weather report and choose a summer day that's as sunny and windless as possible; like you, whales and dolphins enjoy nice weather and are most likely to surface then. May through August are the best months, when whales are attracted to the small creatures feeding near the sun-warmed surface of the water. Windy weather or rough seas can turn the trip into four hours of seasickness, and you likely won't see more than a dolphin or two. From November to February, I'd skip the trip entirely. Dress warmly (though boat operators usually have extra outerwear to loan).

Be aware that whale-watching trips are a big commitment of time and money—best for those with a serious interest in the creatures. For a guaranteed, up-close look at (artificial) whales, stop by the expensive but enjoyable Whales of Iceland exhibit near Reykjavík's harbor.

BIRDS AND BIRDING

Adorable, chubby little puffins—with their black-and-white markings and cartoonish beaks—are fun to watch. They usually arrive in Iceland in early summer, then take off again at summer's end—making the window for seeing them quite short. (For more on puffins, see the sidebar on the next page.)

The biggest puffin populations are in the Westman Islands (with about half of Iceland's estimated 10 million puffins—and one-fifth of the world's puffins); along the South Coast (particularly around the Dyrhólaey promontory, and farther east, at Ingólfshöfði cape); and along the Westfjords (at Látrabjarg, Hornbjarg, Hornstrandir, and Breiðafjörður). The islet called Lundey ("Puffin Island")—with a relatively small population of about 20,000 puffins—is ideally situated just a short boat trip from downtown Reykjavík, and a handy destination for a puffin cruise from the Old Harbor. Perhaps Iceland's best puffin experience is at the Westman Islands' Sæheimar Aquarium, where you can usually meet a real-life puffin named Tóti, who was rescued as a stranded puffling by local kids.

Birders find plenty of other seabird species to get excited about in Iceland. Along with puffins, the auk family includes the guillemot, the murre, and the razorbill (all of which have a black body and white belly, but lack that cute orange beak). Arctic terns are sleek flyers—gray on top, white on bottom, with a black crown and a reddish beak. They're notorious for aggressively dive-bombing tourists who wander too close to their nests, then pulling up at the last second. Arctic terns have the longest migration in the animal kingdom: They spend their summers in the Arctic...and then, come fall, fly to the "southern summer" in the Antarctic (over its life, an Arctic tern might fly as many as 1.5 million miles). Rounding out the flock are seagull-like fulmars and kittiwakes. Iceland has several freshwater bird species as well, including ducks, oystercatchers, and golden plovers.

For a one-stop look at (taxidermy-style) examples of all Icelandic bird species, head north to Sigurgeir's Bird Museum near Mývatn (see page 307).

ICELANDIC HORSES

Icelandic horses are small, strong, and docile, and descend from the ponies originally brought to Iceland in the Settlement Age. (Viking Age settlers carefully selected only the smallest yet strongest horses for the journey—able to fit on their ships, but capable of working hard once in Iceland.) Today, Icelandic horses are exported to enthusiasts worldwide, but since A.D. 982, no horses have been imported to the island—so every one you see is a purebred. Icelandic horses are renowned for their unique gaits: In addition to

Puffins

Iceland's unofficial mascot is the Atlantic puffin *(Fratercula arctica)*—that adorably stout, tuxedo-clad seabird with a too-big orange beak and beady black eyes. Some 10 million puffins summer in Iceland—the largest population of any country on earth.

Puffins live most of their lives on the open Atlantic, coming to land only to breed. They fly north to Iceland between mid-May and early June, raise their brood, then take off again late in August. Puffins mate for life and typically lay just one egg each year, which the male and female take turns caring for. A baby puffin is called—wait for it—a puffling.

To feed their pufflings, puffins plunge as deep as 200 feet below the sea's surface to catch sand eels, herring, and other small fish. Their compact bodies, stubby wings, oil-sealed plumage, and webbed feet are ideal for navigating underwater. Famously, puffins can stuff several small fish into their beaks at once, thanks to their agile tongues and uniquely hinged beaks. This evolutionary trick lets puffins stock up before returning to the nest.

Stocky, tiny-winged puffins have a distinctive way of flying. To take off, they either beat their wings like crazy (at sea) or essentially hurl themselves off a cliff (on land). Once aloft, they beat their wings furiously—up to 400 times per minute—to stay airborne. Coming in for a smooth landing on a rocky cliff is a challenge (and highly entertaining to watch): They choose a spot, swoop in at top speed on prevailing currents, then flutter their wings madly to brake as they try to touch down. At the moment of truth, the puffin decides whether to attempt to stick the landing; more often than not, he bails out and does another big circle on the currents...and tries again...and again...and again.

Each August, the puffins head south at night, following the moon. On the Westman Islands, pufflings are often distracted by the town lights and crash-land on streets and rooftops. Local children collect them and bring them to the aquarium, which allows them an overnight rest before being released into the wild to try again.

In addition to seeing puffins along the summer coastline, you may occasionally see them on restaurant menus. With such abundant numbers, Iceland doesn't protect the puffin. Considered by some Icelanders to be a delicacy, puffin tastes like chicken...but cuter.

the typical walk, trot, and gallop, Icelandic horses employ the *tölt*, which is fast and extremely smooth, and the *skeið*, a high-speed "flying pace." This "five-gaited" status is their claim to fame.

Even if you're not an equestrian enthusiast, a horseback ride is a nice way to enjoy the outdoors for a couple of hours, much

as Icelanders have for centuries. Horseback riding is big business, and dozens of farms all over Iceland offer rides for travelers—including a cluster just outside Reykjavík. Browse and book on company websites: Íslenski Hesturinn (The Icelandic Horse, tel. 434-7979, http:// islenskihesturinn.is), Viking Horses (mobile 660-9590, www.vikinghorses.is), Laxnes (tel. 566-6179, www.laxnes.is), and Íshestar (tel. 555-7000, www.ishestar.is).

It's usually a half-day affair, either morning or afternoon. If you're based in Reykjavík, they'll pick you up, drive you out to the farm, outfit you with a helmet and riding gear, give you about an hour and a half on horseback, and drop you off afterwards, all for about 12,000-15,000 ISK (some tours throw in lunch; Laxnes and Íshestar lower the price if you drive out yourself). Beyond the Reykjavík area, your scores of options include some in dramatic surroundings: in the broad valley of Skagafjörður, through the glacial rivulets of Þórsmörk, along the beaches of the South Coast, and so on. Wherever you ride, check the weather forecast before booking.

For just a glimpse of an Icelandic horse, watch for roadside paddocks all around the island. Or head to the Reykjavík Family Park and Zoo (see page 111), ideally at feeding time. On weekends, the zoo lets little kids trot around the horse paddock, accompanied by a keeper.

Hiking

Iceland is a wonderland for hikers, whether you're taking an easy stroll from your car to a waterfall, or embarking on a grueling but dramatic multiday trek. Before heading out on a challenging hike, make sure you have proper equipment, water, maps, and advice from an experienced local.

Be aware of current weather conditions—and don't underestimate the impact of Iceland's howling winds and bone-chilling (even in summer) temperatures. Read "The Many Ways Iceland Can Kill You" sidebar (earlier in this chapter).

EASY HIKES

Throughout this book, I've focused on easy hikes that offer a big reward for minimal effort—mainly starting from a parking lot and looping through an accessible slice of Icelandic scenery. More details on each of these are given in the individual chapters. Some of my favorite, easy car hikes include the loop through Þingvellir along the Golden Circle route; the hikes up to the South Coast glaciers at Sólheimajökull and Skaftafell; the hike up to the lighthouse at Dyrhólaey promontory, on the South Coast; and walking up to Eldfell volcano on the Westman Islands. Along the Ring Road, there's a variety of enjoyable options around Mývatn lake—including the pseudocraters at Skútustaðir, the forested peninsula at Höfði, and the lava pillars at Dimmuborgir. Other Mývatn hikes include the Námafjall thermal field and adjacent hill-climb just over the mountains from the lake, and the hike out to the volcanic cone at Leirhnjúkur. Also consider the crater hikes described in the "Volcanoes" section, earlier.

Each of the great **waterfalls** I've described in Iceland comes with a hike—some short, some long—and often an opportunity to climb up to a higher vantage point: Gullfoss on the Golden Circle, Seljalandsfoss (and its neighbor Gljúfrabúi) on the South Coast, Skógafoss on the South Coast, Hraunfossar and Barnafoss in West Iceland, and along the Ring Road—Goða-foss and Dettifoss in North Iceland, and Svartifoss in the southeast.

THERMAL BATH HIKES

To combine a hike with a natural thermal bathing experience, you can walk about an hour up the valley called **Reykjadalur,** just above the town of Hveragerði (an hour from Reykjavík and on the route of both the Golden Circle and the South Coast day trips). Your reward is a thermal river where you can recline in warm, rushing water. Less of a hike, and less rewarding, is **Seljavallalaug,** a tepid pool tucked into the side of a mountain about a 15-minute hike from the South Coast road. At both, expect minimal, grubby changing areas and plenty of adventurous hikers.

SERIOUS HIKES

For serious hikers, Iceland offers dozens of premier hiking destinations—many in the Highlands, and inaccessible with a standard car. The two below are perhaps the best-known; for either you'll need a high-clearance four-wheel drive vehicle, or you can ride in a specially equipped excursion bus.

Perhaps the best combination of quality hiking and accessibility is **Þórsmörk,** a volcanic landscape with glorious mountain, valley, and canyon walks; the moderately challenging hike up to Valahnúkur is spectacular. Þórsmörk is a short detour from the South Coast, but most people get there via excursion bus from Reykjavík (5 hours each way; for more on Þórsmörk, see the South Coast chapter).

More remote is **Landmannalaugar,** in the Highlands about 120 miles east of Reykjavík (much of it on difficult-to-traverse, gravel-and-rock roads; about 4.5 hours one-way, open only in summer). In this vivid area—striped with volcanic hues—a petrified lava field from 1477 butts up against pointy peaks, with excellent trails and some natural thermal pools. Hikes abound: You could trek to the crater lake called Ljótipollur ("Ugly Puddle"); huff your way up the extremely colorful Brennisteinsalda, with high-altitude views and an optional detour to the Stórihver thermal area near the top; or opt for an easier walk to the big lake called Frostastaðavatn.

To reach Landmannalaugar, you'll need a 4x4 vehicle, or you can join an excursion (typically Aug-Sept, starting at 20,000 ISK, offered by various outfits). You can also take a bus operated by Iceland On Your Own (www.ioyo.is), Trex (www.trex.is), or Iceland By Bus (www.icelandbybus.is). While you can get a glimpse of the area in a very long day trip from Reykjavík, serious hikers overnight at the Landmannalaugar hut/campground.

Both Þórsmörk and Landmannalaugar are key stops along a variety of popular multiday hikes (with overnights in staffed huts) that traverse the glacial landscape of the south. One of the most popular routes, called **Laugavegur,** takes three to five days (34 miles over challenging terrain) and connects Þórsmörk and Landmannalaugar. Another favorite is the two-day, 14-mile **Fimmvörðuháls** hike, from Þórsmörk south, over the saddle between Eyjafjallajökull and Mýrdalsjökull, to Skógar on the South Coast—right over the site of the first stage of the 2010 Eyjafjallajökull eruption.

For something closer to the capital, you could ascend **Esja**—the big, long ridge that looms just north of Reykjavík. The most popular hike here is the four-mile round-trip to Steinn ("The Stone"), with an elevation gain of 650 feet (don't attempt this in cold weather).

For details on these, and good overall information about hiking, see the websites of FÍ (the Iceland Touring Association, www.fi.is) and NAT (Nordic Adventure Travel, www.nat.is). Companies offering guided hikes in Iceland include Icelandic Mountain Guides (www.mountainguides.is) and Trek Iceland (www.trek.is).

Other Outdoor Experiences

To reach spectacular scenery without the climb, you can choose from a variety of wheeled tours. Tours by **mountain bike,** by **ATV,** or by **"Super Jeep"** (a monster 4x4 vehicle that can go just about anywhere) give you access to some of the more remote areas mentioned earlier.

Various companies also offer **rafting and kayaking tours,** either in the canyon just below Gullfoss (the thundering waterfall on the Golden Circle), or in North Iceland on two rivers that drain the Hofsjökull glacier, south of Sauðárkrókur in the Skagafjörður region. Companies include Arctic Rafting (www.arcticrafting.com) and Viking Rafting (www.vikingrafting.is).

For divers, **scuba diving or snorkeling at Silfra**—a fissure flooded with crystal-clear glacial water, at Þingvellir on the Golden Circle—is a highlight (see the Golden Circle chapter).

Northern Lights

The northern lights are a magical, occasional, serendipitous sight on clear, crisp nights in Iceland from about the end of August to the middle of April. You can't really plan to see the northern lights—they don't always appear, and when they do, are often ob-

Nature's Light Show

Like floating curtains of translucent cloth, the northern lights arc across Iceland's wintery sky in shades of green, pink, purple, and even red. The lights are caused by charged particles from the sun that collide with the earth's upper atmosphere and cause it to glow. If these particles were able to hit earth's surface, the radiation would be catastrophic, damaging our DNA and increasing the risk of cancer. Fortunately, the earth's magnetic field deflects most of these particles; but near the poles, where the field is weakest, some can seep through, creating the northern lights. They are strongest along a ring-shaped band that crosses Iceland, Greenland, northern Canada, Alaska, Russia, and northern Scandinavia, and diminish as you move farther north toward the magnetic pole. Their intensity varies with the sunspot cycle; the last maximum was in 2013, and the next will be in 2025.

Iceland is a good place to see the northern lights, but not the best; its advantage is that it's relatively easy to get to, and its main disadvantage is its frequent cloudy weather. Perhaps that's why there's no mention of the phenomenon in the Icelandic sagas. However, a few Icelandic folk traditions mention the lights: For example, pregnant women avoided looking at the northern lights for fear their babies would be born cross-eyed. While other ancient people also saw the northern lights as a sign of war or famine, today they are a tourist attraction—and a reminder that life on our fragile planet depends on the protection of a magnetic field.

scured by cloud cover. While often visible in Reykjavík, the northern lights stand out better farther from the center of town and in the countryside, where there's less light pollution. All things being equal, spending a night or two in a more remote area could increase your chances.

The dreamy northern lights images that you see are done using long exposures and sometimes Photoshop (tweaking the aurora colors to a Kermit-the-Frog green). What you'll actually see will probably be closer to the color of a Thai green curry—more coconut milk than Kermit.

With all the interesting things to do in Iceland, it would be a shame to spend your energy chasing after the northern lights every evening. I suggest planning your trip as if you won't see them, and considering it as a bonus if you do. Whether you'll see the lights or not is mostly out of your control, but consider the tips below to improve your odds.

Come during aurora season. Visit Iceland in aurora season (from a little before the fall equinox to a little after the spring equinox). Some say that September/October and February/March are the best months. At the least, they have longer days and nicer temperatures, so you can enjoy regular sightseeing more. If you're planning to rent a car, go in fall, when the road conditions are better.

Maximize your chances. It's easy to miss the northern lights simply by not bothering to look for them.

On any clear, dark night, go outside and scan the sky every half hour or so up until bedtime. You can follow the aurora and cloud-cover forecast on the Icelandic weather service's English-language website (http://en.vedur.is; click on "Weather," then "Aurora forecasts"). The American aurora forecasts at www.swpc.noaa.gov also cover Iceland.

See the lights without a car. If you're staying in Reykjavík and you don't have a car, consider taking a northern lights bus tour (around 7,000 ISK). Tours only run when conditions look good—call around dinnertime to find out. You'll leave town at 21:00 or 22:00 and you won't be in bed until almost four hours later. Read a few reviews before you go, and remember that even if the forecast is good, you may see nothing at all. (If so, the bus company will likely give you a voucher for another trip—not much help on a short visit.) For some, the trip is a nice chance to snuggle up with a travel partner on a bus and listen to an entertaining tour guide who serves hot cocoa. For others, it's a disappointing few hours of yawning and wishing they'd turned in early.

See the lights with a car. If you're staying in Reykjavík and have a car, you could put together your own northern lights tour by driving out into the suburbs or a little way into the countryside. Þingvellir (see the Golden Circle chapter) and Kleifarvatn (see the Blue Lagoon & Reykjanes Peninsula chapter) are plenty dark and within a 45-minute drive of town. If you stay within greater Reykjavík, drive out toward the tips of Seltjarnarnes or Álftanes (by Bessastaðir, the presidential residence), where city lights are a little dimmer.

REYKJAVÍK

REYKJAVÍK

Reykjavík, the tiny capital of a remote island-nation, is unexpectedly cosmopolitan, with an artistic, bohemian flair. It lacks world-class sights, yet manages to surprise and delight even those who use the city mostly as a home base for exploring Iceland's natural wonders.

The city's downtown streets are lined with creative restaurants, quirky art galleries, rollicking bars serving everything from craft beer to designer cocktails, and shops selling stuffed puffins, local knitwear, and Gore-Tex parkas. Reykjavík is a colorful enclave in a stark landscape: It seems every wall serves as a canvas for a vibrant street-art mural, and each corner is occupied by a cozy, art-strewn, stay-awhile café. In the old town center, colorful timber-frame houses clad in corrugated metal sheets huddle together amid a sprinkling of landmarks—such as the striking Hallgrímskirkja church, which crowns the town's highest point.

Reykjavík, like the rest of the country, has old roots. Viking Age farmers settled here in the ninth century. Until the 1750s, this area remained nothing more than a sprawling farm. As towns started to form in Iceland, Reykjavík emerged as the country's capital. Today, the capital region is a small city, home to two out of every three Icelanders—a population similar to that of Berkeley, California, or Fargo, North Dakota. The northernmost capital city in the world—which straddles the European and American hemispheres—feels more New World than Old.

With the recent tourism boom, these days Icelanders tend to work, live, and shop elsewhere, and make fun of Reykjavík's downtown core with all its "puffin shops" selling souvenirs. But that doesn't mean you should avoid downtown: Visitors find just about everything they need in this small, walkable zone. You can take in the vibe of the pithy city in a leisurely two-hour  stroll, and it's an enjoyable place to simply hang out. While museums aren't a priority here, those seeking sights can easily fill a day or two.

Step into Hallgrímskirkja's serene church interior, and ride the elevator up its tower for a view over Reykjavík's rooftops. Learn about this little nation's proud history at the National Museum, and about the city's humble Viking Age roots at the Settlement Exhibition—built around the surviving walls of a 10th-century longhouse. Art lovers can visit a half-dozen galleries highlighting Icelandic artists (early-20th-century sculptor Einar Jónsson is tops). Naturalists can go on a whale-watching cruise, or ride a ferry to an island getaway. Modern architecture fans can ogle the award-winning Harpa concert hall, then walk along the shoreline to the iconic *Sun Voyager* sculpture.

Explore the city's pricey but well-done private museums: At Whales of Iceland, ogle life-size models of gigantic marine mammals; at the Saga Museum, meet the Viking protagonists of the Icelandic sagas face-to-waxy-face; and at the Aurora Reykjavík exhibit, watch mesmerizing time-lapse footage of the northern lights. More sights await in the suburbs, including another city view at a domed building called the Pearl, and family-friendly activities (open-air museum, zoo, botanic gardens). To recharge, the capital area has plenty of relaxing—and very local—thermal swimming pools.

But don't focus too much on the capital. On a short summertime getaway to Iceland, I might not even devote a full day to Reykjavík. Instead, use the city as a springboard for Iceland's glorious countryside sights, taking advantage of its accommodations, great restaurants, and lively nightlife. Even on a longer visit, drivers may prefer sleeping at a distance, dropping into town only for occasional sightseeing, strolling, and dining. To save money and have a more

Greater Reykjavík

Faxaflói

Lundey

Akurey   Engey   Viðey   Geldinganes

Seltjarnarnes

IMAGINE PEACE TOWER

See Reykjavik Maps

Örfirisey   Old Harbor

SUÐURSTRÖND

HARPA

SKARFAGARÐAR CRUISE TERMINAL

SELTJARNARNES POOL

LAUGARVEGUR   41

SHORELINE STROLL

HRINGBRAUT

ZOO

GRAY LINE BUS TERMINAL

Reykjavík

BSÍ BUS TERMINAL

SÆBRAUT

49

MIKLABRAUT

Reykjavik City

THE PEARL

BÚSTAÐAVEGUR   49   VESTURLANDS-

Nauthólsvík Beach   40

SLEDDING HILL

B #16

BESSASTAÐIR (PRESIDENT'S RESIDENCE)

KÓPAVOGS POOL   413

ÁRBÆJARSAFN OPEN-AIR FOLK MUSEUM   41

ÁLFTANES POOL

Kópavogur

FÍFUHVAMMSVEGUR

MJÓDD STRÆTÓ BUS TERMINAL

Ellíðaár

HAFNARFJARÐARVEGUR

SMÁRALIND SHOPPING MALL   413

Hliðsnes

ÁLFTANESVEGUR

VIFILSSTAÐAVEGUR

Garðabær

410

See Detail Map   40

Vifilsstaða-vatn

Hafnarfjörður   41

IKEA

#1 B   VIKING VILLAGE

STRAUMSVÍK ALUMINUM PLANT

To Keflavik Airport & Blue Lagoon   #1   41

B

ÁSVALLALAUG POOL   To Íshestar Horse Farm

local experience, consider sleeping in suburban Reykjavík—which has fewer hotels, but ample Airbnb options.

PLANNING YOUR TIME

On a short visit, savor Reykjavík's strolling ambience in the morning and evening, maybe drop into one or two sights early or late, and use your precious daytime hours to tour sights in the countryside (see the Near Reykjavík chapter for an overview of your

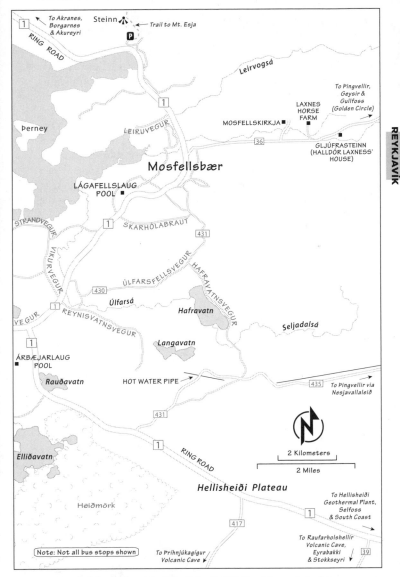

options). My self-guided Reykjavík Walk offers a helpful town orientation (and crash-course in Iceland) that can be done at any time of day or night.

On a longer trip—or in winter (when countryside options are limited)—Reykjavík warrants more time. The following schedule is designed to fill two full days in Reykjavík itself. With less time, mix and match from among these options. My plan ignores weather—in practice, let the weather dictate your itinerary. If it's blowing hard and drizzling, prioritize indoor sights. Use the good weather well.

Day 1: Start with my self-guided walk around downtown, and (if the line's not too long) ride up the tower of Hallgrímskirkja church. Then find a nice lunch in the Laugavegur/Skólavörðustígur area. Walk down to the *Sun Voyager* sculpture for a photo op, then follow the shoreline to the Harpa concert hall (peek in the lobby, and stop by the box office to survey entertainment options). Follow the moored boats around to the Old Harbor, where you can comparison-shop whale watching and other boat tours for tomorrow. Then continue along the harbor to the Grandi area, where you can drop into your choice of exhibits: Whales of Iceland, Saga Museum, Maritime Museum, or Aurora Reykjavík. Return to the downtown area for dinner and after-hours strolling.

Day 2: Begin your day at the Settlement Exhibition. If that compact exhibit whets your appetite for Icelandic history, take a walk along the Pond (the city's little lake) to the National Museum. After lunch, take your pick of activities: boat trip (either whale or puffin watching, or simply a ride out to Viðey Island); suburban sights in Laugardalur (botanic garden, zoo) and/or Árbær Open-Air Museum, with a stop at the observation deck/museum called the Pearl; or explore the city's many art museums. In the late afternoon, unwind with the Icelanders in one of Reykjavík's thermal swimming pools, before another dinner in the center.

If you're in town on a weekend, squeeze in a visit to the Kolaportið flea market, downtown.

Orientation to Reykjavík

Reykjavík's population is about 125,000, but the entire capital region has nearly double that (220,000). The compact core of Reykjavík radiates out from the main walking street, which changes names from Austurstræti to Bankastræti to Laugavegur as it cuts through the city. You can walk from one end of downtown Reykjavík (Ingólfstorg square) to the other (the bus junction Hlemmur) in about 20 minutes. Just northwest of downtown is  the mostly postindustrial Old Harbor zone, with excursion boats, salty restaurants, and a few sights.

Greater Reykjavík is made up of six towns. Hafnarfjörður ("harbor fjord"), to the south, has its own history, harbor, and downtown core. Kópavogur and Garðabær, between Reykjavík and

Hafnarfjörður, are 20th-century suburbs. Mosfellsbær, once a rural farming district along the road running north from Reykjavík, has turned into a sizable town of its own. And Seltjarnarnes is a posh enclave at the end of the Reykjavík Peninsula. While I haven't recommended specific hotels or restaurants in these neighborhoods (except in Hafnarfjörður)—finding an affordable Airbnb in one of these areas can provide a very local home base.

TOURIST INFORMATION

The city-run **TI** is in City Hall, by the Pond (daily 8:00-20:00, Tjarnargata 11, tel. 411-6040, www.visitreykjavik.is). It has three desks: one for impartial information; the "Guide to Iceland" desk, which sells tours and excursions; and a "Safe Travel Iceland" desk, which offers advice and answers questions about driving, weather, and other risks and concerns. Around downtown you'll see several booking services billed as tourist information offices. These are primarily tour-sales offices, but can be helpful.

The *Reykjavík Grapevine,* a free informative English-language paper and website, provides a roundup of sightseeing hours, music listings, helpful restaurant reviews, and fun insights into local life. They also publish a quarterly *Best of Reykjavík* booklet with lots of reviews (www.grapevine.is). The local blog IHeartReykjavik.net also has helpful insights about both the capital region and all of Iceland.

Sightseeing Pass: The **Reykjavík City Card** may make sense for busy museum sightseers on a longer stay, but is not worth it for a short visit. It covers bus transport, city-run museums, Reykjavík swimming pools, and some other attractions (24 hours-3,700 ISK, 48 hours-4,900 ISK, 72 hours-5,900 ISK; sold at hotels and City Hall TI).

HELPFUL HINTS

Money: You'll use credit cards more than cash in Iceland. If you do need cash, several big banks downtown have ATMs, and can exchange money (banks closed Sat-Sun). The downtown branch of Landsbankinn at Austurstræti 11 is convenient and along my self-guided walk.

Useful Bus App: If you'll be using public buses, use the **Strætó app** to avoid having to carry exact bus fare. Download the app, then change the default language to English under "Settings." At the prompt to enter your mobile number, include "001" for the US country code. You'll receive a PIN number on your mobile phone—once you enter the PIN, you can enter your credit card details to buy bus tickets.

Pharmacy: A downtown pharmacy is at Laugavegur 16 (Mon-Fri 9:00-18:00, Sat 11:00-16:00, closed Sun, tel. 552-4045, www.

REYKJAVÍK

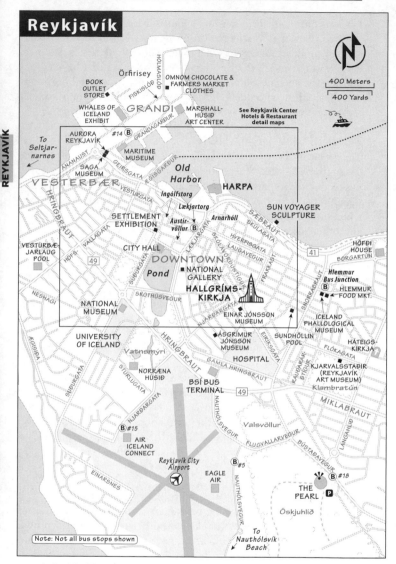

Reykjavík

Örfirisey

BOOK OUTLET STORE

OMNOM CHOCOLATE & FARMERS MARKET CLOTHES

WHALES OF ICELAND EXHIBIT

GRANDI

MARSHALL-HÚSID ART CENTER

See Reykjavík Center Hotels & Restaurant detail maps

#14 B

AURORA REYKJAVÍK

MARITIME MUSEUM

SAGA MUSEUM

Old Harbor

HARPA

To Seltjarnarnes

VESTERBÆR

SUN VOYAGER SCULPTURE

HRINGBRAUT

Ingólfstorg

Lækjartorg

Arnarhóll

SETTLEMENT EXHIBITION

Austur-völlur B

VESTURBÆJARLAUG POOL

CITY HALL

DOWNTOWN

HÖFDI HOUSE

41

Pond

NATIONAL GALLERY

Hlemmur Bus Junction

B HLEMMUR FOOD MKT.

NESHAGI

HALLGRÍMS-KIRKJA

NATIONAL MUSEUM

EINAR JÓNSSON MUSEUM

ICELAND PHALLOLOGICAL MUSEUM

UNIVERSITY OF ICELAND

Vatnsmýri

ÁSGRÍMUR JÓNSSON MUSEUM

SUNDHÖLLIN POOL

HÁTEIGS-KIRKJA

HRINGBRAUT

HOSPITAL

KJARVALSSTADIR (REYKJAVÍK ART MUSEUM)

NORRÆNA HÚSID

GAMLA HRINGBRAUT

Klambratún

BSÍ BUS TERMINAL

49

MIKLABRAUT

B #15

Valsvöllur

AIR ICELAND CONNECT

Reykjavík City Airport

EAGLE AIR

B #5

B #18

THE PEARL

P

EINARSNES

Öskjuhlíd

Note: Not all bus stops shown

To Nauthólsvík Beach

N

400 Meters

400 Yards

lyfja.is). For a pharmacy with longer hours, try the ones at Lágmúli 5 in outer Reykjavík (tel. 533-2300) and Smáratorg 1, under the Læknavakt after-hours medical service near the Smáralind shopping mall (tel. 564-5600).

Local Guidebook: Look for historian Guðjón Friðriksson's great little book *Reykjavík Walks*, which describes six building-by-building routes around the downtown center.

Laundry: The downtown **Laundromat Café,** has four washers and four dryers in its basement (long hours daily, Austurstræti 9,

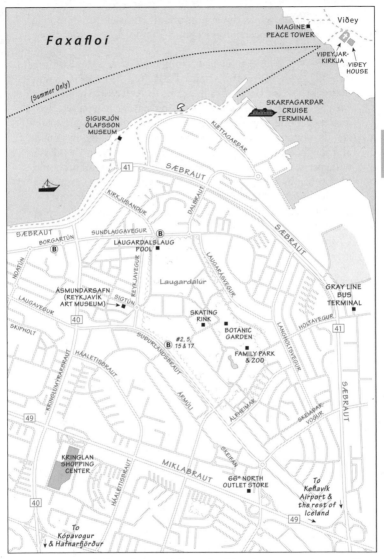

www.thelaundromatcafe.com). It's also a popular comfort-food restaurant (described later in this chapter—but check before you go; it's rumored to be closing down).

Bike Rental: WOW Citybike provides basic rent-and-return bikes at several self-service stations around the city center (400 ISK/one-way trip up to 30 minutes; www.wowcitybike.com). For a better-quality and longer-term rental, **Reykjavík Bike Tours** rents from its location on the pier in the Old Harbor (3,500 ISK/4 hours, 4,900 ISK/24 hours; in summer daily at least

9:00-17:00, in winter by appointment; Ægisgarður 7, mobile 694-8956, www.icelandbike.com). They also run tours (see "Tours in Reykjavík," later).

Taxis: The two long-established companies are **Hreyfill** (tel. 588-5522, www.hreyfill.is) and **BSR** (tel. 561-0000, www.taxireykjavik.is). Both offer flat rates to Keflavík Airport. For early-morning rides, call the evening before to reserve. Icelanders generally order taxis by phone, but there are a few taxi stands downtown and at major transportation hubs. In general, though, taxis are expensive—even a short ride in Reykjavík will cost 2,000 ISK—so use them only when there's no better option (cabbies expect payment by credit card but not a tip). Services such as Uber and Lyft don't operate in Reykjavík.

Online Translation Tip: A few of the websites I list in this chapter are in Icelandic only. To view them in English, use Google's Chrome browser (for automatic translation) or paste the URL into the translation window at Translate.google.com.

GETTING AROUND
By Car

North Americans will feel at home in Reykjavík, as it's largely a car city. If you'll be renting a car to explore the countryside, you may want to keep it for part of your time in Reykjavík. Outside of downtown, parking is generally free and easy.

That said, you don't need a car to enjoy your visit. And if you are staying in the center (inside the street called Hringbraut) and visiting only downtown sights, a car can be a headache. But many interesting and authentic things to do in town are outside the center, accessible only by car or bus. If you plan to have your own wheels in town, consider looking for accommodations with free parking a little outside the center.

Parking: Downtown, on-street parking is metered (Mon-Fri 9:00-18:00, Sat 10:00-16:00; free outside these times). Pay with credit cards or coins at machines (look for the white and blue "P" sign), and display your ticket on the windshield. Parking in the P1 zone is the most expensive (275 ISK/hour); parking in P2 through P4 costs about 150 ISK/hour. You can prepay for an entire day, so even if overnighting in the center, you don't have to worry about returning to feed the meter. A few coin-op-only parking meters still survive.

There are several small public parking garages downtown (check up-to-the-minute availability at www.bilastaedasjodur.is/#bilahusin). The Traðarkot garage at Hverfisgata 20 is the best option and close to the end point of my Reykjavík Walk (80-150 ISK/hour, daily 7:00-24:00). Progressively closer in, but typically full on weekdays, are the Kolaport garage, near the Harpa concert hall at Kalkofnsvegur 1; the Ráðhúsið garage, underneath City Hall at Tjarnargata 11; and—closest to my Reykjavík Walk's starting point—the Vesturgata garage at Vesturgata 7 (on the corner with Mjóstræti).

You can also park just outside downtown in a neighborhood with free on-street parking, such as behind Hallgrímskirkja church or near the BSÍ bus terminal. A free parking lot is along Eiríksgata at the top of the hill by Hallgrímskirkja church, but it's often full. Or look for metered on-street parking closer in (along Garðastræti and its side-streets, just a couple of blocks above Ingólfstorg). There's also plenty of free parking in the Grandi box-store zone to the far side of the Old Harbor.

By Public Transportation

Greater Reykjavík has a decent bus *(strætó)* system. In this late-rising city, buses run from about 6:30 on weekdays, 8:00 on Saturdays, and 10:00 on Sundays, with last departures between 23:00 and 24:00. Service is sparse on evenings and weekends, when most buses only run every half-hour.

Bus routes intersect at several key points, notably Hlemmur, at the eastern end of Laugavegur, Reykjavík's downtown shopping street; Lækjartorg, at the western end of Laugavegur; Mjódd, in the eastern Reykjavík suburbs; and Fjörður, in the town of Hafnarfjörður. The English journey planner at Straeto.is makes using the system easy, and recognizes addresses without Icelandic characters (you can omit all the accent marks and use *th, d,* and *ae* instead of *þ, ð,* and *æ*). To get help from a real person, call 540-2700.

You can pay for the bus in cash (440 ISK), but few do this, and drivers don't give change. Instead, buy a pass, a shareable perforated strip of paper tickets, or use the Strætó app (app described in "Helpful Hints," earlier; one-day pass-1,560 ISK; three-day pass-3,650 ISK; 20 tickets-8,300 ISK and more than most visitors will need). Buses are also covered by the Reykjavík City Card (described earlier).

Tickets and passes are sold at 10-11 convenience stores, most swimming pools, information desks at the Kringlan and Smáralind shopping malls, and at the Mjódd bus junction (but not from bus drivers). Without a pass, ask the driver for a free transfer slip if you need to change buses.

Tours in Reykjavík

While you'll see bus tours advertised in Reykjavík, I wouldn't take one. The city is easy and enjoyable by foot.

Reykjavík at a Glance

▲▲▲Thermal Swimming Pools Bathe with the locals at more than a dozen naturally heated municipal pools. See page 114.

▲▲Hallgrímskirkja Iconic Guðjón Samúelsson-designed Lutheran church, with crushed-volcanic-rock exterior, serene and austere interior, and bell tower with sweeping views. **Hours:** Daily 9:00-21:00, Oct-April until 17:00. See page 85.

▲▲National Museum of Iceland Well-curated Icelandic artifacts that illustrate the nation's history. **Hours:** Daily 10:00-17:00, mid-Sept-April closed Mon. See page 96.

▲▲Harpa Boldly modern harborfront concert hall, with a fun-to-explore lobby and regular schedule of cultural events. **Hours:** Lobby open daily 8:00-24:00. See page 100.

▲▲Whales of Iceland Pricey but captivating exhibit with life-size models of the gentle giants in Icelandic waters. **Hours:** Daily 10:00-18:00, off-season until 17:00. See page 105.

▲The Settlement Exhibition Modern museum showcasing the actual ruins of a millennium-old, Viking Age longhouse. **Hours:** Daily 9:00-18:00. See page 89.

▲Kolaportið Flea Market Lively, market hall just off the Old Harbor, with fun food section. **Hours:** Sat-Sun 11:00-17:00. See page 92.

▲Einar Jónsson Museum and Garden Talented sculptor's house and studio, with free back garden decorated with his works. **Hours:** Tue-Sun 10:00-17:00, closed Mon. See page 95.

On Foot

I Heart Reykjavík, run by local blogger Auður and her associates, offers excellent two-hour small-group walking tours that start at Hallgrímskirkja church and end in front of the parliament building. While you'll get a good historical overview of the city, this tour's strength is its personal approach and insights on daily life in Reykjavík (5,500 ISK/person, at least one morning tour per day, more in summer, book on website, tel. 511-5522, www.iheartreykjavik.net, hello@iheartreykjavik.net).

CityWalk, more conventional and typically with bigger groups, has two-hour tours starting in front of the parliament building several times a day year-round. While advertised as "free," you pay whatever you feel the tour is worth; book in advance on their website. They also run a pub crawl (2,500 ISK/person, Fri-Sat

▲*Sun Voyager (Sólfar)* Modern, harborfront sculpture by Jón Gunnar Árnason evoking Iceland's earliest settlers. See page 100.

▲**Old Harbor** Modern harbor with waterfront eateries and sightseeing cruises. See page 101.

▲**Saga Museum** Viking Age mannequins reenact the legendary early-history sagas. **Hours:** Daily 10:00-18:00. See page 104.

▲**Aurora Reykjavík** Modest but enjoyable exhibit on the northern lights, starring a mesmerizing film of the aurora borealis. **Hours:** Daily 9:00-21:00. See page 105.

▲**The Pearl (Perlan)** Domed building in the suburbs with fine views over Reykjavík's skyline and the new Museum of Icelandic Natural Wonders. **Hours:** Observation deck and museum open daily 9:00-19:00. See page 109.

▲**Viðey Island** An easy ferry ride to a smattering of attractions, including the John Lennon Imagine Peace Tower (lit in fall). Ferries depart daily in season from the Old Harbor (none off-season) and Skarfagarðar (off-season Sat-Sun only). See page 110.

▲**Árbær Open-Air Museum** Collection of old buildings in the suburbs, offering a glimpse of traditional lifestyles. **Hours:** Daily 10:00-17:00, Sept-May by guided tour only. See page 112.

at 22:00) and a running tour (mobile tel. 787-7779, www.citywalk. is, citywalk@citywalk.is).

For something a little different, take the 2.5-hour **"Walk the Crash"** tour with Magnús Sveinn Helgason, a journalist and historian. Starting at the parliament building, he'll walk you around downtown and relay a lively inside story of Iceland's 2008 financial crash—one of the largest in world history—and how the country has recovered since. Magnús worked for the government commission that investigated the crash, so he knows his stuff (3,500 ISK/person, 1-2 tours a week, usually Mon and/or Fri—email or check website for times, www.citywalk.is, magnus@citywalk.is).

Food Tours: To learn more about Icelandic cuisine and cooking—from traditional dishes to modern interpretations—you can take a three- to four-hour guided walk with stops at a half-dozen local eateries. Two companies offer the tours (each one around 15,000 ISK): **Wake Up Reykjavík Food Tour** (www.wakeupreykjavik.com) and **Your Friend in Reykjavík** (www.yourfriendinreykjavik.com).

By Bike

Reykjavík Bike Tours takes you on a 2.5-hour, fairly flat guided bike tour that starts on the Old Harbor pier and does a circuit through downtown and all the way over to the university and residential areas on the other side of the peninsula. This is a nice way to get to know more of the city than the downtown core (7,500 ISK, mid-May-Sept daily at 10:00, off-season Fri-Sat only at 10:00 or 11:00, confirm times by phone or on website; Ægisgarður 7, mobile 694-8956, www.icelandbike.com).

Reykjavík Walk

This self-guided walk, rated ▲▲▲, introduces the highlights of downtown Reykjavík, as well as some slices of local life, in about two hours. While a few indoor sights may be closed early or late, the walk can be done at any time—allowing you to fit it in before or after your day-trips. The walk starts at Reykjavík's central square, Ingólfstorg, and finishes at Hallgrímskirkja, the big, landmark church on the hill. As Reykjavík is likely your first stop in Iceland, I've designed this walk as a crash course not only for the city, but for the whole country—introducing you to names, customs, stories, and themes that will come in handy from here to the Eastfjords.

Getting There: By **bus,** the Ráðhúsið, MR, and Lækjartorg stops are each a five-minute jaunt from the beginning of this walk (it's easy to find Ingólfstorg; the main street, Austurstræti, runs right into it). If coming by **car,** see "Getting Around," earlier, for parking options.

• *Begin on the modern, sunken square called...*

❶ Ingólfstorg (Ingólfur's Square)

While this somewhat dreary square isn't much to look at, it packs a lot of history and myth. Ingólfstorg is named for Ingólfur Árnason, the early Scandinavian explorer who—according to the Icelandic sagas—settled at Reykjavík in A.D. 874.

In the middle of the square, look for the two nondescript **stone pillars** (one of them marked *874*). These recall the much-told legend about Ingólfur: As he sighted the southeast coast of Iceland, he followed an old Scandinavian custom and threw the two carved wooden pillars from his best chair overboard—vowing to establish his farm wherever they washed ashore. In the meantime, he set up a temporary settlement on the South Coast and sent two of his slaves on a scavenger hunt all over the island. Three years later (in 874), they discovered the pillars here. Ingólfur called this place Reykjavík, meaning "Smoky Bay"—likely for the thermal vapor he saw venting nearby.

While the details of this story are a mix of fact and legend (see the "Sagas of the Icelanders 101" sidebar in this chapter), archaeologists confirm that the original Reykjavík farm was just a few steps from where you're standing. And for most of its history, Reykjavík remained nothing more than a farm—set between the sea and a pond a few hundred yards inland (we'll go there in a few minutes). But in the 18th century, Reykjavík gradually emerged as the logical seat of Iceland's government.

Ingólfstorg was not an open space until 1944, when a big hotel that used to stand here burned down. The lot was left vacant and became a seedy hangout where Reykjavík teens would drink, smoke, and do other things they didn't want their parents to know about. Locals called it Hallærisplan (which means, roughly, "Messed-Up Square"). Only in 1993 was it cleaned up, redesigned, and respectably renamed. Today, this square is designed for skateboarders, and hosts outdoor concerts and performances in summer. Lining the square are cafés and fast-food joints where you can pick up a hot dog, a slice of pizza, a toasted sub sandwich, or an ice-cream cone (or even a decadent *bragðarefur*—a giant cup of soft serve with mix-ins, like a supersized McFlurry).

The big, glass-fronted, **eight-story building** that dominates the square represents the latest chapter in Reykjavík's story: its re-

cent tourism boom. Long the headquarters of Iceland's biggest newspaper, those offices recently moved out to the suburbs, and the building is now a hotel. A generation ago, downtown Reykjavík was mostly offices, government institutions, cheap housing, and lots of students. But with the flood of tourism over the last decade, most of these have been replaced by hotels, bars, restaurants, shops, and tour operators; the number of Icelanders who actually live downtown has dropped sharply.

• *Let's take a little back-streets detour. Facing that big building, turn right, then walk to the end of the square. The street leaving the square is...*

REYKJAVÍK

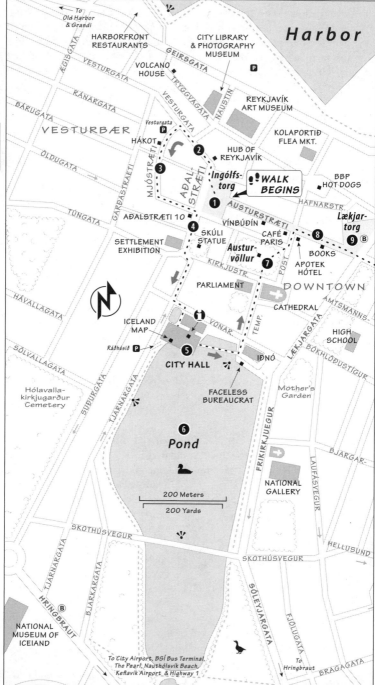

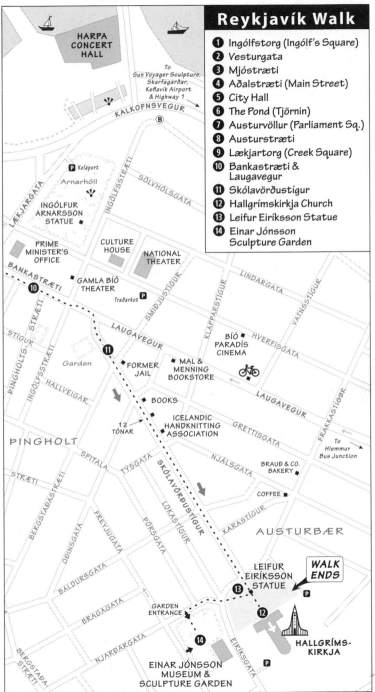

Reykjavík Walk

1. Ingólfstorg (Ingólf's Square)
2. Vesturgata
3. Mjóstræti
4. Aðalstræti (Main Street)
5. City Hall
6. The Pond (Tjörnin)
7. Austurvöllur (Parliament Sq.)
8. Austurstræti
9. Lækjartorg (Creek Square)
10. Bankastræti & Laugavegur
11. Skólavörðustígur
12. Hallgrímskirkja Church
13. Leifur Eiríksson Statue
14. Einar Jónsson Sculpture Garden

❷ Vesturgata, Reykjavík's Original Shoreline

This lovely lane (literally "West Street") is lined by colorful buildings from the early 20th century. The **yellow building** (today the Restaurant Reykjavík) was once the base of the town pier, back when the waterfront came all the way up to this point. The entry to the pier ran under the building's tower (beneath the round window). In 1874, when the king of Denmark visited Iceland, his fleet anchored in the harbor, and he came ashore on little boats right here. Around 1910, land reclamation created the modern harborfront zone, just beyond the taller modern buildings. Today, this so-called Old Harbor area has some appealing sights (see page 101).

In the sidewalk immediately in front of the yellow building, notice the brass plaque marking the **"hub of Reykjavík"**—both the symbolic gateway to the city, and the spot from where the city's address numbers radiate.

Around the left side of the yellow building, you can spot faint remains of the **original wharf,** and a little tidal pool that's still connected, underground, to the harbor. Several recommended restaurants are on or near this square (see "Eating in Reykjavík," later).

• *Now continue along Vesturgata. Just past the bright red building on the left corner, turn left onto...*

❸ Mjóstræti, Back-Streets Reykjavík

Even in the bustling downtown of Iceland's capital, you're never more than a block or two away from a sleepy residential area. Stroll a couple of blocks along Mjóstræti ("Little Street"), appreciating some slices of Reykjavík life.

A block up Mjóstræti, look right up the hill to see a humble cottage called **Hákot.** Built in the 1890s, and beautifully renovated in the 1980s, this is one of a few old houses that survive in the neighborhood. In the 1970s, many houses were knocked down after an expressway was slated to cut through here. Locals protested, and the plans were abandoned.

Continue straight along Mjóstræti, and notice one of Reykjavík's distinctive **fire hydrants**—painted in garish, McDonald's-esque red and yellow. Residents embrace these cheery hydrants, some embellished with faces, as a sort of local symbol.

You'll see many houses sided with vertical **corrugated iron** (despite the name, it's usually steel, galvanized with zinc). Since the late 19th century, corrugated metal sheets have been widely used for siding and roofing in Iceland. It stands up well to the

punishing wind and sideways rain, it doesn't burn, it's easy to maintain, it's cheap and easy to transport to Iceland, and can dress up renovated old houses as well as new ones. Many locals prefer to use brightly saturated hues, perhaps to help cheer them through the gloomy winters. Around town, you may also notice a few houses with boring gray metal: Newer siding needs to weather for a few years to get rough enough for primer and paint to adhere.

As you stroll, notice lots of **propped-open windows** (often one smaller pane built into a bigger window). Icelanders mostly heat their homes with geothermal hot water—harnessing the substantial natural power of their volcanic island. There are radiators in every room, but typically no central thermostat. Heating costs are low, so when things get too warm or stuffy indoors, Icelanders just open the window to create a cross-breeze. For tourists, opening a window also helps vent the sulfur smell that accompanies the city's scalding-hot tap water, which is piped directly into the city from boreholes in the countryside. (Residents are used to the smell and don't even notice it.)

Another way Icelanders use all that hot water is to heat **swimming pools.** Every Iceland town has a municipal thermal pool complex where locals swim laps, relax, and socialize—particularly appealing in the cold and dreary winter months. These basically feel like your hometown swimming pool...except that the water is delightfully warm-to-hot, year-round. Tourists are welcome to join in the fun, and many find it the most local-feeling experience they have in Iceland. (For more about visiting pools, see "Experiences in and near Reykjavík," later.)

Any **cats** roaming? Reykjavík has a relaxed, small-town vibe, and people tend to let their cats wander free by day. Watch for clever little cat doors built into windows and doors. You won't see many dogs, though; until 1984 they were banned in the city for health reasons (for the whole story, see page 365), and condo owners still need permission from their neighbors to keep a dog.

• *After another block, Mjóstræti dead-ends into someone's driveway. Turn left on Brattagata and head downhill. You'll pop out back at the bottom of Ingólfstorg square, on...*

❹ Aðalstræti, Reykjavík's First Street

While today it feels more like an alley, this "Main Street" (as its name means) was Reykjavík's first thoroughfare.

The **one-story, black house** on your right (at Aðalstræti 10) was originally built around 1760 for the textile industry. The current version is a complete rebuild (only the location of the walls is original), but faithful to the original style. The hand pump across the street (under the arcade) is a reminder

that, until 1910, locals used pumps like this one as their sole source of drinking water.

Turn right down Aðalstræti. A few doors down on the right is the Hótel Reykjavík Centrum. When this hotel was built in 2001, workers unearthed the ruins of a 10th-century Scandinavian longhouse—part of the original Reykjavík farm. Today it's the excellent **Settlement Exhibition,** where you can step down into the cellar and walk around the ancient structure (enter at the corner; museum described later, under "Sights in Reykjavík"). The museum's other name—Reykjavík 871±2—refers to a volcanic eruption in A.D. 871, plus or minus a few years, evidence of which was found in the house.

Opposite the hotel, a statue of **Skúli Magnússon** stands in a small square with a few trees. Skúli was an Enlightenment-era entrepreneur whose enterprises seeded settlement at Reykjavík in the mid-1700s—finally transforming it from a farm into a real town, and setting the stage for its eventual capital status. While Ingólfur may have settled in Reykjavík, Skúli put it on the map. The little square was the village cemetery until 1838.

• *Ahead of you, the big yellow building is the former branch of the Salvation Army. Loop around it to the left, following Tjarnargata for a block to Vonarstræti, where you'll see, on your left, a large, modern concrete building with a curved roof and a mossy pond in front. This is the...*

❺ Reykjavík City Hall (Ráðhús Reykjavíkur)

Enter the blocky, curved-roofed, concrete-and-glass building (daily 8:00-20:00, free WCs; use the door at the inner corner of the fountain). The city council meets upstairs, but most city offices are outside the center, and this "City Hall" is more of a ceremonial hall for the city's residents. Its ground-floor space, normally open to the public,

is rented out for concerts, exhibitions, and other cultural events.

A huge wooden **relief map of Iceland** is sometimes displayed in front of the large windows overlooking the little lake known as the Pond. The towns on the map are not labeled, but it's easy to find Reykjavík and the Reykjanes Peninsula: Look for the airport. Pick out the island's major landforms: Fjords ruffle the coastline in the northwest (the Westfjords), the east coast (the

REYKJAVÍK

Eastfjords), and the far-north (Skagafjörður and Eyjafjörður, flanking the mountainous Tröllaskagi— "Troll Peninsula"). Glacier-covered volcanic peaks loom ominously above the South Coast, while the desolate Highlands cover the middle of the country. Trace your

own route through Iceland; spotting the roads and towns around the country is absorbing. Notebooks with topographic maps help you identify fjords, mountains, and rivers. Nearby you may see a second model, with a street map of Reykjavík and elevated models of major architectural landmarks.

Stop by the official **Reykjavík TI** here for help with your sightseeing plans, or to purchase a sightseeing or bus pass.

• *Exit the City Hall next to the TI, and walk across the pedestrian bridge that runs along...*

❻ The Pond (Tjörnin)

This miniature lake feels just right for this small capital of a small country. On sunny days, parents bring small children to feed the ducks and swans that live in the Pond. In the winter, if the temperatures drop to a safe range, snow on the Pond is cleared away to make a skating rink. It's a pleasant one-mile walk all the way around.

At the far end of the pedestrian bridge, you're greeted by a statue of a **faceless bureaucrat** (see photo next page).

The period building next to him is Iðnó, Reykjavík's old theater.

Gaze out to the far end of the Pond, where you'll see some of the **University of Iceland** buildings (that's the science center with the curved glass roof). The country's oldest and largest university, with a total enrollment of around 13,000, was founded in 1911. Before that, students had to go abroad for college (mostly to Denmark)...a reminder of just how recently this country came into its own.

Farther right, rising a couple of stories above the rooftops, is the brown tower of the recommended **National Museum,** where a thoughtfully explained collection of artifacts tells the story of Iceland (described under "Sights in Reykjavík"). Along the right side of the Pond are fine homes built by wealthy families a century ago.

• *Standing next to the bureaucrat, turn your back to the Pond, cross the street, and walk straight up Templarasund. You'll arrive at a lovely little park with a big statue in the middle. Stand by the statue and get oriented to...*

❼ Austurvöllur, Iceland's Parliament Square

Translated roughly as "Eastern Field," Austurvöllur is the political center of this small country. With your back to the statue, the big,

stone building facing the square is Iceland's parliament, the **Alþingi** (pronounced, roughly, "all-thingy"). While Icelanders like to call the Alþingi the "world's oldest parliament," this is an exaggeration. The Alþingi that met at Þingvellir in the centuries after settlement was very different from a modern

democratic parliament. From about 1400 to 1800, it was an appeals court, not a legislature. Then there were 45 years when the Alþingi didn't meet at all. It was reestablished in Reykjavík, in a totally new and different form, in 1845. Finally, in 1874, Iceland received a constitution that gave the Alþingi its first real decision-making power—even though Iceland remained fully part of Denmark.

On the building's gable, notice the crowned *9*, which represents King Christian IX (the Danish ruler in 1881, when the building was erected). Engraved over four of the upstairs windows of the

Alþingi, notice the mythical "four protectors of Iceland"—dragon, eagle, giant, and bull—which also appear on Iceland's coat of arms and many Icelandic coins. (As if to drive home Iceland's closeness to the sea, the flipsides of the coins feature cod, dolphins, crab, and lumpfish.)

The Alþingi's 63 members are a lot for a country of less than 350,000 people. Icelanders vote for a party, not for a person; each party submits an ordered list of candidates, and the top names on the list get seats. There are no public tours of the Alþingi, but if parliament is in session visitors are welcome to sit in the gallery (parliament is on vacation June-mid-Sept; otherwise confirm session times at www.althingi.is—typically Mon 15:00, Tue 13:30, Wed 15:00, Thu and sometimes Fri 10:30). The gallery entrance is around the back of the building, by a fine little walled garden that's open to the public.

Now turn your attention to the statue on the pillar: **Jón Sigurðsson** (1811-1879) was the 19th-century scholar and politician who successfully advocated for Iceland's increased autonomy under the Danish crown. Jón spent most of his life in Denmark, where he politely but forcefully pressed the case for freer trade and a constitution that would reduce the king's power. At the time, many other Europeans were agitating for the same kinds of things, and often took up arms. But Icelanders achieved their goals without firing a shot—thanks largely to the articulate persistence of this one man. The parliament building was finished just a couple of years after Jón's death. In Jón's honor, his birthday—June 17—became Iceland's National Day.

Look around the **square.** Early each summer new turf is laid and flower beds are filled in preparation for National Day ceremonies and speeches. But it was quite a different scene in the winter of 2008-2009: Thousands of Icelanders gathered here to demand the government's resignation in the wake of the country's financial collapse. Protesters banged pots and pans, and pelted politicians with eggs and tomatoes (hence the protest's nickname, the "Kitchenware Revolution"). New elections were called, and the prime minister was censured for failing in his responsibilities. Ólafur Þór Hauksson—a small-town cop who became the unyielding special prosecutor for financial crimes—emerged as something of an international folk hero. A good number of bankers were tried, convicted, and in many cases jailed for their role in the crisis.

Then, in spring 2016, thousands came to this square again after it was revealed that Iceland's then-prime minister had kept some of his considerable family wealth in an offshore account in Panama. Again, new elections were called.

To the left of the Alþingi is Reykjavík's **Lutheran Cathedral** (Dómkirkjan; generally open Mon-Fri 10:00-16:00, closed

Sat-Sun except for services, occasional concerts—look for posters, www.domkirkjan.is). Surprisingly small, it was built in the 1790s and expanded in the 1840s. The city now has larger churches, but the cathedral is still regularly used for weddings, funerals, and the opening of parliament. If you

go inside, you'll find a beautifully tranquil interior, with an upstairs gallery and finely painted ceiling. The centerpiece—directly in front of the main altar—is a marble baptismal font by renowned 19th-century Danish sculptor Bertel Thorvaldsen, whose father was Icelandic.

At the right end of the Alþingi, notice the **statue of a strong woman** on a pillar: Ingibjörg H. Bjarnason (1867-1941), who was

elected Iceland's first female member of parliament in 1922. Iceland has an impressive tradition of honoring women's rights. On October 24, 1975, 90 percent of Icelandic women went on strike to drive home their importance to society. The country ground to a halt. (Icelandic men—who very quickly learned their lesson—gave the protest the tongue-in-cheek nickname "The Long Friday," which is also what Icelanders call Good Friday.) In 1980, Iceland became the first modern, democratic nation to elect a female head of state, when single mother Vigdís Finnbogadóttir became president. She served for four terms (16 years) and remains a beloved figure today.

Facing the Bjarnason statue, at the corner of the park, notice the chunk of rock split in half by **"The Black Cone."** This monument to civil disobedience was placed here (somewhat controversially) in 2012—when memories of those 2009 protests were still fresh and, for some, painful.

• *Exit the square behind Jón Sigurðsson's left shoulder, and go one short block up the street called Pósthússtræti ("Post Office Street"). Pause at the intersection with Austurstræti ("Eastern Street"), in front of Apotek Hótel.*

❽ Austurstræti, Reykjavík's Main Street

Reykjavík's main drag begins about a block to your left (at Ingólfstorg, where we started our walk) and continues about a mile to your right, changing names as it runs through town.

Looking straight ahead, on your right is the red **post office** building. Across the street on the left, the old-meets-new building is **Landsbankinn,** founded as Iceland's national bank in 1886. It was privatized around 2000, failed spectacularly in 2008, and then continued operations under a slightly altered name. Past that, at the end of the block, you'll see a white, boxy building that houses the **Kolaportið flea market** on weekends—a fun browse, even for nonshoppers (see page 92).

Tucked away kitty-corner from the flea market (just down this street and on the right, but not quite visible from here) is Reykjavík's

most-famous **hot dog stand.** In 2004, Bill Clinton was in Reykjavík to speak at a UNICEF event. When the proprietor of this stand offered him a free frankfurter, Clinton—a notorious connoisseur of junk food— just couldn't say no. Camera shutters clicked...and suddenly, eating at Bæjarins Beztu Pylsur ("The City's Best Sausages") became *the* thing to do when visiting Reykjavík. Now people stand in long lines to shell out 600 ISK for what is, by any honest assessment, a fairly average weenie.

Now look up, behind you, at the Art Deco-style facade of the **Apotek Hótel.** This was designed by Guðjón Samúelsson, Iceland's best-known 20th-century architect, who's responsible for many of the major landmarks around town—including his masterpiece church, Hallgrímskirkja.

Facing the hotel, across the street, is **Café Paris,** an old

standby. Look up at the relief on the pediment-like gable, from the 1920s, which shows an imagined scene from the settlement of the country: An established settler—standing in front of his pack animals—shakes hands with a new arrival, whose crew is taking down the mast of his longship. While you may sometimes hear the word "Viking" used to describe those early Icelandic settlers, that's not quite right. They were contemporaries (and actually relatives) of the Vikings, but had a different modus operandi: Rather than

Icelandic Names:
From Magnússon to Gunnarsdóttir

Traditionally, Icelanders' last names were patronymics, formed from the father's name plus "son" or "dóttir." So if you meet a man named Gunnar Magnússon, you know his father's name was Magnús. If Gunnar has a son Jón, he'll be named Jón Gunnarsson. A daughter María will be María Gunnarsdóttir. Get it? (This system was the norm all over Scandinavia until just a few hundred years ago.) Women keep their name at marriage.

Around 1900, fashions changed, and Icelanders started to assume family names and pass them down from generation to generation, like we do in the US. Then the pendulum swung back: In 1925, family names were banned as un-Icelandic, but people who had already taken one were allowed to keep it. (You may run into a few of these today.) Things went so far that for a few decades, immigrants who wanted to take up Icelandic citizenship had to abandon their foreign surname and choose an Icelandic patronymic (this requirement was abolished only in the 1980s). Today, with immigration rising, and many marriages between Icelandic women and immigrant men, family names are on the increase in Iceland again.

These days, Icelanders can choose to form their children's last name from either parent's first name. So, if Gunnar and Katrín have a son, they could give him the last name Katrínarson. But

pillage, plunder, and rape, the first Icelanders were mostly farmers in search of good grazing land.

Now look up the street past Café Paris (back toward Ingólfstorg). On the left side of the street, notice **Vínbúðin**—one of the unobtrusive state-run liquor stores. Only weak beer can be bought at regular stores; every other kind of alcohol can be purchased only here. While nationalized liquor stores are fairly standard in Nordic countries, Iceland has at times taken a particularly hard line against alcohol. From 1915 all the way until 1989—in an attempt to curtail everyone's favorite, cheap "gateway drug"—beer with an alcohol content over 2.25 percent was illegal. Icelanders compensated by mixing spirits—which were, oddly, perfectly legal—with light beer, creating a super-alcoholic faux-brew. Today, as if making up for lost time, Iceland has a burgeoning microbrew culture (see recommendations, including many within a few steps of this walk, on

the country's Personal Names Committee still controls what first names parents can give their children (from a list of 3,500 authorized names). While this seems oppressive, it's largely a grammatical concern—to ensure that names will work within the structure of the Icelandic language. Recently, politicians have moved to abolish the committee. Stay tuned.

All Icelanders address each other by first names, which may seem strangely informal. But in Icelandic, using a person's full first name actually has a ceremonial ring to it. Most Icelanders go by a nickname among family and friends, so Magnús's old schoolmates probably call him "Maggi." But strangers wouldn't dare call him anything less than Magnús. There's no real equivalent of "Mr." or "Ms." in Icelandic.

It's traditional for Icelandic parents to reveal their children's names only when the child is christened (usually a few weeks after birth, but the law lets them wait for up to six months). Many parents choose the name before the birth, but still follow custom and keep it a secret. Others appreciate the chance to get to know their child before deciding. In the meantime, parents use nicknames for their baby, like "The Short One."

What children do get within minutes of birth is a 10-digit identification number, based on their birth date, which follows them through life. This number, called the *kennitala,* is almost like an alternative name, and Icelanders use it very openly and casually to identify themselves to schools, banks, or the power company. Anyone can look up anyone else's ID number and address. This shocks Americans, who are used to keeping their social security number secret. Despite—or perhaps because of—this openness, identity theft in Iceland is practically unknown.

page 125). Also look for the Icelandic firewater called *brennivín.* In another anti-alcohol crusade, originally the *brennivín* bottle came with a health warning in the form of a black skull. While that's long gone, today the drink still carries the tongue-in-cheek nickname "Black Death" *(svartidauði).*

Turn right and walk up Austurstræti. After a few steps, on your right, look for one of the city center's three main **bookstores** (this one is run by Eymundsson—Iceland's answer to Barnes & Noble). Books are clearly valued here: A high percentage of Icelanders are published authors, and every Icelandic living room has shelves of books on display. Books also play a key role in Christmas gift exchanges: The Iceland publishers' association mails a catalog of the year's new releases each fall, just in time for holiday shopping lists.

Just past the bookstore, notice "The Hot Dog Stand"...taking full advantage of its prime location to hijack hungry tourists looking for the famous place around the corner.

• *Across the street from the bookstore is a 10-11 convenience store, useful for bus tickets or a bus pass. At the end of the street, you'll emerge into a square called...*

❾ Lækjartorg (Creek Square)

This square and the adjacent, busy street (Lækjargata) are named for a creek *(lækur)* that ran from the Pond (to your right) down to the sea (to your left) in Reykjavík's early days. It still flows, but was buried in an underground culvert more than a century ago.

As Reykjavík grew in the mid-1700s, the first building constructed of materials more permanent than turf or timber was

not a church or palace but a prison, built across the creek from the village center. (Look across Lækjargata to find the white stone building with five windows on the second story.) Today it's the **office of Iceland's prime minister.** The "no parking" sign out front indicates the spot reserved for the prime minister.

But no matter how high you rise in Icelandic society, you're called by your first name—so President Guðni Th. Jóhannesson is known to Icelanders simply as "Guðni." That's why, in this book, I'm on a first-name basis even with big-name historic Icelanders. This isn't necessarily because Icelanders are more casual than the norm—it's because of the unique way they form their last names. (For more on this tradition, see the "Icelandic Names" sidebar, earlier.)

Flanking the prime minister's office are two streets: **Bankastræti** (on the right) runs uphill for a couple blocks, and then changes its name to Laugavegur. This has long been the main downtown shopping street; we'll head up this way soon. **Hverfisgata** (on the left), a more heavily trafficked commercial street, is where city buses run on their way between the two main bus stops downtown: Lækjartorg (where you're standing) and Hlemmur (just under a mile to the east).

On the hill to the left of Hverfisgata are many government offices, including Iceland's supreme court, ministry of finance, and central bank. The large white building with multiple chimneys is the former city library; today it's the **Culture House,** with a modest exhibit (including a precious 14th-century illuminated manuscript; see page 93). Behind it rises the flyspace of the dark-gray **National**

Theater, whose color comes from crushed obsidian mixed into its roughcast coating—a popular look in Icelandic architecture.

Out by the water, you may just be able to see the corner of the dark, glassy, boxy building called **Harpa**—Reykjavík's concert hall and conference center. Don't trek out to Harpa now; at the end of this walk, you can head to Harpa to enter the hall's futuristic lobby for a good look at its multicolored windows.

• *Cross the busy street and walk uphill on Bankastræti (with the prime minister's office on your left).*

⑩ Bankastræti/Laugavegur, More of Reykjavík's Main Drag

By the end of the 19th century, Reykjavík had expanded, and most people lived on this side of the town's little creek. This stretch became the city's main shopping and business street. Today, most locals shop at malls and in the suburbs, and services along Laugavegur are geared toward tourists.

A half-block up on your left (just past the PM's backyard), notice another old stone building (marked with the *Stella* sign).

This was Iceland's first bank building, built in 1882, which gave Bankastræti its name.

Huff uphill along Bankastræti, noticing the moveable, blue **traffic barriers** (including some shaped like bicycles). In the summer, some stretches of this street are closed to cars to promote strolling—but be careful at intersections, as cross-streets still carry traffic.

As you walk along here, keep a very close eye on street signs; you'll spot tiny plastic **action figures** glued to some of them. This is the work of a mysterious street artist (dubbed Dótadreifarinn—"The Toy Spreader") who sneaks around the city center and glues figurines to signs and ledges, always just out of arm's reach. Spotting these as you stroll can be a fun scavenger hunt.

Also keep your eye out—both along this main strip, and in the residential side streets—for big **street-art murals.** This isn't eyesore graffiti, but quite the opposite: Locals have found that if you supply a blank canvas, it'll be tagged. But if you decorate it yourself, taggers leave it alone. So government and private property owners commission murals like these. Many of the most renowned Icelandic street artists are women. The back lanes are even more highly decorated than the main streets we're seeing on this walk—be sure to explore later.

After two short blocks, pause at the lively intersection where Skólavörðustígur splits off to the right. This is also where the street changes names to **Laugavegur** (roughly LOY-ga-VEH-grr, "Hot Springs Road")—once the walking route for those going to do their laundry in the Laugardalur hot springs east of downtown. We won't walk the entire length of Laugavegur right now, but you'll certainly find plenty of excuses to explore it while you're in town—many of the city's best restaurants, shops, and bars are on or within a few steps of this street. About 10 minutes' walk away, at Laugavegur's far end, is Hlemmur, the main city bus junction. While the entire drag is commercialized, the farther you go up Laugavegur, the less it feels like a tourist circus.

• *From here, head toward the distant church steeple on the angled, uphill street called...*

⓫ Skólavörðustígur Street

This street (SKO-la-vur-thu-STEE-grr, "School Cairn Lane") leads up to Hallgrímskirkja church. The street got its name from

a pile of rocks that Reykjavík schoolchildren set up long ago atop the hill, near where the church is now. A bit broader and brighter than Laugavegur, it's lined with cafés, restaurants, and bookstores. As it's also a bit less congested, and capped with a lovely church steeple, this street is many visitors' (and shoppers') favorite place to stroll in Reykjavík.

Just a few steps up Skólavörðustígur at #4 (on the right), notice the tiny gap between the buildings. If the gate is open, step discreetly into an adorable, private little **garden** facing a bright red house—a tranquil parallel world to the bustle just a few steps away. Many downtown blocks have an interior garden, shared among the surrounding houses. Sometimes, like here, little houses are tucked behind other houses. This was a good way to increase the capacity of your lot in this city of chronic housing shortages (and loosely enforced building regulations).

Back on Skólavörðustígur, continue a block uphill. On the left, you'll see another **old stone building.** It looks a bit like the historic jail we saw earlier—and yes, it's another former jail, built in 1874 (after the city had expanded, and this area was just outside town). This remained in use until summer 2016. Run your fingers over the chunky, volcanic rock in the building's facade.

Just past the jail, also on the left, the boxy three-story building at #11 was a bank, until the financial crisis, and now houses a branch of the Eymundsson bookstore chain.

While the lower end of the street is dominated by big, glitzy shops (like Geysir, with modern Icelandic fashion, or the venerable Rammagerðin handicraft shop), as you continue uphill the shops become smaller, more characteristic boutiques. Ceramic and jewelry shops—often with a small workshop in the back—are popular along here. At #15 (on the left), 12 Tónar is Reykjavík's most beloved music store, specializing in Icelandic tunes. A few doors up at #19 (with the metal balcony) is the Handknitting Association of Iceland's shop, where you can browse expensive but top-quality handmade Icelandic sweaters and other woolens. For more recommendations, see "Shopping in Reykjavík," later.

• *The last couple of blocks of the street are increasingly residential. It's fun to explore the side-streets in this neighborhood, where you'll find more corrugated metal siding, propped-open windows, street art, hidden gardens, and cats. But for now, continue straight uphill until you run right into...*

⓬ Hallgrímskirkja Lutheran Church

After Reykjavík's Catholic minority built their church atop the hill west of downtown in 1929, Lutheran state church leaders felt they needed to keep up. They hired the same well-known architect, Guðjón Samúelsson, and commissioned him to build a taller, bigger response on the higher hill to the east of downtown. His distinctive Hallgrímskirkja (HAHTL-greems-KEER-kyah) was designed in the 1930s, with construction beginning in 1945, but was not completed until the 1980s. On New Year's Eve, this square is one of the best spots in town to watch fireworks.

Exterior: The basalt-column motif soaring skyward on the facade recalls Iceland's volcanic origins. In the winter, as you look up from Skólavörðustígur, light shining out through the windows makes the top of the 250-foot tower glow like a giant jack-o'-lantern.

Guðjón Samúelsson (1887-1950)—an Icelander who trained in Denmark—was Iceland's most influential architect. Arriving back home after finishing his studies in 1919, he was hired as the government's in-house building designer—a plum post that he kept until his death. These were good years for architects, as Iceland urbanized and the availability of concrete opened up new design possibilities. Guðjón's favored aesthetic was the functionalist style typical of the 1920s and 1930s. He attempted to forge a distinctly Icelandic architectural style...and, because he designed so many buildings here, you might say he succeeded. In Reykjavík alone, he designed this church, the main university building, the original National Hospital building, the National Theater, the Sundhöllin swimming pool, the Apotek Hótel we saw earlier, and the Hótel Borg across the square from the parliament building.

Hallgrímskirkja is named for the 17th-century Icelandic poet Hallgrímur Pétursson, who wrote a well-known series of 50 hymns retelling the story of the Passion of Christ.

Interior: Step inside (free, daily 9:00-21:00, Oct-April until 17:00). Temporary art installations fill the entry foyer. The church's

dramatically austere nave is a sleek space culminating in classically Gothic pointed arches—but with virtually no adornments. The glass is clear, not stained, and the main altar is a simple table. Notice how the ends of the pews echo the stairstep steeple outside.

Turn around and face the massive organ, which was "crowdfunded" in 1991; people paid to sponsor individual pipes. (To the right of the door you came in, notice the collection box shaped like an organ pipe—donations for the instrument's upkeep.) The church is a popular venue for organ and choral concerts (look for posters, and see page 124).

Notice that the pews are reversible—the seat backs can be flipped over to face the organ. Not only is this in keeping with Lutheranism—where the most important aspects of worship are the sermon (pulpit) and the music (organ)—but it's very practical. In smaller towns, you can't have both a church and a concert hall—so one building has to do double-duty.

Before leaving, consider riding the elevator (plus 33 steps) to the top of the **tower,** with a fine view over the rooftops. If there's a long line for the small elevator, consider coming back in the evening.

• *Head back outside. Prominently displayed in front of the church is a...*

® Leifur Eiríksson Statue

Known as Leif Erikson (c. 970-1020) to Americans, this Viking Age explorer was—if we can trust the sagas—the first European

to set foot on the American continent. The sagas weave a colorful tale of Leifur's outlaw-family lineage and his clan's explorations. His grandfather, Þorvaldur Ásvaldsson, was exiled from Norway to Iceland, and his father, Eiríkur Þorvaldsson (Erik the Red), was in turn exiled from Iceland—establishing the first settlements on Greenland. Leifur carried on farther west, seeking a mysterious land that had been spotted by another Nordic sailor when he was blown off course.

Around five centuries before Christopher Columbus, Leifur and his crew landed in the New World, very possibly at L'Anse aux Meadows, in today's Newfoundland, where there are ruins of a Viking Age complex. Norsemen may have established more settlements in this area—which they called *Vínland* (meaning either "Land of Wine" or "Land of Meadows") for its relatively lush climate—but if so, they did not last. On his way home, according to the sagas, Leifur rescued the crew of another ship that had been stranded on a small island, and after that he was dubbed "Leifur heppni" (Leif the Lucky). The statue was donated by the US government to mark the Alþingi's 1,000th anniversary in 1930. The inscription delicately acknowledges Leifur as the "discoverer of Vínland"—but not of America.

If it's summertime, in the park flanking Leif the Lucky, look for three types of **flowers** that grow abundantly in this otherwise inhospitable land: the vivid purple Nootka lupine (from Alaska, introduced to Iceland in the mid-20th century to combat erosion); bright yellow European gorse, an alpine shrub with a pungent herbal fragrance in the early summer; and...dandelions. All three are considered weeds in much of the world, but most Icelanders don't remove them. As one local explained, "We're just happy when *anything* grows here."

• *We'll finish our walk with one more hidden sight. With the church at your back, turn left and head toward the bunker-like mansion. You'll curl around the right side of this building, passing a fun little metal cutout that lines up perfectly with the jagged roofline of the church—turn around and try it. Watch for a gate on the left and enter the...*

⑭ Einar Jónsson Sculpture Garden

Iceland hasn't produced many great artists—but Einar Jónsson (1874-1954) was one of the first and most significant. After study-

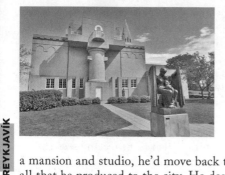

ing in Copenhagen and Rome, Einar made his name working in big European capitals. But, like so many Icelanders, after half a lifetime of living abroad he felt drawn back to his homeland. Einar struck a deal with the Alþingi: If they built him a mansion and studio, he'd move back to Reykjavík and bequeath all that he produced to the city. He designed and built this house back when this was a naked, largely uninhabited hilltop (not even the church was built yet), seeding what has become a desirable neighborhood.

Linger over the 26 bronze works in the sculpture garden (free to enter). Einar's statues—with universal human themes—are taut with tension and angst. Einar was a fearful man, yet also very spiritual; his work suggests glimmers of hope in frightening times. You'll see motifs from Norse mythology and references to Iceland's "hidden people" (elves and the like). The men are mighty warriors, and the women (whose faces are modeled after Einar's wife, Anna) are protectors. Einar and Anna lived in a small, cozy, wood-paneled penthouse apartment at the top of the building's tower. To learn more about Einar, see some plaster casts of his work, and walk through his apartment, you can pay to enter the building (today the **Einar Jónsson Museum**—described on page 95, entrance facing the church).

• *Our walk is over. Both of the two downtown shopping streets— Skólavörðustígur and Laugavegur—are lined with eating options. To quickly get down to Laugavegur (and the Hlemmur bus junction), head down Frakkastígur, which runs to the left as you face the church from the top of Skólavörðustígur; on your way to the main drag, you'll pass an excellent top-end coffee shop (Reykjavík Roasters) and a fine bakery (Brauð & Co). Dining options are described later, under "Eating in Reykjavík."*

*If you follow Frakkastígur down to Laugavegur, then cross it and continue straight downhill through an uninviting condo zone (passing by the recommended Kex Hostel café), you can cross a busy street to reach the city's iconic **Sun Voyager** sculpture. From here, it's an easy five-minute walk (with the water on your right) to the **Harpa** concert hall. The **Old Harbor** zone is just beyond.*

Sights in Reykjavík

In addition to its fine state- and city-run museums, Reykjavík has an assortment of pricey private museums (including Whales of Iceland, Saga Museum, Aurora Reykjavík, and the Phallological Museum). You might expect these to be tourist traps, but they're thoughtfully presented.

DOWNTOWN REYKJAVÍK
Near Parliament and Laugavegur

These sights are all within a short walk of the city's main artery. They're listed roughly from west to east.

▲The Settlement Exhibition (Landnámssýningin)

During downtown construction work in 2001, archeologists discovered the remains of a 10th-century longhouse from the origi-

nal Reykjavík farmstead. These ruins were carefully preserved, and a small, modern, well-presented museum was built around them. This is the most accessible (and most central) place in Reykjavík to learn about Iceland's earliest history.

Some of the oldest building remains here were covered by tephra material from a volcanic eruption; carbon dating has narrowed the time of the eruption to A.D. 871...give or take a couple of years. That's why this museum is also called "Reykjavík 871±2." It's worth paying admission to see what's left of the old Viking Age house and the modern, well-presented exhibits that surround it.

Cost and Hours: 1,600 ISK, covered by Reykjavík City Card, free for kids 17 and younger, daily 9:00-18:00, Aðalstræti 16, tel. 411-6370, www.settlementexhibition.is.

Tours: Admission includes a guided tour on weekday mornings in summer (June-Aug Mon-Fri at 11:00, no tours on weekends or off-season). Skip the free audioguide, which basically repeats posted information.

Visiting the Museum: You'll descend to cellar level and walk around the stone-and-turf wall that survives from the 65-by-26-foot longhouse. The site is explained by a circle of high-tech exhibits on the surrounding walls. You'll learn how Scandinavians first settled the Reykjavík area a little before a volcanic eruption that took place around A.D. 871. This house dates from later (around 930) and may have belonged to the grandson of Reykjavík's semi-legendary founder, Ingólfur Árnason (famous for throwing carved

REYKJAVÍK

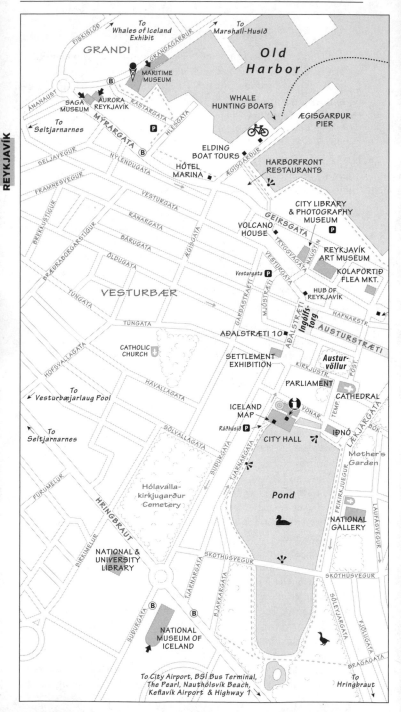

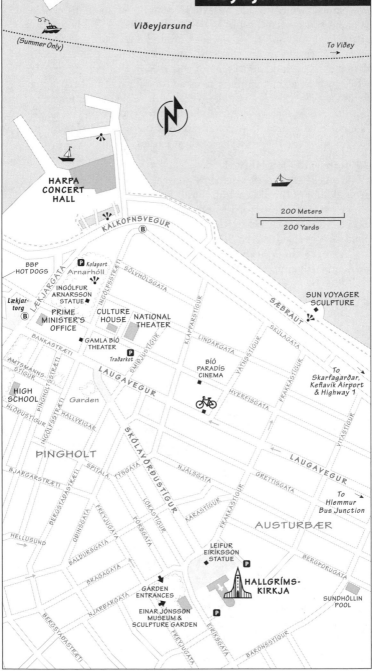

REYKJAVÍK

Reykjavík Center

Viðeyjarsund

(Summer Only)

To Viðey

HARPA
CONCERT
HALL

KALKOFNSVEGUR

200 Meters

200 Yards

BBP
HOT DOGS

Kolaport

Arnarhóll

INGÓLFUR
ARNARSSON
STATUE

Lækjar-
torg

PRIME
MINISTER'S
OFFICE

CULTURE
HOUSE

NATIONAL
THEATER

GAMLA BÍÓ
THEATER

Traðarkot

BANKASTRÆTI

AMTSMANNS-
STÍGUR

HIGH
SCHOOL

Garden

LAUGAVEGUR

BÍÓ
PARADÍS
CINEMA

SKÓLAVÖRÐUSTÍGUR

ÞINGHOLT

BJARGARSTRÆTI

HELLUSUND

BERGSTAÐASTRÆTI

NJÁLSGATA

LOKASTÍGUR

KÁRASTÍGUR

FRAKKASTÍGUR

GRETTISGATA

AUSTURBÆR

SUN VOYAGER
SCULPTURE

SÆBRAUT

SKÚLAGATA

LINDARGATA

VATNSSTÍGUR

HVERFISGATA

FRAKKASTÍGUR

VITASTÍGUR

LAUGAVEGUR

To
Skarfagarðar,
Keflavík Airport
& Highway 1

To
Hlemmur
Bus Junction

BERGÞÓRUGATA

LEIFUR
EIRÍKSSON
STATUE

GARDEN
ENTRANCES

EINAR JÓNSSON
MUSEUM &
SCULPTURE GARDEN

HALLGRÍMS-
KIRKJA

SUNDHÖLLIN
POOL

EIRÍKSGATA

BARÓNSSTÍGUR

pillars overboard to select a building site). The house of a fairly prosperous farmer, it held an extended family of about 10 people. It had a sod roof and a big hearth in the middle. The house was abandoned after only a few decades, around A.D. 1000, perhaps due to damage from a spring that still runs beneath it. Exhibits explain the landscape, flora, and fauna of this area in that era, suggesting why it was an attractive place to establish a farm. You'll see actual items excavated here: a spindle whorl with runic inscriptions, and primitive tools such as keys, fish hooks, arrowheads, and ax heads. A model and a virtual, interactive reconstruction of the longhouse further illustrate the lifestyles of these earliest Icelanders.

▲Kolaportið Flea Market

Reykjavík's flea market, open only on weekends, takes up the dingy ground floor of the old customs building.

Cost and Hours: Free entry, open Sat-Sun 11:00-17:00, closed Mon-Fri, closed or varying hours on major holiday weekends, Tryggvagata 19, tel. 562-5030, www.kolaportid.is.

Visiting the Market: While you'll see plenty of tourists, the market is still aimed largely at locals. It's fun to rummage through the stalls of used books and music, clothing (including knockoff Icelandic sweaters), and collectibles.

The food section serves as a crash course in Icelandic eats. Several stalls offer free samples. Look for the different kinds of smoked fish: *silungur* is trout, *bleikja* is  arctic char, *lax* is salmon, and *makríll* is mackerel. If you're a bit bolder, there's *harðfiskur* (air-dried, skinless white fish that's been pounded flat—eaten as a snack with butter), crunchy fish chips, or dried seaweed (which might be labeled *hollustusnakk*—"health snack"). And if you're even more daring, you can buy a tiny 200-ISK tub containing cubes of the notorious fermented shark, *hákarl* (you'll never eat more than this amount, and the rare restaurant that serves it charges much more).

Also look for other unusual Icelandic eats: horsemeat and horse sausage, and in summer, seabird eggs (typically from guillemots or other *svartfuglar*—birds in the auk family, which also includes puffins and murres). Look in the freezers for cod *(þorskur),* haddock *(ýsa),* and plaice *(rauðspretta),* which are all Icelandic, as well as Asian imports such as *pangasius* (catfish), mussels, and squid. To cleanse your palate, grab some samples at the bakery counter (they might have a layer cake with frosting or jam), or taste-test the many different varieties of chocolate-covered licorice.

Culture House (Safnahúsið)

Filling the stately former National Library building, this downtown branch of the National Museum features a semipermanent,

highly conceptual exhibit with objects from six national institutions. The audioguide (which you can rent, or browse on your phone using the free Wi-Fi) works hard to weave the exhibits together, but ultimately there are few highlights. Come here only if you have a National Museum ticket or Reykjavík City Card, and are curious to explore a fine old building.

Cost and Hours: 2,000 ISK, covered by Reykjavík City Card, includes admission to National Museum; Tue-Sun 10:00-17:00, closed Mon; Hverfisgata 15, tel. 530-2210, www.culturehouse.is.

Visiting the Museum: The exhibit begins with a display of 14 manuscripts of the *Jónsbók*—the law code imposed on Iceland by Norway in the late 1200s, and named "Jón's Book" after the man who compiled it. The earliest one is the priceless *Skarðsbók* from 1363, an illuminated manuscript painstakingly written on vellum (calfskin). As the original Icelandic saga manuscripts are not on public view, this is as close as you'll get to seeing pages from that era...and a very big deal to Icelanders. Other highlights include the elegant old reading room on the second floor; some eye-catching illustrations of Icelandic mountains and rivers by Samúel Eggertsson; and, on the top floor, an exhibit on the great auk—a large, flightless, penguin-like bird that was once abundant in Iceland, but hunted to extinction in the mid-19th century.

▲▲Laugavegur, Reykjavík's Main Drag

The city's main walking street is a delight to stroll—particularly its eastern stretch, Laugavegur. While far from "local" (you'll

rarely spot an Icelander here who doesn't work in the tourist trade), it's enjoyable to wander and browse, with characteristic old houses, vivid street art, tempting cafés and bars, and—yes—plenty of touristy puffin shops. Many visitors wind up doing several laps up and down Laugavegur, picking out new

REYKJAVÍK

details with each pass. I've described a short stretch of Laugavegur on my self-guided "Reykjavík Walk," and listed several businesses along here in the Eating, Shopping, and Nightlife sections.

Icelandic Phallological Museum (Hið Íslenzka Reðasafn)

This gimmicky museum near the Hlemmur bus junction (at the far end of Laugavegur) is a one-room collection of preserved animal penises that can be seen in 15 minutes, plus various depictions of phalluses in folk art. It's impossible to describe (or visit) this place without juvenile jokes, so here goes: You'll see more wieners than you can shake a stick at—preserved, pickled peckers floating in jars of yellow liquid. You'll see a seal's schlong, a wolf's wang, a zebra's zipper trout, a fox's frankfurter, a giraffe's gherkin, a dog's dong, a badger's baloney pony, a squirrel's schwanz, a coyote's crankshaft, a horse's hardware, a reindeer's rod, an elephant's equipment, and lots of whale willies. If you can't get through this description without giggling, maybe you should visit. If you're about to set down this book and write me an angry letter...don't.

Cost and Hours: 1,500 ISK, daily 9:00-18:00, Oct-April from 10:00, Laugavegur 116, tel. 561-6663, www.phallus.is.

Hallgrímskirkja Area

This hilltop zone is marked by the prominent tower of Reykjavík's landmark church.

▲▲Hallgrímskirkja Lutheran Church

Reykjavík's most recognizable icon is the stairstep gable of this fine, modern church, designed in the 1930s by state architect Guðjón Samúelsson. It boasts a sleek interior and a tower with grand views. For more on the church and its interior, see my "Reykjavík Walk," earlier. In the summer, there are regular  performances on its booming organ (see "Entertainment in Reykjavík," later).

Cost and Hours: Church—free; tower—900 ISK, 100 ISK for kids under 15. Church and tower open 9:00-21:00, Oct-April until 17:00. The church sometimes closes for special events. Tel. 510-1000, www.hallgrimskirkja.is.

Tower: The 250-foot-tall tower offers a commanding view of the city. A six-person elevator takes you up to the belfry, where you can look down on the city's colorful roofs amidst the clang of the church bells (cover your ears at :00 and :30 past the hour). Straight ahead, look down over the colorful roofs lining Skólavörðustígur street, which stretches toward the harbor. In the distance, if it's clear, you may see the snow-capped volcanic peak at the end of the Snæfellsnes Peninsula, 50 miles away. The closer mountain, looming to the right, is the 3,000-foot Mount Esja, a popular destination for local hikers. And to the right, the island you see is Viðey, reachable on an easy cruise (see page 103). Ponder the fact that well over half of Iceland's population lives in view of this church. Lines for the elevator can be long—if there's a crowd, swing back later in the day.

▲Einar Jónsson Museum and Garden (Listasafn Einars Jónssonar)

The former home of gifted sculptor Einar Jónsson (1874-1954)—facing Hallgrímskirkja church—has a free sculpture garden out back (described in "Reykjavík Walk," earlier). For a more intimate look at the artist, tour the museum (entrance at the front, facing the church). Inside, you'll see his home, and several large- and small-scale plaster casts for Einar bronzes that decorate the city.

Cost and Hours: 1,000 ISK, Tue-Sun 10:00-17:00, closed Mon, Eiríksgata 3, tel. 551-3797, www.lej.is.

Visiting the Museum: Stepping into the grand **entry hall,** immediately on your right is *Outlaws* (*Útlagar,* 1901). This break-through work, completed while Einar was a student in Denmark, is one of his trademark pieces. It depicts a convicted man who takes his wife's lifeless body to a cemetery before escaping with his child to live in the Highlands. (As many original Icelandic settlers were themselves outlaws—exiled from Norway—this theme is particularly poignant.) Just beyond that, *Dawn* (*Dögun,* 1906) illustrates a scene from an Icelandic folk tale, in which a girl tricks a troll by keeping him talking until the sun rises. He sweeps her up in his arm at the very moment the sun freezes him in stone, and he shakes his fist defiantly.

Then climb the tight spiral staircase to see the intimate **apartment** that Einar and his wife Anna shared—a cozy, human-scale contrast to the beefy building and Einar's dynamic works.

Yet more of Einar's sculptures are **downstairs.** In the red room, the striking *Rest* (*Hvíld,* completed in 1935) is an eerie, over-sized bust of a young man whose face is half-covered by reptilian basalt columns. Beneath his chin stands a sculptor leaning against a giant hammer, taking a break. This recalls the notion (dating back to Michelangelo) that the sculpture already exists within the stone; it's the artist's job to chip away and reveal it. In *The Spell Broken* (*Úr Álögum*, completed 1927), a St. George-like knight—protectively cradling a woman—slays a dragon by driving his sword through its head. In the green room, the evocative *Remorse* (*Samviskubit*, completed 1947) shows a man tormented by tiny, conscience-like beings. One holds his eyes open, the other recites a litany of wrong-doings in his ear, and both ensure he can't escape whatever's wracking him with guilt.

Beyond the Pond

▲▲National Museum of Iceland (Þjóðminjasafnið)

The National Museum presents a thoughtful and manageable look at the history of this island nation, making excellent use of artifacts and a top-notch audioguide that brings meaning to the exhibits. The collection is a bit dry, but rewards those with a serious interest and attention span. There's also a pleasant café and a classy gift shop.

Cost and Hours: 2,000 ISK, covered by Reykjavík City Card, includes admission to Culture House; daily 10:00-17:00, mid-Sept-April closed Mon; Suðurgata 41, tel. 530-2200, www.thjodminjasafn.is.

Tours: Rent the essential audioguide for 300 ISK—or download it for free via the museum's Wi-Fi.

Getting There: The museum is near the far end of the Pond, a pleasant 10-minute walk from City Hall along Tjarnargata; you can also take bus #1, #3, #6, or #14 to the Háskóli Íslands stop. If walking between the harbor area and the museum, you can short-cut along Garðastræti and through Hólavallakirkjugarður, the city's oldest cemetery.

Visiting the Museum: The permanent exhibit fills the two long floors upstairs, telling the story of Iceland. The exhibit is high-tech, loosely chronological, and well-explained in English.

From the ticket desk, head upstairs to begin. You'll see a few objects from the Settlement Age, including candle holders and gorgeous, oversized brass "dome brooches." Much of this floor is dominated by medieval church art, dating from after the island's conversion around A.D. 1000. The darkened room in the center displays vestments, statues, altar tapestries, and bells that were all imported from Europe—a reminder that early Icelanders were hardworking frontier farmers who had to order their luxury goods from "back east." Two locally made exceptions are wooden panels from a c. 1100 *Judgment Day* painting, and a carved crucifix from c. 1200. Nearby, examine the exquisite wood-carved door from the church in Valþjófsstaður (in eastern Iceland), illustrating the story of a knight who slew a dragon to save a lion. Like many precious

Icelandic objects, this door was taken to Denmark for safekeeping; the Danish government returned it in the 1930s, as part of a gift to Iceland in honor of the millennial celebration of the Alþingi.

Near the end of this floor, look for Guðbrandur's Bible—the first-ever Bible in Icelandic (1584). The Protestant Reformation, which began in Europe, also spread to Iceland, and to this day, the majority of Icelanders are Lutheran. The landing at the far end of the hall quickly covers the period of Danish rule, plus temporary exhibits.

The permanent exhibit continues upstairs, covering the 17th century through the present. Look for the drinking horn by Brynjólfur Jónsson, painstakingly carved with Bible scenes (1598). Following the Reformation, the Danish king also headed the Lutheran Church of Iceland, giving him tremendous power. While absolute rule by the king limited his subjects' freedom, it spurred efficiency and economic progress. Exhibits explain how, in 1703, Iceland conducted the world's first census that recorded every person's name (allowing us to know with precision that, in that year, Iceland was home to 50,358 people—99 percent of them farmers and farm workers).

Other exhibits explain how Danes maintained a monopoly on trade in Iceland. Starting around 1750, first the Enlighten-

ment and then the wave of nationalism and democracy that swept Europe also reached these shores—with diverse effects, from the reconstitution of the Alþingi in 1845, to the creation of an Icelandic national costume by a local artist in 1860 (Sigurður Guðmundsson's *skautbúningur*). Meanwhile, the humble people of Iceland toiled along on chilly, smelly farms in the countryside—peer inside a typical farmhouse living room (called a *baðstofa*). Other Icelanders lived off the sea—fishing from basic, small, open rowing/sailing boats, like the one on display, all the way up to the advent of motorized vessels.

Soon Iceland was primed for self-rule, and you'll see the desk of the man who worked hardest to make it happen: Jón Sigurðsson, who loudly agitated in Copenhagen for a national constitution and

an end to the trade monopoly. Nearby, look for "The Blue and White"—an early, unofficial Icelandic flag (missing the current red cross). In 1913, a young Icelander flew the flag from his small boat in Reykjavík harbor, until a Danish coast guard ship seized the "unauthorized" colors. Furious Icelanders demanded that the issue be resolved, and it eventually caught the attention of the Danish king—who agreed that Iceland deserved its own banner. Viewing tests from a distance showed that the blue-and-white flag was too easy to confuse with Sweden's, so the red cross was added. The flag was made official in 1915. Iceland became a sovereign state in 1918, and a fully independent republic in 1944.

The exhibit finishes with a look at modern Iceland. Look for the giant, white trawl wire cutters—a weapon used in the "Cod Wars" between Iceland and the UK (1958-1976), when the two countries squabbled over fishing rights. Finally, an airport conveyor belt displays various trappings of modern Icelandic life.

REYKJAVÍK'S ART MUSEUMS

This small community has a busy arts scene, and the six local museums described next proudly show off Iceland's 20th-century artists. Iceland's artistic tradition goes back only a century or so; most Icelandic artists (even today) traveled abroad to get a solid education. Among the country's impressive artists are the early-20th-century sculptor **Einar Jónsson** (whose former home and gallery, described earlier, faces Hallgrímskirkja church), several good painters and illustrators, and the contemporary mixed-media artist **Ólafur Elíasson** (based in Berlin, but with a studio along Reykjavík's waterfront, described later). The Reykjavík City Card covers all six branches, but I wouldn't dedicate much time here: These museums have a hard time competing with all the nearby natural beauty and interesting history.

National Gallery of Iceland (Listasafn Íslands)

The National Gallery has three branches, each with separate costs and hours. The **main branch** is near the Pond, with five gallery spaces showing off a continually changing selection of pieces from their permanent collection of mainly modern Icelandic artists. They also have a few international pieces—including works by Picasso and Munch—but these are not always on display (1,500 ISK; daily 10:00-17:00; off-season Tue-Sun 11:00-17:00, closed Mon; Fríkirkjuvegur 7, www.listasafn.is).

The **Ásgrímur Jónsson Collection** highlights a rotating selection of works by this early-20th-century painter who specialized in Impressionistic landscapes of his homeland, dynamic illustrations of the sagas, and some later, Expressionistic, Munch-like pieces (1,000 ISK; summer Tue, Thu, Sat-Sun 14:00-17:00; off-season open only Sat-Sun; in his former home at Bergstaðastræti 74—a few blocks southeast of the main branch and Pond).

The **Sigurjón Ólafsson Museum** showcases the heavily stylized, sometimes abstract works of this mid-20th-century sculptor, who studied under both Einar Jónsson and Ásgrímur Jónsson (1,000 ISK; summer Tue-Sun 14:00-17:00, closed Mon; off-season Sat-Sun only, closed Dec-Jan; northeast of downtown near the Skarfagarðar cruise terminal, at Laugarnestangi 17).

Reykjavík Art Museum (Listasafn Reykjavíkur)

This institution has three branches, each with changing exhibits focusing on modern art (for the latest lineup, see www.artmuseum.is). The **main branch,** right downtown and near the Kolaportið flea market at Tryggvagata 17, has an eclectic range of temporary exhibits, but almost always highlights a few works by Pop artist Erró—Iceland's answer to Roy Lichtenstein. The **Kjarvalsstaðir** branch exhibits some works by idiosyncratic modern painter Jóhannes Sveinsson Kjarval, who blended Icelandic landscapes with abstract and surreal flourishes (it's a 10-minute walk south of the Hlemmur bus junction, in the Klambratún park at Flókagata 24). And the **Ásmundarsafn** branch, in the eastern neighborhood of Laugardalur, highlights work by the mid-20th-century, mostly abstract, Miró-like sculptor Ásmundur Sveinsson, displayed in his architecturally striking former home (on Sigtún, near the corner of Reykjavegur).

Cost and Hours: All three museums are covered by a 1,600-ISK ticket for 24 hours, covered by the Reykjavík City Card, and open daily 10:00-17:00. The main branch stays open until 22:00 on Thu, and Ásmundarsafn has shorter hours off-season (13:00-17:00, www.artmuseum.is).

Reykjavík Museum of Photography (Ljósmyndasafn)

This museum features Icelandic photography, both contemporary and historical. It's near the Reykjavík Art Museum's main branch, on the top floor of the downtown City Library (1,000 ISK, covered by Reykjavík City Card, open Mon-Thu 10:00-18:00, Fri from 11:00, Sat-Sun 13:00-17:00, Tryggvagata 15, www.borgarsogusafn.is).

ALONG THE WATERFRONT

These sights are spread along a lengthy stretch of the city waterfront. I've listed them roughly from east to west.

Just Below the Main Drag

These sights are just downhill from Bankastræti/Laugavegur streets.

▲Sun Voyager (Sólfar)

This popular outdoor stainless-steel sculpture is shaped like an old Viking boat, pointing northwest in the direction of the setting sun in summer. This ode to the sun

is a good place to watch the sea, take a selfie, and ponder the promise of undiscovered territory that brought Scandinavians to Iceland more than a thousand years ago—and the impulses that pushed them farther west, to Greenland and Canada. The sculpture, by Icelandic artist Jón Gunnar Árnason, is a few blocks along the shore past Harpa, at the base of Frakkastígur street, about a five-minute walk below Laugavegur; drivers on the westbound waterfront highway will find a handy pull-out right at the sculpture.

▲▲Harpa Concert Hall

One of Reykjavík's newest landmarks, this cutting-edge performing arts and conference center feels too big for such a small city.

That's because the ambitious building was conceived during Iceland's banking mania. When the crash came in 2008, construction had already begun. Some cynics proposed that it be left half-built, as a monument to the greed and excess of unbridled capitalism. In the end, Harpa was finished, but plans for a new residential and commercial quarter around it (including a striking bank headquarters) were shelved. By the time it was completed and opened in 2011, Harpa was hemorrhaging money, kept alive thanks only to huge subsidies (which some Icelanders feel would be better spent elsewhere). Despite the woes, Reykjavík wound up with a fine performance space, and the city will grow into it. In 2013, the building (designed by the Danish Henning Larsen firm), won the EU's prestigious Mies van der Rohe Award—achieving the goal of putting Iceland on the world architectural map.

Harpa's honeycombed facade, designed by Danish-born Icelandic artist Ólafur Elíasson, is the most-loved part of the building: In summer the window panes reflect the light in patterns, and in winter they're illuminated in pretty colors. The choice of location, parroting the harborside opera house cliché that started in Sydney, unfortunately separates Harpa from the rest of downtown across a busy four-lane road. But photographers drool over the building, and find lots of great angles to shoot. Don't miss the view from the far end of the pier that extends to the right of the building, where the facade is reflected in the harbor along with sailboats.

Be sure to step inside, where you're bathed in the light of those many windows. The dominant interior materials are black concrete and red wood, evoking the volcanic eruptions that have shaped Iceland. To enjoy the building's full effect, catch a performance (see options under "Entertainment in Reykjavík," later) or take a tour.

Cost and Hours: Lobby free to enter, daily 8:00-24:00; summer 30-minute tour—1,500 ISK, hourly 10:00-17:00; off-season 45-minute tour—2,200 ISK, 1-2/day; café and gift shop, tel. 528-5000, www.harpa.is.

Old Harbor Area

Reykjavík's Old Harbor—about a 10-minute walk west of Harpa—isn't a creaky, shiplap time capsule, but an industrial-feeling port. Tucked around the busy berths and piers are a few seafood restaurants, kiosks selling boat trips, and (at the far end) a smattering of museums. To get here, walk out from downtown (10 minutes), or take bus #14 to the Mýrargata stop.

▲Exploring the Harbor

To get your bearings at the harbor, stand on the seaward side of the turquoise-colored sheds (which house some recommended restaurants) and face the bob-bing boats. This "old" harbor was built only in the 1910s, on reclaimed land. (For much of its history—back when Reykjavík was a farm, then a small town—there was good anchor-age, but no real harbor.) Today, heavy traffic has moved to the newer container terminal far-

ther along the peninsula. The harbor serves a mixture of excursion boats, small craft, the coast guard (notice the hulking gray ships with red-and-blue trim), and a few fishing trawlers that bring their catch to processing plants. A single small cruise ship can also moor in the harbor (larger ones use the cruise terminal in a different part of town).

On your left is the Ægisgarður pier, lined with ticket offices for several whale-watching tours (described next), as well as bike tours. On your right, across the harbor, you can see the angular, glass facade of the Harpa concert hall. And the dramatic mountain ris-ing up straight ahead is Esja—six miles away and 3,000 feet high.

Stroll out to the end of the **Ægisgarður pier** to comparison-shop excursion boats, and to get a good look at the hodgepodge of vessels that call this harbor home. At the beginning of the pier, an anti-whaling organization would love to talk you out of sampling whale meat. At the far end (on the left), you'll see part of Iceland's whale-hunting fleet moored (look for the black-and-white boats called *Hvalur 8* and *Hvalur 9*)—an odd juxtaposition with the whale watching industry all around you.

Back at the base of the pier, in front of Hótel Marina, is a slip where boats are hauled up to be painted (one of the remain-ing vestiges of the maritime industry here). To extend your visit to the nearby Grandi area—with several sightseeing attractions and eateries—simply follow the footpath between the harborfront and Hótel Marina. For more on this area, see "Grandi," later.

Whale Watching and Other Boat Trips

Whale watching is a popular Reykjavík activity. While it can be en-joyable to get out on the water—and catching a glimpse of a whale is undoubtedly exciting—it's a substantial investment of time and money, particularly given that you may see nothing at all. Before deciding to go on a whale-watching cruise, read the description on page 46. As an alternative to a pricey whale-focused trip, consider a faster and cheaper boat trip—such as to the island of Viðey (see later). And if you want to be assured of seeing "whales"—very up-close—you may prefer a visit to the Whales of Iceland exhibit, a short walk away (described under "Grandi," later). If you're traveling around Iceland, be aware there are also whale-watching opportunities in the north, in the Akureyri area and in Húsavík (both covered in The Ring Road chapter).

The many boat tour companies with ticket booths along the Old Harbor's Ægisgarður pier are fiercely competitive, offering

much the same experience. For the latest prices, schedules, and details, check each company's website, look for brochures locally, or stop by the sales kiosks. The most established outfit is **Elding** ("Lightning," described later); others include **Whale Safari** (www.whalesafari.is), **Special Tours** (www.specialtours.

is), and **Ambassador** (www.ambassador.is). While Elding is typically the most all-around reliable choice, check the latest online reviews to survey the pros and cons of each one. For comparison's sake, I've outlined Elding's offerings here. Prices are typically a bit cheaper if you prebook directly online, where you'll usually find special offers.

Whale Watching: The **classic** whale-watching trip is three hours and runs daily all year, weather permitting (from 6/day July-Aug to 1/day Dec-Jan; adults 11,000 ISK, children 7-15 pay half-price, children under 7 free; Ægisgarður 5, tel. 519-5000, www. elding.is). You'll pay nearly double for an **"express"** option on a "RIB"—a rigid inflatable boat that also includes a high-speed zip across the waves. You'll be issued a warm coverall and goggles for this two-hour thrill ride (20,000 ISK, mid-April-Oct only).

Other Boat Trips: Elding and their competitors also run other seasonal boat trips. The **puffin-watching** cruise (mid-May-mid-Aug only) is shorter (1 hour) and cheaper (6,500 ISK adults) than whale watching—so if you're most interested in riding a boat, it's a reasonable alternative. Cheaper still is Elding's 20-minute ferry service to **Viðey Island,** which gets you out on the water while saving you the overland trip to the Skarfagarðar dock (1,500 ISK round-trip, 2/day, mid-May-Sept only; for more on what to do on the island, see page 110). In the early winter (early Oct-early Dec), when the **Imagine Peace Tower** on Viðey Island is illuminated, Elding offers a two-hour cruise for a closer look (8,500 ISK). Anglers enjoy the **sea-angling** trips (3 hours trying your luck catching cod, haddock, mackerel, and catfish, with an on-board grill party at the end, May-Aug only, 14,200 ISK). And in the dark months, you can take a two-hour, late-evening cruise in hopes of viewing the **northern lights** from the water (11,000 ISK, Sept-mid-April at 21:00 or 22:00).

Volcano House

This attraction, a block off the Old Harbor, features a modest exhibit and a screening room that alternates between two documentaries explaining Iceland's most famous recent eruptions: the Westman Islands in 1973, which swallowed up part of the town of Heimaey (20 minutes); and Eyjafjallajökull in 2010, which halted European air traffic (25 minutes). The movies are interesting, particularly if you're not getting beyond Reykjavík and are curious about Iceland's famous volcanoes, but it's pricey.

Cost and Hours: 2,000 ISK, daily 9:00-22:00, last film begins at 21:00, Tryggvagata 11, tel. 555-1900, www.volcanohouse.is.

Grandi

The long, broad peninsula that juts out beyond the far end of the Old Harbor is an up-and-coming district called Grandi. This former sandbar, built up with landfill, is an odd assortment: A spread-out strip of old warehouses and new big-box stores, but with a lively little waterfront zone (along Grandagarður) where you'll find some excellent eateries, and several sights (which I've listed in the order you'll approach them, if walking from the Old Harbor). At the far tip of the peninsula—a 15-minute walk or short drive away—is a trendy little cultural zone, anchored by the Marshall-húsið arts center.

▲Saga Museum

The Saga Museum is your best bet for an experience focused on the stories of the early Norsemen who turned Iceland's wilderness into a European community (even the National Museum covers the sagas only tangentially). This place does a valiant job of telescoping the sagas into an educational 35 minutes. Though expensive, it's far better than you'd expect for a walk-through of 17 Viking Age mannequin scenes depicting Iceland's Settlement Age. Each scene is rooted in textual evidence from the sagas and well-described by the audioguide (which is academic enough that it might bore younger or less interested visitors). At the end, you can dress up in Viking garb for a photo.

Cost and Hours: 2,100 ISK, 800 ISK for kids 6-12, daily 10:00-18:00, Grandagarður 2, tel. 694-3096, www.sagamuseum.is.

REYKJAVÍK

▲Aurora Reykjavík: The Northern Lights Center

If weather and daylight conditions are imperfect during your visit, this attraction may be more satisfying than trying to see the northern lights in person. You'll walk through some sparse exhibits, including one on legends and superstitions that attempted to explain these once-mysterious dancing lights. Then you'll learn a bit about the science of the phenomenon. But the main attraction is an extremely soothing 22-minute widescreen film featuring time-lapse footage of the aurora borealis at points around Iceland, photographed over eight years of cold nights. In the gift shop, you can slip on a pair of virtual reality goggles and spin around in a chair, tracking the lights as they flutter through the sky. (For more on the northern lights, and how to see them yourself, see the Icelandic Experiences chapter.)

Cost and Hours: 1,600 ISK, daily 9:00-21:00, Grandagarður 2, tel. 780-4500, www.aurorareykjavik.is.

Reykjavík Maritime Museum (Sjóminjasafnið í Reykjavík)

This well-done but fairly dry exhibit considers Reykjavík's connection to the sea. Upstairs is the permanent exhibit, which traces Reykjavík's history from remote farm to bustling capital—partly thanks to its role as a fishing, shipping, and maritime center. Throughout you'll see plenty of well-described artifacts (including full-size boats), and life-size dioramas re-creating various chapters in the city's history. You'll learn why stockfish (naturally dried in the cold Reykjavík wind) was so important on early voyages, how boats gradually evolved from rowing and sailing to industrial trawlers, and how radios and navigational technology improved over time.

Cost and Hours: 1,600 ISK, daily 10:00-17:00, Grandagarður 8, tel. 411-6300, www.borgarsogusafn.is.

▲▲Whales of Iceland

Tucked unassumingly in a box-store zone just a five-minute walk beyond the museum strip, this attraction fills a cavernous ware-

house with life-size models of the whales found in the waters around Iceland. The models are impressively detailed and bathed in a shimmering blue light, and you're invited to wander under and among them, getting an up-close view of the graceful creatures. The essential audioguide (free to download via the exhibit's Wi-Fi) is informative and engaging. Begin with the smaller marine mammals: dolphin, narwhal, orca. Then step

Sagas of the Icelanders 101

As with tales of Beowulf, King Arthur, and Robin Hood, scholars don't know how much of the Icelandic sagas is historically based and how much is fictionalized. But all agree that the sagas are an essential resource for understanding both Iceland's history and the cultural heritage it shares with mainland Scandinavia.

Icelanders have strong narrative traditions. Before they had a written language, legends and laws were passed down orally. With Christianity around A.D. 1000 came the Latin alphabet, which Icelandic scribes used to document their history, writing mostly in their own language.

These historical narratives, known collectively as "the sagas," were written on precious vellum (calfskin) mainly in the 13th and 14th centuries. It was the Icelanders who first wrote down the dynamic stories of the early Norsemen—from myths of Norse gods like Óðinn (Odin) and Þórr (Thor) to early histories of Scandinavian warriors and kings. Like the epic poems of the ancient Greeks, the sagas provide a cultural foundation for the Nordic people, stretching all the way through history to the present.

Here's a simplified overview of some of the most famous or influential sagas and other early writings:

The **Book of Settlements** (*Landnámabók*)—not strictly a "saga"—documents the earliest ninth- and tenth-century settlers in Iceland. This chronicle tells the story of Hrafna-Flóki (the Raven) Vilgerðarson, who followed a bird to Iceland after he'd been blown off-course on his way to the Faroe Islands; and the story of Ingólfur Árnason, who threw two carved pillars overboard and built his settlement where they washed up, founding Reykjavík. Remarkably, the Book of Settlements lists more than 400 different families, where each one settled, their family tree, and vivid stories of what they encountered here. The much shorter **Book of Icelanders** (*Íslendingabók*), written by Ari fróði ("the Wise") Þorgilsson in the early 12th century, gives a concise summary of the history of Iceland up to Ari's own time, including the establishment of the Icelandic Commonwealth and the conversion to Christianity.

The **Saga of Erik the Red** (*Eiríks saga rauða*) and the **Saga of the Greenlanders** (*Grænlendinga saga*), known together as "the Vínland sagas," tell of how Eiríkur rauði ("the Red") Þorvaldsson

(950–c. 1003), banished from Norway, then Iceland, founded a Norse settlement in Greenland; and how his son, Leifur heppni ("the Lucky") Eiríksson, explored what we now know as North America.

Egill's Saga *(Egils saga Skallagrímssonar)* tells the story of Egill Skallagrímsson (c. 904–c. 995). Egill is a fascinatingly complex figure: Swarthy and ugly, he was both a fearsome champion warrior and a tender-souled poet. When he was just seven years old, after losing a game, a furious Egill buried his ax in the head of his opponent—claiming his first of many victims. And yet, Egill composed his first poem at the tender age of three, and went on to author some of the loveliest verse in Icelandic literature (after two of his children died, Egill composed the heartbreaking "Lament for My Sons"). Egill's Saga tells of his tortured relationship with his equally short-tempered father, Skalla-Grímur ("Grímur the Bald"); his friendship and rivalry with his dashing brother, Þórólfr; his relationship with his foster sister, turned-sister-in-law, turned wife, Ásgerður; his run-ins with the powerful witch Gunnhildur; and his clashes with his nemesis, King Harald Fairhair of Norway.

Njál's Saga *(Brennu-Njáls saga)* tells the story of wise Njáll Þorgeirsson and his best friend, the gallant Gunnar Hámundarson. Things take a tragic turn—as they always do in the sagas—as early Iceland's penchant for escalating blood feuds spirals out of control, culminating in several tragic deaths. (Spoiler: The protagonist is also known as Brennu-Njáll—"Burning Njáll.")

The **Saga of the People of Laxárdalr** *(Laxdæla saga)* is a gripping love triangle. Childhood friends Kjartan Ólafsson and Bolli Þorleiksson fall in love with the same woman, the beautiful Guðrún Ósvífrsdóttir. Tragedy ensues.

Icelanders also recorded mythic histories much older than the settlement of Iceland. **Völsunga Saga,** which may have roots in the fifth-century conquests of Attila the Hun, is a sprawling, epic tale of the Völsung clan, including Sigurðr Fáfnisbani ("Slayer of the dragon Fáfnir"), which has inspired artists from Richard Wagner to J. R. R. Tolkien. The two Eddas—the anonymous **Poetic Edda** and Snorri Sturluson's **Prose Edda**—contain ancient poetry that records the myths of the Germanic pagan religion.

Snorri Sturluson (1179-1241)—who also wrote **Heimskringla,** the history of the Norwegian kings—was himself a dynamic figure whose life is described in **Sturlunga Saga.**

For a hefty (and I mean hefty) sample of some of the better-known sagas, pick up *The Sagas of the Icelanders,* a good, brick-like English translation edited by Robert Kellogg.

into a vast space to ogle the majestic giants: pilot whale, humpback whale, sei whale, bowhead whale, minke whale (the one you'll see on local menus—fittingly suspended above the museum café), *Moby Dick*-style sperm whale, and the largest specimen, the blue whale—which can grow up to 110 feet long. You'll also get to see (and heft) a whale's tooth and some baleen. While this is very expensive considering the brief amount of time most visitors spend here, it's legitimately educational and scratches your Icelandic-whale itch.

Cost and Hours: 2,900 ISK, 1,500 ISK for kids ages 7-14, free for kids under 7, daily 10:00-18:00, off-season until 17:00, Fiskislóð 23, tel. 571-0077, www.whalesoficeland.is.

Getting There: The exhibit is a little tricky to find. From the Maritime Museum and recommended Grandi restaurants along Grandagarður, walk to the end of the first long, white-and-turquoise warehouse building with eateries and boutiques, then turn left on Grunnslóð and walk one long block. You can also take bus #14 to the Grunnslóð stop, or drive (free parking right in front).

Marshall-húsið Art Center

Filling a converted fish factory at the far tip of the pier (and of interest mainly to art lovers with a car), this arts center hosts several galleries. The big draw is the gallery of Ólafur Elíasson, the renowned Icelandic artist who was born in Denmark and keeps a (private) studio upstairs here. Ólafur—who helped design Reykjavík's Harpa concert hall—specializes in large-scale, multimedia pieces that combine technical precision with intangible elements like light, water, wind, temperature, and movement. The building also has two other artist-run gallery spaces (The Living Art Museum, www.nylo.is; and Kling & Bang, www.this.is/klingogbang) and Marshall, an appealing **$$$** café/restaurant facing the harbor (same hours as galleries, tel. 519-7766).

Cost and Hours: All galleries are free, Tue-Sun 12:00-18:00, Thu until 21:00, closed Mon, Grandagarður 20, bus #14 to Fiskislóð stop.

Nearby: This far tip of Grandi has started to attract some trendy businesses. Across the street in a nondescript warehouse zone, you'll find the flagship store of **Farmers Market,** with updated Icelandic fashion (closed Sun; city-center branch described under "Shopping in Reykjavík") and **Omnom,** a boutique chocolate factory (closed Sun, www.omnomchocolate.com).

OUTSIDE THE CENTER

You'll need a car, a bus, or a boat to reach the sights in this section.

Just South of Downtown
▲The Pearl (Perlan)

This striking observation deck/restaurant/museum was created in the 1990s at the site of the city's former water storage tanks.

Come here for the view of the city and surroundings from the circular fourth-floor **viewing platform,** which rings a glass dome above the old water tanks. While the Hallgrímskirk-ja tower puts Reykjavík's rooftops at your feet, the Pearl's sweeping views take in the full 360-degree panorama of the city and its backdrop of sea and mountains.

Get your bearings by looking north to the rugged ridge of Mount Esja, then pan left, where you can't miss the spire of Hall-grímskirkja. Farther to the left (if it's clear) you'll spot the snowy white triangle of Snæfellsjökull on the northwest horizon, 75 miles away as the puffin flies. The view to the west is dominated by the bay of Faxaflói, and beyond that is the Denmark Strait. Sail 460 miles due west, and you'll be in Greenland. To the southwest you'll see a few small peninsulas jutting into the bay, and, in the distance, volcanic cones that mark the Reykjanes Peninsula, where the Blue Lagoon and Keflavík Airport lie.

The old tanks below the dome have been converted into a **Museum of Icelandic Natural Wonders,** with informative dis-

plays about Iceland's unique environment. Highlights include a short walk through an artificial 230-foot-long ice cave (chilled to 15°F, but don't worry—they provide warm jackets), and a simulation of what it's like to stand on top of Vatnajökull, Iceland's largest glacier. A planetarium and exhibits covering geology, sea life, birds, earthquakes, volca-noes, and the northern lights are also part of the line-up.

The Pearl is worth a quick stop for driv-ers, who will likely pass by on their way into and out of town. There's a convenient but pricey café on the fourth floor, an expensive restaurant on the fifth (in the dome), and a branch of the Rammagerðin gift shop.

Cost and Hours: Observation deck—490 ISK; exhibit—3,000

ISK, 1,500 ISK for kids 6-15, daily 9:00-19:00, last entry one hour before closing; www.perlanmuseum.is.

Getting There: It's easiest to drive; there's a big, free parking lot. By bus, take #18 from Hlemmur two stops to Perlan. You could also take bus #5 to Nauthólsvegur and walk up the hill along the paths.

Nearby: Around the Pearl is the forested **Öskjuhlíð** hill, with walking paths, World War II ruins (signboards explain them), many rabbits (descended from escaped pets), the temple for Iceland's revived pagan religion (the "first Norse temple built here in a thousand years," www.asatru.is), and a large cemetery, Fossvogs-kirkjugarður.

Northeast of Downtown
▲Viðey Island
On a nice day, spend an afternoon enjoying the views of the sea and the mountains from this island a few hundred yards offshore. It's a sleepy sight, and takes a little work to reach, but it gets you into the Icelandic outdoors inexpensively and without a trip out of town. And the island comes with an interesting history.

Getting There: You have two options for reaching Viðey (schedules below). From the Old Harbor in the city center, Elding runs a direct but infrequent ferry (2/day, summer only, 20 minutes). Or—for a more frequent and much shorter connection—go to the Skarfagarðar ferry dock, by Reykjavík's cruise ship terminal, where small passenger ferries make the five-minute crossing to the island (take bus #16 from Hlemmur six stops to Skarfagarðar). Drivers park for free by the Skarfagarðar dock.

Cost and Hours: The ferry is 1,500 ISK roundtrip from the Old Harbor, 1,200 ISK round-trip from Skarfagarðar, covered by Reykjavík City Card; sights on the island are free. Ferries from the Old Harbor leave daily mid-May-Sept at 11:50 and 14:50 (none off-season); last return from island at 17:30. Hourly ferries from Skarfagarðar leave mid-May-Sept daily 10:15-17:15, last return from island at 18:30; Oct-mid-May Sat-Sun only 13:15-15:15, last return from island at 16:30. Ferry info at tel. 519-5000, www.elding.is.

Visiting the Island: Above the island's dock, the large, restored **house** from the 1750s is the oldest in the capital area. It was originally built for Iceland's Danish governor, but he chose to live in Reykjavík instead. Inside is a modest café, a free exhibit about the island, and a free WC. Next door, look into the small, traditional church, which is almost as old (from the 1760s).

From where you land, you can stroll to either end of the island in about 15 minutes. To the left, the west part of the island is empty grassland except for a series of columnar basalt statues by

American sculptor Richard Serra. To the right, the road through the east part of the island leads to an **abandoned village** that, in the 1920s, had a port almost as important as Reykjavík's. You can enter the old village school, which has a photography exhibit on the island's history.

Next to the café is the **Imagine Peace Tower**—a powerful vertical pillar of light, installed and paid for by Yoko Ono. Each year it shines from October 9, John Lennon's birthday, until December 8, the day he died (www.imaginepeacetower.com).

In Laugardalur, East of Downtown

Though modest by international standards, the Laugardalur (LOY-gar-DA-lurr) valley—just east of downtown—makes a pleasant outing on a nice day and lets you hang out with Icelandic families and their kids. You pay to enter the zoo and amusement area (the adjacent botanic garden is free). A lovely café in the gardens serves meals. There's also an indoor ice rink, and the Reykjavík Art Museum's Ásmundarsafn branch is nearby (see listing, earlier).

Getting There: By bus, take #2, #5, #15, or #17 to the Laugardalshöll stop and walk 10 minutes downhill to the parking lot and entrance.

Family Park and Zoo (Fjölskyldu-og Húsdýragarðurinn)

The park and zoo combines animal exhibits, amusement park rides, and a giant playground area. You'll see Icelandic farm animals—

pigs, cows, horses, sheep—plus a seal pool, birds, reindeer, rabbits, and a small aquarium. The website lists feeding times (click on "Dagskrá"). The park is open all year, but in winter it's a bit desolate, especially on weekdays, and most rides are closed. Quick Icelandic horse rides for little kids are offered year-round (Sat-Sun at 14:00). If you're hungry, you can grab a meal at the nondescript café, or stop by one of the hot-dog or ice-cream stands and enjoy a picnic at the outdoor tables with grills.

Cost and Hours: 860 ISK, covered by Reykjavík City Card, less for kids; rides cost about 250-750 ISK, or buy a day pass for 2,200 ISK; daily 10:00-18:00, mid-Aug-May until 17:00; Múlavegur 2, 411-5900, www.mu.is (yes, that's the Icelandic word for "moo").

Botanic Garden (Grasagarður)

Next to the Family Park and Zoo, the city-run botanic garden showcases local trees, herbs, flowers, and other plants. Buried in the garden is the excellent **Flóran café** (described later, under "Eating in Reykjavík"), which makes a visit worthwhile even on a rainy day (free, daily 10:00-22:00, Sept-April until 15:00, tel. 411-8650, www.grasagardur.is).

Nearby: Follow the parkland five minutes downhill from the gardens past the ponds and bridges to an open grassy area. Here you can see the remains of the washing troughs and channels where city folk used to do their laundry in hot spring water, all the way up to the 1970s. Outdoor posters tell the story, and give you a feel for how fast the country has modernized.

Ice Rink (Skautahöllin)

Next to the parking lot for the zoo and gardens is the city's indoor ice rink with public skating most afternoons—a useful bad-weather option (entry including skate rental-1,500 ISK, less for kids; closes for a few weeks in summer, confirm current hours on website; Múlavegur 1, tel. 588-9705, www.skautaholl.is).

FARTHER EAST OF REYKJAVÍK

The first listing, for the open-air museum, is just on the outskirts of town. The other listings are farther east, roughly on the way to or from the Golden Circle loop. If you're efficient, you may be able to squeeze one of these into your Golden Circle day trip, or see the Hellisheiði Power Plant on the way to the South Coast. Or you can consider these as easy side-trips from the capital—each is about a 30-minute drive from downtown.

▲Árbær Open-Air Museum (Árbæjarsafn)

Reykjavík's open-air museum is a modest collection of old buildings and farm animals—meant to help visitors envision Icelandic life in the 1800s. Homes hold period furnishings and reward those with the patience to poke around and ask questions; while everything is described in English, exhibits seem designed for Icelandic families. At the far edge of the property, the four attached houses (one with a sod roof) are the only ones that were  originally located here; walking through them, you can see how each successive generation added their own wing. The grounds—tucked next to a subdivision, with a highway rumbling along the horizon—are underwhelming, especially if you've visited the lush open-air museums elsewhere in northern Europe. But the exhibits compensate.

Make an effort to time your visit to coincide with the 13:00

hour-long guided tour (included in admission). Note that off-season (Sept-May), this tour is the only time you can enter the museum. In December, in the weeks before Christmas, the museum opens with a holiday spirit on Sundays from 13:00 to 17:00.

Cost and Hours: 1,600 ISK, covered by Reykjavík City Card, free for kids under 17. Museum open daily 10:00-17:00, Sept-May by guided tour only—daily at 13:00. Café (waffles and snacks) open June-Aug daily 11:00-17:00 and on the Sundays before Christmas. Kistuhylur 4, tel. 411-6300, www.borgarsogusafn.is.

Getting There: The museum is at the end of the street called Kistuhylur, just off the busy highway 49. The easiest bus connection from downtown is #16 from Hlemmur to the Strengur/Laxakvísl stop.

Halldór Laxness House (Gljúfrasteinn)

Iceland's most famous author, Nobel Prize winner Halldór Laxness (1902-1998), lived in a house called Gljúfrasteinn ("Canyonstone"). The house has been preserved as a museum; an audioguide explains each room. The backyard borders on a rushing stream.

Cost and Hours: 900 ISK, daily 9:00-17:00; Sept-Oct and March-May Tue-Sun 10:00-16:00, closed Mon; Nov-Feb Tue-Fri 10:00-16:00, closed Sat-Mon; tel. 586-8066, www.gljufrasteinn.is.

Getting There: It's one of the last houses on the right as you drive up the Mosfellsdalur valley on highway 36, about 25 minutes from downtown Reykjavík. You can easily combine Laxness's house with a visit to Þingvellir, but doing the house plus the whole Golden Circle in a day is too much.

Background: Born in Reykjavík, Halldór Guðjónsson was the eldest son of parents who started life poor. His father worked in road construction, and bought a farm at Laxnes in Mosfellsdalur when Halldór was three. Halldór grew up in the valley and started to write as a teenager. Like many Icelanders of his time, he took a surname (based on the farm where he grew up) instead of using his traditional patronymic. In the 1920s and 1930s he traveled in Europe and America, and converted to Catholicism. In 1945, he settled at Gljúfrasteinn, close to where he grew up, with his second wife. Here he lived comfortably, but not lavishly.

Over his lifetime, Laxness wrote more than a dozen novels, some brilliant...and others barely readable. *Independent People* (in Icelandic, *Sjálfstætt fólk*) is the best known. He also wrote short stories, plays, poetry, travel books, memoirs, and other nonfiction. In his writing, Laxness concerned himself strongly with social justice and the struggles of working people. Icelanders on the political right forbid their children to read his books, and cringed when he received the Nobel Prize; those on the political left loved him and felt he told the truth. In the end, no one could deny that he was a gifted writer and a person of insight and compassion.

Geothermal Exhibition at Hellisheiði Power Plant (Hellisheiðarvirkjun)

Less than a half-hour's drive from Reykjavík on the way to Selfoss, this is the only one of Iceland's seven geothermal energy plants where visitors can get a good look at some of the powerful turbine machinery at work. The hot water from the ground is piped to homes for heating, and it drives the turbines that generate electricity. (Most of Iceland's electricity, though, is produced by dams rather than geothermal sources.) But the plant isn't all good: It releases hydrogen sulfide—carrying the aroma of rotten eggs—that east winds blow into Reykjavík.

At the exhibit, you can see turbine rooms through big windows, read posters on how geothermal energy works, and see a couple of films. Free guided tours run several times a day if enough visitors gather (typically 5-person minimum).

Cost and Hours: 1,450 ISK, Mon-Fri 8:00-17:00, Sat-Sun from 9:00, confirm hours before heading out, tel. 591-2880, www.geothermalexhibition.com.

Getting There: The plant is on highway 1 about halfway across the Hellisheiði plateau that forms the pass between Reykjavík and the South Coast. Look for a turnoff marked *Hellisheiðarvirkjun*—you can't miss the plant, with steam rising from its towers.

Experiences in and near Reykjavík

▲▲▲Thermal Swimming Pools

There are well over a dozen thermal swimming pools to choose from in the greater Reykjavík area, each one run by the local municipality. The more recently built pools in the suburbs are typically more spacious, with more elaborate waterslides and at least one weatherproof indoor pool, making them worth a short drive or bus ride. Any Icelander you ask will have a favorite pool and be able to rattle off its advantages and disadvantages. The recommended pools below are definite winners. (The famous Blue Lagoon is 45 minutes' drive from downtown—and described in the Blue Lagoon & Reykjanes Peninsula chapter—but that's quite a different experience...much more tourist-oriented, and much more expensive, than the pools described here.)

How to Visit: For essential tips on visiting Iceland's thermal pools, read the "Pool Rules" sidebar on page 42. For background on thermal pools and helpful resources, see page 41.

Cost: Pools in Reykjavík charge 950 ISK. The pools in Seltjarnarnes and Hafnarfjörður provide the same experience but charge only 600 and 550 ISK. In Reykjavík, a shareable 10-entry ticket costs 4,400 ISK, which saves money with only five entries (for example, a couple visiting three times). These are adult rates—kids get in for less.

Hours: On weekdays, most swimming pools in the capital area open early in the morning (before 7:00) and stay open until at least 20:00, except on Fridays, when most close around 18:00. Weekend hours are a little shorter (at least 9:00-17:00 or 18:00). Note that most pools close on national holidays. Pools are most crowded after work and school, in the late afternoon.

Pools in and near Reykjavík

Nondrivers staying downtown can walk to either of the first two listings. The website for all Reykjavík pools is Reykjavik.is.

Sundhöllin, Reykjavík's oldest swimming pool, is the only one within the downtown zone and the only indoor pool within easy reach of the center. It was built in the 1930s, and parts of it have an antique feel, though it's well-kept. An outdoor wing was added in 2017, with a lap pool, kiddie pool, and new women's dressing room (Barónsstígur 45a, 5-minute walk from Hlemmur bus junction, limited free street parking in front, tel. 411-5350).

Vesturbæjarlaug, a 20-minute walk from downtown (or take bus #11, #13, or #15), is a compact 1960s-era pool in a residen-

tial area near the university, and a good all-around pool choice for those staying downtown. Though close enough to the center to catch tourists, it has a predominantly neighborhood feel. It's outdoor-only, with a small lap pool, a wading area, hot pots, and a sauna (corner of Hofsvallagata and Melhagi, free parking in front or on the street nearby, tel. 411-5150). If you're swimming here, grab a drink or meal at the recommended Kaffihús Vesturbæjar café across the street.

Árbæjarlaug, far from the center, wins the award for the nicest modern design (from the 1990s). A dome covers its small indoor section, the outdoor hot pools are especially comfortable, and there's a good water slide. It's near some pleasant-enough hiking trails, as well as the Árbær Open-Air Museum and the road from Reykjavík to Selfoss and the south. It's better on weekends, as the indoor section is mostly reserved for children's swim lessons on weekdays (Fylkisvegur 9, bus #5 or #16 to Fylkisvegur stop, tel. 411-5200).

Laugardalslaug, the country's largest pool, is a bit industrial-feeling, with outdoor-only facilities. A bus ride from the center, it's next to the official Reykjavík youth hostel and sports complex. It's a good option if you're staying nearby, if you want to go swimming late on a weekend evening, or on major holidays like Christmas or New Year's Day, when it's typically the only pool open (Sundlaugavegur 30, bus #14 to Laugardalslaug stop, tel. 411-5100).

In Seltjarnarnes: Sundlaug Seltjarnarness, a 10-minute drive or bus ride from the center on #11 (or a 40-minute walk), is a small, cozy, newly renovated residential pool frequented mostly by locals. It's outdoor-only, and has easy parking, nice views, a modest water slide, and a cozy wading and lounging area (on Suðurströnd in Seltjarnarnes; bus #11 to Íþróttamiðstöð Seltjarnarness stop, tel. 561-1551, www.seltjarnarnes.is).

Indoor Bathing in Hafnarfjörður: The best indoor pool in the capital area, and overall the best family pool, is **Ásvallalaug,** on the outskirts of the town of Hafnarfjörður. From downtown Reykjavík, it's a 20-minute drive by car (on the way to the airport), or a long 45 minutes by direct city bus. There's a full-size lap pool, a large wading pool, a large and shallow family pool, a good water slide, and hot pools. It's a great bad-weather destination with a big parking lot (Ásvellir 2, Hafnarfjörður, bus #1 to Ásvallalaug stop, tel. 512-4050, www.hafnarfjordur.is). You could stop in downtown Hafnarfjörður to eat afterward (see recommendations on page 148), or drive to the cheap cafeteria at IKEA, which is on the way back to Reykjavík.

Heated Beach: Nauthólsvík

Nauthólsvík, maintained by the city of Reykjavík, is an artificial beach *(ylströnd)* in a sheltered part of the shoreline, where you can bathe in an area heated with excess geothermal water from the city's heating system. This can be fun on a nice summer day, although you'll find better facilities and services at the regular pools (free, possible charge for changing facilities; daily 10:00-19:00, limited hours and 600 ISK charge mid-Aug-mid-May, off Nauthólsvegur, bus #5 to Nauthóll/HR stop, free parking, or walk from here to the Pearl, tel. 511-6630, www.nautholsvik.is).

Also Consider...

Lágafellslaug, a large, new pool in the town of Mosfellsbær (about 9 miles northeast of downtown Reykjavík), has a small indoor section. It's convenient if driving between Reykjavík and the Golden

Circle (Þingvellir) or the north (toward Akureyri; Lækjarhlíð 1a, Mosfellsbær, tel. 617-6080, www.mosfellsbaer.is).

Álftaneslaug, with a high waterslide and the country's only wave pool, is in the formerly separate town of Álftanes (on the peninsula due south of Reykjavík). This pool cost so much to build that the town went bankrupt and merged with neighboring Garðabær (Breiðmýri, Garðabær, tel. 550-2350, www.gardabaer.is).

Sundlaug Kópavogs, an older pool in the town of Kópavogur, is handy for those staying nearby (Borgarholtsbraut, Kópavogur, tel. 570-0740, www.kopavogur.is).

More Experiences
Horseback Riding
Several horse farms on the outskirts of Reykjavík run riding tours for tourists; see the Icelandic Experiences chapter for details.

Volcanic Cave Tours
Two pricey excursions inside a volcano cave are close to Reykjavík: At **Þríhnjúkagígur** (a.k.a. "Inside the Volcano"), 30 minutes from the capital, you're lowered down into an extinct magma chamber (very expensive, at around $400 per person). More affordable (at $100) is **Raufarhólshellir** (a.k.a. "The Lava Tunnel"), where you can walk through a petrified lava tube (about 45 minutes from Reykjavík). A similar tour at **Víðgelmir**—a.k.a. "The Cave"—is more impressive, but much farther away from Reykjavík; consider taking it if you'll be in the West Iceland region. For more on these options, see the Icelandic Experiences chapter.

Shopping in Reykjavík

While you'll find plenty of shopping opportunities, don't expect any bargains: Iceland has almost no manufacturing industry of its own, so many items are imported and quite expensive. My shopping advice emphasizes items that are produced or at least designed in Iceland.

Store Hours: Most shops are open at least Mon-Fri 10:00-18:00; on Saturdays, many close earlier. Sundays are unpredictable—larger or tourist-oriented shops remain open, while others close. In general, touristy shops on the main shopping streets downtown (Laugavegur and Skólavörðustígur) have longer hours in the evening and on Sundays.

WHERE TO SHOP
Downtown Reykjavík seems designed for shoppers—you'll find plenty of temptations as you window-shop along the main drag, **Laugavegur.** Dozens of stores along here run the gamut from

gaudy "puffin shops" to high-end craft and design boutiques; a few highlights are mentioned in the next section.

Don't be so mesmerized by Laugavegur that you miss **Skólavörðustígur,** the charming street leading up from Lan-gavegur to Hallgrímskirkja. It's lined with more authentic-feeling small boutiques. I've listed some of my favorites in the next section, but here's a quick rundown: Near the bottom are large branches of Geysir (fashion), Rammagerðin (top-end souvenirs), and Eymundsson (books). Farther up—especially

around the intersection with Týsgata—you'll find an enticing assortment of one-off boutiques, including the 12 Tónar record shop and the Handknitting Association of Iceland.

Jewelry is a popular item along here, including at **Orrifin** (with funky style, at #17B) and **Fríða** (#18). This street also specializes in ceramicists; look for **Stígur** (a collective showcasing the work of seven artists, at #17) and **Kaolin** (at #5). It also has some eclectic fashion boutiques, such as **Yeoman** (at #22). **Nikulásarkot** features delicate, handmade dolls and ornaments infused with Icelandic folk culture (at #22). Many of these stores have their own little workshops attached, where you can watch artisans at work.

WHAT TO BUY
Sweaters and Other Icelandic Fashion

At the top of many shopping lists is a handmade Icelandic wool sweater *(lopapeysa).* Knitting is a major pastime in this nation where sheep outnumber people, and where hobbies get you through the dreary winter months. Traditional Icelandic designs—often with classy one- or two-tone patterns radiating from the neck—are both timeless and stylish. A good, handmade sweater starts at around $200; they tend to be bulky, so you'll need room in your luggage.

Classic Sweaters: The best place for a traditional sweater (as well as other knitwear and yarn) is the cozy little **Handknitting Association of Iceland** (Handprjónasambandið) shop; browse their website before you go (Mon-Sat 9:00-18:00, Sun from 10:00, Skólavörðustígur 19, tel. 552-1890, http://handknit.is). They also have a more souvenir-y location on the main drag (Laugavegur 53, closed Sun).

Secondhand Sweaters: For a quality sweater at a lower price (closer to $100-120), consider buying secondhand. For a big, well-stocked vintage clothing shop, stop by **Spúútnik** on the main drag (Laugavegur 28) or their second location, **Fatamarkaður** (at the Hlemmur bus junction, Laugavegur 118). Or, to support a good cause while you shop, the **Red Cross** charity shop has three very central locations (at Laugavegur 12B, Laugavegur 116, and Skólavörðustígur 12). Note that these places line up conveniently—allowing you to comparison-shop easily in about a 10-minute stroll along Laugavegur. There's also a **Salvation Army** branch at the corner of Garðastræti and Ránargata. You'll find plenty of sweaters at the **Kolaportið flea market**—but don't expect top quality there (Sat-Sun only, see listing on page 92).

Stylish Sweaters (and Other Fashion): Icelandic design-ers enjoy updating traditional sweater designs. **Farmers Market** has a full range of fashionable clothes, including sweaters (www. farmersmarket.is). Their downtown outpost is called Farmers & Friends (Laugavegur 37), while their flagship store is at the far end of the Old Harbor's Grandi pier, near the Marshall-húsið arts center (Hólmaslóð 2). **Geysir**—another modern Icelandic fashion designer with several branches downtown (including at Skólavörðustígur 7 and Skólavörðustígur 16, www.geysirshops. is)—also has contemporary sweater styles, as do various one-off boutiques along Laugavegur.

Other Clothes: 66°North, Iceland's best-known outerwear brand, is *the* place to buy waterproof shells and puffy vests. A big, convenient location is right on the main drag (Mon-Sat 9:00-21:00, Sun from 10:00, Laugavegur 17). For a better deal, drivers can head to their suburban outlet store with deep discounts (buried in the back of the Skeifan shopping zone, Mon-Fri 8:00-21:00, Sat from 10:00, Sun from 12:00, Faxafen 12, bus #5 to Fen stop, tel. 535-6676, www.66north.is).

For high-end local fashion—a notch dressier than Farmers Market and Geysir, described earlier—check out **Kiosk,** a co-op run by local designers (just off the main drag at Ingólfsstræti 6, www.kioskreykjavik.com).

Icelandic Souvenirs

Visitors enjoy browsing for keepsakes emblazoned with the Icelan-dic flag, or an outline of the country. Other popular items include stuffed puffins, whales, and polar bears (they don't live in Iceland, but every now and then, a stray bear drifts across from Greenland on an iceberg). Laugavegur and adjoining streets seem to specialize in tacky souvenir outlets; most of what you'll find is overpriced and

REYKJAVÍK

made in China. Here are a few better options for more authentically Icelandic souvenirs.

Locally produced and inexpensive, edible souvenirs may be your best bet. **Icelandic candy** is unusual and hard to get outside of Iceland, but easily found at discount grocery stores (Bónus and Krónan), which are generally cheaper and have a better selection than the duty-free airport shops. Cooks on your shopping list might enjoy some of the wide variety of flavored **Icelandic sea salts** (including birch-smoked, seaweed, black lava, and arctic thyme).

Gift shops at the **National Museum** and the **Harpa** concert hall are a little more sophisticated than the norm (see listings in "Sights in Reykjavík").

Rammagerðin, a venerable, high-end boutique, offers extremely expensive but good-quality Icelandic handcrafts and design (www.rammagerdin.is). The main branch—with a row of taxidermied puffins looking out the window—is in the heart of the main shopping zone at Skólavörðustígur 12; other branches are just up the street at Skólavörðustígur 20, at Bankastræti 9, at the Pearl, and at the airport ("Iceland Gift Store").

Iceland, like other Scandinavian countries, has a knack for clean, eye-pleasing design; several shops along the main drag specialize in the works of local designers. The **Kraum** design shop shares a space with the "Around Iceland" booking center at Laugavegur 18; in the back is a small, free exhibit about Icelandic reindeer (www.kraum.is). **Hrím Eldhús** has a fun selection of upscale kitchen gadgets and housewares—a mix of Icelandic and international (Laugavegur 32); their sister shop just up the street, **Hrím Hönnunarhús,** has a more eclectic selection (Laugavegur 25, www.hrim.is).

Bookstores

Some English-language books on Iceland are available much more cheaply back home from Amazon or other online retailers; others are hard to find outside the country.

Mál og Menning, along Laugavegur, is Reykjavík's most enjoyable-to-browse bookstore.

In the big atrium, tables are piled with intriguing choices, including many English books and travel guides, and there's a tiny café upstairs (Mon-Fri 9:00-22:00, Sat-Sun 10:00-22:00, Laugavegur 18, tel. 552-3740, www.bmm.is).

Two downtown branches of **Eymundsson,** Iceland's answer to Barnes & Noble, are at Austurstræti 18 and Skólavörðustígur 11 (same hours as Mál og Menning, www.eymundsson.is).

Those with a car or bike can visit the **publishers' outlet store** in the Grandi neighborhood beyond the Old Harbor, which has a large selection of books, maps, and posters offered at a 15 percent discount (Mon-Fri 10:00-18:00, Sat 11:00-15:00, closed Sun, Fiskislóð 39, tel. 575-5636, www.forlagid.is).

REYKJAVÍK

Other Ideas

12 Tónar, downtown at Skólavörðustígur 15, is a local institution. Their shop specializes in Icelandic music, and they run their own label—making this a beloved outpost for indie music lovers (Mon-Sat 10:00-18:00, Sun from 12:00, www.12tonar.is).

Greater Reykjavík's two big **shopping malls** (Kringlan and Smáralind) are convenient for drivers and give you a nontouristy look at Icelandic commercial life.

Entertainment in Reykjavík

PERFORMANCES AT HARPA

Iceland's cutting-edge arts center (described earlier, under "Sights in Reykjavík") has several venues, big and small, that offer enter-

tainment options every night of the year. Three serious musical ensembles are based at Harpa: the **Iceland Symphony Orchestra** (Sinfóníuhljómsveit Íslands, http://en.sinfonia.is), the **Icelandic Opera** (Íslenska Óperan, http://opera.is), and the **Reykjavík Big Band,** a large jazz ensemble (Stórsveit Reykjavíkur, www.reykjavikbigband.com). All three regularly perform in the 1,800-seat main hall, called Eldborg. Harpa's smaller halls (200-1,100 seats) host many types of performances. Check the schedule for a chance to combine a show with a visit to the most architecturally exciting building in Iceland (box office open Mon-Fri 9:00-18:00, Sat-Sun from 10:00, often later during performances, https://en.harpa.is).

Among the shows at Harpa are likely to be the following tourist-oriented options (all designed for an English-speaking au-

Icelandic Music

For centuries, there were few instruments in Iceland, and it was hard to organize an ensemble in a land with difficult travel and no towns or villages. What little music Icelanders had was mostly vocal, using simple melodies in minor keys, lyrics from old ballads and verses, sometimes accompanied by primitive string instruments. At Christmastime, Icelanders danced holding hands in a line while singing traditional verses. When the Pietist movement gained ground among Lutherans in the mid-1700s, music and dance were frowned upon.

But over time, that changed—especially in the 20th century, as Icelanders became wealthier and better tied into European culture. Young Icelanders started to take music lessons, sing in choirs, and play in bands, and both classical and popular music blossomed. Today, Icelanders love to sing along to local folk songs at birthdays or Christmas parties.

The best-known modern Icelandic musician is Björk Guðmundsdóttir—known worldwide by her first name alone. Born in 1965 in Reykjavík to two politically active parents (her father was the head of the Icelandic electricians union for years), Björk sang in choirs as a child. She gained fame as the lead singer of the Sugarcubes, then struck out on her own in 1993. Björk is known for her eclectic musical style, unique voice (which strikes some ears as discordant), energetic performances, and avant-garde fashion sense (most famously, the swan-shaped dress she wore to the 2001 Oscars). Björk has also dabbled in acting, taking home the Cannes Best Actress prize for her lead performance in the 2000 Lars von Trier film *Dancer in the Dark*. While Björk's music

dience). While these may change, each one has been running for several years (though sometimes only in summer). All are entertaining and (aside from the first and last) designed to give visitors insights into Icelandic culture.

Reykjavík Classics is a daytime concert offering a 30-minute presentation of some "greatest hits" of classical music (Mozart, Beethoven, etc.) performed by a smaller ensemble from the symphony. As it's short and always in the main hall, it's an affordable way to experience Harpa without investing too much time and money...but there's very little Icelandic about it (3,000 ISK, usually at 12:30 or 15:30, www.reykjavikclassics.com).

Pearls of Icelandic Song presents a collection of traditional tunes sung by operatically trained soloists with piano accompaniment. The formal presentation of these informal songs may not be to everyone's taste, but it's authentically Icelandic (3,900 ISK, usually at 18:00 in the main hall, www.pearls.is).

Icelandic Sagas: The Greatest Hits is a frenetic two-person show that attempts to compress centuries of deep and complex Ice-

is not for everybody, her fans are devout. To get a taste for Björk, some of her early albums in Icelandic are available for free on YouTube and well worth listening to. Try *Gling-Gló* (roughly, "Ding Dong"), with accessible but typically idiosyncratic interpretation of jazz standards. Later in her career, Björk moved to England, but still spends a lot of time in Iceland.

Over the last decade or so, other Icelandic bands have become known internationally. Sigur Rós and, more recently, Of Monsters And Men specialize in soaring, bombastic soundscapes (fitting for their dramatic homeland) that often turn up in Hollywood epics. Singer-songwriter Ásgeir is attempting to become the next Icelander to break out in a big way.

Icelandic music fans shouldn't miss the Icelandic Museum of Rock 'n' Roll, a five-minute drive from Keflavík Airport (see page 174). The 2013 book *Blue Eyed Pop* is also good (buy it at the museum, or from the website of the author, Gunnar Lárus Hjálmarsson, better known as Dr. Gunni; http://blueeyedpopdotcom1. wordpress.com).

Two annual festivals showcase the latest in Icelandic pop music. Iceland Airwaves takes place in Reykjavík in late October/ early November (www.icelandairwaves.is). Aldrei Fór Ég Suður (which loosely translates as "I never moved to Reykjavík") fills Ísafjörður, the largest town in the Westfjords, with young visitors for a few days at Easter (www.aldrei.is). There's also Eistnaflug, a heavy metal festival each July in the eastern town of Neskaupstaður (www.eistnaflug.is).

landic heritage into 75 minutes, with plenty of humor and costume changes. While designed to be more entertaining than educational, you'll come away with a somewhat better appreciation for Iceland's history (4,900 ISK, usually at 20:15 in the Northern Lights Hall, www.icelandicsagas.com).

How to Become Icelandic in 60 Minutes is a crowd-pleasing one-man comedy show designed to offer outsiders some humorous insights into the Icelandic psyche (4,500 ISK, usually at 19:00 in the smaller Kaldalón, www.h2become.com).

Múlinn Jazz Club hosts weekly jazz performances in an intimate setting (2,000 ISK, typically Wed at 21:00, www.facebook. com/mulinnjazzclub).

OTHER PERFORMANCES

The Gamla Bíó theater—a classic old cinema in the heart of town—periodically presents **Saga Music 101**. A contemporary songwriter has written music designed to tell some of the saga stories with English lyrics (4,700 ISK, Wed at 20:00, www.sagamusic101.com).

The theater hosts other performances, too (check www.gamlabio. is), and its recommended rooftop bar—Petersen Svítan—is a fine venue for a before- or after-show drink.

Various **churches** around Reykjavík present low-key concerts. The big, landmark Hallgrímskirkja offers concerts (mainly on their huge organ) about four times weekly in summer (late June-late Aug, as part of the "International Organ Summer"), and sporadically at other times of year (www.hallgrimskirkja.is). And the cathedral—the modest building next to the parliament, downtown—hosts occasional concerts in its intimate, lovely space (www.domkirkjan.is).

Movies: Bíó Paradís, a beloved art-house cinema just off the main drag downtown, shows international films in their original language with Icelandic subtitles, as well as Icelandic films with English subtitles. Locals kick off weekend revelry at their throwback film series every Friday night—camp classics, '80s movies, interactive screenings (like the *Rocky Horror Picture Show*), and so on. Their bar/café is a popular hangout. The movie lets out just as things are getting rolling outside (Hverfisgata 54, tel. 412-7711, www.bioparadis.is).

NIGHTLIFE

Reykjavík is renowned for its crazy nightlife. It's pretty simple: Just go downtown any Friday or Saturday night and hit your choice of bars and clubs. Typically, Icelanders come here only on weekends. Many young Icelanders drink at home first (less expensive) before heading downtown between 23:00 and midnight. Higher-end drinking places—hotel cocktail bars, craft-beer specialists, and the like—tend.to close on the "early" side...which, in Reykjavík, means midnight on weeknights and 1:00 in the morning on weekends. Harder-partying places stay open until 3:00 or later.

I've recommended some well-established watering holes (see map on page 140)—but this scene changes quickly. For a more timely take, pick up the latest issue of the *Reykjavík Grapevine* (or read it online at www.grapevine.is) to find what's in, what's on, and which bands or DJs are playing where. The *Grapevine* also publishes a list of best happy hours—good to know about in this pricey city.

If you want company, go on a **guided pub crawl** such as the one offered by CityWalk (2,500 ISK, Fri-Sat at 22:00, mobile tel. 787-7779, www.citywalk.is).

Upscale Cocktails

These options are for those who'd prefer a more sophisticated scene, and don't mind investing in a pricey (2,000-2,500 ISK) but wellcrafted cocktail in a memorable setting.

Sophisticated Art Deco Vibe: Right in the heart of town, **Apotek** fills the ground floor of a landmark hotel by renowned architect Guðjón Samúelsson. This borderline-stuffy place loves to brag about their many "best cocktails" awards and generous happy-hour deals (half-price drinks 16:00-18:00). A bit more sedate than the rowdy party scene all around it, this is a nice choice for a genteel drink. They also serve a full menu of food—including a decent lunch special—but better restaurants are nearby; come for the drinks and the ambience (daily 7:00-late, Austurstræti 16).

Rooftop Bar: To reach **Petersen Svítan** ("The Petersen Suite"), you'll slip through a side door next to the classic Gamla Bíó theater, then ride the elevator up to a rooftop deck. You can sit in the Old World interior, but the main draw is the large outdoor area, overlooking city rooftops—a delight on warm evenings. Don't miss the spiral stairs up to an even higher deck (open daily from 16:00, happy hour until 20:00, Ingólfsstræti 2a).

By the Harbor: Slippbarinn ("Dry Dock Bar") is one of the best places in town for quality, creative cocktails. The menu is vividly described and fun to peruse, with a few mainstays and lots of seasonal concoctions. A mellow hangout by day, at night it's a big, boisterous, and colorful party. It sprawls through the spacious, creative, industrial-mod lobby of the Icelandair Hótel Marina, right along the harborfront, facing the namesake dry dock (daily 11:30-late, also serves food, occasional DJs or live music, Mýrargata 2).

Craft Beer

Iceland has a burgeoning craft beer scene, including high-end bars where you can focus on sampling local brews. While some proudly feature Icelandic beer, most acknowledge the limits of local brewers and make a point to also offer a carefully curated range of imports. Most craft-beer bars have several taps and a chalkboard listing what's on today. Figure on paying 1,000-1,800 ISK for a pint.

Skúli Craft Bar, named for the statue of the original Reykjavík developer on the downtown square it faces, has a great section of Icelandic craft beers. The prices are high, but the glassy, modern, aboveground space feels inviting and attracts a few locals along with the tourists. At the bar—in front of an illuminated wall displaying bottles like trophies—you can choose between Icelandic brews (marked with red-and-blue stripes) and imports. They also have pleasant outdoor tables (Mon-Thu from 15:00, Fri-Sat from 14:00, Sun from 16:00, happy hour until 19:00, Aðalstræti 9, tel. 519-6455).

MicroBar fills a straightforward cellar with happy drinkers (mostly tourists, thanks to its main-drag location) enjoying an even wider selection of microbrews. They specialize in Icelandic beers—with 14 on tap, and more than 100 in bottles—and is the only craft beer place I saw that offers 5- or 10-beer sampler boards; this being

Iceland, you'll pay dearly for each sip (daily from 16:00, happy hour 17:00-19:00, Vesturgata 2, tel. 865-8389).

Mikkeller & Friends, at the top floor of an old house, focuses on Scandinavian craft brews (Mikkeller is a Danish brewery), with a big chalkboard menu of 20 choices. They take their beer (and themselves) very seriously, but it's an appealing setting—you'll feel like you're in a friend's attic lounge—and a good place to get beyond Icelandic beers (Sun-Thu from 17:00, Fri-Sat from 14:00, Hverfisgata 12—head to the top floor, passing a good pizzeria partway up, tel. 437-0203).

Ölstofa Kormáks og Skjaldar ("Kormákur and Skjöldur's Tavern") is a nice hybrid of the beer-geek places mentioned earlier, and the lowbrow Laugavegur scene described next. Because it's tucked away, it feels more local than most Laugavegur bars, with a *Cheers* vibe and a table often filled by regulars. While they do have taps and bottles from local brewers, their draft selection is limited (all from the same brewery, Borg Brugghús); visit for the atmosphere, not a deep dive into Icelandic brews (daily from 15:00, Laugavegur 59).

Lively Late-Night Bars

These places really get rolling late at night on weekends (though you're welcome to stop by earlier in the evening, when they can already be quite crowded on weekends). Come for Reykjavík's famous social weekend experience, not the drinks.

Kaffibarinn is a classic dive bar right in the center. It's a local institution that still attracts a largely Icelandic clientele. Filling an old house, it can feel crowded and gets pretty wild on weekends; for a mellower visit, check it out on a weeknight (daily from 15:00, good happy-hour deals before 20:00, live DJ at prime times, Bergstaðastræti 1, tel. 551-1588).

Right along the busiest stretch of Laugavegur, you can't miss **Lebowski Bar,** with neon lights, a Dude-Walter-and-Donny bowling theme, 16 versions of white Russians...and, one would assume, owners very nervous that the Coen Brothers' legal team will catch on. It's rollicking, rowdy, and popular with young Americans (open long hours daily and nightly, Laugavegur 20b, tel. 552-2300).

A block from Ingólfstorg toward the river is a cluster of rowdy, hole-in-the-wall bars for late-night revelry. **Húrra** is the all-around favorite, with a big dance floor and great DJs (Tryggvagata 22, tel. 571-7101). **Paloma** is a late-late-late night option with a basement dance floor and a vaguely nautical vibe; it's bigger than most, so it feels less claustrophobic (Naustin 1). And **The Dubliner** is the city's most central Irish pub (Hafnarstræti 1).

In addition, several of the places listed under "Eating in Reykjavík," later, can be good places to grab a drink, including the hipster/vegetarian café **Kaffi Vínyl,** the lowbrow pub **Íslenski Barinn,** and **Kex Hostel.**

Sleeping in Reykjavík

Reykjavík is an expensive place to spend the night. With its recent spike in tourism, the city is bursting at the seams, demand is soaring, and lots of new places are opening up (or old places expanding) each year—some of them great, others not.

I've focused my listings on relatively established hotels offering good value. Given how pricey Reykjavík's hotels are (especially in the center), I'd also give guesthouses and private rentals (such as on Airbnb) a serious look; youth hostels are especially good for solo travelers. Real hotels are very expensive, especially in the center, and can easily cost $400 a night in summer. Guesthouses (figure $200 a night) and Airbnb (closer to $100 a night) give you more value for the money and a more local experience.

Whatever you do, book any accommodations well in advance, as the best places sell out early for the peak summer months, or if your trip coincides with a major holiday.

In Iceland, prices drop a lot if you are willing to share a bathroom. If a place has the option of a shared bathroom, I've noted that in the listing—a shared bath often knocks down the price considerably.

Without a car, stay downtown. It's more convenient for restaurants, nightlife, much of the worthwhile sightseeing, and bus-excursion pickups. With a rental car, it can make better sense to stay outside the downtown core—where lodgings cost less and parking is easy. There are fewer hotels and guesthouses in the suburbs, but Airbnb and other rentals are abundant.

For car travelers, the outlying community of Hafnarfjörður is a nice compromise. It has its own downtown core and quaint old houses, but free parking and less noise and traffic than Reykjavík. It's strategically situated for those driving to and from the airport, the Golden Circle, the Blue Lagoon, and the South Coast.

City buses run to every corner of the metropolitan area, although some parts are a long ride (with a transfer) from downtown. When scoping out a place to stay, check bus access by plugging the address into the journey planner at www.straeto.is and seeing how long it takes to get to the main downtown stops (Lækjartorg and Hlemmur).

I rank accommodations from **$** budget to **$$$$** splurge. To get the best deal, contact small hotels and guesthouses directly by phone or email. If you go direct, the owner avoids a roughly 20 percent commission and may be able to offer you a discount. For more information and tips on hotel rates and deals, making reservations,

REYKJAVÍK

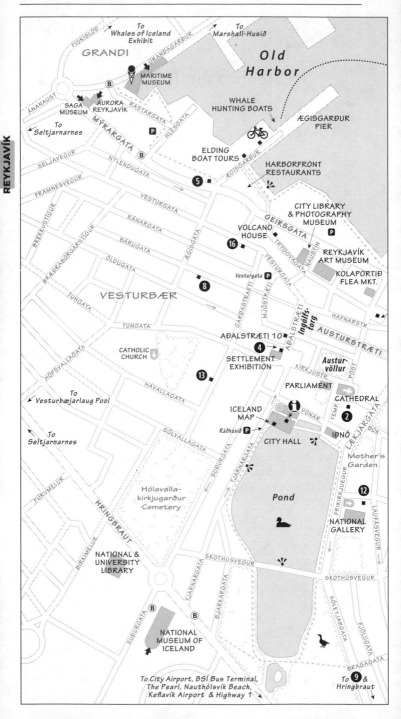

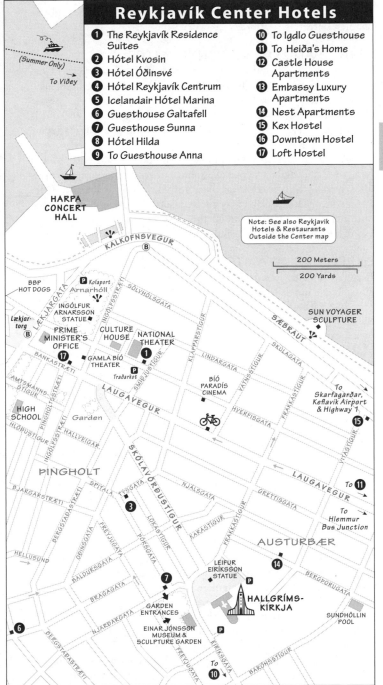

Reykjavík Center Hotels

1. The Reykjavík Residence Suites
2. Hótel Kvosin
3. Hótel Óðinsvé
4. Hótel Reykjavík Centrum
5. Icelandair Hótel Marina
6. Guesthouse Galtafell
7. Guesthouse Sunna
8. Hótel Hilda
9. To Guesthouse Anna
10. To Igdlo Guesthouse
11. To Heiða's Home
12. Castle House Apartments
13. Embassy Luxury Apartments
14. Nest Apartments
15. Kex Hostel
16. Downtown Hostel
17. Loft Hostel

REYKJAVÍK

Note: See also Reykjavik Hotels & Restaurants Outside the Center map

200 Meters
200 Yards

HARPA CONCERT HALL

(Summer Only)
To Viðey

KALKOFNSVEGUR

BBP HOT DOGS
Kolaport
Arnarhóll
Ingólfur Arnarsson Statue
PRIME MINISTER'S OFFICE
GAMLA BÍÓ THEATER
CULTURE HOUSE
NATIONAL THEATER
SÖLVHÓLSGATA
SÆBRAUT
SUN VOYAGER SCULPTURE
Lækjartorg
BANKASTRÆTI
Traðarkot
BÍÓ PARADÍS CINEMA
LINDARGATA
SKÚLAGATA
AMTSMANNS-STÍGUR
LAUGAVEGUR
HVERFISGATA
HIGH SCHOOL
Garden
ÞINGHOLTSSTRÆTI
INGÓLFSSTRÆTI
HALLVEIGAR.
HLÖÐUSTÍGUR
SKÓLAVÖRÐUSTÍGUR
To Skarfagarðar, Keflavík Airport & Highway 1
15
ÞINGHOLT
SPITALA.
TÝSGATA
NJÁLSGATA
GRETTISGATA
LAUGAVEGUR
To 11
BJARGARSTRÆTI
BERGSTAÐASTRÆTI
LOKASTÍGUR
ÞÓRSGATA
KÁRASTÍGUR
FRAKKASTÍGUR
To Hlemmur Bus Junction
HELLUSUND
ÓÐINSGATA
FREYJUGATA
AUSTURBÆR
14
BALDURSGATA
LEIFUR EIRIKSSON STATUE
BERGÞÓRUGATA
BRAGAGATA
HALLGRÍMS-KIRKJA
SUNDHÖLLIN POOL
6
NJARÐARGATA
GARDEN ENTRANCES
EINAR JÓNSSON MUSEUM & SCULPTURE GARDEN
EIRÍKSGATA
BARÓNSSTÍGUR
BERGSTAÐASTRÆTI
To 10

finding a short-term rental, and chain hotels, see the Practicalities chapter.

AIRBNB AND OTHER RENTAL SITES

I've intentionally listed fewer hotels and guesthouses than I normally would for a city of Reykjavík's size. That's because here, even more than elsewhere, I find Airbnb and other short-term rentals to be a much better value than hotels. The bottom line: Iceland is expensive, and staying in nontraditional accommodations can have the single biggest impact on your travel budget.

Airbnb lists plenty of options in the downtown core, and is handy for finding less-expensive suburban accommodations (easier for drivers), while providing a more authentic look at Icelandic life. A search for "Reykjavík" may turn up some of these, but for more options, search for the name of the separate town: Hafnarfjörður, Garðabær, Kópavogur, Mosfellsbær, or Seltjarnarnes.

EXPENSIVE DOWNTOWN HOTELS

If you're going to spend a lot of money, you might as well do it with class. These hotels each offer something special.

$$$$ The Reykjavík Residence Suites, next to the National Theater, occupy a fine former private home that was built in 1912 by a local bigwig who later became prime minister. When the king of Denmark visited in 1926, this is where he stayed. It's been converted into 10 top-end suites, each with a kitchenette (Hverfisgata 21, tel. 546-1200, www.rrsuites.is, info@rrsuites.is). The same outfit also rents regular hotel rooms in a less historic location a couple blocks away, at Hverfisgata 45.

$$$$ Hótel Kvosin, across the street from parliament and the cathedral in a building from 1900, has 24 big suites with full kitchenettes and fine art on the walls (Kirkjutorg 4, tel. 571-4460, www.kvosinhotel.is, desk@kvosinhotel.is).

$$$$ Hótel Óðinsvé, with 50 stylish rooms and 10 apartments in a blocky shell, sits in a pleasant residential area a short walk from the lively Skólavörðustígur shopping and dining street (Þórsgötu 1, recommended Snaps Bistro on-site, tel. 511-6200, www.hotelodinsve.is, odinsve@hotelodinsve.is).

$$$ Hótel Reykjavík Centrum boasts a great location, in view of the parliament, in a modernized building with a period facade and 89 rooms. The Settlement Exhibition on Reykjavík's early history is in the basement, centered on archeological ruins found when the hotel was built in 2001 (Aðalstræti 16, tel. 514-6000, www.hotelcentrum.is, info@hotelcentrum.is).

$$$ Icelandair Hótel Marina is at the Old Harbor in a long, skinny building that spent many years as the post office's sorting facility. This hotel's location is more interesting and convenient than the other Icelandair hotel, the Natura, and it's also home to the recommended Slippbarinn cocktail bar (Mýrargata 2, tel. 560-8000, www.icehotels.is, marina@icehotels.is).

GUESTHOUSES AND SMALL HOTELS

These smaller, less expensive properties are generally in converted residential buildings without elevators. Most of these listings give you the option of sharing a bathroom, which brings down the price substantially. When comparing prices, remember to factor in breakfast and parking costs.

Closer In

$$$ Guesthouse Galtafell is on a quiet street in a handsome neighborhood a block above the Pond, a convenient five-minute walk from both downtown and the BSÍ bus terminal. One of Iceland's richest merchants and fishing magnates built this attractive house with its crenellated roof in 1916. Breakfast is served in a cozy, art-filled dining room in the main house (free parking, Laufásvegur 46, mobile 699-2525, www.galtafell.com, info@galtafell.com).

$$$ Guesthouse Sunna, around the corner from the big Hallgrímskirkja church, is big and feels more like a hotel than a guesthouse. It offers a range of rooms with shared or private bath—some with kitchens—and some with lots of stairs. There's limited free parking in their courtyard (Þórsgata 26 at the corner of Njarðargata, tel. 511-5570, www.sunna.is, sunna@sunna.is).

$$$ Hótel Hilda has 15 rooms, many quite small and tight, and all with private bath. It's in a pleasant, fairly quiet residential neighborhood just a five-minute walk west of downtown. Parking in the immediate vicinity is scarce (Bárugata 11, tel. 552-3020, www.hotelhilda.is, info@hotelhilda.is).

Farther Out

For locations, see the map on page 132.

$$ Guesthouse Anna is conveniently just a hundred yards from the BSÍ bus terminal, where many airport buses and day trips depart. Even so, it feels quiet and residential, and it's about a 10-minute walk from the parliament building and Laugavegur. Of the 12 rooms, 7 have private bathrooms. There are bright, south-facing common spaces and a nice backyard. The modern building was built to house the Czechoslovak Embassy, which closed after the fall of communism (free on-street parking, Smáragata 16, tel. 562-1618, www.guesthouseanna.is, info@guesthouseanna.is).

$ Igdlo Guesthouse (the name is Greenlandic for "igloo") is on the outskirts of downtown, about a 5- to 10-minute walk from the BSÍ bus terminal, in a converted small apartment building on a dead-end street near a busy road. It's a bit hostel-like—all rooms

REYKJAVÍK

REYKJAVÍK

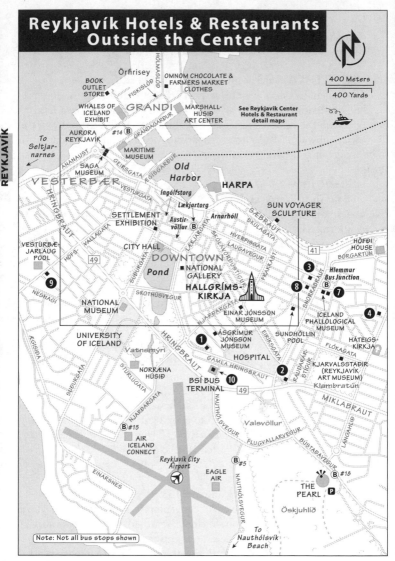

Reykjavík Hotels & Restaurants Outside the Center

400 Meters
400 Yards

Örfirisey

BOOK OUTLET STORE

OMNOM CHOCOLATE & FARMERS MARKET CLOTHES

WHALES OF ICELAND EXHIBIT

GRANDI

MARSHALL-HÚSIÐ ART CENTER

See Reykjavík Center Hotels & Restaurant detail maps

AURORA REYKJAVÍK #14 B

To Seltjarnarnes

SAGA MUSEUM

MARITIME MUSEUM

Old Harbor

HARPA

VESTERBÆR

Ingólfstorg

Lækjartorg

SUN VOYAGER SCULPTURE

SETTLEMENT EXHIBITION

Austir-völlur B

Arnarhóll

HÖFÐI HOUSE

41

VESTURBÆ-JARLAUG POOL

CITY HALL

DOWNTOWN

Pond

NATIONAL GALLERY

HALLGRÍMS-KIRKJA

Hlemmur Bus Junction

9

3

8

7

NESHAGI

NATIONAL MUSEUM

SKOTHÚSVEGUR

EINAR JÓNSSON MUSEUM

ICELAND PHALLOLOGICAL MUSEUM

4

UNIVERSITY OF ICELAND

Vatnsmýri

ÁSGRÍMUR JÓNSSON MUSEUM

SUNDHÖLLIN POOL

HÁTEIGS-KIRKJA

1

HOSPITAL

NORRÆNA HÚSIÐ

BSÍ BUS TERMINAL

10

49

2

KJARVALSSTAÐIR (REYKJAVÍK ART MUSEUM)

Klambratún

MIKLABRAUT

B #15

Valsvöllur

AIR ICELAND CONNECT

Reykjavík City Airport

EAGLE AIR

B #5

B #18

P

THE PEARL

Öskjuhlíð

EINARSNES

Note: Not all bus stops shown

To Nauthólsvík Beach

share a bathroom, and most rooms have multiple beds. The exterior and location are ho-hum, but prices are low, downtown is a 15-minute walk away, and there's usually plenty of free on-street parking (kitchen, laundry facilities, rental bikes, family rooms, Gunnarsbraut 46, tel. 511-4646, www.igdlo.com, booking@igdlo. com).

$ Heiða's Home rents 14 tight double rooms (no sinks), with shared bathroom and kitchen facilities. It's close to the Hlemmur bus junction, occupying an older building along a busy urban-

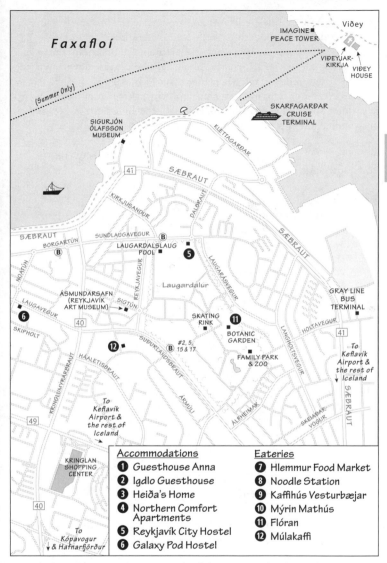

Faxaflói

Viðey

IMAGINE
PEACE TOWER

VIÐEYJAR-
KIRKJA

VIÐEY
HOUSE

(Summer Only)

SIGURJÓN
ÓLAFSSON
MUSEUM

SKARFAGARÐAR
CRUISE
TERMINAL

KLETTAGARÐAR

SÆBRAUT

KIRKJUSANDUR

DALBRAUT

SÆBRAUT

SÆBRAUT   BORGARTÚN

SUNDLAUGAVEGUR

LAUGARDALSLAUG
POOL ❺

REYKJAVEGUR

Laugardalur

LAUGARÁSVEGUR

GRAY LINE
BUS
TERMINAL

NÓATÚN

ÁSMUNDARSAFN
(REYKJAVÍK
ART MUSEUM)

SIGTÚN

SKATING
RINK   ⓫

BOTANIC
GARDEN

HOLTAVEGUR

LANGHOLTSVEGUR

LAUGAVEGUR ❻

SKIPHOLT

SUÐURLANDSBRAUT

#2, 5,
15 & 17

FAMILY PARK
& ZOO

ÁRMÚLI

To
Keflavík
Airport &
the rest
of Iceland

HÁALEITISBRAUT

ALFHEIMAR

SÆBRAUT

SKEIÐARVOGUR

KRINGLUMÝRARBRAUT

❿

To
Keflavík
Airport &
the rest of
Iceland

KRINGLAN
SHOPPING
CENTER

To
Kópavogur
& Hafnarfjörður

<u>Accommodations</u>	<u>Eateries</u>
❶ Guesthouse Anna	❼ Hlemmur Food Market
❷ Igdlo Guesthouse	❽ Noodle Station
❸ Heiða's Home	❾ Kaffihús Vesturbæjar
❹ Northern Comfort Apartments	❿ Mýrin Mathús
❺ Reykjavík City Hostel	⓫ Flóran
❻ Galaxy Pod Hostel	⓬ Múlakaffi

feeling street at the east end of downtown (no breakfast, pay on-street parking, lots of stairs, Hverfisgata 102, tel. 553-6435, mobile 692-7654, www.heidashome.is, heida@heidashome.is).

APARTMENTS
These apartments are good for a longer stay, or if you want your own kitchen.

$$ Castle House Apartments at Skálholtsstígur 2a and **Embassy Luxury Apartments** at Garðastræti 40 offer a dozen well-appointed, mostly one-bedroom apartments with kitchenettes in two super downtown locations well-described on their shared website. They also have cheaper studio apartments dubbed **Northern Comfort** in a lesser location at Skipholt 15, a bit outside downtown (pay on-street parking, tel. 511-2166, http://4.is, 4@4.is).

$$ Nest Apartments rents four units in a three-story building in a quiet spot not far from Laugavegur. The basement is generously called the "ground" floor (2-night minimum, cheaper if you stay a week, pay on-street parking, Bergþórugata 15—see map on page 129, mobile 893-0280, www.nestapartments.is, nest@nestapartments.is).

HOSTELS

¢ Kex Hostel ("Cookie")—filling an old cookie factory—is a popular choice for backpackers. While a bit pricey, it's big, close to downtown, and has a popular café that's frequented even by nonguests (lots of stairs, pay on-street parking, Skúlagata 28, a 7-minute walk from the Hlemmur bus junction—see map on page 129, tel. 561-6060, www.kexhostel.is, info@kexhostel.is).

"Official" HI Hostels: These three **¢** listings belong to the Hostelling International network (website for all: www.hostel.is). **Reykjavík City Hostel** is a 45-minute walk or easy bus ride from downtown, conveniently next to the Laugardalslaug swimming pool and close to the Family Park and Zoo (private rooms available, bike rental, playground, free parking, Sundlaugavegur 34—see map on page 132, bus #14 to Laugarásvegur stop, tel. 553-8110, reykjavikcity@hostel.is). **Downtown Hostel** is better suited to travelers without a car (private rooms available, Vesturgata 17—see map on page 129, bus #14 to the Mýrargata stop, tel. 553-8120, reykjavikdowntown@hostel.is). **Loft Hostel** is even more urban, occupying the top floor of a downtown building just uphill from the prime minister's office (elevator, Bankastræti 7—see map on page 129, near the Lækjartorg bus stop, tel. 553-8140, loft@hostel.is).

¢ The Galaxy Pod Hostel offers something different: Guests sleep in individual capsules, which give a little privacy and space to lock up valuables. The capsules are a good value for solo travelers, but two people traveling together will do better in a two-bed room at one of the HI hostels listed earlier. It's in an uninteresting neighborhood, a half-hour's walk or short drive from Parliament (elevator, breakfast optional, free parking, Laugavegur 172—see map on page 132; bus #2, #5, #14, #15, or #17 to Gamla sjónvarpshúsið; tel. 511-0505, www.galaxypodhostel.is, bookings@galaxypodhostel.is).

OUTSIDE REYKJAVÍK, IN HAFNARFJÖRÐUR

If you're renting a car and using Reykjavík as a base for day trips to sights in the countryside, you may find it easier to stay outside downtown in the southern suburb of Hafnarfjörður (HAHP-nar-FYUR-thur). While calling this area "charming" is a stretch, it does get you into a car-friendly zone away from the crowds, and gives you a glimpse of an authentic Icelandic

neighborhood, with restaurants and services in walking distance. And it's strategically located between downtown Reykjavík and points south: the airport, the Blue Lagoon, and the Golden Circle and South Coast.

Hafnarfjörður Town: Tucked just behind Hafnarfjörður's harborfront promenade is its little downtown core—a largely pedestrianized area with lots of big, modern buildings and a few historical ones. On its outskirts are rows of high-rise condos and some cozy cottage neighborhoods. Wherever you go, parking is easy.

Hafnarfjörður has good swimming pools (Ásvallalaug is one of the area's best), about a dozen restaurants and cafés downtown (including some real gems—see my recommendations in "Eating in Reykjavík," later), a big-box-store zone near the main road—handy for groceries and other shopping, and its own little TI (in the City Hall building, Mon-Fri 8:00-16:00, Sat-Sun 11:00-17:00, Vesturgata 8, www.visithafnarfjordur.is).

Hafnarfjörður doesn't have much in the way of sights, but there are some nice places to stroll (such as Hellisgerði, a small park off Hellisgata), and a surprisingly good little town history museum (Vesturgata 6, http://museum.hafnarfjordur.is).

Route Tips for Drivers: Downtown Reykjavík is a 15-minute drive away, or a 25-minute ride on bus #1; airport buses stop in the center, but don't offer door-to-door pickup.

If you stay here and drive the Golden Circle or South Coast day trips, Breiðholtsbraut (highway 413) is a useful shortcut from Reykjanesbraut (highway 41) over to highway 1 in the direction of Selfoss. Your GPS or map app will guide you; otherwise, from highway 41, follow the signs for highway 413 toward highway 1.

Sleeping in Hafnarfjörður: While I've listed a few traditional accommodations (hotel, B&B, and hostel), you'll often get a better value via Airbnb. Before booking anything with a Hafnarfjörður address, check a map to make sure it's near downtown, rather than in the industrial zone to the east.

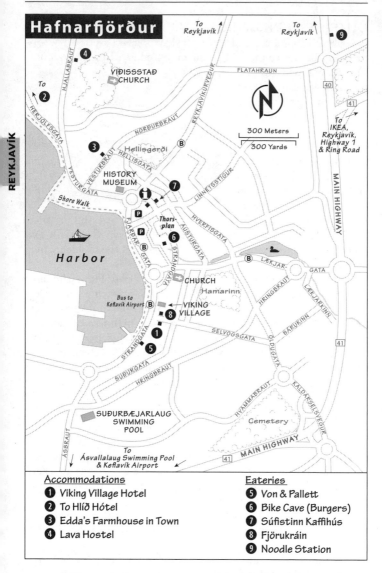

Hafnarfjörður

To Reykjavík
To Reykjavík

VIÐISSTAÐ CHURCH

To

FLATAHRAUN

N

300 Meters
300 Yards

To IKEA, Reykjavík, Highway 1 & Ring Road

Hellisgerði

HISTORY MUSEUM

Shore Walk

Thorsplan

Harbor

LÆKJAR-GATA

CHURCH
Hamarinn

Bus to Keflavík Airport

VIKING VILLAGE

SELVOGSGATA

SUÐURGATA

HRINGBRAUT

SUÐURBÆJARLAUG SWIMMING POOL

Cemetery

To Ásvallalaug Swimming Pool & Keflavík Airport

MAIN HIGHWAY

REYKJAVÍK

Accommodations

1 Viking Village Hotel
2 To Hlíð Hótel
3 Edda's Farmhouse in Town
4 Lava Hostel

Eateries

5 Von & Pallett
6 Bike Cave (Burgers)
7 Súfistinn Kaffihús
8 Fjörukráin
9 Noodle Station

$$ Viking Village Hótel, part of the cheesy Viking-themed Fjörukráin restaurant complex, has Viking-esque common areas, but most of its 41 rooms are straightforward, on the small side, and full of heavily varnished wooden furniture; some feel a bit dated. They also have bunk-bedded cabins that sleep up to six (with private baths)—potentially cost-effective for families or small groups. There's a free sauna and hot pots, and the airport bus stops nearby (Strandgata 55, tel. 565-1213, www.fjorukrain.is, booking@

vikingvillage.is). Their "Fishermen's Village" annex, called **$$$ Hlíð Hótel,** is a little compound of woody, waterfront cabins on a rustic, sparsely populated point just north of Hafnarfjörður (a 15-minute drive from the main hotel; 20 minutes from downtown Reykjavík). It feels remote, yet is still close to the city (same contact information).

¢ **Edda's Farmhouse in Town,** in a charming and historic residential zone a short walk from downtown, has three simple, tidy rooms with a shared bathroom, and includes homemade breakfast. It's a "farmhouse" because Edda has cats, dogs, and rabbits (Vesturbraut 15, tel. 565-1480, mobile 897-1393, ekaritas@simnet.is).

¢ **Lava Hostel,** a 15-minute walk north of downtown Hafnarfjörður, is smaller and more intimate than the hostels in Reykjavík. This nonprofit hostel raises funds for the local Boy Scout troop; they also manage the adjacent campsite. As the name suggests, it's in the midst of an old lava flow (free parking, Hjallabraut 51, tel. 565-0900, www.lavahostel.is, info@lavahostel.is).

HOTELS NEAR THE AIRPORT

It usually makes better sense to stay in Reykjavík (even when arriving or departing at odd hours). Still, given the 45-minute distance between the city and the airport, staying out here does make arrival and departure quicker: Late-night arrivals won't have to blearily pick up a rental car, or wait for an airport bus to slowly fill and rumble into town. Hotels and Airbnb lodgings in Keflavík and Njarðvík, the towns near the airport, are also a bit cheaper than in Reykjavík. But basing yourself out here makes for a much longer drive to the sights on your full days in Iceland, and drastically reduces your choice of bus tours if you're not using your own wheels. A taxi from the airport into Keflavík town can cost as much as 5,000 ISK, so figure that into your budget. For locations, see the map on page 150.

$$ Hótel Aurora Star, a hundred yards from the terminal, is the only hotel right at the airport, with 72 rooms. It's undistinguished but gets the job done; has family rooms, free parking, and a restaurant; and starts serving breakfast at 5:00. Prices are less expensive than downtown Reykjavík hotels, but still pricey by international standards (Blikavöllur 2, Keflavík, tel. 595-1900, www.hotelairport.is, airport@hotelairport.is).

$ Hótel Keflavík, near the harbor in the center of the town of Keflavík, also offers breakfast from 5:00 and free transport to (but not from) the airport. If you arrive on an early-morning transatlantic flight and get a rental car, you could have breakfast here and watch the town wake up (Vatnsnesvegi 12, Keflavík, tel. 420-7000, www.kef.is, stay@kef.is).

¢ **Alex Guesthouse,** a large one-story structure on a semirural lot between the airport and Keflavík, has two types of rooms: hotel-style rooms with shared bath and kitchen, and in summer, wooden cabins with private bath. They offer limited free transport to the airport and start serving breakfast at 4:30 (Aðalgata 60, Keflavík, tel. 421-2800, www.alex.is, alex@alex.is).

Eating in Reykjavík

Iceland's tourist boom has equipped Reykjavík with a surprisingly good range of dining options. You'll dine well here—and it's easier

than you might think to eat out without emptying your wallet. My best budget tip is to have your main meal at lunch: If you stick to drinking water, you can come away from a near-gourmet seafood lunch downtown only a little more than $25 poorer. Then, for dinner, save by picnicking, having a light meal at a café, grabbing a cheap takeout or fast-food meal, or finding a restaurant that doesn't increase its prices in the evening—they do exist. For a few specific leads on cheap eats, see the "Budget Bites" sidebar in this section.

I rank restaurants from $ budget to $$$$ splurge, based on average main-course dinner prices; many restaurants also offer a few cheaper items (like burgers or pizza). That said, you get what you pay for—in my experience, a $40 dinner is substantially better than a basic $25 dinner. For a memorable meal, consider splurging on a fixed-price, multicourse dinner (8,000-10,000 ISK). For details on restaurant pricing, dining in restaurants and cafés, and a rundown of Icelandic cuisine, see the Practicalities chapter.

DOWNTOWN RESTAURANTS

Reykjavík's restaurants—from mom-and-pops to swanky splurges—serve weekday lunch specials for about 2,000-3,000 ISK (this may be a fixed "fish of the day," but sometimes you can choose among several options). Many places close for lunch on weekends—or, if open, have a pricier menu. Fancier restaurants become more expensive (sometimes *much* more expensive) at dinnertime.

Given the large tourist crowds, virtually any downtown restaurant (particularly in the $$$ or $$$$ price range) can book up during the busy summer months. In peak season, it's always smart to book ahead.

I've organized my listings along Reykjavík's main tourist spine, divided into three zones: to the east, along Laugavegur (the main shopping and nightlife drag) and the intersecting Skólavörðustígur (leading up to the big church); a 10-minute walk west, around Ingólfstorg and the parliament area; and a 10-minute walk farther west, near the Old Harbor area.

Along Laugavegur and Skólavörðustígur

$$$$ Sjávargrillið ("The Seafood Grill") is a respected seafood house with a corner location right along Skólavörðustígur. Chef Gústav Axel Gunnlaugsson grills up delicious fish, lobster, and lamb meals. In addition to reasonable lunch specials and blow-out fixed-price dinners, they have a nice selection of lighter main courses for smaller appetites...and budgets. The cozy, tight interior is decorated with Icelandic driftwood gathered during Chef Gústav's culinary travels (Mon-Sat 11:30-14:30 & 17:00-22:30, Sun 17:00-22:30, Skólavörðustígur 14, tel. 571-1000).

$$$ Snaps Bistro is more Parisian-posh than Icelandic-kitsch, with a menu of mostly French-inspired dishes. The lively, sophisticated, glassed-in setting is just far enough off the main drag to attract locals alongside the tourists—particularly at lunchtime on weekdays, when their filling and artfully prepared fish-of-the-day special may be the best deal in town (around 2,000 ISK). They accept reservations only until 18:30, and it's busy at dinner—reserve to eat early, or plan to wait a bit (Sun-Thu 11:30-23:00, Fri-Sat until 24:00, Þórsgata 1, tel. 511-6677, www.snaps.is).

Hverfisgata 12: This classic old house, on a corner just a few steps from the main drag, hides several options for eating and drinking. From street level (along Hverfisgata), go up the stairs and let yourself inside. You'll find a cocktail bar in the basement; in the middle of the building is the **$$ Pizza Place with No Name** (good 3,000-ISK pizzas, daily 11:30-23:00, tel. 437-0203); and upstairs is the recommended **Mikkeller & Friends** bar, focusing on Scandinavian microbrews. If you're confused about which seating goes with which business...so is everyone else, so don't be afraid to ask. All have tables in comfortable wood-paneled rooms.

Just around the corner in the same building, at street level, is **$$$$ Dill**—one of Iceland's finest restaurants (and the recipient of its only Michelin star). In a clean, concrete-minimalist space, they serve up excellent, high-end, New Nordic-inspired dishes, at prices that aren't drastically higher than many other "upper-mid-range" places in this pricey town (five courses-12,000 ISK, seven courses-14,000 ISK). They often book up weeks or months ahead—reserve as early as possible (Wed-Sat 18:00-23:00, closed Sun-Tue, enter on Ingólfsstræti—look for shelves of preserve jars in the window, tel. 552-1522, www.dillrestaurant.is).

Ostabúðin ("The Cheese Shop") is a popular choice right near the bottom of Skólavörðustígur. In the **$$ deli,** you can assemble a

REYKJAVÍK

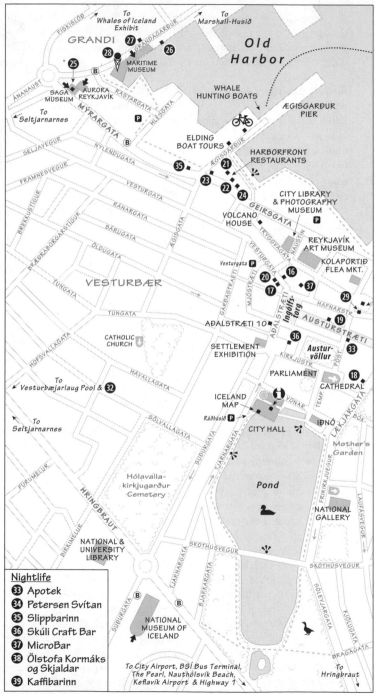

To
Whales of Iceland
Exhibit

To
Marshall-Husið

GRANDI

Old
Harbor

MARITIME
MUSEUM

SAGA
MUSEUM

AURORA
REYKJAVÍK

To
Seltjarnarnes

WHALE
HUNTING BOATS

ÆGISGARÐUR
PIER

ELDING
BOAT TOURS

HARBORFRONT
RESTAURANTS

CITY LIBRARY
& PHOTOGRAPHY
MUSEUM

VOLCANO
HOUSE

REYKJAVÍK
ART MUSEUM

KOLAPORTIÐ
FLEA MKT.

Vesturgata

VESTURBÆR

AÐALSTRÆTI 10

Ingolfs-
torg

AUSTURSTRÆTI

CATHOLIC
CHURCH

SETTLEMENT
EXHIBITION

Austur-
völlur

To
Vesturbæjarlaug Pool & 32

PARLIAMENT

CATHEDRAL

To
Seltjarnarnes

ICELAND
MAP

CITY HALL

IÐNÓ

Ráðhúsið

Hólavalla-
kirkjugarður
Cemetery

Mother's
Garden

Pond

NATIONAL
GALLERY

NATIONAL &
UNIVERSITY
LIBRARY

Nightlife

33 Apotek
34 Petersen Svítan
35 Slippbarinn
36 Skúli Craft Bar
37 MicroBar
38 Ölstofa Kormáks
   og Skjaldar
39 Kaffibarinn

NATIONAL
MUSEUM OF
ICELAND

To City Airport, BSÍ Bus Terminal,
The Pearl, Nauthólsvík Beach,
Keflavík Airport & Highway 1

To
Hringbraut

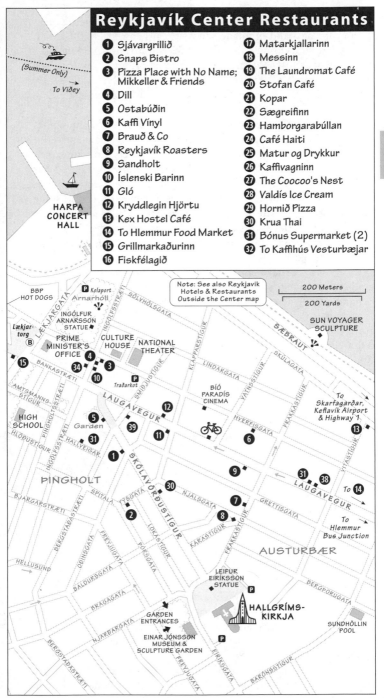

Reykjavík Center Restaurants

1. Sjávargrillið
2. Snaps Bistro
3. Pizza Place with No Name; Mikkeller & Friends
4. Dill
5. Ostabúðin
6. Kaffi Vínyl
7. Brauð & Co
8. Reykjavík Roasters
9. Sandholt
10. Íslenski Barinn
11. Gló
12. Kryddlegin Hjörtu
13. Kex Hostel Café
14. To Hlemmur Food Market
15. Grillmarkaðurinn
16. Fiskfélagið
17. Matarkjallarinn
18. Messinn
19. The Laundromat Café
20. Stofan Café
21. Kopar
22. Sægreifinn
23. Hamborgarabúllan
24. Café Haiti
25. Matur og Drykkur
26. Kaffivagninn
27. The Coocoo's Nest
28. Valdís Ice Cream
29. Hornið Pizza
30. Krua Thai
31. Bónus Supermarket (2)
32. To Kaffihús Vesturbæjar

REYKJAVÍK

HARPA CONCERT HALL

(Summer Only)
To Viðey

Note: See also Reykjavik Hotels & Restaurants Outside the Center map

200 Meters
200 Yards

SUN VOYAGER SCULPTURE

BBP HOT DOGS
Kolaport
Arnarhóll

INGÓLFUR ARNARSSON STATUE

Lækjar-torg

PRIME MINISTER'S OFFICE

CULTURE HOUSE

NATIONAL THEATER

HIGH SCHOOL

Garden

BÍÓ PARADÍS CINEMA

To Skarfagarðar, Keflavík Airport & Highway 1

ÞINGHOLT

AUSTURBÆR

To Hlemmur Bus Junction

HELLUSUND

LEIFUR EIRÍKSSON STATUE

HALLGRÍMS-KIRKJA

SUNDHÖLLIN POOL

GARDEN ENTRANCES

EINAR JÓNSSON MUSEUM & SCULPTURE GARDEN

pricey gourmet picnic, with cheese and meat, olives, baguettes, pestos and spreads, and premade sandwiches (Mon-Fri 10:00-18:00, Sat 11:00-16:00, closed Sun). Their **$$$ restaurant** next door has a full menu of artfully presented international dishes. It's well-priced at lunch, but gets expensive at dinnertime (Mon-Fri 11:30-21:00, Sat from 12:00, Sun from 17:00; both are at Skólavörðustígur 8, tel. 562-2772).

$ Kaffi Vínyl, the only real vegan restaurant downtown, is worth considering even for carnivores. The hipster-chic ambience includes mismatched furniture, old record players, and an extensive record collection (live DJs spin mostly mellow tunes Wed-Sat after 20:00). The chalkboard menu lists an eclectic selection of flavorful hot sandwiches; for a heartier meal, pay extra to add some "Oumph" meat substitute. As they also have a full bar with beer and creative cocktails, this is also a cozy spot for an evening drink (Mon-Fri 9:00-23:00, Sat from 10:00, Sun from 11:00, Hverfisgata 76, tel. 537-1322).

Hipster Corner: For a pastry-and-coffee break downtown, head to Frakkastígur street—between Hallgrímskirkja church and Laugavegur—where two of Reykjavík's most appealing little eateries are separated by a grungy but colorful square. The exterior of artisanal bakery **$ Brauð & Co** ("Bread & Co.") is slathered with a wild graffiti mural, but inside the pastry chefs work like clockwork—churning out hot-from-the-oven cinnamon rolls *(snúður)*, danishes *(vínarbrauð)*, croissants, sourdough loaves and rolls, and seasonal pastries. Get it to go and head for the little square just up the road (daily 6:00-18:00, Frakkastígur 16, tel. 776-0553). Conveniently, that's also where you'll find **Reykjavík Roasters,** the city's best, top-end gourmet coffee shop, where each grind of  beans is weighed to ensure a perfect pull. Flip through their vintage record collection while you wait, or just hang out in the bohemian-chic interior (Mon-Fri 8:00-18:00, Sat-Sun 9:00-17:00, at intersection of Frakkastígur and Kárastígur, tel. 517-5535). Reykjavík Roasters also has a larger, less crowded second location beyond the Hlemmur bus junction (same hours, Brautarholt 2).

$$ Sandholt, a refined, upscale-feeling bakery has great pastries (including homemade croissants and danishes), and serves breakfast and light lunches at tables in the back (daily 7:00-21:00, Laugavegur 36, tel. 551-3524).

$$ Íslenski Barinn ("The Icelandic Bar"), a small and casual tavern, attracts tourists looking to try very traditional, no-frills

Icelandic fare—including some exotic items, such as fermented shark. You'll pay dearly for a small vial, and eat only a nibble. More palatable pub grub (burgers) and a wide range of drinks make it a popular pub-crawl stop. This feels like a lowbrow alternative to some of the pricier, more pretentious places nearby (daily 11:30-late, Ingólfsstræti 1a, tel. 517-6767).

$ Gló, a local vegetarian chain, is a smart choice for a quick, inexpensive, healthy meal in the center. While it's technically a cafeteria, the inviting space—filling the upstairs of a characteristic old Reykjavík house just steps off the main street—is classy and inviting (Mon-Fri 11:00-21:00, Sat-Sun 11:30-21:00, Laugavegur 20b).

$$ Kryddlegin Hjörtu ("Spiced Hearts") serves Icelandic-Indian cuisine, with some vegetarian options, a cheap soup-and-salad lunch buffet, and prices that remain affordable at dinner (Mon-Sat 11:30-21:00, Sun 17:00-22:00, Hverfisgata 33, tel. 588-8818).

$$ Kex Hostel runs a big café open to nonguests, serving breakfast, burgers, lunch specials, and reasonably priced dinners in an ex-industrial space with lots of nooks and couches and a water view (daily 7:30-10:00 & 12:00-23:00, close to Hlemmur and the *Sun Voyager* sculpture at Skúlagata 28, tel. 561-6060).

Hlemmur Food Market (Hlemmur Mathöll): Located at the Hlemmur bus junction at the far end of Laugavegur, this food hall gathers lots of great Reykjavík eating under one roof, with stalls from several respected local restaurants. Check the website for vendors; for foodies, it merits the 10-minute walk from the downtown core (Laugavegur 107, www.hlemmurmatholl.is).

Near Ingólfstorg

$$$$ Grillmarkaðurinn ("The Grill Market"), tucked on a courtyard along Austurstræti, is a worthwhile splurge. It has a rustic-industrial, two-story setting, with big split-log counters and a lively energy. The whole place smells like rich smoke, and their charcoal grill imbues powerful flavor. Their creative dishes allow curious travelers to sample traditional Icelandic "nov-

elty foods" in a way that feels modern and palatable rather than eating on a dare. Their trio of sliders feature a few bites each of puffin, minke whale, and Icelandic lobster, and their grilled minke whale steak comes on its own little hibachi. The service is helpful and without pretense. You can eat here more affordably at lunch on weekdays (reservations recommended, Mon-Fri 11:30-14:00 &

17:00-22:30, Sat-Sun 17:00-22:30, Lækjargata 2a, tel. 571-7777, www.grillmarkadurinn.is).

$$$ Fiskfélagið ("The Fish Company") is in the quaint Vesturgata area just off Ingólfstorg square. It fills the dark, stony cellar of a historic house; in the summer, it has outdoor seating in a sunken courtyard by a gurgling pool. Their French-trained chefs meld a variety of cuisines—including Mediterranean and Asian—with a respect for Icelandic ingredients and traditions. They offer weekday lunch specials, a few sushi options, and eclectic fish and non-fish main dishes. Reserve ahead, especially on weekends (Mon-Sat 11:30-14:30 & 17:30-22:30, Sun 17:30-22:30, closed for lunch Sat off-season, Vesturgata 2a, tel. 552-5300, www.fiskfelagid.is).

$$$ Matarkjallarinn ("The Food Cellar"), also at Vesturgata, manages to be one of Reykjavík's most popular restaurants despite being in a nearly windowless cellar. It's nicely decorated and feels more contemporary and sleek than its neighbor Fiskfélagið. While pricey at dinner, it's more affordable at lunch—with set-priced meals and a good-value daily fish combo (Mon-Fri 11:30-15:00 & 17:00-23:00, Sat-Sun 17:00-23:00, Aðalstræti 2, enter from Vesturgata, tel. 558-0000).

$$ Messinn, in a bright space on busy Lækjargata, features an appealing menu of fish and seafood, including "fish pans" served in sizzling skillets. Portions are large—even shareable. With a pleasant, woody Westfjords ambience, it's a bit more casual and less expensive than some of the fancier places I list in this area. Reserve ahead (daily 11:30-15:00 & 17:00-22:00, Lækjargata 6b, tel. 546-0095, www.messinn.com).

$$ The Laundromat Café is more café than launderette, and a handy place to enjoy comfort food (burgers, sandwiches, and fish) whether or not your laundry is spinning downstairs. The open-feeling space—decorated with photographs of laundromats around the world, big maps, and a bookshelf bar—is understandably popular with travelers—but it's rumored to be closing, so check before you go (Mon-Fri 8:00-23:00, Sat-Sun from 9:00, Austurstræti 9).

$$ Stofan Café ("Living Room") is straightforward, central, and popular. With a cozy living-room vibe overlooking a colorful (and touristy) slice of Reykjavík, it's a tempting place to escape the drizzle for a soup or sandwich. While you'll find better deals at lunch, prices are reasonable at dinnertime (daily 9:00-23:00, Vesturgata 3, tel. 546-1842).

Old Harbor Area
$$$ Kopar ("Copper"), looking out over the harbor from one of the turquoise sheds, emphasizes fish and shellfish but also serves lamb and horse. They have competitively priced weekday lunches

and more expensive dinners (Mon-Fri 11:30-14:00 & 17:00-22:30, Sat-Sun 17:00-22:30, Geirsgata 3, tel. 567-2700).

$ Sægreifinn ("The Seabaron") is a local institution, beloved for its affordable lobster soup and its late, colorful owner (who lives on in the form of a creepy wax statue in the dining room). Now the old man's daughter runs the place and keeps things simple: Line up at the register; order your soup and/or seafood skewers (including whale); then find a seat at a shared table in the sprawling interior. If you stop by on the first Saturday of the month in winter and notice a peculiar odor, they're cooking up a batch of *skötustappa*—putrefied skate wings in a sheep-innards stew (daily 11:30-23:00, children's play area, Geirsgata 8, tel. 553-1500).

Quick Meals at the Harbor: For a fast and affordable bite, try **$ Hamborgarabúllan** (look for "Burger Joint" signs; part of the local Tommi's chain) for a good-sized burger (daily 11:30-21:00, Geirsgata 1, tel. 511-1888). **$ Café Haiti,** Icelandic with a Caribbean twist, has inexpensive lamb and fish soups, plus sandwiches and a big coffee selection (long hours, Geirsgata 7b, tel. 588-8484).

At the Far End of the Harbor, in Grandi

The peninsula called Grandi—which defines the far (western) end of the harbor area—has sprouted some trendy eateries, which are a notch less touristy and "ye olde" than choices closer to the whale-watching piers.

$$$ Matur og Drykkur ("Food and Drink"), inside the Saga Museum, prides itself on time-tested recipes that other restaurants

might dismiss as old-fashioned. Here, chefs update those traditional dishes for modern tastes. Try the trademark "halibut" soup (not made with halibut—which is illegal, for complicated reasons), cod's head (more delicious than you'd imagine), or arctic char smoked over burning sheep's dung (ditto). You'll also find lots of barley and seaweed on the menu. Despite the casual, rustic bistro ambience, the food is high-end and dinner can be spendy (when reservations are important); it's much more affordable at lunch, and pairs well with daytime sightseeing nearby (daily 11:30-15:00 & 17:00-22:00, Grandagarður 2, tel. 571-8877, www.maturogdrykkur.is).

$$ Kaffivagninn ("The Coffee Cart") perches on a pier overlooking bobbing boats. The understated nautical decor is charming, and the seaward glassed-in patio is tempting on a sunny day. The main dishes are Icelandic home-cooking classics like fish cakes, *plokkfiskur* (fish gratin or hash), and cod, plaice, and arctic char filets; on weekdays, soup and coffee are included (Mon-Fri 7:30-18:00, Sat-Sun from 9:30, Grandagarður 10, tel. 551-5932, http://www.kaffivagninn.is).

$ The Coocoo's Nest is a somewhat trendier-feeling café just across the street from Kaffivaginn, and lacks its view. But it does have a cozy, split-level, stay-awhile interior and a tempting, brief menu—ideal for escaping the elements and enjoying soup, salad, or sandwiches. It serves a rotating menu—tacos one night, pizza the next, then Italian (Tue-Sat 11:00-22:00, Sun until 16:00, closed Mon, Grandagarður 23, tel. 552-5454).

Ice Cream: Valdís, a couple of doors down, offers creative flavors. The name is a pun—it's a girl's first name, but can also be read as "Power Ice Cream" (daily 11:30-23:00, Grandagarður 21).

OUTSIDE DOWNTOWN
These places are best for drivers (all have free parking) but can also be reached by bus.

West and South of Downtown
$ Kaffihús Vesturbæjar, an inviting neighborhood café across the street from the Vesturbæjarlaug swimming pool, is the kind of place that makes you want to hang out and pretend you live here. They serve good lunches from a small menu chalked on the board. While I wouldn't make a special trip, it's definitely worth a visit if you happen to be nearby (Mon-Fri 8:00-23:00, Sat-Sun from 9:00, hot food served 11:30-15:00 & 17:00-21:00, at Melhaga 20 at corner of Hófsvallagata, walk or take bus #11 to Melaskóli or #15 to Vesturgarður, easy parking, tel. 551-0623, www.kaffihusvesturbaejar.is).

$ Mýrin Mathús, a grill restaurant set unatmospherically inside the BSÍ bus terminal, is worth a visit mostly if you want to eat *svið* (sheep's head) served with mashed potatoes and turnips. You'll get a half sheep's head grinning at you on a plate (neatly sawed down the midline, brains not included), and a fork and a knife. You eat the cheek meat; those who dare can try the eyeball and tongue. They also dish up other classic Icelandic stick-to-your-ribs fare all day long, like fish cakes, salted lamb, and stuffed cabbage. These dishes come with soup and beverages (Mon-Fri 7:30-21:00, Sat-Sun 6:00-21:00, *svið* and other hot food served daily 10:30-20:30, small kids eat free with their parents, Vatnsmýrarvegur 10, tel. 552-1288, see map on page 132).

Near the Botanic Garden
For locations, see the map on page 132.

$$ Flóran, the relaxing café inside Reykjavík's botanic garden, has an eclectic, inventive menu, with main dishes and meal-

Budget Bites

If you're trying to stretch your budget—or want a low-key dinner option—here are some ideas. I normally don't recommend international chains, but if you're on a tight budget in this expensive country, inexpensive and familiar comfort food can hit the spot.

Pizza is a bad value at lunch but competitive at dinner, when a 2,500-ISK one-person pizza starts to look cheap compared to a 5,000-ISK entree at sit-down restaurant. Pizza joints downtown include the hip $$ **Pizza Place with No Name** (at Hverfisgata 12, a bit pricier) and the venerable $$ **Hornið** (at Hafnarstræti 15, close to Parliament and Lækjartorg). For a cheap meal, locals call $ **Domino's,** with multiple outlets (including a central one at Skúlagata 27, near Hlemmur; easy ordering in English online or call 581-2345, locations and offers at www.dominos.is).

Just like back home, Reykjavík's suburban **IKEA** store has a handy and very cheap $ **cafeteria.** Local families pack in for inexpensive (if small) main dishes, including Swedish meatballs and Icelandic *plokkfiskur* (fish gratin or hash). Downstairs by the cash registers are Reykjavík's least-expensive hot dogs and soft-serve ice cream. IKEA is just off the main route from Reykjavík to the airport, the Blue Lagoon, and the Ásvallalaug swimming pool (daily 9:30-20:30, Kauptún 4 in the suburb of Garðabær, bus #21 to the IKEA stop—catch it at Mjódd or in Hafnarfjörður).

As in other expensive European cities, **international food** can be a good value here. $ **Noodle Station,** a small local chain, serves just one dish: big portions of a vaguely Vietnamese noodle soup, with your choice of beef, chicken, or vegetables. There's a location close to the Hlemmur bus junction (Laugavegur 86—see map on page 132), and another in a strip mall on the main road through Hafnarfjörður. For a larger selection of Asian dishes, consider $ **Krua Thai,** a couple of blocks downhill from the big Hallgrímskirkja church (daily 11:30-21:30, Skólavörðustígur 21a—see map on page 141), tel. 551-0833).

Of course, the absolute cheapest option is to assemble a picnic at a **supermarket.** Discount supermarket **Bónus** has two downtown branches, at Hallveigarstígur 1 and Laugavegur 59 (both open Mon-Thu 11:00-18:30, Fri 10:00-19:30, shorter hours Sat-Sun). **Hagkaup** runs several 24-hour supermarkets (closed on holidays) including one a 10-minute drive from downtown at Skeifan 15. There are also supermarkets in the Kringlan and Smáralind indoor shopping malls, outside the center.

sized salads. Eat outdoors on a nice day, or in the warm, greenhouse-like interior. Befitting the location, they grow some of their own vegetables and herbs (daily 10:00-22:00, early May and Sept until 18:00, closed Oct-April; take bus #2, #5, #15, or #17 to the Laugardalshöll stop and walk 10 minutes downhill to the parking lot and garden entrance; tel. 553-8872).

$ **Múlakaffi** serves old-style Icelandic cuisine with all the polish of a 1970s school lunchroom. You can stuff yourself for about 2,000 ISK, even at dinnertime. Choose a main dish at the counter—it might be fish cakes, cod cheeks, or pasta with meat sauce—then help yourself to as much soup, salad, bread, butter, and coffee as you like (dishes are listed at www.mulakaffi.is). This place has been here—in a commercial zone amidst office blocks and strip malls—for decades. You'll see tradespeople here on a midday break and older men who meet to chat and read the papers together (Mon-Fri 7:30-20:00, Sat 10:00-14:00, closed Sun, Hallarmúli 1, bus #2, #5, #15, or #17 to Nordica stop, tel. 553-7737).

Farther Out, in Hafnarfjörður

This bedroom community, about 15 minutes' drive south of Reykjavík, isn't worth going out of your way to get a meal. However, if you're sleeping in Hafnarfjörður—or passing through on your way back from side-trips to the Blue Lagoon, South Coast, or Golden Circle—it can be easier to grab a bite here than to look for parking downtown. See the "Hafnarfjörður" map, earlier, for locations.

$$ **Von** ("Hope") is the top choice for foodies. This small, ambitious restaurant serves modern fish and meat dishes and is proud of their seafood and ox cheek. Local office workers come for good weekday lunch specials (reservations recommended for dinner, Tue-Sat 11:30-14:00 & 17:30-21:00, Sun 11:30-14:00, also open Sun evenings June-Aug, closed Mon year-round, Strandgata 75, along the water at the south end of downtown, past the fake stave church, tel. 583-6000, www.vonmathus.is).

$ **Pallett,** an inviting hangout café in the same complex as Von, is run by an Icelandic-British couple. They serve great coffee, affordable soup and sandwiches, and—on weekends—a full traditional English breakfast at midday (Mon-Fri 8:00-23:00, Sat-Sun from 10:00, Strandgata 75, tel. 571-4144).

$ **Bike Cave** is a casual hamburger restaurant tucked in the town center, with a spacious interior (including a glassy winter garden) and intriguing burgers (daily 9:00-22:00, Strandgata 34, tel. 571-3144).

$ **Súfistinn Kaffihús** is a simple, two-story café with soups, sandwiches, and quiches on the old main street, close to the town library (Mon-Fri 8:00-23:30, Sat from 10:00, Sun from 11:00, Strandgata 9, tel. 563-3740).

$$$ **Fjörukráin**
("The Waterside Tavern")
is a Viking-themed din-
ner-only restaurant, often
busy with groups (you
can't miss it—look for the
Norwegian stave church-
like roof). It's kitschy and
the prices are high for
what you get, but the in-

terior is a work of art and a visit can be fun (daily 18:00-22:00,
Strandgata 55, tel. 565-1213).

Reykjavík Connections

BY PLANE
Keflavík Airport (International Flights)

Keflavík Airport (pronounced KEPP-la-VEEK, code: KEF, tel.
425-6000, www.kefairport.is) is Iceland's only real international
airport and the center of Icelandair's hub-and-spoke operation that
carries thousands of passengers a day between North America and
Europe. The airport's status as a transfer point gives Icelanders a
much broader range of flight options, all year long, than they would
otherwise have in this small country. Budget carrier Wow Air and
several other airlines also serve the airport. Extra flights are added
each summer to carry European tourists to Iceland—during sum-
mer months, the airport can get very crowded.

Arrival and departure areas are both on the ground floor, on
opposite sides of the main terminal building. You'll find a couple
cafés and a convenience store, car rental offices, a tax-refund desk,
and ATMs, but no TI. A 24-hour bank is located inside (after se-
curity) where you can change any leftover Icelandic crowns when
you leave the country—they're hard to exchange outside Iceland.
The airport has free Wi-Fi.

Nearby Gas Stations: When returning a rental car be aware
that the airport itself has only a couple of teeny self-serve pumps
hidden near the car-rental return. It's smarter to fill up in down-
town Keflavík or at the bigger gas stations a five-minute drive away
along the main road from Reykjavík.

The Orkan gas station along the main road, next to the Bónus
supermarket, can't process US chip-and-signature credit cards at
the pump but sells prepaid gas cards inside its 24-hour shop. The
N1 station in downtown Keflavík takes signature cards, but has
shorter hours.

Breakfast Near the Airport: Many flights from the US arrive
early in the morning. Hótel Keflavík, near the harbor in the town

REYKJAVÍK

REYKJAVÍK

Keflavík Airport Area

DUUS MUSEUM

Faxaflói

To Sandgerði [459]

To Garður [45]

[41]

GAS STATION

[41]

AÐALGATA

MAIN TERMINAL ❶

❸

K E F L A V Í K

RENTAL CARS ❶

Ⓑ Strætó Bus #55

❷

N-1 GAS STN.

DEPARTURES Ⓑ

Ⓑ ARRIVALS

Ⓟ

Ⓟ

R E Y K J A N E S B Æ R

ICELANDIC ROCK & ROLL MUSEUM

RUNWAYS

REYKJANESBRAUT

NJARÐARBRAUT

GRÆNÁS-VEGUR

Lava Fields

VIKING WORLD MUSEUM

NJARÐARBRAUT

SETTLEMENT AGE ZOO

Lava Fields

ÁSBRÚ (FORMER US BASE)

SUPERMARKET

ORKAN GAS STN.

[41]

To Reykjavík & Blue Lagoon (via Highway 43)

1 Kilometer

[44]

1 Mile

Ⓝ

❶ Hotel Aurora Star
❷ Hótel Keflavík
❸ Alex Guesthouse

To Hafnir & Grindavík (via Highway 425)

Not all gas stations shown

of Keflavík, offers a buffet open to nonguests (no reservations needed, 2,800 ISK, daily 5:00-10:00, Vatnsnesvegi 12, tel. 420-7000). The Viking World museum on the Reykjanes Peninsula also does a breakfast buffet that includes admission (see page 174).

Getting Between Reykjavík and Keflavík Airport

The airport is about a 45-minute drive from downtown Reykjavík (30 minutes from Hafnarfjörður). For details on renting a car, see page 409. Without a rental car, your options are private airport buses, shared door-to-door van service, taxis, or an infrequent public bus.

Don't worry about making an early flight: The whole system is designed for people to get from Reykjavík with plenty of time to make a 7:00 or 8:00 departure. Buses, shuttles, and taxis are ready to go by 3:00 or 4:00 in the morning.

By Airport Bus: Two companies—Reykjavík Excursions and Gray Line—run buses between Reykjavík and the airport. Buses run whenever there are flights, even at odd hours. From the airport, buses typically depart when full, which can mean a wait.

From Reykjavík, buses depart according to a schedule that varies depending on the flight density.

Reykjavík Excursions runs the **Flybus** (tel. 580-5400, www. flybus.is) between the airport and the company's terminal in Reykjavík (called BSÍ, at Vatnsmýrarvegur 10, about a 10- to 15-minute walk from downtown).

Gray Line runs **Airport Express** buses (tel. 540-1313, www. airportexpress.is) to and from their terminal at Holtavegur 10, next to a Bónus supermarket in a distant part of Reykjavík.

Taking these buses makes good financial sense for solo travelers and for families, as children ride free or at a sizable discount. But the buses can be slow, disorganized, and stressful. The companies try to fill every seat. At busy times, the aisle will be crowded with hand bags, the luggage compartment will be jammed full, and boarding may be a mob scene. Bring patience.

Both companies have desks in the airport arrivals hall where you can buy tickets; you can also book and pay in advance online. A round-trip ticket (about 4,000 ISK) saves over two one-ways (about 2,500 ISK).

Gray Line's regular price is a tad cheaper, but Reykjavík Excursions tickets are discounted if you buy them from the flight attendant on board Icelandair. (Icelandair and Reykjavík Excursions have a longstanding business alliance, so you won't hear or read a word about Gray Line on Icelandair flights.)

In Reykjavík, the buses stop primarily at each company's main transfer point, but Gray Line also picks up and drops off downtown for no extra charge. En route between Reykjavík and the airport, both companies' buses stop on request at the bus shelter across from the Viking Village Hótel in downtown Hafnarfjörður (at Strandgata 55). If you need to be picked up there, pay in advance and reconfirm with the company, as buses bypass this stop if there are no requests.

Door-to-Door Service: For an extra 500 ISK each way, each company will tack on the transportation between their transfer point and major hotels and hostels in central Reykjavík. This usually involves a separate minibus trip between the transfer point and the hotel, and takes about 30 extra minutes. It's cheaper than a taxi, and easier than taking the city bus. The transfer procedures can be confusing (you'll need to carry your luggage from one bus to the other). If you're staying in an Airbnb, put in a nearby hotel as your pick-up and drop-off point, then walk from the hotel to your lodgings. If you're staying way out in the suburbs, the transfer service may not serve any point near you.

By Taxi: Groups of at least four adults (who can split the cost) save time and pay only a little more to take a taxi to or from the airport. Anyone up for paying extra to avoid the craziness of the airport buses should also consider a taxi. Reykjavík's two main taxi companies both offer fixed-price service to and from the airport for about 15,000-16,000 ISK (1-4 passengers) or 19,000-21,500 ISK (5-8 passengers). If you reserve in advance, they'll wait for you at the airport with a sign. When reserving, tell them your destination and ask their advice; if your starting or ending point is in the southern part of the capital area (for example, in Hafnarfjörður), using the meter may be cheaper than these fixed rates. Contact **Hreyfill** (tel. 588-5522, www.hreyfill.is) and **BSR** (tel. 561-0000, www.taxireykjavik.is). Other smaller taxi and transfer companies may offer slightly lower rates.

By Public Bus: Strætó, the public bus company, runs buses (#55) between downtown Reykjavík and Keflavík Airport every 1-2 hours, taking about 70 minutes. At some times of the day and on weekends, they run only between the airport and the Fjörður stop in Hafnarfjörður, where you change to bus #1. The public bus is meant more for commuters than for international travelers and goes infrequently, but it's the cheapest way into town and has space for luggage. As it's considered a long-distance route, you can pay the bus driver with a credit card (1,760 ISK or four bus tickets; connecting city buses are free if you ask the drive for a transfer slip). For schedules, see www.straeto.is (enter the airport as "KEF" in the journey planner).

The Strætó bus stop is out in the open air along row A of the car rental lot. To find it, walk out from the arrivals side of the terminal under the roofed walkway, then hang a left and look for the tiny "S" sign (it's not signposted from inside the arrivals hall).

Reykjavík City Airport

Reykjavík's domestic airport (code: RKV) is just south of downtown. Planes landing from the north fly directly over Parliament at a height of only a few hundred feet. While the runways are long enough to land an Icelandair 757, the airport is only used for smaller planes flying domestic routes and to the Faroe Islands and east Greenland. Check-in at the pint-sized terminals feels informal; arriving even an hour early feels like overkill, and there's no security checkpoint for domestic flights.

It's important to know that the airport has two terminals on *opposite* sides of the runway. If you go to the wrong terminal, you'll have to take a taxi to get to the other (you can't walk). Air Iceland Connect uses the larger main terminal on the *west* side of the runways (take bus #15 to the Reykjavíkurflugvöllur stop). If you're flying on Eagle Air—for example, to the Westman Islands—you'll go from a separate, smaller terminal on the *east* side of the runways (take bus #5 to the Nauthólsvegur stop; the terminal is behind the

Icelandair Hótel Reykjavík Natura and the control tower). Parking is free at both terminals.

To make an early-morning domestic flight, before buses start running, call a taxi (reserve the night before; see the taxi recommendations earlier, under Keflavík Airport). Figure about 2,000 ISK for a taxi between downtown and either terminal (or between terminals). When you get in the taxi, remember to specify which airline/terminal you're heading to.

BY BUS

Reykjavík has several bus stations. Buses run by **Reykjavík Excursions,** including all of their excursion buses and the scheduled FlyBus to the airport, use the old **BSÍ** bus terminal at Vatnsmýrarvegur 10, about a 15-minute walk from downtown (or take bus #1, #3, #5, #6, #14, or #15 to BSÍ). Two smaller companies, Sterna Travel and TREX, also use BSÍ for their scheduled and excursion buses.

Buses run by **Gray Line** use their terminal at **Holtavegur 10,** in the Reykjavík suburbs near the container-ship harbor. Gray Line runs minibuses to hotels around town to pick travelers up and shuttle them to the terminal. You can get within a five-minute walk of the terminal by public bus (#12 or #16 to the Sund or Holtagarðar stops), but it's easier to use their shuttles.

Long-distance buses run by **Strætó,** Iceland's public bus service, depart from the Mjódd bus terminal in the eastern Reykjavík suburbs. It's next to a small indoor shopping mall, also called Mjódd (MEE-ohd). Many city bus routes stop at Mjódd, including #3, #4, #11, #12, #17, #24, and #28 (no extra charge for transfer ticket).

Strætó's downtown city bus junction at **Hlemmur** doesn't serve long-distance routes, but is a good place to catch a bus to the long-distance terminal at Mjódd.

BY CRUISE SHIP

There's no scheduled boat service from Reykjavík, but cruise ships frequently stop here in summer. The cruise ship terminal is at Skarfagarðar, a five-minute drive east of downtown; by bus, take #16 to the Klettagarðar/Skarfagarðar stop. Smaller cruise ships occasionally use a berth in the Old Harbor, just steps from downtown. The weekly ferry from Iceland to Denmark leaves from Seyðisfjörður, in eastern Iceland (see the "Transportation" section of the Practicalities chapter).

NEAR REYKJAVÍK

NEAR REYKJAVÍK

Most visitors to Iceland settle into a home base, typically Reykjavík, and see most of the countryside on day trips. The destinations in the following chapters—all in western or southern Iceland—are all doable as day trips from Reykjavík, whether you rent a car or join an excursion.

Two of the best side-trips for getting a glimpse of Iceland's dramatic landscape are the Golden Circle (linking historical and geological wonders, in the country's lava-rock interior) and the volcano-and-glacier-lined South Coast (where you can hike up to the face of a glacier, stroll along black sand beaches, and walk behind a thundering waterfall).

There's also the famous Blue Lagoon spa—a serene, milky-blue oasis in a volcanic landscape—and the West Iceland region around Borgarnes, with an eclectic variety of sights. My favorite "Back Door" destination is the Westman Islands, just off Iceland's South Coast, where you can see the effects of a recent volcanic eruption and perhaps meet a real, live puffin.

Below, I've given you a few tips for planning side-trips on your own with a car, as well as your options for joining guided excursions.

Summer Bonus: In summer you'll enjoy very long hours of daylight; from early June to mid-July it never really gets dark. You can pack a day full by sightseeing close to your home base in the

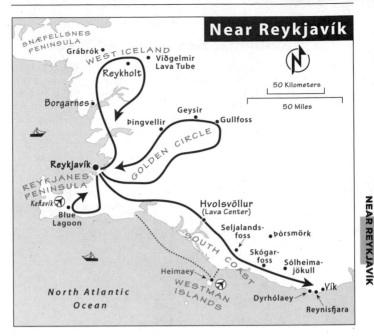

morning, then setting out on a side-trip in the late afternoon. In the peak of summer, for example, it's possible to leave Reykjavík for the Golden Circle as late as 16:00, see most of the sights along that route, and be back in town before the sun goes down.

Winter Wake-up: In winter, daylight is brief (as short as 4 hours). If roads are clear, it's smart to leave Reykjavík in the dark and time your arrival at the first attraction for sunrise. Be alert to weather conditions, as roads may close due to snow, high winds, or ice.

Car vs. Excursion: Although a car rental may seem pricey (roughly $350 for a one-week rental in summer, plus insurance, fuel, tolls, and parking), consider this: Per person, the bus transfer to and from the airport is $40; you'll pay $100 for a basic Golden Circle excursion and $150 for the South Coast. If you're in Iceland for three nights, and take two day-trip excursions, you'll spend close to $300 (double that for a couple). Suddenly a rental car doesn't seem that expensive.

WITH A CAR

For travelers day-tripping on their own by car, in each chapter I've outlined detailed self-guided driving tours with suggested hour-by-hour schedules and opinionated descriptions to help you assess your options and plan your drive.

My directions assume you're staying in Reykjavík. But if you

Decoding Icelandic Place Names

Most Icelandic place names are simply a pileup of geographical features. For example, the word for the famous tongue-twister volcano Eyjafjallajökull can be broken down into three smaller words meaning "Island-Mountain Glacier." You can learn a lot about a place simply by decoding its name (and often just its suffix). For example, if you see *fjörður*, expect a dramatic seaside setting; *vík* is on the water, but less thrilling; *fjall* is mountainous; and *hver* means things could get steamy. Here are some of the building blocks:

á	river, stream	*fell*	hill, mountain
akur	field	*fjall*	mountain
ár	river	*fjara*	beach, shore
austur	east	*fjörður*	fjord
bær	town	*fljót*	large river
bjarg	cliff	*flói*	gulf, bay
borg	outcrop, fortification	*flúðir*	rapids
braut	avenue	*foss*	waterfall
brú	bridge	*gata*	street
bú	estate, farm	*gerði*	fence, hedge
dalur	valley	*gígur*	crater
eldfjall	volcano (fire mountain)	*gljúfur*	canyon, gorge
ey	island	*grænn*	green
eyja	island	*heiði*	treeless highland, heath, sometimes "pass"
eyri	point, spit	*hellir*	cave

prefer sleeping outside the city, you can drive to these day-trip destinations from a home base anywhere in the southwestern part of the country—for example, from along the South Coast; from the Reykjavík suburb of Hafnarfjörður; or from Keflavík, near the international airport.

Before heading out, be sure to read the tips on driving in Iceland in the Practicalities chapter.

WITH AN EXCURSION

A variety of companies offer excursions around Iceland. These are great if you want to sit back, enjoy the scenery, and learn from a knowledgeable guide (or, in a few cases, a well-produced recorded commentary). With careful planning, you can cobble together half-

hlíð	mountainside, slope	*sandur*	sandy area
holt	hill	*skagi*	peninsula
höfn	harbor	*skarð*	mountain pass
hraun	lava	*skógur*	forest
hús	house	*staður*	place, farm, town
hver	hot spring	*stígur*	trail
hvítur	white	*stræti*	street
jökull	glacier	*strönd*	coast, sandy beach
krókur	hook, river bend	*suður*	south
laugar	hot spring, pool	*svartur*	black
lækur	creek	*tún*	hay field
lón	lagoon	*vatn*	lake (also "water")
mýri	swamp, marsh	*vegur*	road
nes	promontory, headland	*vestur*	west
norður	north	*vík*	bay, inlet
reykur	steam	*völlur*	field, plain (plural vellir)

These place name elements recur throughout the country, and in a few cases entire names are recycled (for instance, there's a Reykholt near Borgarnes in western Iceland, and another near Geysir along the Golden Circle). When that happens, the place name might get an add-on modifier for clarity. The town of Vík ("Bay"), on the South Coast, is called Vík í Mýrdal (the "Bay in Marshy Valley") to distinguish it from other less-visited Víks around the country. And if you're heading for Borgarfjörður Eystri (literally the "more eastern Borgarfjörður"), don't follow your GPS to plain old Borgarfjörður...nearly 400 miles to the west.

and full-day excursions that will get you to many of Iceland's top sights.

The most popular excursion destinations are the Golden Circle, the Blue Lagoon, the South Coast, the Snæfellsnes peninsula (north of Reykjavík), and the Reykjanes Peninsula (south of Reykjavík). In winter, you'll find evening trips in search of the northern lights. Some tours run all year, but winter offerings are generally sparser.

Most excursions start

in Reykjavík, but there are also options from Akureyri, Mývatn, and other small towns around the Ring Road (see the Ring Road chapter for specific recommendations).

You may see tours advertised for the glacier lagoons and Skaftafell National Park in Southeast Iceland; while these are amazing sights, they're too far from the capital for a reasonable day trip (at least 10 hours round-trip from Reykjavík)—you'll spend far more time in the bus than at your destination. Save these for another trip...when you come back and drive around the Ring Road. Or, if you're serious about glaciers, add an overnight or two in the southeast and do it right.

BIG VS. SMALL COMPANY

The two biggest players are **Reykjavík Excursions** (www.re.is, owned by Icelandair and promoted on their flights) and **Gray Line** (www.grayline.is). Their offer-ings are slick and consistent, but the 50-seat buses are typically jam-packed (though Gray Line offers some minibus departures). An advantage, though, is predictability and price; what these tours lack in intimacy they make up for in efficiency and lower ticket costs.

Several smaller outfits are more personal, generally use smaller vehicles—and charge a little to a lot more. Well-established and respected companies include family-run **Nicetravel** (www.nicetravel.is); environmentally focused **Geo Iceland** (www.geoiceland.com); small-bus, small-group **Iceland Horizon** (www.icelandhorizon.is); and pricey, boutique **Season Tours** (www.seasontours.is).

Choosing an Excursion: For starters, look at each company's brochure and website. As the offerings are constantly in flux, check reviews on TripAdvisor.com (in the "Things to Do" section) for recent firsthand accounts. Guide to Iceland (www.guidetoiceland.is), a consortium of several travel outlets, can be a good one-stop source for tours; they also have a booking desk at the Reykjavík TI.

Add-on Options: Beyond the standard sightseeing loops, excursion companies mix and match a staggering variety of add-on activities: hiking, caving, horseback riding, snorkeling, glacier walking, and snowmobiling. The possibilities are endless: You can do the Blue Lagoon on the way to the airport; add the Fontana baths in Laugarvatn, snorkeling, or an ATV ride to a Golden Circle trip; or go on a tour of *Game of Thrones* shooting locations.

Prices: Excursions run from about $80 to $250 (more for boutique experiences). For example, an express, six-hour Golden Circle tour costs about $100; a 10-hour South Coast tour costs around $150; and a bus trip to the Blue Lagoon, including the hefty admission, runs at least $120.

When to Book: For the standard tours—such as the Golden Circle or South Coast—you generally don't need to book a seat more than a day or two in advance, so you may want to wait until you arrive in Iceland—and can check the weather report. One exception is the Blue Lagoon, which can fill up faster than other excursions. Your hotel may be happy to book these tours for you (be aware that they get a commission).

More specialized tours (ice caving, glacier hikes) can book up quite a bit earlier; for these, keep an eye on online booking calendars, which typically count down the number of slots available for each tour. If it looks like they're selling fast, book yours before it's too late.

WITH AN UNGUIDED EXCURSION

A number of private companies run regularly scheduled buses throughout Iceland's countryside—offering transportation to otherwise difficult-to-reach, remote areas, but without any guiding. Developed primarily to get hikers to trailheads, some of these buses can also work for independent travelers who want to put together day trips on their own. For more information, see the "Transportation" section of the Practicalities chapter.

BLUE LAGOON & REYKJANES PENINSULA

The Blue Lagoon—arguably Iceland's most famous attraction—is tucked into a jagged volcanic landscape in the middle of nowhere, about a 45-minute drive south of downtown Reykjavík and not far from the international airport. People flock here from around the globe to soak, splash, and bob in the lagoon's thermal and, yes, milky-blue waters. While many visitors consider the Blue Lagoon a must, others disagree—it's pricey, time-consuming, and not everyone's cup of tea.

The Blue Lagoon and Keflavík Airport both sit on the Reykjanes (RAKE-ya-NESS) Peninsula, which extends into the sea south of Reykjavík. A few low-impact sights are scattered around the volcanic terrain beyond the Blue Lagoon—including Kleifarvatn lake; the thermal fields at Seltún; Grindavík, a humdrum town with some good lunch options; and Keflavík, the peninsula's main town. While the scenery is more impressive in other parts of the country, a quick drive around Reykjanes provides those on a tight time frame with an efficient glimpse of the Icelandic landscape.

PLANNING YOUR TIME

Be aware that the Blue Lagoon requires reservations—you can't just show up and hope to slip in. To have your choice of slots, book several days ahead.

Blue Lagoon Strategic Strike: Given the Blue Lagoon's proximity to the international airport, a smart, time-saving strategy is to schedule your visit to coincide with your flight: If arriving on a morning flight, hit the Blue Lagoon on your way into Reykjavík. Or if you're flying out in the afternoon, soak in the Blue Lagoon on your way to the airport. If you have a layover of several hours, it

Blue Lagoon: To Visit or Not to Visit?

Travelers are split on the Blue Lagoon. For some, a visit to this iconic thermal pool is the highlight of their time in Iceland. For others, it's outrageously expensive and overrated. Here are the pros and cons:

On one hand, the Blue Lagoon is a unique and memorable travel experience, thanks to its stunning volcanic setting, silky-blue water, and luxury-spa class. While you could visit any municipal swimming pool in Iceland to splash in hot water, the Blue Lagoon is as refined as those are functional—it is, in a sense, the ultimate expression of Icelandic thermal bathing. And it's simply fun: sipping a drink, smearing fancy mud on your face, and feeling pebbles under your feet as 100°F water ebbs your stress away. As a bonus, it's easy to reach on the way to or from the airport.

On the other hand, the Blue Lagoon is expensive (absurdly so to Icelanders), overly crowded with an almost exclusively touristic clientele, grossly commercial, and inconveniently located for those staying in Reykjavík. The reservation requirement is cumbersome, and the minerals in the water can wreak havoc on your hair. If you believe that one big pool of hot water is pretty much the same as any other, you'll be much happier to pay one-tenth of the price to enjoy one of Reykjavík's many municipal swimming pools—which also offer a far more authentic cultural experience. (For more on the municipal pool experience, read the description on page 114.)

may not be worth the trouble to go all the way into Reykjavík—but a visit to the Blue Lagoon (or sights in the town of Keflavík) makes a far better alternative to hanging out at the airport.

Combining the Blue Lagoon with the Reykjanes Peninsula: If you're staying longer in Reykjavík and want to make a day of it, book your Blue Lagoon reservation for 13:00 and follow this plan.

10:00	Leave Reykjavík for Kleifarvatn lake (45 minutes)
11:00	Visit Kleifarvatn and Seltún geothermal field
11:30	Drive to Grindavík (30 minutes) and have lunch
12:45	Drive to the Blue Lagoon (10 minutes)
13:00	Soak in the Blue Lagoon—aaah
16:00	Return to Reykjavík—or, before heading home, take in one of the museums in the town of Keflavík

Blue Lagoon

While Iceland has a wide variety of thermal baths, the Blue Lagoon's setting amongst rocky lava makes it unique. Bathing at the Blue Lagoon is, for many travelers, the ultimate Icelandic experience, and worth ▲▲▲.

If you're excited to visit the Blue Lagoon (Bláa Lónið), you're not alone: The sight's popularity and don't-miss-it reputation have driven prices way up. The lagoon has expanded, but at a pace that can't keep up with tourist demand (over 3,000 people visit each day). Reservations are required, and some slots sell out days in advance. (The bottleneck isn't the lagoon itself, but the number of lockers.) While the reservation requirement is a hassle, it keeps the lagoon from getting too congested—even on the busiest days, you can find pockets of hot water where you can escape the tour groups. Once inside, you can stay as long as you want.

The Blue Lagoon is a delight. Nestled in a lunar-like landscape, this steamy oasis is a sprawling hot-water playground for grown-ups. Chunky rocks disappear beneath the opaque water, where they're coated with white silica slime. The naturally heated water is thoroughly relaxing. You'll smear mineral deposits on your

face, while giggling at your fellow silica-masked bathers. The hardest "work" you'll have to do is keeping your Icelandic microbrew or *skyr* smoothie above the water, as you behold the surrounding rocks hissing like teakettles. Before leaving the lagoon, some travelers are already planning their next layover in Iceland...giving them juuust enough time for a future soak.

GETTING THERE

With a Car: If you're renting a car—and traveling with others who can split the cost—you'll save by driving to the lagoon over going by bus. It's about 45 minutes from downtown Reykjavík, and only 15 minutes from Keflavík Airport, off highway 43, on the way to the town of Grindavík. Some signs use only the Icelandic name: *Bláa Lónið.* The lagoon's huge parking lot is free.

By Excursion Bus: Both **Reykjavík Excursions** and **Gray Line** sell packages that include standard admission and round-trip travel between Reykjavík and the lagoon for about 11,700 ISK. You're allowed to use your return ticket to continue to Keflavík Airport instead of going back to Reykjavík (luggage storage is available at the Blue Lagoon—see page 167). Buses run hourly

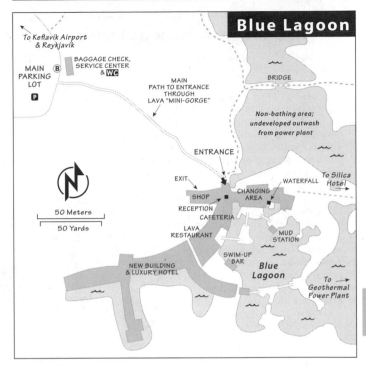

Map labels:
Blue Lagoon
To Keflavík Airport & Reykjavík
MAIN PARKING LOT
BAGGAGE CHECK, SERVICE CENTER & WC
MAIN PATH TO ENTRANCE THROUGH LAVA "MINI-GORGE"
BRIDGE
Non-bathing area; undeveloped outwash from power plant
ENTRANCE
EXIT
WATERFALL
To Silica Hotel
CHANGING AREA
SHOP
RECEPTION
CAFETERIA
LAVA RESTAURANT
MUD STATION
NEW BUILDING & LUXURY HOTEL
SWIM-UP BAR
Blue Lagoon
To Geothermal Power Plant
50 Meters
50 Yards

between Reykjavík and the Blue Lagoon but less frequently between the lagoon and airport—check schedules carefully and plan ahead (Reykjavík Excursions tel. 580-5400, www.re.is; Gray Line tel. 540-1313, www.grayline.is). Note that these companies have access to the same time slots for the Blue Lagoon as individuals—if the lagoon is sold out in one place, it'll be sold out everywhere.

ORIENTATION TO THE BLUE LAGOON

Cost: Prices vary with demand. Most visitors opt for the **standard** package (typically 7,500 ISK, but can be as low as 5,400 ISK in off-peak hours). If you choose this package, you'll need to bring your own towel or rent one for 700 ISK. For an extra 2,000 ISK, the **comfort** package bundles towel rental, a dollop of green algae mud for your face (otherwise 450 ISK), and a free drink from the bar in the lagoon (otherwise 500-1,200 ISK). For another 2,000 ISK, the **premium** package adds bathrobe and slipper rental.

Hours: Daily 8:00-22:00, June-Aug until 23:00 or 24:00, Oct-Dec until 20:00, last entry one hour before closing. You need to leave the water at closing time, but have another 30 minutes after that to dress.

Information: Tel. 420-8800, www.bluelagoon.com.

The Origin of the Blue Lagoon

The Blue Lagoon dates only from the early 1970s, when the local power authority drilled for hot water to heat homes on the Reykjanes Peninsula. They hit a good high-temperature source, but as often happens, the water wasn't suitable for piping directly into home radiators—it was salty (due to sea-water intrusions) and had a high mineral and clay content. Instead, they set up a heat-exchange system where the geo-thermal water was used to heat fresh, cold water that could then be piped to homes. After running through the system, the partly cooled geothermal water was simply dumped into the lava field near the plant.

Within a few years, locals realized this was a great place for a free dip and started to bathe in the water. Silica clay gives the water its milky texture, and sunlight gives it a blue appearance. (The name "Blue Lagoon"—borrowed from the notori-ous 1980 Brooke Shields movie—was originally used in jest.) Authorities caught on, fenced off the lagoon, built a changing shed, and started to charge admission, which at first was no more than at a local swimming pool. Word spread, and within a few years the lagoon had become a major tourist attraction. The power authority privatized

the lagoon, controversially selling it to a group of local politi-cians. They raised capital and did an admirable job developing and marketing the lagoon, adding cosmetics lines, a gift shop, a hotel, and a fancy restaurant.

Today, almost all the Blue Lagoon's guests are tourists; only a small percentage are Icelanders, who find the facil-ity too expensive and distant and don't like what it does to their hair. Meanwhile, three similar premium pools in Iceland have sprung up: **Fontana** (at Laugarvatn, on the Golden Circle route); **Mývatn Nature Baths** (partway around the Ring Road, in North Iceland); and **Krauma** (at Deildartunguhver, in West Iceland—see page 263). These somewhat cheaper, less up-scale alternatives are farther afield and lack the lava setting (though Mývatn comes close); most travelers stick with the original.

Reservations: Book as far in advance as you can to get the widest selection of times. You have to commit to an entry time when you book, but once you're in the lagoon, you can stay until closing time. Evening entries are cheaper and less likely to be sold out. Tickets are only partially refundable, and changing a reservation costs 1,400 ISK. If you're running ahead of schedule for your reservation, you can try to enter earlier—if it's not too crowded, they may let you in (no promises).

Arrival and Luggage Storage: The lagoon's parking lot is connected to the main building by a 100-yard-long path cut through the lava field. A small building near the parking lot has a WC, pay luggage storage, and a waiting room for those taking buses from the lagoon.

Eyewear and Jewelry: Avoid wearing valuable eyeglasses in the water; if you must, secure them with a strap (if they fall off, you won't be able to find them in the opaque water). Be careful not to rub delicate lenses while they're in the Blue Lagoon water, as the clay can scratch them—instead, wait to rinse them in freshwater when you get out. (On a bright day, a pair of cheap sunglasses makes the lagoon more pleasant.) Because the water is opaque, there's no need for goggles. Leave jewelry in your locker to avoid tarnishing.

Hair Concerns: As with ocean water, the minerals in the Blue Lagoon leave your hair dry and brittle. The effect goes away within a day or two. Don't stress about this too much—the lagoon is more fun if you relax and let your hair get wet. Still, especially for those with long hair, it's smart to slather on the free conditioner (from dispensers in the shower stalls) before and after you bathe, or keep long hair tied up and out of the water. A bathing cap offers the best protection. In addition to conditioner, the lagoon provides free body wash and the use of hair dryers.

Kids: Children under age two are not allowed in the Blue Lagoon, and the facility is not really designed for kids (no slides, kiddie pools, or play areas). The water is opaque, so if a child goes under, you won't be able to see him or her. The same goes for toys, glasses, goggles...and anything else that might slip out of little hands.

Eating: The main building has an overpriced **$ self-service cafeteria**, plus the expensive, sit-down **$$$$ Lava Restaurant** (reservations recommended, same contact info as lagoon). You can get much more value by eating in Grindavík, a 10-minute drive away (described later in this chapter).

Sleeping: The lagoon runs the nearby **$$$$ Silica Hotel** and the preposterously expensive **Retreat suites**. If you want to stay close, you'll find lower prices in towns like Keflavík and Grindavík (see "Hotels near the Airport" in the Reykjavík chapter).

Expect Changes: The Blue Lagoon is undergoing an ambitious expansion project. While the lagoon itself and the changing areas will remain essentially the same, they're adding a new wing with in-water spa treatments and a 60-room luxury hotel.

Looking without Bathing: If you're in the area and just want a peek at the dreamy setting, you can park, enter the main building, and visit the gift shop, cafeteria, and restaurant without a ticket. There's a good view of the bathing area from the cafeteria. A path from the parking lot leads through the non-bathing section of the lagoon. Also, as you drive toward the complex, there's a point where the water from the power plant comes up through the lava and right up to the road; you could get out for a photo, if you can pull off without blocking traffic.

VISITING THE BLUE LAGOON

The procedures for a visit to the Blue Lagoon are basically the same as at other Icelandic pools (see "Pool Rules" sidebar on page 42). Watch the helpful video on the website (www.bluelagoon.com), which walks you through the process.

As you enter, you'll get an electronic wristband that serves as your locker key (and lets you charge drinks, face mud, and other extras—pay when you leave). Once in the **changing area,** follow green lights to available lockers. Attendants are also there to direct you. Once you've changed and showered (in a private cabin, if you prefer), head out to the lagoon.

The **lagoon** is *big.* The water ranges from waist to chest deep. The temperature varies more than in a regular swimming pool, with hot and cool spots—the average is around 100°F. While the water is not chlorinated, new water continually circulates into the lagoon—refilling the entire pool about every 40 hours. Bathers congregate by the warm spots where the hot water enters. Splish and splash around, exploring the nooks and crannies of the interconnected pools. There are many hidden areas to explore, including a little roofed grotto, and a few areas with benches that resemble hot pots at the municipal baths. Find the scalding, thundering waterfalls, and dare yourself to linger beneath them. There's also a sauna and a steam room.

The **bar** is in the far-right corner of the lagoon. Be sure to stay hydrated; look for water fountains under the bridges.

At the **mud station** (to the left), there are three options:

Every bather is entitled to a free ladleful of the **white** silica mud that collects in the lagoon. Smear this exfoliant on your face, let it set for about 10 minutes, then wash it off. Bathers who bought a "comfort" or "premium" ticket also get a blob of **greenish** algae, which supposedly reduces wrinkles and rejuvenates the skin (same procedure: wear for 10 minutes, then rinse). You may also see roving attendants handing out a **black** "lava scrub" face wash. (Keep all of these out of your eyes.) While it adds to the experience, all that mud is really just a sales pitch for the extremely expensive spa products for sale inside.

After you've showered and dressed, pay for any extras you indulged in. At the **exit** turnstile, touch your wristband to the panel, then insert it in the slot. Now comes the hard part: Try to keep your relaxed body awake for the drive back to your hotel or the airport.

Reykjanes Peninsula Driving Tour

The Reykjanes Peninsula has enough sights to fill a day trip, and it's easy to combine with a visit to the Blue Lagoon. It's not the most scenic or historic part of Iceland—don't visit this area at the expense of more dramatic scenery only a bit farther away, such as the Golden Circle or South Coast. But Reykjanes is handy for those who don't have time to venture far beyond the airport area.

My self-guided driving plan assumes you'll tour the peninsula first and visit the Blue Lagoon later, but it works just fine in reverse, too. The major excursion bus companies all offer guided tours of the peninsula for about 12,500 ISK.

FROM REYKJAVÍK TO THE BLUE LAGOON

This loop route is fairly straightforward. First, you'll drive about 45 minutes to the rugged Kleifarvatn lakeshore, with some interesting natural features (especially the Seltún geothermal field). Then you'll loop along the peninsula's south coast to Grindavík (about 30 minutes), a harbor town with some appealing lunch options. From there, it's a 10-minute drive to the Blue Lagoon. When you're done bathing, you can head straight back to Reykjavík (45 minutes), or consider a quick detour to some of the museums in Keflavík. (To see my suggested timing for this route, see page 164.)

• *Leaving the city, drive south on highway 41 through* **Hafnarfjörður**—*a suburb of Reykjavík that feels like its own small town—following the route toward the airport.*

As you crest the hill at the end of Hafnarfjörður, look ahead to see the red-and-white towers of the aluminum plant at **Straumsvík***. This was Iceland's first metal smelter, opened in 1969. Before you reach the smelter, follow the signs for* Krýsuvík *and turn left on highway 42. Continue as it makes several turns through an industrial area.*

Reykjanes Peninsula

- - - - Recommended Driving Route

The forbidding-looking mountains ahead of you enclose your destination, the lake called Kleifarvatn. A low pass winds through the mountains to the lake; for these few miles, the road isn't paved—drive slowly as you dodge potholes.

Kleifarvatn Lake

Kleifarvatn (CLAY-vahr-VAHT) lake offers a nice sample of Iceland's distinctive volcanic scenery. In good weather, you can walk along the black sand beach and even dip your toes in the water. There's something peculiar about Kleifarvatn: It has no outlet (it's fed by underground springs, and the water level varies). The area around the lake is totally undeveloped, and is a good (if lonely) place to look for the northern lights on clear, dark nights. There's a small parking lot near the end of the first long

stretch of sandy beach, as well as parking lots at the overlooks from the headlands a little farther on. Don't drive off-road here.

• *A little past the end of the lake, take the turnoff to the right and park to explore the...*

▲Seltún Geothermal Field

This steaming, bubbling, boiling (and very smelly) landscape hints at the geothermal power just underfoot. A boardwalk and marked

paths take you on a 15-minute circuit through the field. Stay on the path, as the water and steam here are boiling hot. Partway through the loop, you can climb steeply up to a hilltop viewpoint overlooking the entire area, with Kleifarvatn lake just  beyond—but the up-close boardwalk stroll through the steam zone is plenty satisfying. The environment here is not just natural, but also the product of botched attempts to exploit the geothermal field for energy—first in the 1750s, and most recently in the 1940s. In 1999, one of the boreholes from the last attempt got plugged up and exploded violently, creating a 30-foot crater now filled with water (at the first overlook). There are picnic benches here, and a WC (in summer).

• *Just after leaving Seltún, watch on the left for the Grænavatn parking lot. **Grænavatn** ("Green Lake") is a small lake that was formed inside a volcanic crater. It's worth a quick stop for a look at its green water (the color comes from algae at the bottom) and surrounding jagged hilltops.*

Continue south on highway 42 until it tees at highway 427, where you'll turn right. About 10 minutes from Seltún, you'll see a dirt road branch off to the left, signposted Krýsuvíkurbjarg. This road (too rough for two-wheel-drive cars) leads out to a high coastal cliff with a large seabird colony. Hikers not in a hurry could park along the shoulder of the dirt road and walk out (about 2.5 miles each way).

Highway 427 continues through attractive, moss-covered lava fields and then traverses a dark, inhospitable upland before arriving in the town of Grindavík.

Grindavík Town

Grindavík (pop. 2,000) is important for its harbor, which was improved in the 20th century and is one of the few usable ones on Iceland's southern coast. Follow *Höfnin* signposts to reach the harbor, where you'll see fishing boats moored and large fish-processing factories. If you like, spend a few more minutes driving around

History of the Reykjanes Peninsula

The Reykjanes Peninsula is geologically new and active, and the extensive lava fields here have at most a thin layer of vegetation. (Looking at it from an approaching plane, or on Google Maps, you'll see lots of brown.) During Iceland's early centuries, when farming was the mainstay of the economy, few people lived here. But the peninsula was a good base for rich offshore fishing grounds. As fishing became more important, the temporary settlements on the peninsula became permanent. Villages sprang up, particularly at Keflavík and Njarðvík on the north side, and at Grindavík in the south. Many of the people who settled here were poor and landless, and today's Icelanders, perhaps wrongly, still think of the peninsula as a proletarian region with little "old money" wealth—no sheep, no fine churches.

During World War II, military planners realized that the broad, flat wastelands near the town of Keflavík were an ideal place for an air base. Planes crossing the Atlantic could refuel here efficiently, and there was space for very long runways (long enough to land a space shuttle). After the war, the US military established a base next to the airport. Until 2006, when the base was closed, up to a few thousand Americans lived there, in a mostly self-contained community. The military base and the airport became the peninsula's largest employers, and the towns of Keflavík and Njarðvík grew.

this spread-out town; keep an eye out for the old church, the new church, the police station, the primary school, and the municipal swimming pool.

Sights in Grindavík: The town museum, **Kvikan** ("Salt-fish Museum"), backs up to the harbor. It has exhibitions on the town's history (including life-size dioramas of the fishing industry), the history of salted cod (once the backbone of the local economy), Icelandic geology and geothermal energy, and novelist Guðbergur Bergsson (b. 1932), who was born here but has spent much of his life in Spain. The building also serves as the local TI, dispensing maps and brochures, and there's a contemporary art exhibition space upstairs. While nicely presented and fairly interesting, the museum is worth visiting only if you have time to kill before your Blue Lagoon appointment (1,500 ISK; daily in summer, Oct-April Sat-Sun only, Hafnargata 12a, tel. 420-1190, www.grindavik.is/kvikan).

Eating in Grindavík: The unassuming **$ Bryggjan** café at the harbor specializes in lobster soup, served with bread and butter and coffee or tea; they also have sandwiches and cakes. It's cozy, and decorated with fishing gear and memorabilia from both Grindavík and the Faroe Islands (the owner is half Faroese; daily 7:00-23:00, Miðgarður 2, tel. 426-7100). **$ Hjá Höllu** ("Halla's Place") is a popular local lunch joint with a small, inventive, ever-changing menu that includes vegetarian options—ask them to translate. It's on the town's main road, in the tiny mall next door to the Nettó supermarket, which also houses a liquor store, pharmacy, and hair salon—enter from inside the mall (Mon-Fri 8:00-17:00, Sat from 11:00, closed Sun, Víkurbraut 62, tel. 896-5316, www.hjahollu.is). For something more formal, try the **$$ Salthúsið** sit-down restaurant, a block behind Nettó, with a spacious, woody interior and a deck that's inviting on a nice day (daily 12:00-22:00, off-season until 21:00, Stamphólsvegur 2, tel. 526-9700, www.salthusid.is).

Onward to the Blue Lagoon

The Blue Lagoon is a 10-minute drive north of Grindavík: Hopefully you've timed things so that you arrive promptly for your reservation.

• *Road signs direct you to* **Bláa Lónið** *along highway 426, which winds through the lava around the west side of the mountain called Þorbjörn.*

It's also fine to take highway 43, going north past the **Svartsengi geothermal plant**, *which feeds the lagoon. The plant is not open to the public, but you can make an unmarked turn off highway 43 and drive up as far as the visitor parking lot, getting a view of the red-painted water pipes that deliver hot water to area communities, and the turbine halls that generate electricity. (To actually visit a geothermal power plant, plan a trip to Hellisheiðarvirkjun, between Reykjavík and Selfoss; see page 114.)*

Even if you're not getting wet at the Blue Lagoon, you can park for free at the complex and have a look around.

FROM THE BLUE LAGOON TO KEFLAVÍK AND BACK TO REYKJAVÍK

From the Blue Lagoon, most travelers get on the road to Reykjavík. If you're tempted to drive around the desolate **southwestern tip** of the Reykjanes Peninsula, note that the route is less interesting than it looks on the map. Both the Reykjanesviti lighthouse, and the nearby path up to the headland, are closed to visitors; the Gunnuhver geothermal area is impressive but Seltún is better; and the bridge over a tectonic fissure, which claims to let you "walk between continents," is gimmicky. I'd skip this circuit, but if you do travel it, follow the *Reykjanesviti* signs down paved road 425 to Gunnuhver (don't take the Gunnuhver turnoff before that, which leads down a mucky dirt road).

• To **return to Reykjavík** from the Blue Lagoon, head out to highway 43 and head north. After about 10 minutes, highway 43 tees into highway 41, the main road between Keflavík and Reykjavík. Turn right to head straight back to Reykjavík (about 45 minutes from the Blue Lagoon).

To stop in **Keflavík and Njarðvík** (described below), follow highway 43 as described above, but instead of turning right on highway 41, turn left. You'll soon see the towns of Keflavík and Njarðvík on your right (about a 15-minute drive from the Blue Lagoon).

Keflavík and Njarðvík (Reykjanesbær)

The peninsula's main settlement (pop. 15,000) isn't a must-see, but has some attractions that can easily fill a few hours. Once separate towns, Keflavík and Njarðvík have grown together; in the 1990s they merged governments under the new name Reykjanesbær.

In 2006, the town expanded even more when the US military left its base near the airport and turned the area over to civilian use. That neighborhood is now called **Ásbrú;** if you're curious, you can follow signs into it and drive around (turning off highway 41 at a roundabout). The streets still have English names and you can drive past the old military PX, the base's theater, and the yellow-painted housing blocks.

Keflavík and Njarðvík have several museums that can be a good end to this driving tour. To reach them, turn off highway 41 and head into town, following signs for the museums. For a map of this area, see the end of the Reykjavík chapter.

Icelandic Museum of Rock 'n' Roll: This chronicles the coming-of-age of Icelandic pop music, from the 1930s to the present. The museum fills a large space in the local music school and concert-hall complex. Exhibits cover the biggies (Björk, Sigur Rós, and Of Monsters and Men), as well as many Icelandic musicians who aren't known internationally (Páll Óskar Hjálmtýsson and Björgvin Halldórsson). The free videoguide with headphones lets you watch and listen to the performers. There's also a small theater that screens documentary films, and a drum set you can try out. The museum sells coffee and candy bars, but doesn't have a real café (1,500 ISK, daily 11:00-18:00, Hjallavegur 2, Reykjanesbær, tel. 420-1030, www.rokksafn.is).

Viking World: This museum houses the *Icelander,* a replica of the medieval Scandinavian ship unearthed at Gokstad, Norway in the 1880s (the original is in Oslo). While the boat itself is worth seeing, the rest of the attraction—with a few artifacts, some conceptual exhibits,

and a Viking dress-up area—lacks substance. The museum opens early and offers a breakfast buffet (museum—1,500 ISK, museum and breakfast—1,800 ISK, daily 7:00-18:00, breakfast until 11:00, Víkingabraut 1, tel. 422-2000, www.vikingworld.is). More interesting is the **"Settlement Age Zoo"** (Landnámsdýragarður) just across the parking lot—a cute (and free) petting farm, with animals living in miniature sod-roofed huts (early May-mid-Aug daily 10:00-17:00).

Duus Museum: At the northwestern end of Keflavík, this local history and art museum has a collection of more than 100 model boats made by a retired local sea captain (1,500 ISK, daily 12:00-17:00, Duusgata 2, tel. 420-3245, http://sofn.reykjanesbaer. is/duusmuseum).

• *When you're ready to head back, it's a straight, 45-minute shot directly to Reykjavík along highway 41.*

GOLDEN CIRCLE

The Golden Circle is Iceland's classic day trip. If you have just one day to see the Icelandic countryside from Reykjavík, this route offers the most satisfying variety of sightseeing and scenery per miles driven. And you'll be in good company: Travelers dating back to the Danish king Christian IX, who visited Iceland in 1874, have followed the same route outlined in this chapter.

The Golden Circle loop includes this essential trio of sights: Þingvellir, a dramatic gorge marking the pulling apart of the Eurasian and North American tectonic plates (and also the site of the country's annual assembly in the Middle Ages); Geysir, a bubbling, steaming hillside that's home to Strokkur, Iceland's most active geyser; and Gullfoss, one of Iceland's most impressive waterfalls. You can round out the trip by adding any of several minor sights, taking a dip in a thermal bath, or going snorkeling or scuba diving at Þingvellir. This chapter explains your options and links them with driving directions.

Note that the Golden Circle loop is well-trod and extremely touristy. Long lines of tour buses and rental cars follow each other around the route each day, and you'll see the same faces more than once. Despite the crowds, the attractions hold their appeal.

On Your Own or with an Excursion: Driving the Golden Circle in your own car offers maximum flexibility, but some may find it more relaxing to join an organized bus trip. The tour companies listed on page 161 offer full-day Golden Circle tours (10,000-15,000 ISK depending on group size). Reykjavík Excursions and Gray Line also offer half-day trips—but these cost only slightly less, rush you through the sights, and are worth it only if you're short on time.

Golden Circle Driving Tour

The entire circuit involves about four hours of driving, not including stops. The basic self-guided route is simple: From Reykjavík, you can take your pick for the first leg of the drive (straightforward vs. scenic), either 40 minutes or one hour to Þingvellir. After touring Þingvellir, it's about an hour to the thermal fields at Geysir, then 10 minutes farther to the gushing Gullfoss

waterfall. From there, you'll backtrack to Geysir and circle back around to Reykjavík in about 1.75 hours, passing a few lesser sights (the most interesting of which is the Kerið crater). My suggested route goes clockwise—starting with Þingvellir—but it can also be done in the other direction.

PLANNING YOUR DRIVE

Here's a suggested plan (with stops) for those wanting to get an early-ish start and be home in time for dinner:

9:00   Leave Reykjavík and head for Þingvellir national park, taking the scenic Nesjavallaleið route (1 hour)

10:00   Visit Þingvellir

11:30   Drive from Þingvellir to the village of Laugarvatn (30 minutes) and have lunch

13:00   Head to Geysir geothermal field (20 minutes), and watch Strokkur erupt a couple of times

14:00   Drive to Gullfoss (10 minutes) and visit the waterfall

15:00   Head in the direction of Selfoss (1 hour), stopping briefly at Skálholt Church and Kerið crater (or any other sight along the way that interests you—all described later)

16:30   Return to Reykjavík (about 45 minutes from Selfoss)

Golden Circle Tips

This drive is peppered with additional sights and activities; you can easily alter my suggested plan to suit your interests. In addition to the sights described in this chapter, this route also passes by the Halldór Laxness house (commemorating an esteemed Icelandic author) and the Hellisheiði Power Plant (both covered in the Reykjavík chapter). Visiting every possible sight could take two or three days. Before setting out, review the possibilities, prioritize,

and come up with a plan that hits what you want to see in the time you have. Here are some things to consider:

Avoiding Crowds: The geothermal field at Geysir—the smallest sight—is the most crowded spot on the route. An early start helps keep you ahead of the tour buses; in summer, when days are long, you could instead do this trip in the afternoon/evening, when crowds are lighter (see "Evening Options," later).

Activities: Several activities along the Golden Circle require extra time—and in some cases, prebooking. To allow time for any of these, skip some of the minor sights along the drive. The Silfra fissure, at Þingvellir, provides top-notch **scuba or snorkeling** opportunities (book well in advance—see details on page 190). Several horse farms are just outside Reykjavík, making it easy to incorporate **horseback riding** into your Golden Circle spin (again, this should be pre-arranged—see page 47). There are also several **thermal baths** along the way (see sidebar later in this chapter).

Evening Options: In the summer, some intrepid travelers—determined to wring the absolute maximum travel experience out

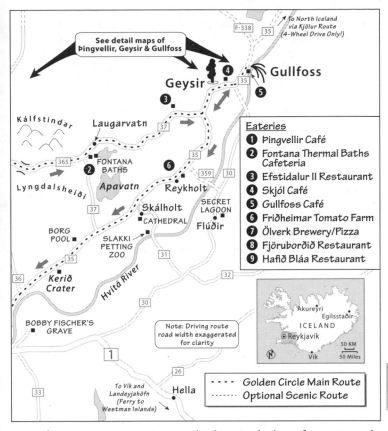

See detail maps of Þingvellir, Geysir & Gullfoss

To North Iceland via Kjölur Route (4-Wheel Drive Only!)

Geysir

Gullfoss

Kálfstindar

Laugarvatn

FONTANA BATHS

Lyngdalsheiði

Apavatn

Reykholt

Skálholt

CATHEDRAL

SECRET LAGOON

Flúðir

BORG POOL

SLAKKI PETTING ZOO

Kerið Crater

Hvítá River

BOBBY FISCHER'S GRAVE

Note: Driving route road width exaggerated for clarity

To Vík and Landeyjahöfn (Ferry to Westman Islands)

Hella

Eateries

1 Þingvellir Café
2 Fontana Thermal Baths Cafeteria
3 Efstidalur II Restaurant
4 Skjól Café
5 Gullfoss Café
6 Friðheimar Tomato Farm
7 Ölverk Brewery/Pizza
8 Fjöruborðið Restaurant
9 Hafið Bláa Restaurant

Akureyri Egilsstaðir

ICELAND

Reykjavík

Vík

50 KM
50 Miles

- - - - Golden Circle Main Route
.... Optional Scenic Route

GOLDEN CIRCLE

of every moment—set out on this loop in the late afternoon...making the most of the abundant daylight. And since the major Golden Circle sights (Þingvellir, Geysir, Gullfoss) don't technically "close," you can visit them essentially anytime—plus, they're less crowded in the evening (some of the lesser sights and thermal baths do have closing times). Another fine evening activity is to have a memorable dinner in the countryside at one of my recommended restaurants—stretching your day and allowing a late return to Reykjavík.

With More Time: If you have an extra day or two, consider splitting the Golden Circle into shorter, more manageable day trips: For example, on one (highbrow) day you could do Þingvellir along with the Halldór Laxness house and the Fontana baths, and on the next (nature-focused) day you could do Geysir, Gullfoss, and the hike to the Reykjadalur thermal river.

Weather and Road Conditions: The route crosses three mountain passes (Mosfellsheiði or Nesjavallaleið, then Lyngdalsheiði, and finally Hellisheiði). These passes can be icy and slippery, especially from October to April. Check the road conditions map at Road.is before you start off. In treacherous conditions, take a bus tour and leave the driving to pros. If you do drive the Golden Circle in winter, it's smart to set off from Reykjavík an hour before sunrise so you get maximum value out of the daylight hours.

If highway 365 (Lyngdalsheiði, between Þingvellir and Laugarvatn) is closed or in bad shape, you can avoid it by taking a long way around on lowland roads (highways 36 and 35). This adds about a half-hour to the trip, which makes it difficult to cram the entire Golden Circle into a short winter day. You may need to lower your expectations, and do only part of the circuit (either Þingvellir or Geysir/Gullfoss).

Name Note: Be aware that there are two Reykholts in Iceland: one here on the Golden Circle, and the other about 100 miles away, in West Iceland.

Golden Circle Loop

Below, I've linked the main stops with driving directions. Let's get started.

FROM REYKJAVÍK TO ÞINGVELLIR

There are two ways to get from Reykjavík to Þingvellir: through Mosfellsheiði (highway 36) or along the road called Nesjavallaleið (highway 435). Nesjavallaleið takes a little longer (one hour) and is narrow and curvy in parts (with many blind summits), but is much more scenic. Because of its high elevation, Nesjavallaleið is open only from May to September. If it's closed, it will appear in red on the road conditions map at Road.is. The Mosfellsheiði route is kept open all year. If conditions are appropriate and you're confident driving in Iceland, I'd definitely take Nesjavallaleið.

Option 1: A Straight Shot via Mosfellsheiði

You'll start this 40-minute route heading north out of Reykjavík on highway 1 toward Borgarnes and Akureyri, then turn right on highway 36 just past the town of Mosfellsbær, following the *Þingvellir* signs. This leads up through Mosfellsdalur ("Moss Mountain Valley") and over a low, broad pass (900 feet above sea level) to Þingvellir.

The Mosfellsdalur valley is still rural, with several horse farms. As you drive through, look left up the hillside (or turn up the side road called Mosfellsvegur) to see the unusual church called **Mosfellskirkja,** designed

Thermal Bathing Along the Golden Circle

If you're trying to pack the maximum Icelandic experience into your Golden Circle day, consider adding a visit to a thermal bath. This loop drive passes near four extremely different options (each one described in this chapter). Skim these options before you depart, to strategize where you might squeeze in a dip...and remember to bring your swimsuit and towel (or rent one—available at all listed here except Reykjadalur).

Fontana Thermal Bath, in Laugarvatn, is the upscale choice. While not as ritzy as the Blue Lagoon, it's a "premium" option that feels a notch up from standard municipal swimming pools.

The Secret Lagoon, in Flúðir (a 10-minute detour from the main Golden Circle route, near Reykholt), is a big, rustic outdoor pool packed with young travelers unwinding after a busy day of sightseeing. This is the only bathing experience on this route where it's smart to prebook.

Borg swimming pool is a municipal facility right along the main road between Reykholt and Selfoss—nothing fancy, but cheap, handy, and (more than the others listed here) authentically Icelandic.

Reykjadalur—the "Smoky Valley" above the town of Hveragerði—is the adventurous choice: It's a remote, steaming, natural thermal river that requires a one-hour hike each way.

Of course, if you're heading home to Reykjavík at the end of your Golden Circle day, you can have your pick of the capital area's many **public swimming pools** (options are described on page 114); two good suburban pools, Lágafellslaug and Árbæjarlaug, are on the outskirts of town and convenient to the Golden Circle route.

Before visiting any of these, be sure to get up to speed by reading the "Pool Rules" sidebar on page 42.

GOLDEN CIRCLE

by architect Ragnar Emilsson in the 1960s. It's full of triangular shapes—including the bell tower and roof—as a reference to the Trinity.

Note that this route passes by the former home of Iceland's most famous author, **Halldór Laxness** (open to tourists; for details see page 113). Otherwise, it's a (fairly dull) straight shot to Þingvellir. When you begin to see the Þingvallavatn lake—Iceland's largest—on your right, you know you're getting close.

Option 2: Scenic and Rugged via Nesjavallaleið

This one-hour route—more with photo stops—is much more interesting than Mosfellsheiði. It climbs high up (to about 1,500 feet) over a craggy mountain range, descends steeply past the Nesjavel-

lir geothermal plant, and then narrows as it hugs the shore of Þingvallavatn lake. Most of Nesjavallaleið (NESS-ya-VAHT-la-laythe) was built as a service road for a giant hot water pipe that feeds Reykjavík's heating system.

Start out by leaving Reykjavík south on highway 1 toward Selfoss. As the town thins out into countryside, turn left following a small sign for highway 435 and *Nesjavellir*. The road crosses the giant **hot-water pipe,** then curves around to follow straight along it. You'll drive parallel to the pipe—and some high-tension wires— for quite some time. In August and September, the bracken along the sides of this road is a good place to look for blueberries and crowberries. The road rises and eventually hits a ridge, part of a volcanic system called Hengill; from here the road climbs in a series of bends. Before the crest, you can stop at a pullout in the small, mountain-ringed Dyradalur valley, with signboards and picnic benches; an important path for travelers once led through the gully you see at the end of the valley (called Dyrnar—"The Doors").

As you come over the ridge, you'll see the **Nesjavellir geothermal power station** far below you. This plant, built in the early

1990s, sends 250 gallons of boiling water through the pipe to Reykjavík every second, and also generates electricity. For a better look, take your pick of two overlooks: one at the end of a little dead-end side lane, and the other reached by short paths from a parking lot by the side of the road. (Another power plant—Hellisheiði, at the conclusion of this Golden Circle spin—has a real visitors center; see page 114.)

The highway descends steeply into the valley, ending at a T-junction with highway 360, where you'll turn left toward Þingvellir. (Note that if you're doing the Golden Circle in reverse, highway 435 is signposted here only as *Hengilssvæði*.)

Now the road winds tightly along the shore of **Þingvallavatn** lake, with fine views, no guardrails, and several narrow, blind summits. You'll pass some nice summer homes. Building here is forbidden, but houses constructed before the ban were grandfathered in. Eventually, the road leaves the lake and ends at a junction with highway 36, where you'll turn right; from this junction, it's another four miles to Þingvellir.

▲▲▲Þingvellir

The gorge at Þingvellir (THING-VETT-leer), dear to all Icelanders, is both dramatic and historic. It's dramatic because you can readily

see the slow separation of the North American and Eurasian tectonic plates— the earth's crust is literally being torn apart. And it's historic because, during the Settlement Age, it was here at "Assembly Plains" (as its name means) that chieftains from the dif-

ferent parts of Iceland gathered annually to deal with government business (at a meeting called the AlÞingi). Today the area has been preserved as a national park. Visitors can walk along the rifts created by the separating plates, stand at the place where the original Icelanders made big decisions, hike to a picturesque waterfall, see a scant few historic buildings, and even go for a snorkel or scuba dive into a flooded gorge (book ahead).

Orientation to Þingvellir

Cost and Hours: Park—free and always open, tel. 482-2660; visitors center—free and open daily 9:00-20:00, Sept-May until 18:00, tel. 482-3613, www.thingvellir.is.

Arrival at Þingvellir: Regardless of which route you took from Reykjavík, you'll wind up on the same road as you approach Þingvellir. You can park on either the upper (west) or the lower (east) side of the Öxará river. The two sides are no more than a half-mile apart if you use the footbridges over the river, but a five-mile drive by car. Parking is 500 ISK for the entire day (machines take credit cards; if you have trouble paying, go into the visitors center for help).

The first turnoff you'll reach is the large **P1 parking lot** on the upper side, with a pay WC; on maps, this spot is sometimes called Hakið. If it's not too crowded, it's easiest to park here, stop in at the visitors center, get oriented at the overlook, then hike down to the sights.

If you can't find a spot at P1, continue a few miles to the intersection with the park offices/café; turn right—onto road 361—to reach several **smaller parking lots** on the lower side (P2, P4, P5, and a lot for Silfra divers). This area is less congested and more convenient for picnicking. (Lot P3, which you'll see along the main

GOLDEN CIRCLE

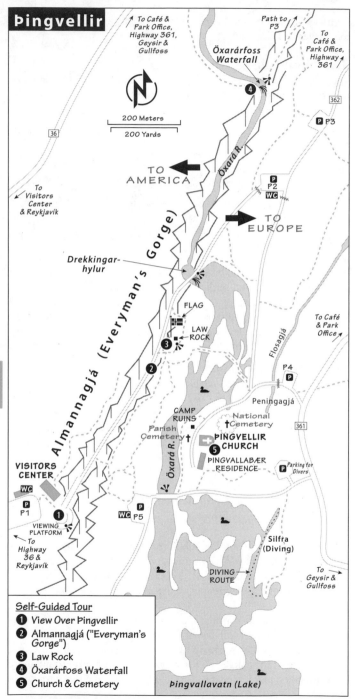

Þingvellir

To Café & Park Office, Highway 361, Geysir & Gullfoss

Path to P3

To Café & Park Office, Highway 361

Öxarárfoss Waterfall

④

362

P3

200 Meters
200 Yards

36

Öxará R.

TO AMERICA

P2
WC

To Visitors Center & Reykjavík

TO EUROPE

Drekkingar-hylur

FLAG

LAW ROCK

③

②

Flosagjá

To Café & Park Office

P4

Peningagjá

CAMP RUINS

National Cemetery

361

Parish Cemetery

ÞINGVELLIR CHURCH

⑤

ÞINGVALLABÆR RESIDENCE

Parking for Divers

VISITORS CENTER

WC

P1

① VIEWING PLATFORM

To Highway 36 & Reykjavík

Öxará R.

WC P5

Silfra (Diving)

DIVING ROUTE

To Geysir & Gullfoss

Self-Guided Tour
① View Over Þingvellir
② Almannagjá ("Everyman's Gorge")
③ Law Rock
④ Öxarárfoss Waterfall
⑤ Church & Cemetery

Almannagjá (Everyman's Gorge)

Þingvallavatn (Lake)

GOLDEN CIRCLE

road between P1 and the others, is designed for hikers who want to take the Langistígur path, which descends into the fissure near the big Öxarárfoss waterfall.)

If you're with a group, consider drawing straws and having the loser drop everyone off at P1 (allowing them the convenience of a one-way stroll); the driver can park at one of the lower lots and hike up to meet the group.

Length of This Visit: For a quick visit, you can enjoy the overview, hike the gorge, and see the Law Rock in less than an hour. Add a half-hour to hike up to the waterfall (about a mile one-way from P1), and a half-hour to cross the river to the church (the least interesting and most skippable).

Eating: In good weather, Þingvellir is a nice place for a picnic. There are benches, wooded areas, and free portable toilets near P2 and P5. If you want to picnic here, B.Y.O.—the visitors center (at P1) has a very basic **$ snack stand** with premade sandwiches. Otherwise, the only eatery nearby is the **$ café** at the national park office a couple of miles away, at the junction of highways 36, 361, and 550. It's small and sometimes crowded, but acceptable in a pinch (daily 9:00-22:00, Sept-May until 18:00).

Self-Guided Tour

This plan assumes that you're parking at the upper P1 lot (even if you park elsewhere, hike up here to begin your visit since it offers a nice overview). Start at the **visitors center,** where you'll find a modest and free exhibit with helpful maps for getting your bearings.

• *Exiting the visitors center, walk over to the overlook with the railing.*

❶ **View Over Þingvellir:** Look down at the lake and the land that's subsided to its north. You can see how the Öxará ("Ax River")

empties into the lake. Þingvellir's church (and some ruins of the old chieftains' encampments) lies just across the river below you. The five-gabled farm building dates from 1930.

Directly below you is Þingvellir's **great fissure;** look at how the North American and Eurasian tectonic plates are moving apart. Imagine pulling a big, chewy cookie apart very slowly; you'd start to see cracks in the dough, and eventually crumbs would start to slide into the gap. Here, you can see long, narrow fissures in the earth, running roughly north-south. The lake itself sits in the largest fissure of all. The lake bed (and the land to the north and south) basically has slid into the gap between the

plates. The deepest parts of the lake bed are actually below sea level.
• *Follow the boardwalk as it switchbacks down between the cliffs,
descending through the little side channel that leads into...*

❷ **Almannagjá** ("Everyman's Gorge"): As you walk, you're
tracing the boundaries of continents. To your left is America. To

your right is Europe. You
may see brochures claim-
ing that at Þingvellir you
can "touch America with
one hand and Europe
with the other," or jump
between the continents.
The idea inspires fun photographs, but it's not quite
true: The whole area is
shaped by the interaction between the two tectonic plates, and no
single fissure forms the boundary between them.

On the left, the vertical cliff face is original rock as it was laid
down by volcanic eruptions and compressed over the eons. On the
right, you can see how the rock—once even with the cliff on your
left—has fallen away into the gap due to the subsidence that also
created the lake. On the right (fallen) side of the gorge, you can
scramble out to various walkways and viewpoints.
• *As you approach the valley floor, follow the boardwalks to the right to
stand in the area just below the flagpole. This marks the likely location
of...*

❸ **The Law Rock** (Lögberg): Within about 60 years of the first
settlements, Iceland was home to somewhere between 10,000 and
20,000 people—almost all of them farmers,
scattered across the island on isolated home-
steads. In about A.D. 930, local chieftains
(goðar) began to gather at an annual meeting
called the Alþingi ("all-thing"), which took
place more or less where you're standing.
For this reason, Þingvellir can be thought
of as Iceland's first capital. Today, this site
remains important for Icelanders—it's their
Ancient Agora, their Roman Forum, their
Independence Hall.

Gaze over the marshy delta below you,
and time-travel back a thousand years. It's
the middle of June, and you're surrounded
by fellow chieftains, some having traveled on
horseback more than two weeks, over challenging terrain, just to be
here. Each chieftain has brought along an entourage of *þingmenn*

(assemblymen). The field below you is dotted with temporary turf huts.

The meeting is about to begin, and you're immersed in a hairy mosh pit of hundreds—maybe thousands—of unwashed Norsemen (and Norsewomen). The collective body odor is overwhelming. But for two weeks, you've all agreed to set aside your grudges and work together to find consensus on critical issues of the day. This is your one chance all year to learn the latest news and gossip. And while everyone's here, there are sure to be some big parties, business wheeling and dealing, marriages arranged...and, quite likely, some duels. Merchants, tradesmen, and panhandlers are milling about, trying to drum up a little business. The whole event has a carnival-like bustle.

The crowd quiets with the appearance of the *allsherjargoði* (grand chieftain)—a direct descendant of Ingólfur Árnason (who was, according to the sagas, the first Icelandic settler of Reykjavík). As the high priest of the Norse pantheon, the *allsherjargoði* calls the assembly to order, and sanctifies the proceedings before the gods. Then the "law speaker" *(lögsögumaður)* takes his position at the Law Rock and recites the guidelines for the assembly, outlines the broad strokes of Icelandic law, and recaps the highlights of last year's session. The acoustics created by the cliff behind him help bounce his voice across the throngs; other speakers, strategically located at the back of the crowd, carefully listen to, then repeat, whatever the law speaker says.

As the Alþingi continues, the law speaker also presides over the Law Council *(Lögrétta)*, on the opposite riverbank. A more select group of chieftains reviews and debates existing legislation, and weighs in on legal disputes, and the law speaker is responsible for memorizing whatever is decided. (Mercifully, he serves only a three-year term.) Eventually, Christianity brings literacy and the Latin alphabet, and the law speaker's role gives way to that of a sort of "high attorney"—*lögmaður.*

The Alþingi gatherings took place throughout the Commonwealth Era. But things changed after 1262, when the chieftains entered into union with Norway—pledging fealty to the Norwegian king under an agreement called the Old Covenant. The Alþingi still convened annually at Þingvellir, but morphed into an appeals court; it continued this way until 1798.

Þingvellir became a national park in 1930, to celebrate the millennial anniversary of the first Alþingi. And in 1944, the mod-

GOLDEN CIRCLE

Iceland's Conversion to Christianity

In A.D. 1000 (or 999, depending on how you reckon the calendar), the Alþingi had its most important session. Iceland's longtime ally Norway—whose king had recently converted to Christianity—was exerting tremendous pressure on Iceland to follow suit. When Norwegian missionaries failed to convert the entire island, the impatient king took several Icelandic traders hostage. Losing its primary trade partner would have been devastating to Iceland, and at the next summer's Alþingi, all hell broke loose between the pro- and anti-conversion factions. Civil war was in the air.

Eventually, both sides agreed to let the law speaker, a pagan named Þorgeir Ljósvetningagoði, make the decision for all of Iceland. According to the sagas, Þorgeir covered himself with a fur pelt and slept on it (literally) for one night and one day. Upon emerging, he addressed the assembly with his decision: Iceland was now Christian, but Icelanders could still worship their pagan gods privately, and continue a few key pagan practices (including the consumption of horse meat, the infanticide of unwanted children, and animal sacrifices to the old gods). And so, in one fell swoop, Þorgeir brought Iceland into the Christian fold, and averted a conflict with Norway that could well have wiped out the island's still-fragile civilization. This stands as one of the most peaceful mass religious conversion in history.

ern, independent Republic of Iceland was proclaimed right here. The stands below the flag are for official ceremonies; one of the information boards at the railing displays photographs of some of these ceremonies.

By the way, those original settlers couldn't possibly have known that the place they selected for their gathering also happened to straddle America and Europe. They chose this site mainly because it had recently been seized from a convicted murderer and designated for public use. Þingvellir is also fairly central (relatively accessible in summer from every corner of Iceland) and had ample water, grazing lands, and firewood to supply the sprawling gatherings. Its location along the cusp of continents is just one of those serendipities of history.

• *Follow the wide, gravel path straight ahead, and cross the river on a small bridge over a waterfall (the bottom end of Öxarárfoss, which we'll visit next). To your left is* **Drekkingarhylur** *("Drowning Pool"), where women suspected of witchcraft were drowned between the late-16th and mid-18th centuries.*

If you're short on time, you could turn back here. Ideally, continue along the path. After about 300 yards, just before reaching parking lot P2, branch off on the small path to your left. Follow it for a few minutes as it crests the rise to your left. Then, a hundred yards to your left, is the large waterfall called...

❹ **Öxarárfoss:** This is where the river—which rises up on the plateau—plunges over the cliff face into the valley. Old sagas say that the early settlers changed the course of the river to improve the water supply at Þingvellir, but no one is exactly sure whether this is true and how that might have been done.

• *You've already seen the most interesting parts of Þingvellir—you can head back the way you came (past the P2 lot). With more time, cross the footbridges on your left (below the Law Rock) to reach the...*

❺ **Church and Cemetery:** The current **church** was built in 1859, but there were churches here for centuries before. The origi-

nal church was supposedly built using timbers sent here from Norway's St. Olaf (King Olav II, 995-1030). If the church is open, step inside to see the humble, painted interior (generally closed Sept-May). Local parishioners lie in the small cemetery in front of the church. The multigabled house just beyond it, called **Þingvallabær,** was built in 1930 as a residence for the local priest, who was also the park warden. It's now used for ceremonial functions.

Behind the church, the round, elevated area up the stairs is a **cemetery** lot. This was planned as a resting place for national heroes, but the idea never took off, and only two people (well-known writers) were ever buried there.

Along the riverbank near the church, the **mounds** contain the remains of the temporary dwellings that were set up here each year for the annual assembly. From here, looking back the way you came, enjoy great views of the sheer cliff that defines the fissure.

• *Between the church and the river, a waterside path allows further exploration. Following this path takes you to the P5 lot, where a steep shortcut (on a rocky path through the woods) leads back up to the P1 lot where you started. (Also nearby is Silfra, a favorite destination of divers—described next.) For an easier route, you can backtrack along the river, then take the bridge on your left to reach the Law Rock, then hike back up through Everyman's Gorge.*

Silfra Snorkel or Dive Trip

One of the many fissures at Þingvellir, Silfra is renowned among snorkelers and scuba divers for the clarity of the water. Thanks to the purity of the glacial water that fills it, you can see underwater for more than a hundred yards.

To snorkel or dive in Silfra, you'll need to join a tour (such as those offered by Dive.is, the largest operator). Snorkelers must

be relatively fit and comfortable in the water, while divers need to be certified and experienced. There have been a few fatal accidents at Silfra in recent years (even involving snorkelers)—don't overestimate your abilities.

The water is a constant 35-39°F, so you'll be outfitted with some serious gear: a neoprene dry suit, hood, gloves, fins, mask, and snorkel. (The better companies have basic changing cabins in the parking lot; otherwise, there's limited privacy.) The suit keeps your body warm enough, but expect your face to go numb and your hands to get cold. After changing into your gear, you'll walk a few minutes to the entry stairs and descend into the fissure with your guide. A gentle drift current slowly takes you along the fissure and into a lagoon, where you'll need to kick against the current to U-turn to the metal exit stairs. You'll be in the water for about 30-40 minutes (prices for Dive.is: 20,000 ISK for guided snorkeling, extra 5,000 ISK for pickup in Reykjavík, 35,000 ISK for package that includes pickup, Silfra, and bus tour of Golden Circle, more for divers; tel. 578-6200, www.dive.is).

Getting There: Silfra is at the lakeshore near the east bank of the river. The entry point to Silfra is between parking lots P4 and P5. Follow the directions on page 183 (turning off onto road 361 to reach this area) and look for the designated lot.

FROM ÞINGVELLIR TO GEYSIR AND GULLFOSS

This section of the drive circles around the far end of the lake, where you can clearly see the intercontinental rift—as if God dropped his hoe and dredged out a tidy furrow between America and Europe.

• *Leaving Þingvellir, return to highway 36 and continue east for about 10 minutes around the lake's north shore, crossing smaller fissures. Soon you'll pass the intersection with road 361 (a right turn here takes you back to Þingvellir's lower parking lots) and, immediately after that, the* **national park office,** *with a café.*

*Continuing along the east side of the lake, you'll reach a point where highway 36 turns off to the right. Stay straight toward Laugarvatn on highway 365. This road crosses an upland heath called **Lyngdalsheiði** at about 750 feet above sea level (if the road is closed, see "Weather and Road Conditions" under the "Golden Circle Tips" on page 177 for an alternate route).*

*On your left, enjoy some otherworldly, craggy mountain scenery— the **Kálfstindar ridge**. A half-hour after leaving Þingvellir, you'll reach a roundabout. Follow signs onto route 37 toward Geysir (not Selfoss) to descend into the sleepy, unassuming village of Laugarvatn.*

Laugarvatn

Set by a small lake of the same name, Laugarvatn was long the home of Iceland's college for sports teachers (the program has now been moved to Reykjavík), and has many summer cottages owned by the country's labor unions for use by their members. There are hot springs in and around the lake, and Fontana, a nicely designed premium bath, makes good use of them.

Fontana Thermal Baths: Sitting right along the Laugarvatn lakeshore, Fontana is one of Iceland's few "premium" baths (and

worth ▲)—a step up in comfort (and price) from municipal swimming pools, and a bit more tourist-oriented. Beyond the visitors center—with ticket desk, changing rooms, and a good cafeteria—is the outdoor bathing area, overlooking the lake. The complex has three modern, tiled pools, artfully landscaped with natural boulders, as well as a steam room (where you can hear the natural hot spring bubble beneath your feet), and a dry sauna. To cool off or get a change of pace, bathers are encouraged to take a dip in the thermal waters of the lake (4,200 ISK, mid-June-mid-Aug daily 10:00-23:00, mid-Aug-mid-June daily 11:00-22:00, tel. 486-1400, www.fontana.is).

For some, Fontana may be a good alternative to the Blue Lagoon—it's cheaper, smaller (easier to navigate), less pretentious, much less crowded, and doesn't require reservations. But it's also less striking—more functional than spa-like—and lacks the Blue Lagoon's romantic, volcanic setting. Thermal bath fans may want to do both. You can fit the Golden Circle and a leisurely soak at Fontana into a single day if you sightsee quickly and skip the minor stops.

"Thermal Bread Experience": Fontana follows the Icelandic tradition of baking sweet, dense rye bread right in the thermal sands at its doorstep. Twice daily, you can pay to join the baker as they dig up a pot of bread, then taste it straight out of the ground (1,500 ISK, daily at 11:30 and 14:30). But note that you can eat the very same bread as part of their regular lunch buffet.

Nearby Thermal Beach: The lake in front of Fontana—heated by natural hot springs—is free to bathe in (at your own risk). Facing the lake, head right to find a small, black sand beach next to the fenced-off geothermal area (keep well clear of this area of boiling-hot water). The water near the springs is warm, but it gets colder as you go

deeper. At a minimum, consider rolling up your pants and dipping your feet. On the wooden walkway between the geothermal plant and the lakeshore, notice—but don't touch—little boiling pools in the mud.

Eating in or near Laugarvatn: This village is a good place for lunch along the Golden Circle route. One of the best options is

the **$$ Fontana Thermal Baths cafeteria,** in the bath's entrance lobby, and open to the public (no bath entry required). You can get unlimited soup and bread for 1,500 ISK, or spring for their full 3,500-ISK lunch buffet (more expensive at dinner, daily

12:00-14:30 & 18:00-21:00). There are a few other places to eat in town and a small grocery store.

Or consider driving 10 more minutes to **$$ Efstidalur II** ("Uppermost Valley"), a large, family-run restaurant located on a dairy farm just off highway 37 between Laugarvatn and Geysir. The upstairs section specializes in burgers and has pricier main courses. Downstairs is the ice cream counter, with windows overlooking the cows in the barn. It's a popular, bustling place—family-friendly and often crowded with groups (daily 11:30-21:00, mid-Sept-mid-May until 20:00, well-signposted up a gravel driveway, tel. 486-1186, www.efstidalur.is).

• *From Laugarvatn, highway 37 leads 20 minutes onwards to the geothermal field at Geysir (passing the Efstidalur II eatery described earlier). Along the way, the road changes numbers to highway 35.*

▲▲Geysir Geothermal Field

When people around the world talk about geysers, they don't realize they're referencing a place in Iceland: Geysir (GAY-sear), which literally means "the gusher." While the original Geysir geyser is no longer very active, the geothermal field around it still steams, boils, and bubbles nonstop, periodically punctuated by a dramatic eruption of scalding water from the one predictably active geyser, Strokkur. Watch Strokkur erupt a couple times, look at the rest of the field, use the WC, and then continue on.

Cost and Hours: Free and always open.

Safety Warning: Make sure to keep children very close; hold their hands whenever possible. Impress upon them that they should not touch any of the water, which is boiling hot, and that they must stay behind the ropes. At Strokkur, standing upwind will keep you out of any spray.

Arrival at Geysir: Approaching Geysir, you'll see the geothermal field on your left, and a visitors complex with parking lots on your right. Park as close to the geothermal field as you can (the lots at the far end of the visitors center are closer to the best geyser action), then walk across the road and explore.

Services and Eating: Across the road from the geothermal area is a complex with a clothing and souvenir store, free WCs, a golf course, two hotels, and a handful of restaurants at different price ranges. While these are OK, I'd opt for one of the Laugarvatn eating options (described earlier), or wait for **$ Skjól** ("Shelter"), a café connected to a hostel and campground along highway 35 between Geysir and Gullfoss (just before the junction with highway 30). Talkative owner Jón Örvar is known for making good, affordable, splittable pizzas; he also serves other simple meals like burgers and fish-and-chips. This place attracts many hikers and outdoorsy folk (June-Aug daily 9:00-14:00 & 18:00-23:00, shorter hours off-season, mobile 899-4541, www.skjolcamping.com).

Visiting Geysir: The geothermal field itself lacks the boardwalks and other maintenance you would normally expect at a sight this popular. That's due in part to a dispute between the government (which owns part of the site) and private landowners, who have been bickering publicly for years about whether to charge for parking and admission. Outdoor signboards explain the geology.

The area's centerpiece is a geyser called **Strokkur** ("Butter Churn"), which erupts about every 10 minutes (but don't set your

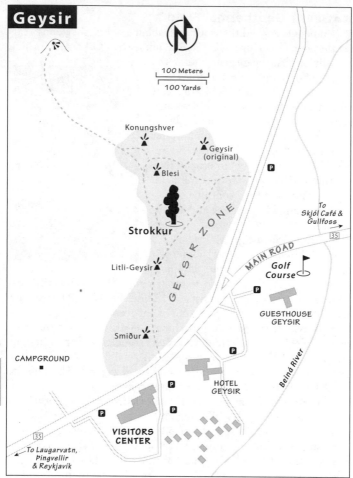

GOLDEN CIRCLE

watch by it). The eruptions themselves, which shoot about 50 feet in the air, are relatively short—in every sense—and won't wow anyone who has seen Old Faithful at Yellowstone. What's nice about Strokkur, though, is the short wait between gushes, and how close you can get. Each eruption is a little different. It's surreal to stand around in a field with people who have come from the far reaches of the globe, just to share this experience...of staring at a hole in the ground. Everyone huddles in a big circle around Strokkur, cameras aimed and focused, waiting for the unpredictable spurt. When it finally happens, it's over in a couple of seconds, as abruptly as it started. After each show, the crowd thins out a bit, and new arrivals shuffle in to take their place, shoulder-to-shoulder, cameras cocked, waiting...waiting...waiting.

Just a few yards up the hill above Strokkur, check out a few other **fumaroles and hot pools,** including Konungshver and the colorful Blesi. The miniature Litli-Geysir, along the path from the main parking lot, bubbles and boils but doesn't erupt.

Steaming uneasily off to the side is the **original "great" Geysir.** This was the only one known to medieval Europeans, and is the origin of the word *geyser*. It was dormant for most of the 20th century, but after a nearby earthquake in 2000 it started erupting occasionally. It blows higher and longer than Strokkur, but rarely and unpredictably, so don't expect to see anything. (Geysir is on the far side of the field if you're coming from the main parking lot; there's another, smaller parking lot close to it.)

For a commanding view over the Geysir area, continue past Konungshver, climb over the stile, and make your way 10 minutes up to the top of one of the rocky outcroppings that overlook the geothermal field and surrounding terrain. The snowy mass of Vatnajökull looms to the west.

• *From Geysir, continue to the Gullfoss waterfall, a straight shot 10 minutes onward along highway 35.*

▲▲Gullfoss Waterfall

The thundering waterfall called Gullfoss (GUTL-foss, "Golden Falls") sits on the wide, glacial Hvítá river, which drains Iceland's interior. The waterfall has two stages: a rocky upper cascade with a drop of about 35 feet, and a lower fall where the water drops about 70 feet straight down into a narrow gorge. Somewhat unusually for a waterfall, the gorge runs transverse to the fall line, effectively carrying the water off to the side. Dress warmly: Cold winds blow down the valley, and the spray from the falls can soak you. Winter visitors should watch for slippery areas. If you have ice cleats, this is a good place to put them on.

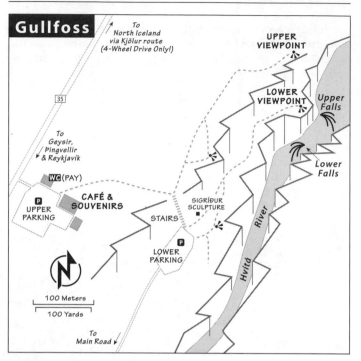

Gullfoss

To North Iceland via Kjölur route (4-Wheel Drive Only!)

To Geysir, Þingvellir & Reykjavík

35

WC (PAY)

UPPER PARKING

CAFÉ & SOUVENIRS

STAIRS

LOWER PARKING

SIGRÍÐUR SCULPTURE

UPPER VIEWPOINT

LOWER VIEWPOINT

Upper Falls

Lower Falls

Hvítá River

100 Meters

100 Yards

To Main Road

Cost and Hours: Free and always open, tel. 486-6500, www.gullfoss.is.

Arrival at Gullfoss: Two different viewing areas—connected by a wooden staircase—let you admire the falls; each has its own

free parking lot and viewpoints. Both are equally worth seeing, but if you're short on time, focus on the lower one—which lets you get up close and feel the spray. To quickly hit the lower viewpoint, as you approach the area, just after the blue *P* sign, watch for the unmarked right turn to the lower parking lot. With more time, continue to the official, well-signed upper parking lot, with pay WC, café, and gift shop (with free WCs for customers).

Eating: The large **$ café** by the upper parking lot serves soup (their bottomless bowl of lamb soup is popular), salad, and sandwiches (daily 9:00-21:30, Sept-May 10:00-18:00).

Visiting the Waterfall: From the upper parking lot, boardwalks lead along the edge of the plateau, high above the falls, to a

couple of good **upper viewpoint** spots. On a clear day, you can see glaciers in the distance. The view upriver gives a sense of Iceland's vast, lonely interior Highlands.

From here, stairs lead down to the **lower viewpoint.** This area gets you close to the falls. It's closed in winter, when ice can make it dangerous (don't try it). A narrow trail leads through the spray from the falls to a level area between the upper and lower stages of the waterfall. If you walk out here with children, keep them close.

It would be easy to dam or divert the river above the falls for electricity generation. In the early 1900s, British investors tried to buy the waterfall, but their plans fell through. The government acquired the land and the falls have been left in their natural state. Near the base of the staircase, look for the relief sculpture of **Sigríður Tómasdóttir,** a local farmer who helped thwart plans for the dam.

FROM GULLFOSS BACK TO REYKJAVÍK

This stretch features a few mildly interesting stops to consider on the way (all described next)—but if you're in a hurry, these are skippable. It's about one hour from Gullfoss to Selfoss, then another 45 minutes back to Reykjavík (without stops).

For a late lunch, consider **$$ Friðheimar** ("Peaceful Homes"), a very popular, borderline-pretentious tomato farm 30 minutes from Gullfoss, offering lunch daily (12:00-16:00) right in the greenhouse, surrounded by rows of tomato plants, with pots of fresh basil on each table. The brief menu is all tomato: tomato soup with bread, fresh pasta with tomato sauce, and tomato ice cream or cheesecake with green tomato sauce (popular with tour groups—reservations strongly recommended, along highway 35 in the village of Reykholt—just north of junction with highway 31, tel. 486-8894, www.fridheimar.is).

• *From Gullfoss, turn back along highway 35 and pass by Geysir again. Shortly after Geysir, make a left turn to stay on highway 35 toward Reykholt and Selfoss. Your next big stop along the route is the Kerið crater (see page 200), about 45 minutes from Gullfoss. Along the way, consider the detours described next.*

GOLDEN CIRCLE

Sights Just Off the Golden Circle

The next three sights—a thermal pool, a church, and a petting zoo—are short detours from highway 35 and the main Golden Circle route.

Secret Lagoon (Gamla Laugin)

Claiming to be the "oldest swimming pool in Iceland" (from 1891), the Secret Lagoon is a big, rustic, three-foot-deep, 100°F pool in front of a dilapidated old house (with a modern entrance/ changing facility). The pool is surrounded by an evocative thermal landscape; a boardwalk leads around the pool, past steaming and simmering crevasses. Green-houses stand nearby. Compared to the over-the-top-romantic Blue Lagoon, or even Reykjavík's mu-

nicipal swimming pools (which are one-third the price), this is a very straightforward experience: Its proximity to the Golden Circle and clever marketing make it more popular than it probably should be. On the other hand, the bathers here seem very happy—sipping drinks, bobbing on colorful pool noodles, happy to enjoy this après-Golden Circle hangout. Far from "secret" (it's included on several day tours from Reykjavík), the pool can get quite crowded with a younger clientele. It's smart to reserve ahead online—when it's full, it's full.

Cost and Hours: 2,800 ISK, daily 10:00-22:00, Oct-April 11:00-20:00, last entry one hour before closing, tel. 555-3351, www.secretlagoon.is.

Getting There: The Secret Lagoon is a 10-minute drive off the main Golden Circle route. From highway 35, just before the village of Reykholt, turn left at highway 359, signed *Flúðir*. Follow this about five miles into the small village of Flúðir, watching on your left for the turnoff to *Hvammur* and *Gamla Laugin*. The Secret Lagoon is tucked amid the big greenhouses, on your right.

Skálholt Church

This church was the old seat of the bishopric of southern Iceland. The current church was built in the 1960s and is flanked by a retreat center run by Iceland's Evangelical Lutheran state church. Unless you're heavily into Icelandic history, this is a low-key site—worth a few minutes only if you want to mix something non-geological into your day.

Cost and Hours: Church entry-free, 300 ISK donation requested if visiting crypt—OK to put foreign bills in the box; daily

9:00-18:00, pay WC in complex next to church, tel. 486-8870, www.skalholt.is.

Getting There: About 30 minutes south of Gullfoss on highway 35, detour left onto highway 31 for a couple of minutes, following *Skálholt* signs through farm fields. The church is just over the hill, overlooking a lake-and-mountain panorama.

Visiting the Church: As you drive up, you can see from the rich farmland around the church how it was able to support a medieval religious community. Almost nothing is left of the original

buildings, many of which were destroyed by earthquakes in the late 18th century. It's peaceful here, and tour buses bypass the place. The locally designed stained-glass windows in the church are very colorful.

If you visit, be sure to go downstairs to the **crypt,** with a small exhibit of historical and archaeological artifacts. There's also a period sketch of the 18th-century church, which survived the earthquakes but was torn down soon after. From the crypt, you can exit directly outdoors through the only original part of the building, a short tunnel (a feature also found in some other medieval Icelandic buildings). An old-style, turf-roofed wooden chapel on the grounds is usually open (but empty).

Slakki Zoo

Slakki is a combination petting zoo and indoor minigolf complex, housed partly in cute buildings meant to look like a typical old-style Icelandic farm. It's best for little kids between ages two and seven. There's a decent café, tiny playground, and good photo ops, and kids can get to know a big, noisy, green parrot. Families with small children could make this their main target for a Golden Circle day trip...and still manage to glimpse some of the better-known sights on the way.

Cost and Hours: Adults-1,000 ISK, kids-500 ISK, daily 11:00-18:00 in summer, May and Sept Sat-Sun only, closed Oct-April, off Skálholtsvegur in the hamlet of Laugarás, tel. 486-8783.

Getting There: The zoo is less than a mile past Skálholt Church along highway 31.

• *To continue to the Kerið crater on highway 35, after passing Skálholt, drive about 15 minutes, then watch for the little Kerið sign, which comes up very quickly (you might see an Icelandic flag and people hiking along a ridge on your left as you approach).*

GOLDEN CIRCLE

▲Kerið Crater ("The Tub")

The most worthwhile stop on the way back to Reykjavík is a volcanic cone, from an eruption about 6,500 years ago, that has collapsed and filled with water—creating a tiny crater lake. It's right next to (but not visible from) the road. It's vividly colorful: red walls draped with green vegetation, overlooking deep aquamarine-blue water. You can see it in a single glance, take a half-hour to walk around the rim, or descend 150 feet down a set of stairs to the surface of the lake.

As Kerið (KEH-rithe) is on private land, it's unusual among Iceland's outdoor sights in charging admission (which caused a great stir when it was announced). But it's cheap, and the owners have improved the parking lot and pathways; most visitors find it worth the cost.

Cost and Hours: 400 ISK when staffed, not staffed at night or in darkness, mobile tel. 823-1336, www.kerid.is.

Nearby: About five minutes north of the crater is the **Borg public swimming pool,** in the Borg sports complex at the junction of highways 35 and 354, between Skálholt and Kerið—look for the water slide just past the main turnoff into the hamlet of Borg (1,000 ISK; June-late-Aug Mon-Fri 10:00-22:00, Sat-Sun until 19:00; otherwise Mon-Thu 14:00-22:00, Sat-Sun 11:00-18:00, closed Fri; tel. 480-5530, www.gogg.is).

• *As you head south from Kerið toward Selfoss on highway 35, you'll drive past a dramatic slope on your right. Look at the mountainside to see the huge boulders that have slid down the slope over the ages—and see if you can spot the one lonely summer house taking its chances among them. About 15 minutes after Kerið, you'll reach...*

Selfoss

Selfoss (pop. 7,000) is the largest town in southern Iceland, and set next to rapids on the Ölfusá river. (The water that flows over Gullfoss winds up here.) The Golden Circle route bypasses the town center, which is fine as there's not much to see, but you can easily drive across the bridge if you need to stop for supplies. Chess fans enjoy visiting the grave of troubled grandmaster Bobby Fischer in the Laugardælakirkja churchyard a mile northeast of Selfoss (for details, see page 208 in the South Coast chapter).

Eating near Selfoss: If you're in the mood for langoustine-by-the-sea, it's about a 15-minute detour to two *humar*-focused restaurants: **Fjöruborðið,** in the seaside village of Stokkseyri, and **Hafið**

Bláa. For more on these options—including how to get to them from Selfoss—see page 221 in the South Coast chapter.

• *It's a 45-minute drive from Selfoss back to Reykjavík. At the main roundabout in Selfoss, turn right onto highway 1. Soon after leaving Selfoss, on the left you'll see* **52 white crosses** *at the base of a conical hill (Kögunarhóll). These commemorate motorists and pedestrians killed on this busy, poorly lit road—statistically one of Iceland's most dangerous— between 1972 and 2006. Consider this a sobering reminder to drive with extra caution.*

In a few minutes, you'll approach the small town of **Hveragerði.** *While the town itself (pop. 2,000) is dreary, it sits at the mouth of a val- ley with evocative hillsides and offers an opportunity to hike to a thermal river (Reykjadalur); the town also has a great brewery/pizzeria (both described later). To stop at these, turn off highway 1 and follow the main drag all the way through Hveragerði. You'll come out at the upper end of town and keep going, following* Reykjadalur *signs about 2.5 miles, until the road dead-ends at the Reykjadalur parking lot, with a little café and basic WCs.*

▲Reykjadalur Thermal River

This natural thermal area—literally "Steamy Valley"—is aptly named. For outdoorsy hiker/bathers, Reykjadalur (RAKE-yah-

dah-lrr) is worth ▲▲. The hike to the river is just over two miles one way along a well-maintained path, with a 600-foot el- evation gain (allow at least three hours total for this experience).

Stepping out of your car at the end-of-the-road parking lot, you're surrounded by steaming hillsides. From here, cross the bridge, then hike approximately one hour up the valley. Eventually you'll reach some basic changing cabins next to a hot stream. The water is shallow—you'll need to lie down to be sub- merged—but wonderfully warm. Reykjadalur is far from undis- covered, so you'll likely have plenty of company. Relax and enjoy the experience...but remember it's an hour's hike back down to your car. The little café in the parking lot, Dalakaffi, is a nice place for cake and coffee (Sun-Fri 13:00-18:00, Sat from 11:00, www. dalakaffi.is).

Warning: Stay on marked paths at all times. This entire area is very geologically active, and anyone wandering off the path could end up stepping into a hidden, underground pool of boiling water.

Eating in Hveragerði: The main reason to visit nearby Hveragerði is to eat at **$$ Ölverk** ("Beerworks"), a wonderful little microbrewery/pizzeria tucked in a dreary strip mall a couple of blocks into town. In addition to a chalkboard menu of their own beers, and some others by local brewers, they dish up tasty pizzas from a brick oven. Casual and family-friendly, it works well for an easygoing, memorable dinner on your way back to Reykjavík (daily 11:30-23:00, take the main road through Hveragerði and watch for the pizzeria on your right at Breiðumörk 2b, tel. 483-3030, www. olverk.is).

• *Leaving Hveragerði, the road climbs steeply in a series of wide bends to a high upland plateau (1,200 feet) called...*

Hellisheiði

This plateau separates southern Iceland from the Reykjavík area. The weather can be dodgy up here, so check the road conditions in advance. About halfway across the plateau, you'll see pipes and steam from **Hellisheiðarvirkjun,** a geothermal plant owned by the Reykjavík energy utility; if it's not too early or late in the day, you could stop at the visitors center (see page 114). From here, it's less than 30 minutes—across a lunar landscape—to Reykjavík. On your way into town, consider stopping in the suburb of **Hafnarfjörður** for dinner (see recommendations in the Reykjavík chapter).

SOUTH COAST

To bask in a land of mountains, glaciers, and rugged coastal scenery, head for Iceland's South Coast. Within about a 2.5-hour drive of Reykjavík, you'll find black sand beaches, dramatic promontories, gushing waterfalls, glacial tongues just finishing their slow-motion 500-year journey, museums on folk culture and volcanoes, and rolling green farm fields dotted with sheep, cows, and Icelandic horses.

All of this sits in the shadow of two glacier-topped volcanoes: Eyjafjallajökull and the even more powerful Katla. The towns here are humble, with sparse sights and services, but Vík—at the far end of this day's drive—has a beautiful setting.

The South Coast rivals the Golden Circle as Reykjavík's best side-trip: It's arguably even better for outdoorsy types, offering more nature activities and a top hiking destination, the mountain ridge called Þórsmörk. However, unlike the Golden Circle, you'll head home the way you came—making the scenery a rerun.

As a Day Trip: You can do the South Coast on your own—following the **driving tour** outlined in this chapter—or with a **bus excursion** in a single long day (about 10 hours) from Reykjavík. Various companies offer full-day guided excursions year-round (prices range from about 13,000 ISK to 19,000 ISK based on the group size; see the Near Reykjavík chapter for a list of tour companies). These don't pack in as many stops as this chapter outlines, but some tours offer the option of adding on a glacier hike or other activities.

As an Overnight: While most people visiting this area are day-tripping from Reykjavík, the South Coast can also be used as a home base (see recommendations later in this chapter, under "Sleeping on the South Coast"). For instance, if doing the long, clockwise Ring Road route, you could make the South Coast your final overnight, as it's the ending point of that drive. Or you could do the Golden Circle drive from Reykjavík, but instead of looping back to the city, end that drive here on the South Coast, where you can spend a night or two (from here, you can head straight to Keflavík Airport for your departure flight, without returning to Reykjavík).

Spending two full days here opens up several sightseeing options. For example, if the weather's good, you can day-trip by boat from Landeyjahöfn to the Westman Islands (see that chapter). Or you can devote a day to the trails at Þórsmörk, which presides over a volcano-ringed glacial valley (described later in this chapter). Accessible only via specially equipped 4x4s or public buses equipped with monster-truck tires, Þórsmörk rewards hikers with stunning, panoramic views over cut-glass peaks and ruddy valleys.

South Coast Driving Tour

This self-guided driving tour links up the main attractions along the South Coast, in the order you'll reach them from Reykjavík. (Those ending their clockwise Ring Road drive will see these sights in the opposite order. Just hold the book upside down.) It's about a 2.5-hour drive each way between Reykjavík and the far point of this area, the town of Vík. Adding in time for a few necessary side roads, plan on at least six hours behind the wheel, plus about five hours to visit sights along the way. Figure on about 11 hours for the full experience.

The basic plan: From Reykjavík, make good time on highway 1 across the desolate Hellisheiði plateau, then through the towns of Hveragerði, Selfoss, Hella, and Hvolsvöllur (where the Lava Centre is worth a visit on the return drive). Just beyond—1.5 hours after leaving the capital—you'll cross the river called Markárfljót and enter the most striking part of the drive. The stops along this stretch are captivatingly Icelandic: Hike  behind the thundering Seljalandsfoss waterfall, ogle the glacier-capped volcano called Eyjafjallajökull, and pause in Skógar to see another towering waterfall and a good folk museum. Next, hike up close to the chilly tongue of Sólheimajökull glacier, enjoy the views from the Dyrhólaey promontory, and stroll along the black sand beaches at Reynisfjara. Just beyond those sights, the village of Vík has a big gas station and restaurants, offering a good pit stop before starting the 2.5-hour return drive back to Reykjavík.

PLANNING YOUR DRIVE
This plan is designed to efficiently link the highlights of Iceland's South Coast:

9:00	Leave Reykjavík and head for your first stop: the Seljalandsfoss waterfall (1.75 hours)
10:45	Visit Seljalandsfoss waterfall
11:15	Drive to Skógar (30 minutes) to visit the waterfall and folk museum, and have lunch
14:00	Head for Sólheimajökull (15 minutes from Skógar) to see a glacier
15:15	Drive to Dyrhólaey promontory (15 minutes); with time and energy, hike to the lighthouse
16:00	Depart for Reynisfjara (25 minutes) and walk the black sand beach
17:00	Start the drive back toward Reykjavík, stopping in Hvolsvöllur (1 hour)
18:00	Tour the Lava Centre in Hvolsvöllur (open until 19:00)
19:00	Drive back to Reykjavík (1.5 hours), and consider stopping for dinner en route

South Coast Tips
There are a number of adjustments you can make to this suggested plan. Consider the following:

With Less Time: To make it a shorter day, skip the Skógar Folk Museum and Dyrhólaey.

With More Time: If you're willing to leave earlier or get back later, your day will be more leisurely. For example, rather than driving straight through and dining late in Reykjavík, you could enjoy a countryside dinner on your way back (for ideas, see "From Vík Back to Reykjavík," at the end of the drive).

If overnighting on the South Coast, you can add more sights: Stop at the visitor center of the Hellisheiðarvirkjun geothermal power plant, check out Bobby Fischer's grave, see the Gljúfrabúi waterfall, visit the Eyjafjallajökull exhibition, or spend time in the village of Vík.

Hiking at Þórsmörk: The mountain valley of Þórsmörk is a hiker's delight, but it takes the better part of a day to experience. You can either do it as a long day trip from Reykjavík, or, if sleeping along the South Coast, you can catch a bus from Hvolsvöllur.

Weather Warnings: Visiting waterfalls and glaciers can be cold and wet; dress warmly and bring waterproof clothing and footwear. Also, be aware of the risk of blowing sand (which can

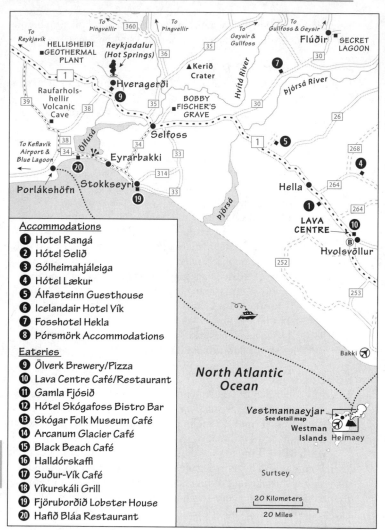

To Reykjavík

HELLISHEIÐI
GEOTHERMAL PLANT

Raufarhols-
hellir
Volcanic Cave

To Keflavík
Airport &
Blue Lagoon

Þorlákshöfn

360 To Þingvellir To Þingvellir

Reykjadalur
(Hot Springs)

35 36

▲Kerið
Crater

Hveragerði

BOBBY
FISCHER'S
GRAVE

Selfoss

Eyrarbakki

Stokkseyri

To Geysir &
Gullfoss

35

Gullfoss & Geysir

Flúðir

SECRET
LAGOON

30

Þjórsá River

Hvítá River

30

26

268

5

4

264

Hella

LAVA
CENTRE

264

10

B

Hvolsvöllur

252

253

North Atlantic Ocean

Bakki

Vestmannaeyjar
See detail map
Westman
Islands Heimaey

Surtsey

20 Kilometers

20 Miles

Accommodations
1 Hotel Rangá
2 Hótel Selið
3 Sólheimahjáleiga
4 Hótel Lækur
5 Álfasteinn Guesthouse
6 Icelandair Hotel Vík
7 Fosshotel Hekla
8 Þórsmörk Accommodations

Eateries
9 Ölverk Brewery/Pizza
10 Lava Centre Café/Restaurant
11 Gamla Fjósið
12 Hótel Skógafoss Bistro Bar
13 Skógar Folk Museum Café
14 Arcanum Glacier Café
15 Black Beach Café
16 Halldórskaffi
17 Suður-Vík Café
18 Víkurskáli Grill
19 Fjöruborðið Lobster House
20 Hafið Bláa Restaurant

damage your rental car's finish, at your expense). There is a small sandy patch (just a few hundred yards long) at the bridge where highway 1 crosses the Markárfljót river, just before the Seljalandsfoss waterfall. Check the weather before you go (at en.vedur.is) and consider alternative plans if very high winds are forecast. For more information see "Driving Hazards" in the Practicalities chapter.

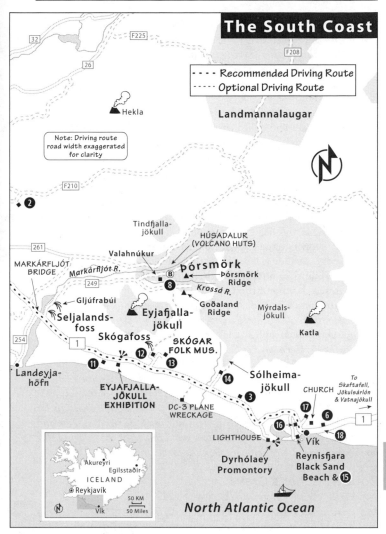

To Skaftafell, Jökulsárlón & Vatnajökull

To the South Coast and Back

FROM REYKJAVÍK TO SELJALANDSFOSS

Once you've left Reykjavík, it's less than a two-hour drive east along highway 1 to the Seljalandsfoss waterfall. Along the way, you'll pass some functional towns—Hveragerði, Selfoss, Hella, and Hvolsvöllur—which have a few minor sights not worth going out of your way for. The one exception is the excellent Lava Centre in Hvolsvöllur, the only place between here and Seljalandsfoss that's definitely worth a stop. You could see it on your way out, or save it for your return drive.

• *Just a few minutes after leaving Reykjavík's suburban sprawl on highway 1, you'll find yourself at...*

Hellisheiði

The 1,200-foot pass called Hellisheiði is a starkly desolate volcanic landscape, where you could easily encounter bad weather in April or October. If you have time, consider a stop at the **Hellisheiðarvirkjun geothermal power plant,** with an exhibit on geothermal energy (see page 114).

Soon after the plant, you reach the edge of the plateau and drop down on a switchback road. In good weather, you'll enjoy great views over the southern lowlands. Below you is the town of **Hveragerði,** at the head of an evocative valley misty with steam vents. (The town's name, aptly, means "hot spring enclosure.") The top end of this valley is where intrepid bathers can hike an hour up to the thermal river at **Reykjadalur.** For a description of the thermal area, see the end of the Golden Circle chapter.)

• *About 10 minutes past Hveragerði, you'll reach the large town of Selfoss (population 7,000), with a full range of services. If you don't want to stop, stay on highway 1, which crosses a river and then heads east as it skirts the northern edge of Selfoss (keep left at the main roundabout, following signs toward Vík and Hella).*

But if you're intrigued by American chess grandmaster Bobby Fischer, you may want to consider a brief detour to see his grave. At the east end of Selfoss (the far end, if coming from Reykjavík), a sign for Laugardælakirkja points north along a side road. Turning off here and driving less than a mile brings you to a small church at the Laugardælur farm (you'll practically drive through the farmyard).

Bobby Fischer's Grave

American chess champion Bobby Fischer was buried here after his death in Iceland in 2008. His gravestone is easy to find, just inside the churchyard gate. When the eccentric, reclusive Fischer came to Iceland in 1972 to face Russian grandmaster Boris Spassky for the world chess championship, he struck up a friendship with Sæmundur Pálsson, the policeman assigned to chauffeur him around. In 2004, Fischer landed in prison in Japan and was due to be extradited to the US on tax evasion charges. (He was in trouble with the IRS for playing chess in Serbia during the Yugoslav wars.) Sæmundur

and a small group of friends arranged for the Icelandic parliament to grant Fischer citizenship and chartered a plane to pick him up in Japan. They brought him to Reykjavík, where he lived quietly until his death. This basically merciful act eased the last years of an ill and elderly man. Some think that the American government silently condoned the operation to avoid the discomfort of putting Fischer on trial.

If you're interested in seeing Fischer memorabilia, visit the tiny information center about him on the main street in Selfoss (1,000 ISK, daily 13:00-16:00, closed mid-Sept-mid-May, Austurvegur 21, mobile 894-1275, www.fischersetur.is).

• *From Selfoss, follow highway 1 east across a lush plain, eventually passing through two small towns, Hella and Hvolsvöllur (KVOLS-vurt-lur). Each town has about 1,000 people, a grocery store, a couple of places to eat, a thermal swimming pool, and gas stations with WCs (you'll also find several recommended accommodations nearby). Right along the main road through Hvolsvöllur is the...*

▲Lava Centre

This state-of-the-art attraction rivals the excellent Volcano Museum in the Westman Islands, and uses cutting-edge exhibits to explain Iceland's volcanic heritage. It's well-presented and enjoyable for all ages and interest levels—worth the pricey ticket. As it's open fairly late, consider stopping here on your way back to Reykjavík.

Cost and Hours: 2,200 ISK, 700 ISK extra for 12-minute film, daily 9:00-19:00, can't miss it along the main highway 1 at the western edge of Hvolsvöllur, tel. 415-5200, www.lavacentre.is.

Eating: The Lava Centre has a **$ café** (with an affordable soup buffet, and takeaway salads and sandwiches) and a cafeteria-style **$$ restaurant.** You can eat here even if you're not visiting the museum (both open until 21:00—later than the exhibit).

Visiting the Museum: In the free-to-enter **lobby,** you'll find a large virtual map of Iceland identifying minor earthquakes over the last 48 hours. Smaller screens let you watch eyewitness accounts of various eruptions. Check out the cross-section of soil excavated at this site, striped with ash and tephra deposits from eruptions over time. (The lobby also has free WCs and a branch of the Rammagerðin gift shop with expensive, high-quality Icelandic souvenirs.)

SOUTH COAST

After buying your ticket, head down a long timeline corridor to the interactive **exhibit.** You'll see a towering, glowing mantle plume (an underground geyser of lava), and stand over eerie and mesmerizing simulated lava flows on tabletops. Throughout, touch-screens invite you to learn more about volcanoes, and darkened corridors between the rooms add to the experience—with simulated ash clouds, noisy eruptions, and trembling floors. In the "Volcano View" room, you'll stand in the middle of wrap-around, wall-to-ceiling virtual footage of what eruptions in this area would look like up close.

You can pay extra for the **cinema,** where a 12-minute film with a booming soundtrack and dramatic music shows off high-definition footage of spitting and flowing lava; historic photos and videos of past eruptions; and aerial eye-candy scenery of volcanic landforms around Iceland.

• *From Hvolsvöllur, it's about a 15-minute drive to the bridge over the Markárfljót river. Directly after the bridge, turn left onto highway 249, and then take the first right into the pay parking area for the Seljalandsfoss waterfall (with a basic café and WCs).*

▲▲Seljalandsfoss Waterfall

Seljalandsfoss (SELL-yah-lahnds-foss) tumbles over its cliff into a pool, with a cave-like walkway just behind it. The 210-foot-high

falls aren't that powerful—but they are handsome. The water comes from Eyjafjallajökull, the glacier capping the volcano that erupted in 2010. In good weather, a one-way path lets you walk around the back of the waterfall; in icy conditions, skip it (it's closed off in winter). If you do walk the path, wear a water-proof jacket and shoes—the path is damp and uneven, and you'll be sprayed steadily.

Before starting off, visually trace the entire path around this one-way loop to be sure you're up for it. The easy part is circling down around behind the cascade. The return trip is the hard part, as it requires climbing up steep rocks and tiptoeing through deceptively deep mud puddles to the top of an old staircase that allows an easy drop down to street level.

Photographers: The sun shines on the falls in the afternoon; in the mornings the mountain shadows them. For the best light, consider visiting in the afternoon, on your way back to Reykjavík.

Optional Add-On: A 30-minute side-trip takes you to another waterfall called **Gljúfrabúi** (GLYOO-vrah-BOO-ee, lit-

erally "Canyon Dweller"). This waterfall, much smaller than Seljalandsfoss, drops into a hollow within the rock and then exits (as a stream) under a tall, narrow, natural archway. To catch a glimpse, walk 10 minutes on the gravel path left of Seljalandsfoss past several minor cascades. From outside, you can only see the very top of the falls. To see a little more, hike up to the archway (on a challenging trail with handholds). To get close to the falls, you have to wade several yards, at your own risk, along the normally shallow but swift-flowing stream as it exits the arch (you'll want high rubber boots and full rain gear). On a typical day trip from Reykjavík, Gljúfrabúi isn't really worth it, but nature lovers or those with more time may enjoy it.

FROM SELJALANDSFOSS TO VÍK

This stretch—less than an hour's drive without stops—is lined with attractions and detours that can easily fill the rest of your day.

• *Leaving Seljalandsfoss, return to highway 1 and continue east. If the coast is clear, look out to sea, where the horizon is fringed with the jagged cliffs of the* **Westman Islands** *rising up just offshore. These islands were formed by volcanoes, including a very recent and dramatic eruption in 1973, which consumed a third of the main town's houses and expanded the island's size by about 20 percent. Aside from the eruption, the Westman Islands are known among Icelanders for their fishing industry, seabird colonies (including lots of puffins in the summer), and folk music (to visit them, see the Westman Islands chapter). About 15 minutes' drive beyond Seljalandsfoss you'll reach the...*

Eyjafjallajökull Area

Eyjafjallajökull is the name of the glacier that tops the volcanic mountain peak you're driving under (the mountain itself is called Eyjafjöll). This volcano thrust Iceland onto the world stage for a week in April 2010, as the ash it ejected high into the atmosphere settled over Europe, halting international air travel. For details, see the sidebar.

• *You'll soon pass a restaurant, worth considering for lunch.*

Eating near Eyjafjallajökull: Located at a roadside farm-

Eyjafjallajökull: The Volcano that Stopped Europe in Its Tracks

The Icelandic volcano called Eyjafjallajökull (EH-ya-FYAH-tla-YUR-kutl) erupted in the spring of 2010, famously disrupting airline flights all over Europe.

The first, short stage of the eruption started late on the night of March 20, 2010, at Fimmvörðuháls, the saddle between the Eyjafjallajökull and Mýrdalsjökull glaciers (where the hiking path crosses between Skógar and Þórsmörk). Tongues of red-hot lava, some as much as 600 feet high, shot up along a short fissure. This was a real "tourist eruption": The curious could view the show by helicopter, or even hike up toward it, in relative safety.

The Fimmvörðuháls eruption died down within a few weeks, and for all anyone knew the whole thing was over. But then came the eruption's second stage, much more violent and dangerous, as the earth opened right in the middle of the glacier. On April 14, a column of black soot and smoke shot four miles into the sky, meltwater rushed down the slopes, and ash rained over the downwind countryside—covering fields, cars, and roofs. The ash blocked out the sun and put livestock in danger. Flights across Europe were cancelled because of the fear that windborne ash would disable jet engines. Paradoxically, Iceland's Keflavík Airport (upwind of the volcano) mostly stayed open throughout the entire eruption.

The second stage lasted until late May, and by August, the volcano was dormant. Thankfully, despite its international infamy, the Eyjafjallajökull eruption caused little real damage—other than dumping a considerable amount of ash on the nearby countryside. Its main legacy was confronting the world with how difficult long Icelandic words are to pronounce. If you'd like to master the pronunciation of Eyjafjallajökull, several YouTube videos offer a tutorial...or you can use its nickname: "E15" (that's E followed by 15 letters).

Eyjafjallajökull had an even bigger impact on tourism. Some experts believe that those headlines in 2010 reminded the world not only that Iceland exists, but that it's a geologically fascinating place. They credit Eyjafjallajökull, in part, for the recent spike in international visitors.

So, when's the next eruption on the South Coast? Historically, eruptions of Eyjafjallajökull have been followed by eruptions of Katla (under Mýrdalsjökull)—which last blew its top in 1918 and, according to volcanologists, is overdue. Stay tuned...

stead, **$$ Gamla Fjósið** ("Old Cowshed") specializes in simple but satisfying dishes made with beef raised right here—delicious steak sandwiches, burgers, and soup. It fills an actual, rustic old cowshed with mismatched furniture under rafters. If you avoid the overpriced fish and seafood dishes, it's a decent value (daily 11:00-21:00, closed off-season, Hvassafell, tel. 487-7788).

• *After passing the restaurant, you'll reach a large shed on the south side of the road that houses the...*

Eyjafjallajökull Erupts Exhibition: Here you'll find a small room with a poster exhibit and a 20-minute film in English about the 2010 eruption. The film focuses on the experiences of the family at the Þorvaldseyri farm across the road (they run the exhibit). While it pales in comparison to the big, slick Lava Centre up the road in Hvolsvöllur, this exhibit offers a somewhat more intimate look at the eruption, and can brighten up a rainy day (850 ISK; June-Aug daily 9:00-18:00, shorter hours off-season, closed Sat-Sun in winter; tel. 487-5757, www.icelanderupts.is). Just beyond the exhibition, and across the road, look for a **pullout** with picnic benches and informational plaques (next to the Þorvaldseyri farm's driveway).

Thermal Bath Detour: From here, hardy bathers can consider a detour to **Seljavallalaug,** a very rustic thermal swimming pool (from 1923) built right into the side of a mountain slope. Some people enjoy the pool's scenic and remote location, which requires a 15-minute hike up a desolate valley. Don't expect a sleek and sanitary experience: The pool is unstaffed and has very limited services (grubby changing rooms), and the water is warm rather than hot. But backpackers and campers looking to take a memorable dip enjoy the detour. (From highway 1, just beyond the exhibition pullout, watch on the left after the bridge for road 242 to *Raufarfell,* then follow signs for *Seljavellir* to the end of the road, where you can park and hike.)

• *Continuing along highway 1, watch on the left after about four miles for a building embedded into the side of a massive rock at a farm.*

Drangshlíð: While I'm not much for Iceland's "hidden people" legends (see sidebar on next page), this sight is intriguing enough to warrant some fantastical stories. The structures here are cowsheds, and said to be peopled by elves who look after the livestock...and prefer to do it without human interference. According to legends, the farmer would leave hay and an empty milk bucket outside the sheds. And then later, he'd discover that the cows had been fed and milked. As it's private property, it's best not to try to visit up close.

• *Soon after Drangshlíð, watch on the left for the turnoff to a small settlement called...*

Iceland's Hidden People *(Huldufólk)*

Icelandic folk tales often speak of "hidden people" *(huldufólk)*—mystical sprites, elves, and other little creatures who inhabit a parallel universe.

No Photo Available

According to legend, these hidden people look, dress, and live much like humans, only smaller. They're farmers and fishers, and typically live inside rocks and hillsides. Hidden people are invisible to normal humans—unless they choose to be seen.

Most hidden people have no interest in humans, they sometimes need our help and they aren't shy about retaliating if disturbed. (After experiencing mysterious equipment malfunctions, construction projects have been known to reroute a road or carefully move a boulder—or even consult a mystic to negotiate with the hidden people.). And some mischievous hidden people take advantage of humans. For example, a truculent elderly elf might be switched out for a human baby as a changeling—to make him some poor Icelander's problem.

Tales of Icelandic hidden people date back to the earliest years of the Settlement Age. It's no coincidence that the stories told in this rugged, sparsely inhabited land feature many instances where showing generosity to a stranger is richly rewarded—promoting a "we're all in this together" ethic essential for survival in this challenging environment.

You may see polls suggesting that most Icelanders believe in hidden people (or at least refuse to rule out their existence). A few Icelanders even claim, matter-of-factly, to have seen an elf walking across their lawn. But many Icelanders—particularly younger ones—roll their eyes at talk of hidden people. In their view, these "beliefs" are exaggerated by the media, by local tour guides, and in guidebooks like this one.

But even if today's Icelanders don't really believe in elves, some may sense concentrated pockets of mysterious energy here and there. Tales of hidden people remind Icelanders to fear and respect nature—and on this island of volcanoes, earthquakes, and steaming geysers, nothing could be more rational.

In the 19th century, a pair of Brothers Grimm-style scholars—Jón Árnason and Magnús Grímsson—collected Iceland's tales of hidden people. To read a variety of vivid folk stories, search for "hidden people folktales" at www.grapevine.is; for a more scholarly compendium, books in English include J.M. Bedell's *Hildur, Queen of the Elves: And Other Icelandic Folk Tales.* For a concise overview, see Alda Sigmundsdóttir's *The Little Book of the Hidden People* or *Icelandic Folk Legends.*

Skógar

Skógar (SKOH-ar, "Woods") was originally the site of a local district school. There are two main attractions here: the Skógafoss waterfall (which you can't miss, on your left) and the Skógar Folk Museum (to the right).

▲▲Skógafoss Waterfall

This waterfall, on a river that drains down from Eyjafjallajökull, is much broader and more powerful than Seljalandsfoss. And yet, it's less spectacular, and you can't walk behind it. Park in the free lot (with pay WC) and gaze up at the water plunging over the side. A stairway climbs all the way up to the top of the falls (about 500 steps); it offers another perspective on the falls and lets you see the river up top. Skip the stairs if you're in a hurry or just not up for the climb. The stairway is actually the start of a long, popular trail that continues all the way up over the saddle between the Eyjafjallajökull and Mýrdalsjökull glaciers, and over to Þórsmörk (requires good preparation; for more on the Þórsmörk area, see the end of this chapter).

Eating at Skógafoss: $$ Hótel Skógafoss Bistro Bar is the best of a cluster of restaurants near the falls. The dining room and outdoor deck have a nice view, and they have a fine menu of lamb, fish dishes, burgers, and soup (daily 11:00-21:00, until 22:00 in summer, tel. 487-8780).

▲Skógar Folk Museum

This large and impressive collection, with both indoor and outdoor areas, is worth the entry price for those who'd like to mix some museum-going into their scenic South Coast day.

Cost and Hours: 2,000 ISK, daily June-Aug 9:00-18:00, Sept-May 10:00-17:00, tel. 487-8845, www.skogasafn.is. The museum has a café (closes one hour before museum), and lets nonguests use the WC for a small fee.

Visiting the Museum: The museum has three sections. The main ticket desk and café are in the biggest building (farthest from the waterfall), along with the **museum of Icelandic transport and communications.** A one-way route snakes through a huge hall cluttered with artifacts, all described in English. In addition to lots of shined-up old cars and rescue equipment, you'll wander past neatly arranged piles upon piles of all kinds of devices—like radio transmitters—and entire walls lined with first-generation cell phones.

The smaller, adjacent building is a typical **regional history museum.** The three floors have old household goods, farm implements, local archaeological finds, an 1855 fishing boat with a photo of its crew, and many other items. Compared to similar museums elsewhere, the sheer volume of stuff here impresses—where other such museums might have one spinning wheel, Skógar has a dozen, all lined up in a row.

Behind the two buildings is a small **open-air museum** with original buildings that were moved here, including two sod-roofed farmsteads (with stone walls and labyrinthine passages), an old timber house, and a school building—all traditionally furnished. The little church itself is not old—it was built here in the 1990s—but the furnishings inside are original, salvaged from other churches in the region.

• *From Skógar, your next stop is Sólheimajökull, a glacier tongue that spills downhill from the much larger Mýrdalsjökull (skippable if you'll also be seeing the stunning glacier lagoons—about 2.5 hours farther down highway 1 and described in the Ring Road chapter). To visit the glacier, continue on the main road. Less than 10 minutes past Skógar, look for signs to* Sólheimajökull. *Turn off the main road, drive for five minutes along paved highway 221, then park in the lot at the end of the road.*

▲Sólheimajökull Glacier

Sólheimajökull (SOHL-HAY-ma-YUR-kutl, "Sun-homes Glacier") is one of Iceland's most accessible places to get up close to (and, often, actually even touch) a glacier. Allow about an hour for a quick visit.

From the parking lot (pay WCs at the café), walk 15 minutes toward the glacier (dress warmly—it's colder by the glacier than at the parking lot). At first you walk on a wide, rocky gravel track. You'll then see a sign telling you not to proceed farther. There are several reasons for this: Melting ice under sand can create a quicksand-like phenomenon, poisonous volcanic gas can be released from under the glacier, ice calving off the glacier can create small tidal waves on the lagoon, rock can slide down the slope, and people can simply slip and fall into the cold lagoon.

Despite these dangers, most visitors choose to keep going, walking across uneven ground to the glacier itself (the helmeted glacier hiking groups that you may see come every day). If you choose to continue past the sign, use common sense, stay near other visitors, and keep in mind that the end of the glacier tongue is always changing, making it impossible to predict the ice and meltwater conditions. In recent years, it's been easy to walk right up next to the ice and give it a loving pat. But rock falls or rushing streams may force you to stay back and look from a distance.

If you've never seen a glacier before, you may be surprised at how dirty it is. Brilliant whites alternate with sections where the surface is covered in black dust. The glacier has been steadily receding over the past few years. You can watch a good time-lapse sequence of its extent at www.extremeicesurvey.org.

Something else to ponder: A generation ago, the glacier reached all the way to the parking lot (saving visitors a long hike). American politicians may squabble over global climate change, but Icelanders can tell you that there's no question their glaciers are receding. In western Iceland, the Okjökull glacier receded to the point that it lost its glacier status—now it's just called "Ok." That's not OK.

Hiking on the Glacier: For most visitors, just looking at the glacier is a fine experience. But if you want to climb on it, you should be properly outfitted and in the safety of a group. Many

companies have excursions of varying lengths and difficulty that take you up on Sólheimajökull and equip you with an ice ax and crampons (about 25,000 ISK). Some companies offer glacier hikes as a day trip from Reykjavík, but you can also join an excursion on-site (look for sales kiosks in the Sólheimajökull parking lot—but ideally, book a day or two ahead). For excursion companies, see the "Glaciers" section of the Icelandic Experiences chapter.

Eating at Sólheimajökull: The little **$ Arcanum Glacier Café** occupies converted shipping containers next to the parking lot. It has a limited menu, but it's fine in a pinch (daily 9:30-17:30, tel. 547-1500).

Nearby: You might hear about **Sólheimasandur**, a desolate beach where you can see the remains of a DC-3 plane that crash-landed in the 1970s (everyone survived). The rusty fuselage lies close to the sea on the sandy wastes near the turnoff to Sólheimajökull. But unless you're an aviation nut, skip it: It's a dull 2.5-mile hike each way, there's nothing to see besides the empty fuselage, and the landowners discourage visitors.

• *Return to highway 1 and continue east another 10 minutes, then turn onto highway 218. Drive about five minutes, cross the causeway, then take the left fork. (The right fork heads up the hill to the lighthouse, but regular cars can't make it up.) You'll come to a parking lot for...*

▲Dyrhólaey Promontory

Dyrhólaey (DEER-hoh-la-AY) is a promontory with a lighthouse, natural sea arches, and picturesque offshore rocks. If you're in a hurry and won't have time for the lighthouse hike (about 10 minutes each way), Dyrhólaey is skippable. You'll get similar scenery at Reynisfjara beach, our next stop at the far end of this same bay.

Dyrhólaey (literally "Door-hill Island") is not really an island, but it's only barely connected to the mainland by a couple of sandbars and a road causeway. At the parking lot, short paths lead up to several overlooks. Enjoy the sweeping views over black sand beaches, stretching from this perch all the way to Reynisfjara. In the early summer, the cliffs around you teem with seabirds (including, often, puffins)...birders love Dyrhólaey. Obey the warning signs: The beaches below the parking lot are permanently chained off after several tourists were swept out to sea by sneaker waves.

The main payoff for visitors to Dyrhólaey is hiking up along the cliffs about a half-mile to the **lighthouse** for more views (follow signs). The lighthouse was recently converted into a top-end boutique hotel. Stay back from the cliff edge as you make your way up, as rock falls have taken a few tourists with them over the past several years. It can also be quite windy here.

Note that from early May to late June, part or all of Dyrhólaey may be closed to car traffic (and maybe even to hikers) to protect nesting birds. While they typically keep it open during the daytime (9:00-19:00), it depends on nesting conditions. Even if it's open, avoid getting too close to nests; Arctic terns aggressively dive-bomb tourists who accidentally wander near their eggs.

• *Next up: the black sand beach of Reynisfjara. Return to highway 1 and continue east almost 10 minutes, then turn right onto paved (though potholey) highway 215, following signs for* Reynishverfi *(the village next to the beach). Along the way you'll drive through a broad, lush, green farmland delta that feels more Celtic than Icelandic. In the pastures, cows moo contentedly—a relatively rare sight in Iceland, where they're mostly kept indoors. Another 10 minutes brings you to a big parking lot with pay WCs and a beach café. From the parking lot, it's just a couple minutes' walk to...*

▲Reynisfjara Black Sand Beach

Tucked under grassy mountains, at the far end of the bay from Dyrhólaey, Reynisfjara (RAY-nis-fyah-rah) is worth ▲▲ on a nice, calm day. The beach here changes frequently with the ocean currents. The sand can bank up higher, or be partially swept away. The tide has an effect, too. In exceptional conditions, a very high tide can flood the parking lot. In winter, all but a thin strip of black sand may be covered by snow.

Looking out to sea, on your left you'll see dramatic **basalt formations**—splintered columns of volcanic rock, evocative of the famous Giant's Causeway in Ireland. Kids enjoy scrambling up the uneven stair-steps formed by the splintered rock, and anyone can easily explore the shallow caves formed by the columns.

Just beyond the basalt caves are the jagged **Reynisdrangar sea stacks,** also formed by volcanic activity. Scanning the horizon to the right, you'll see all the way to the Dyrhólaey promontory.

Caution: The beach is inviting...but very dangerous. The sea is extremely strong here, with an undertow, and tourists have drowned. Frequent sneaker waves—huge, unexpected surges of water—swamp areas of the beach that looked dry a minute before. It's fine to walk along the black sands, but stay well back from the water—*much* farther back than you think is safe—and never turn your back to the sea (not even for a selfie). Make sure that children also understand the rules.

Eating at Reynisfjara: $ Black Beach Café, also known as Svarta Fjaran, is a cafeteria-type place serving simple grill meals. With outdoor seating just off the beach, it's an inviting spot to nurse a beer (daily June-Aug 11:00-22:00, Sept-May until 18:00, tel. 571-2718, www.blackbeach.is).

• *If you're tired or short on time, head back to Reykjavík now—you've seen the best of the South Coast. Otherwise, continue on to one more town to refuel and refresh for the 2.5-hour trip back.*

Vík

A 10-minute drive over a low pass beyond the Reynisfjara turnoff, Vík (pop. 300, also known as Vík í Mýrdal) is Iceland's southernmost village and the endpoint of this tour. Vík enjoys a stunning setting—huddled up against a craggy cliff, with green pastures all around and a pointy steeple overlooking the town center from its plateau perch. But the town itself is almost painfully practical, with very little charm. It's not an inviting place to lin-ger, and most people use it as a turnaround spot for a rest and a bite to eat before returning to Reykjavík.

If the weather's good you can turn off to reach the village **church** on your way into town (watch for road marked *Suðurvíkurvegur* on left). While the church itself is as humble as its town, the parking lot around it offers fine views over Vík, the adjacent cliffs, the jagged dragon's-teeth sea stacks just offshore, and the long stretches of South Coast not covered in this chapter. (If you're intrigued, sights along the Southeast Coast are covered in the Ring Road chapter.) The recommended Suður-Vík restaurant is near the church.

Continuing into town, turn off the main road onto the street called Víkurbraut (on the right). In the Brydebúð building—an 1831 storefront that was moved here from the Westman Islands—the tiny but crowded **TI** has a free exhibit on the Katla volcano (irregular hours, Víkurbraut 28, tel. 487-1395).

Across the street from the TI is the little **Skaftfellingur Museum,** a warehouse displaying the rickety remains of a beloved local ship. The *Skaftfellingur* was built in 1918, went into service during World War II, and was decommissioned in 1963. The museum works hard to spin nostalgic stories about Vík's town heritage. One exhibit identifies the many shipwrecks that have occurred in the treacherous waters off Iceland's South Coast (500 ISK, June-Sept daily 10:00-18:00, shorter hours off-season).

There's little point in perusing the real estate ads here. Vík is directly below Mýrdalsjökull and the Katla volcano, which is due for another eruption. If the volcano erupts, melting water will rush down the slopes, creating a massive, downhill tidal wave that will deluge everything from Sólheimajökull glacier to well past the town of Vík; those present might have only a few minutes to evacuate. The village church, high on a hill, is supposed to be the safest point.

Eating in Vík: $ Halldórskaffi, a busy, convivial café that shares the Brydebúð building with the TI, serves reasonably priced meals (daily 12:00-21:00, tel. 487-1202). **$$ Suður-Vík,** up the road near the church (go left at the fork), offers slightly finer dining in a fun, cheery, attic-like space, with fine views over the town and cliffs from the deck. While their à la carte menu is pricey, they also offer cheaper pizzas (daily 12:00-21:00, Suðurvíkurvegur 1, tel. 487-1515). The N1 gas station on the main road at the east end of town has a cheap, grubby roadside grill called **$ Víkurskáli,** which serves up burgers and deep-fried fish (daily 11:00-21:00).

FROM VÍK BACK TO REYKJAVÍK
Dinner Options

It's about 2.5 hours—back the way you came on highway 1—to return to the capital. Along the way, consider dinner at one of these restaurants (listed in the order you'll reach them as you drive back):

In the Eyjafjallajökull Area: Gamla Fjósið is a good place to stop for burgers and other beef dishes.

In Hvolsvöllur: If you're stopping at the **Lava Centre** on the way home, it's easy to grab a basic bite in their café/restaurant.

Lobster Detour near Selfoss: These places, about 15 minutes south of Selfoss, highlight *humar* (a.k.a. langoustine or Norway lobster). In Selfoss, head south on highway 34 (at the main roundabout, turn off for *Þorlákshöfn, Eyrarbakki,* and *Stokkseyri).* When you hit the coast, turn east on highway 33, to the village of Stokkseyri. Overlooking the water, **$$$$ Fjöruborðið** ("The Water's Edge") is a venerable, nautical-themed lobster house with simple but good dishes. It's not cheap—a meal-sized bowl of lobster soup is 3,500 ISK, or you can pay (dearly) by weight for a sizzling skillet of *humar* tails. But it's a memorable way to sample this coastal delicacy. There's no view despite its waterside location (daily 12:00-22:00, reservations recommended, Eyrarbraut 3a, tel. 483-1550, www.fjorubordid.is).

Another *humar*-focused restaurant is **$$$ Hafið Bláa** ("The Blue Sea"), perched scenically on a ridge by the beach and also about 15 minutes from Selfoss. The food is slightly cheaper than at Fjöruborðið, with more non-lobster dishes. And while it's not as well-regarded, the setting is far more striking: From the airy, modern dining room, you look north into

the delta of the Ölfusá river, and south over crashing waves and a black sand beach that's good for a stroll before or after dinner (daily 12:00-22:00, Óseyrartangi at the Ölfusá Bridge, 816 Ölfus—

follow directions above, but keep going on highway 34 rather than turning off on highway 33, tel. 483-1000, www.hafidblaa.is). From this area, it's less than an hour's drive back to Reykjavík (hop on highway 33/34 west, then north on highway 39 to rejoin highway 1 near the Hellisheiðarvirkjun power plant).

In Hveragerði: Consider dinner at the wonderful **Ölverk** pizzeria and microbrewery in Hveragerði (see the end of the Golden Circle chapter).

In Hafnarfjörður: An efficient, close-to-home option is to stop off in Hafnarfjörður for dinner on your way through Reykjavík's suburban sprawl (see recommendations in that chapter).

Sleeping on the South Coast

For locations, see the map on page 206.

Near Hvolsvöllur: Named after the river it backs up to, **$$$$ Hotel Rangá** is a classic-feeling, high-end luxury resort with 51 woody, rustic, and unpretentious rooms and inviting, lodge-like public spaces. They also have an observatory and offer a "northern lights wake-up service" in case of any late-night light shows. You'll also find a hot tub to relax in, a pricey restaurant, and a comfy bar with overstuffed leather chairs and reasonable prices. If you're looking to splurge on the South Coast, this is the place (5 minutes west of Hvolsvöllur on highway 1 at Suðurlandsvegur, tel. 487-5700, www.hotelranga.is, hotelranga@hotelranga.is).

$$$ Hótel Selið ("Summer Pasture"), remote and restful, has eight modern rooms attached to a big red barn up a gravel road from highway 1, between Hella and Hvolsvöllur (about 15 minutes from either). Owner Hrafn ("Raven") runs the place with pride and is generous with travel tips (simple dinners available for guests—book ahead, on road 264—watch for turnoff from highway 1 near Hotel Rangá, tel. 487-8790, www.hotelselid.is, selid@hotelselid.is).

Near Skógar: My favorite accommodation in this area, **$$ Sólheimahjáleiga** is a country-classy gem. This working farm—conscientiously run by the same family since 1875—is a tidy little compound with 300 sheep and 20 rooms split between new and old buildings. There's a shared kitchen for guests to use, and dinner is available on request (cheaper rooms with shared bath, just off the main road between Skógar and Vík, tel. 864-2919, www.solheimahjaleiga.is, booking@solheimahjaleiga.is).

Near Hella: $$ Hótel Lækur ("Creek") has 21 rooms filling a renovated old barn and a modern annex (full restaurant, 15-minute drive down a gravel road north of main highway connecting Hella and Hvolsvöllur, near village of Hróarslækur, tel. 466-3930, www.hotellaekur.is, laekur@hotellaekur.is).

$$ Álfasteinn Guesthouse is a sod-roofed country home that oozes atmosphere. The main house has several (cheaper) rooms with shared bath, and there are also two separate guest cottages with bath. Ágúst Rúnarsson— the well-traveled host—is a wealth of information who understands travelers' needs and also guides mountain adventures (5.5 miles west of Hella—turn

off at the *Ásamýri* sign, then take the first right, tel. 772-8304, www.icelandmagic.is, icelandmagic@icelandmagic.is).

Big Chain Hotels: Along the South Coast, you'll also find large, tour group-oriented hotels operated by big chains: **$$$ Icelandair Hotel Vík** (44 rooms, tel. 487-1480, www.icelandairhotels.com, info@icehotels.is) and **$$ Fosshotel Hekla,** just north of highway 1 between Hella and Selfoss (42 rooms, tel. 486-5540, www.fosshotel.is, bookings@fosshotel.is).

Þórsmörk

Þórsmörk (THORS-murk)—literally "Thor's Woods"—is a rugged mountain valley immersed in a dramatic glacial landscape. This is one of Iceland's premiere hiking destinations, with a well-marked network of trails that let you gain elevation for thrilling views over volcanoes, glaciers, and valleys.

Þórsmörk is tucked in between three glacier-topped volcanoes: Eyjafjallajökull (the famous "E15"), Mýrdalsjökull (Iceland's fourth-largest glacier), and the small Tindfjallajökull. It's flanked by the wide Markárfljót river valley to the north, and the Krossá river valley to the south. The mountain ridge just south of the Krossá (near the Básar hut/bus stop) is called Goðaland ("Good Country")—but in practice, the entire area is known as "Þórsmörk."

For most visitors, half the fun of Þórsmörk is getting there: It's accessible only on gravel roads that ford several rushing rivers and streams. While some intrepid drivers (with specially equipped 4x4s) attempt visiting Þórsmörk on their own, for the rest of us,

SOUTH COAST

jacked-up buses on monster-truck tires provide a memorable journey.

Þórsmörk requires the better part of a day, and most visitors do it as a long day trip from Reykjavík. The information here is designed to help travelers doing Þórsmörk in one busy day—with an emphasis on its most rewarding hike, to the stunning Valahnúkur viewpoint (with 360-degree panoramas). While not time-consuming, this hike is moderately challenging and very steep in parts. If you're not physically up for the climb, you may want to skip Þórsmörk—although the bus ride in and out is fun, and the area is scenic, there's not much for nonhikers to do.

GETTING THERE

By Car: To reach Þórsmörk, turn off highway 1 north on road 249, pass the Seljalandsfoss waterfall (buses stop here for a photo op), then continue north to where the road turns to gravel. From there, the route hooks east and goes under several streams as it works its way along—and eventually through the middle of—the Krossá river to Þórsmörk. Throughout its course, the river splinters and remerges, and the flow can vary dramatically; the drive into Þórsmörk is never the same twice.

Drivers who have a full-size 4x4 vehicle, and really know what they're doing, can attempt Þórsmörk on their own—but before you do, check current conditions (www.safetravel.is), watch some YouTube videos to fully understand what you're committing to, and be sure your car-rental company is OK with the idea.

By Bus: The one-way journey from Reykjavík to the Þórsmörk Volcano Huts takes up to five hours. Three companies run very expensive bus services to Þórsmörk (summer only): **Iceland On Your Own** (part of Reykjavík Excursions; 3/day June-Aug, 1/day in May and Sept, www.ioyo.is); **Iceland by Bus** (1/day late-June-early-Sept, www.icelandbybus.is); and **Trex** buses (2/day mid-June-late-Sept, www.trex.is). Buses begin in Reykjavík and make a  few stops on their way to and from Þórsmörk. If you're overnighting along the South Coast, you can catch the bus at the N1 gas station in Hvolsvöllur (about the halfway point on the bus ride). Figure around 15,000 ISK round-trip from Reykjavík. While you can theoretically just hop on the bus, it's smart to book a day or two ahead (once you're confident that the weather is good enough to justify the trip).

Stops Along the Way: On the way into Þórsmörk, most buses stop for a stretch-your-legs photo op at **Gígjökull**, a glacial tongue of Eyjafjallajökull. In the 2010 eruption, melted glacier water came pouring down Gígjökull, flooding this area and silting up what had been a dreamy glacier lagoon. You can also see a gigantic rock split cleanly in half—a reminder of the geological power at play here.

The primary bus stop is **Húsadalur** (also known as the **Volcano Huts**), facing the broad Markárfljót valley, with a little café, shop, and information point. It's a popular launchpad for day hikes—the challenging Valahnúkur hike and the easier saddle hike to Langidalur both begin here.

The other stops are in the narrower, adjacent Krossá valley: **Stakkholtsgjá,** a stop made by request only, is where you can hike up a scenic canyon. **Langidalur,** just over the ridge from Húsadalur, faces the Krossá valley and the Goðaland ridge. It's home to the Skagfjörðsskáli hut, from where you can cross over Þórsmörk either on the steep Valahnúkur route, or on the easier saddle trail. The **Básar/Goðaland** hut is the end of the line, at the base of the Goðaland ridge, on the opposite side of the Krossá from Langidalur.

HIKING IN ÞÓRSMÖRK

This section focuses on hikes for day-trippers. Those overnighting have many more options—get information at the various huts,

and invest in a good hiking map (available at huts for 1,000-1,500 ISK). Þórsmörk is also a stop along several multiday hiking routes. Check trail conditions before heading out.

Hiking Options: Most people hop off the bus at Húsadalur, hike from the Volcano Huts over Valahnúkur, descend to Langidalur, then return on the easy saddle trail back to Húsadalur. With more time, consider riding the bus all the way to Básar, hiking across the Krossá to Langidalur, then summiting Valahnúkur and descending to Húsadalur for your return bus at the Volcano Huts; you'll miss the wooded saddle hike, but the variety gained by hiking across the river valley more than makes up for it. Stakkholtsgjá is a fine hike, but bus schedules can make it hard to

SOUTH COAST

combine with others in the area. See below for more details on each of these options.

▲▲▲Valahnúkur
(Moderately Challenging with Spectacular Scenery)

The main reason to come to Þórsmörk is for this glorious hike, offering stunning views in every direction. But the trail makes you earn it: While the hike isn't long (less than one mile from either valley to the summit), it's extremely steep in stretches (with an overall gain of 1,500 feet). The footing varies—stone steps, wooden steps, gravel—but it's mostly stable. You can hike to Valahnúkur from the Volcano Huts (Húsadalur) or from Langidalur. Either way, follow the well-marked *Valahnúkur* trail up, up, up, enjoying higher and higher views. Near the summit, the ladder-like trail gets vertiginous, but keep going and take plenty of breaks.

From the top, scan the horizon for the three glacier-topped volcanoes that surround Þórsmörk, the adjacent Goðaland range, and glacial valleys that fan out into the horizon. The smaller valley just to the right of the Krossá is the Hvanná. Look just above this, to the saddle of land between the two big glaciers (Eyjafjallajökull and Mýrdalsjökull); this is Fimmvörðuháls, where the first stage of the big 2010 Eyjafjallajökull eruption took place. On the steep trail back down, watch your footing and take your time. Figure about 1.5 hours to summit Valahnúkur and make it back down the other side.

▲Saddle Trail Between Húsadalur and Langidalur (Easy)

The easiest ascent over the Þórsmörk ridge connects two low-lying valleys: Langidalur ("Long Valley") and Húsadalur ("House Valley"). The terrain is pretty but mostly wooded, without dramatic views. Hikers use this trail mainly for an easy return to the Volcano Huts after tackling Valahnúkur, but it's also a nice option for those seeking an easier hike (figure 45 minutes or less, one-way). Along the Húsadalur, among the jagged volcanic formations just above the Volcano Huts, a side-trail leads to Snorraríki—a cave burrowed into a wall that's carved with modern names and old runic inscriptions (to reach the cave itself, you'll need to scale a wall with stone footholds).

▲Rocky Stroll Across the Krossá River (Easy)

The Krossá river carves its way through a rocky landscape between Básar (at the base of the Goðaland ridge) and Langidalur (at the base of the Þórsmörk range). This is the same river you'll crisscross on your way to and from this area, but the 30-minute hike across this valley gives you a closer look. As you walk across the desolate expanse, keep an eye out for two or three

movable bridges, which are strategically placed to help hikers cross (marked with yellow arrows). The footing is uneven but walkable—a mix of sand, pebble, and ankle-twisting rock of every color.

▲▲Stakkholtsgjá Canyon Hike (Moderate)

This narrow valley, with walls up to 300 feet high, cuts a mossy mile-and-a-quarter deep into the cliff. Plan on 1.5 hours round-trip for this hike. While mostly level, the footing is uneven, and the canyon's river is always in flux—you'll likely have to step, or even jump or wade, across a swift current (wear proper footwear). Where the stream forks, bear left. The ever-narrowing canyon culminates at a cave-like enclosure with a gushing waterfall. For a closer look, you'll have to scramble up some slippery rocks. Unfortunately, this hike's location—not easily walkable to the other trailheads—makes it tricky to combine with other hikes in the area. Stakkholtsgjá is a good compromise for reasonably hardy hikers who don't mind uneven footing and want a scenic walk, but aren't up for the steepness of Valahnúkur. Note that buses stop here by request only; before getting off, clearly establish the return bus time with your driver.

SLEEPING AND EATING IN ÞÓRSMÖRK

Serious hikers enjoy settling in for a few days to explore Þórsmörk. Your options are the ¢ **Volcano Huts** at Húsadalur, with a variety of private rooms, dorms, cottages, and camping (www.volcanohuts. com); the ¢ **Skagfjörðsskáli** hut, at Langidalur, with dorms, camping, and a private cottage (www.fi.is); and ¢ **Básar,** with dorms and camping across the valley from Skagfjörðsskáli in the Goðaland foothills (www.utivist.is).

Services are sparse in Þórsmörk. The only real restaurant is the $ **cafeteria** at the Volcano Huts. It's smart to bring a picnic to enjoy at your leisure—there are plenty of glorious viewpoints.

SOUTH COAST

WESTMAN ISLANDS

Vestmannaeyjar

The Westman Islands are my favorite "Back Door" destination in Iceland: a highly scenic, relatively undiscovered island experience. On clear days, the islands' sharp cliffs hover like a seductive mirage just offshore from the touristy South Coast. Those who make the trip discover that this pint-sized archipelago packs in an appealing variety of experiences: a gorgeously set small town with engaging museums and good restaurants, an up-close look at a quite recent volcanic eruption, a dramatic approach by air or sea, craggy bird cliffs (including puffin colonies in the summer), and a living, breathing mascot puffin you can usually meet in person. The islands are a bit of a project to reach, but worth the trouble for travelers spending more than a few days in Iceland.

Among Icelanders, the Westman Islands (Vestmannaeyjar, VEST-mah-nah-AY-ar) have various claims to fame: They're known for their recent volcanic activity (and excellent Volcano Museum), busy fishing industry, large populations of seabirds that love the steep cliffs, and musical traditions celebrated in a huge annual music festival. Puffins are an unofficial mascot for all of Iceland, but (in summer) they are particularly abundant here on the Westman Islands.

The "Westman" Islands, which actually lie south of the mainland, are named for some Irish slaves who fled to the islands after killing their master, according to the sagas. In Old Norse, the Irish were called *Vestmenn* (Westmen), so a better translation might be the "Irishmen's Islands."

Only one island—called Heimaey (HAME-ah-AY)—is inhabited, and that's the one you'll be visiting. You can get there by boat, by plane, or by a combination of the two. But I'll be honest:

The reason the Westman Islands aren't swamped with tourists is that reaching them is weather-dependent, particularly off-season. Planes are grounded when it's too foggy or windy, and boats stay moored when the weather or harbor conditions are bad. Patience and flexibility are essential. Keep close tabs on the weather and have a Plan B in mind.

PLANNING YOUR TIME

Given the potential disruption in getting here (or getting home), planning a Westman Islands trip is tricky. Whatever you do, leave a couple days' buffer between your trip to the islands and your flight departing Iceland, in case you get stuck here unexpectedly. Other than that, the main choice is whether to spend the night or come for the day.

Overnight or Day Trip?: An **overnight** in the islands gives you the flexibility to go later in the day, and can be easier on your budget (it's cheaper to eat and sleep on the island than in Reykjavík). Staying two nights gives you a full, undisturbed day to relax, but might be overkill if you're spending less than a week in the country. Note that it works well to overnight on the Westman Islands in conjunction with a visit to the South Coast; the Landeyjahöfn ferry dock is a short drive from that area's top attractions (about 10 minutes south of the Seljalandsfoss waterfall).

You can **day-trip** here from Reykjavík—or from the South Coast—in a rushed but still worthwhile visit. If home-basing on the South Coast, ideally budget two days; use the day with nicer weather for your Westman Islands trip. By **boat,** your only practical one-day option is to leave from Landeyjahöfn harbor on the South Coast (see overview map on page 207). You'll have to drive or ride a bus to the ferry first thing in the morning, and reverse the trip in the evening. By **plane** from Reykjavík or the South Coast, take a morning flight out and a late afternoon flight back. Note that flying from Reykjavík works best Monday through Friday (flight schedules make day-tripping difficult to impossible on Sat-Sun).

GETTING TO THE WESTMAN ISLANDS

Flying is pricey, but it's quick and handy for those looking for an efficient side-trip from Reykjavík. The ferry makes sense for those spending time on the South Coast. Both options are equally scenic, and are more or less equally weather-dependent.

By Plane

From Reykjavík: Eagle Air flies 19-seat turboprop planes from Reykjavík City Airport, near downtown—*not* the international Keflavík Airport (2-3 flights/day Sun-Fri, 1/day on Sat June-Aug only, priced in euros—about €105-150 each way, cheaper online

fares sell out quickly, tel. 562-
4200, www.eagleair.is). A day
trip on Eagle Air is the most
efficient way to see the islands.
But if the morning departure is
cancelled due to bad weather,
you've lost your only shot at
going (they'll normally refund
the entire round-trip fare).

The Eagle Air terminal is
on the *east* side of the runways, behind the Icelandair Hotel Reykjavík Natura and the control tower. (Don't confuse it with the Air
Iceland Connect terminal that serves most domestic flights.) To
reach Eagle Air by public transport, take bus #5 to the Nauthólsvegur stop. For early morning flights, take a taxi (best to arrange
taxi the night before). As there's no security check, you can show up
a half-hour before departure (if sleeping in downtown Reykjavík,
have the taxi pick you up about an hour before your flight).

From the South Coast: Nine-seat planes operated by a small
charter operator, **Atlantsflug,** make the five-minute flight to the islands from the tiny airport at Bakki, near the Landeyjahöfn harbor
(two-hour drive from Reykjavík, one-hour drive from Vík, parking
available, no public transport to airport). The return flight gives you
just six hours on the island—making it a tight day trip (1-2 flights/
day, 8,500 ISK one-way, tel. 478-2406, www.flightseeing.is, click
on "Vestmannaeyjar").

Luggage Limits: Both Eagle Air and Atlantsflug permit just
15 kilos (33 pounds) of luggage; you may need to leave some of your
gear in Reykjavík or hidden in your car.

By Ferry

The weather determines which of two ports the Herjólfur ferry
uses: The 40-minute crossing from the newer **Landeyjahöfn** is
more comfortable, convenient, and closer to the islands, but only
runs in summer (and is about a two-hour drive from Reykjavík).
Some sailings (including all off-season trips) depart from the older
Þorlákshöfn—which is closer to Reykjavík (45-minute drive), but
about three seasickness-inducing hours from the islands.

Weather Disruptions: The Landeyjahöfn harbor, built in
2010, has a significant problem: Ocean currents sweep sand into
its mouth, which then must be dredged clear—and that's possible
only in summer. Rough seas add to the risk of grounding in the
shallow harbor entrance. The result: The ferry *tries* to sail to/from
Landeyjahöfn from about May to September, and the rest of the
time it uses Þorlákshöfn. In unfavorable weather or harbor condi-

tions, summer sailings may move back to Þorlákshöfn—sometimes on short notice.

To check harbor conditions and book tickets, visit www. herjolfur.is (to talk to a real person, call 481-2800). In Vestmannaeyjar, on Heimaey Island, ask about conditions at the boat ticket office at the harbor (open whenever boats sail).

Walk on or drive on?: On a short visit, it's easy to see the main sights in town by foot. To see the rest of the island, you can either bring your car on the ferry, or join the recommended Eyja Tours minibus tour (see "Helpful Hints," later). One advantage of driving on is that you're not stuck if the return ferry must use a different port due to weather issues. Car slots tend to sell out, so reserve a space a few days in advance (often before the weather forecast is very clear).

Sailing from Landeyjahöfn: When Landeyjahöfn is working well, the short, inexpensive crossing to the islands is a pleasure (1,320 ISK/person, 2,120 ISK/car). Typically there are four sailings a day in each direction—two in the morning and two in the evening. Reserve a ferry ticket in advance, even if you're just going by foot (morning departures from Landeyjahöfn and evening departures from Vestmannaeyjar can sell out). At most times, reserving a day or two in advance is usually enough. During festival times (see later, under "Helpful Hints"), reservations are essential and should be made as far in advance as possible.

To reach Landeyjahöfn by public transportation, take bus #52 from Reykjavík's Mjódd terminal (4,400 ISK, timed to work with ferry connections, departs Reykjavík about 9:00, departs Landeyjahöfn about 19:00, 2.5 hours, no bus when ferry is cancelled, tel. 540-2700, www.straeto.is). If driving, check the wind forecast at Landeyjahöfn before parking there. In high winds, blowing sand and gravel could damage your car's finish or even break windows.

Sailing from Þorlákshöfn: It's a three-hour trip from Þorlákshöfn to the islands. This makes a day trip to the islands impractical—it really only works if you stay overnight (3,420 ISK/person, 3,420 ISK/car). To reach Þorlákshöfn by public transportation, take bus #51 to Hveragerði, and then change to bus #71 for Þorlákshöfn (around 1.5 hours, 2,200 ISK).

Heimaey Island

Of the Westman Islands, only one is inhabited: Heimaey (HAME-ah-AY, "Home Island"). The roughly dozen smaller islands surrounding Heimaey are uninhabited. By Icelandic standards, the islands have a wet, warm, and windy climate. Icelanders refer to this area as simply "the islands," and people from here as "islanders."

Orientation to Heimaey Island

The only town on Heimaey—and the only town in the islands—shares the name of the archipelago: **Vestmannaeyjar.** It's fairly humble, but its setting is dramatic: huddled up along its harbor, facing a busy industrial port and steep, scenic cliffs. From here, Vestmannaeyjar climbs gradually uphill, filling a broad plateau between the cliffs to the west and the volcanoes to the east. The main commercial street, called Bárustígur, runs

up from the harbor and holds the TI and many of my recommended eats and sleeps. Puffin-head signposts scattered around town direct you to the various museums and other landmarks.

Tourist Information: The Eymundsson bookstore, at the harbor end of the main drag at Bárustígur 2, serves as the local TI (Mon-Fri 9:00-18:00, Sat 10:00-16:00, Sun from 13:00, www.visitvestmannaeyjar.is).

ARRIVAL IN VESTMANNAEYJAR

By Plane: From the airport, you can take a taxi into town (1,700 ISK—ask the airport staff to call one for you or try Eyjataxi at mobile 698-2038); ask your hotel to pick you up; make friends with a local from the flight and ask for a ride; or on a nice day, and without luggage, walk 1.5 miles from the airport downhill into town (go left from airport, around west side of Helgafell mountain, 35 minutes). To return to the airport, take a taxi instead of walking uphill.

By Boat: If arriving on foot by ferry, follow the blue stripe, then the fish painted onto the pavement. This leads you to the ticket kiosks for various boat and bus tours. The main drag (with the TI, and the start of my self-guided walk) is just uphill from the harbor, roughly behind the Krónan supermarket, about two blocks to the left (look for the Subway and Eymundsson bookshop/TI).

HELPFUL HINTS

Sightseeing Advice for Plane Day-Trippers: If flying in from Reykjavík on a weekday, you'll arrive in the wee hours (before 8:00) and have several hours to kill before the island's museums open (10:00 or later). This is a good time to explore the town and orient yourself with my self-guided walk. Hop on the 11:00 bus trip around the island with Eyja Tours, have a late lunch, then visit the Volcano Museum before heading back to the airport for your flight home (departures generally at 16:30 Mon-Fri, 18:15 Sat-Sun).

Puffin Viewing: The best time to see puffins is from roughly late May to mid-August. They actually arrive around the end of April, but spend only a brief time cleaning their burrows before they go out to sea to mate. In recent years, the number of puffins nesting here has declined, perhaps due to the warming ocean around the islands.

Festivals: On the first weekend in August, the islands host the massive **Þjóðhátíð** (National Festival) in Herjólfsdalur, a picturesque valley near town (fireworks, bonfires, and singing; must buy ticket for festival and book transport to islands well in advance; www.dalurinn.is). The weekend is known for drunkenness and other rowdy behavior, and accommodations book up.

The **Goslok** festival commemorates the end of the 1973 eruption of Eldfell (weekend following July 3). Islanders also celebrate the annual nationwide **Seamans' Day** enthusiastically (usually first weekend in June). These festivals are smaller, but reservations are still essential.

Bus Tours: At **Eyja Tours,** Ebbi runs a delightful two-hour minibus tour of the island every day in summer. This is a great use of your time, offering a good overview of the entire island, lively commentary from a gregarious islander, and just the right balance of information and stops to snap photos and stretch your legs. They have a little ticket office next to the harbor, across from Tanginn restaurant (tour-7,000 ISK/person, includes entry to Sæheimar aquarium; tours run May-mid-Sept at 11:00, 14:00, and sometimes 16:00; smart to prebook July-Aug, may be available off-season—ask, mobile 852-6939, www.eyjatours.is).

Boat Tours: Weather permitting, several companies run boat tours

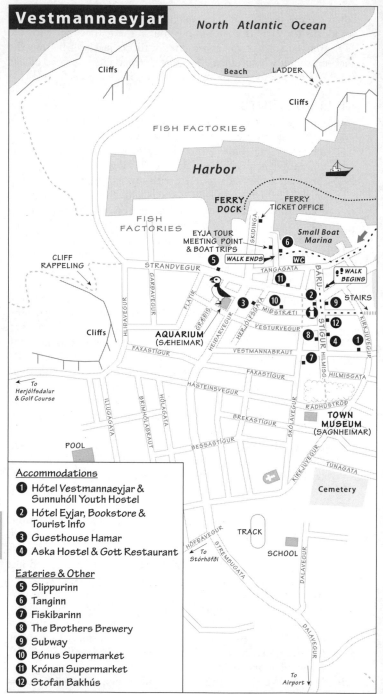

Vestmannaeyjar

North Atlantic Ocean

Cliffs
Beach
LADDER
Cliffs

FISH FACTORIES

Harbor

FERRY DOCK
FERRY TICKET OFFICE

FISH FACTORIES

Small Boat Marina

EYJA TOUR MEETING POINT & BOAT TRIPS
WALK ENDS
WC

STRANDVEGUR
TANGAGATA
SKIÐINGA.
BÁRU-
WALK BEGINS
STAIRS

CLIFF RAPPELING

GARÞAVEGUR
FLATIR
GRÆÐIS.
HEIÐARVEGUR
HERJÓLFSGATA
MIÐSTRÆTI
VESTURVEGUR
STÍGUR
HILMISG.
KIRKJUVEGUR

AQUARIUM (SÆHEIMAR)

Cliffs

HLÍÐAVEGUR
FAXASTÍGUR
VESTMANNABRAUT
FAXASTÍGUR
HILMISGATA

To Herjólfsdalur & Golf Course

ILLUGAGATA
BRIMHÓLABRAUT
HÓLAGATA
HÁSTEINSVEGUR
BREKASTÍGUR
SKÓLAVEGUR
RAÐHÚSTRÖÐ
TOWN MUSEUM (SAGNHEIMAR)

BESSASTÍGUR

POOL

KIRKJUVEGUR
TÚNAGATA
Cemetery

HÖFÐAVEGUR
STREMBUGATA
TRACK
SCHOOL
DALAVEGUR

To Stórhöfði

To Airport

WESTMAN ISLANDS

Accommodations

❶ Hótel Vestmannaeyjar & Sunnuhóll Youth Hostel
❷ Hótel Eyjar, Bookstore & Tourist Info
❸ Guesthouse Hamar
❹ Aska Hostel & Gott Restaurant

Eateries & Other

❺ Slippurinn
❻ Tanginn
❼ Fiskibarinn
❽ The Brothers Brewery
❾ Subway
❿ Bónus Supermarket
⓫ Krónan Supermarket
⓬ Stofan Bakhús

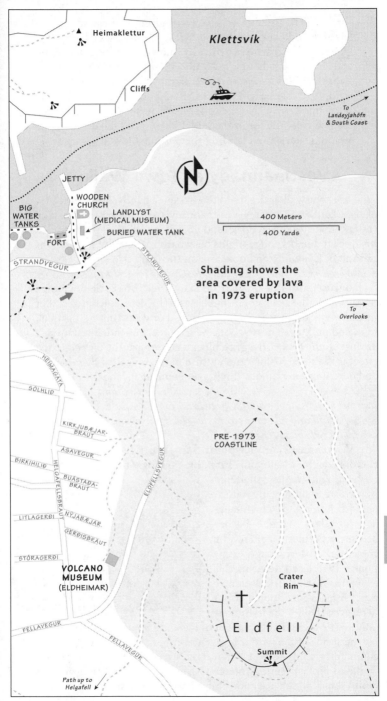

Heimaklettur

Klettsvík

Cliffs

To Landeyjahöfn & South Coast

JETTY

WOODEN CHURCH

LANDLYST (MEDICAL MUSEUM)

BIG WATER TANKS

BURIED WATER TANK

FORT

STRANDVEGUR

STRANDVEGUR

400 Meters

400 Yards

Shading shows the area covered by lava in 1973 eruption

To Overlooks

HEIMAGATA

SÖLHLÍÐ

KIRKJUBÆJAR-BRAUT

ÁSAVEGUR

BIRKIHLÍÐ

HELGAFELLSBRAUT

BÚASTAÐA-BRAUT

LITLAGERÐI

NÝJABÆJAR

GERÐISBRAUT

STÓRAGERÐI

VOLCANO MUSEUM (ELDHEIMAR)

PRE-1973 COASTLINE

Crater Rim

E l d f e l l

Summit

FELLAVEGUR

FELLAVEGUR

ELDFELLSVEGUR

Path up to Helgafell

WESTMAN ISLANDS

that circle the island and give you a glimpse of the smaller is-lets and stacks surrounding it. **Viking Tours** uses a larger ship (7,400 ISK, departures generally mid-May-mid-Sept at 11:00 and 16:00, 1.5 hours, tel. 488-4884, www.vikingtours.is). **Ribsafari** runs more expensive, bumpy tours on small RIBs—rigid inflatable boats (17,900 ISK, 2 hours, mobile 661-1810, www.ribsafari.is). Neither trip visits Surtsey (the island that erupted from the sea in the mid-1960s), as it's too distant from Vestmannaeyjar and landing there is not allowed.

Vestmannaeyjar Town Walk

This 1.5-hour walk is designed to give you a handy ▲▲▲ overview of the island's only town—Vestmannaeyjar—with views from atop the lava that swallowed up several houses, and a stroll past its scant historic landmarks and along its busy harborfront. The walk begins in front of Eymundsson bookstore on the main street.

• *Stand with your back to the water, looking up the street called...*

Bárustígur: This is the little main street of a little town on a little island. The bookstore doubles as a TI, with a helpful staffer inside who can answer your questions between ringing up book sales and pulling espresso shots. Several recommended restaurants are just up the street. The gray, blocky building at the far end of the street is the town history and culture museum (called Sagnheimar and described later, under "Sights on Heimaey Island").

• *Walk one very short block up the street, turn left, and head for the staircase up the side of a bluff. Climb to the top of the stairs, then bear left with the trail and follow it out to the grassy viewpoint where the trail takes a sharp bend to the right.*

Vestmannaeyjar Viewpoint Spin-Tour: Get oriented with this 360-degree visual tour. First, look out over the **harbor,** where boats big and small are sheltered by two steep cliffs with round-ed, green tops. Vestmannaey-jar's excellent natural harbor became even more sheltered by cooled lava after a huge erup-tion in 1973 (see sidebar in this chapter). A sixth of Iceland's total fish exports come from here, even though the island has  only a little more than 1 percent of Iceland's population. The whole northern side of the harbor is given over to fish processing, and the community tends to vote for Iceland's conservative party, which works to protect fishing interests. The harbor is too tight for big cruise ships...which is a good thing for independent travelers.

Just to the left of
the harbor is a towering
cliff where local kids still
learn the age-old skills
needed to collect seabird
eggs or land on the jag-
ged outlying islands. The
islands are rich with bird
life—puffins, of course,
but also fulmars, guille-

mots, and kittiwakes. Starting around age eight, children learn
how to free-climb their way up steep cliff faces and swing on
strategically placed ropes. (Better to learn here, where at worst
they might fall on the soft sod on the ground, instead of the sharp
rocks and cold surf at the base of a sea cliff.) Tucked around the
far side of the cliff (not visible from here) is Herjólfsdalur, a natural amphitheater where this teensy island hosts a gigantic music
festival each summer.

Now pan left, over Vestmannaeyjar's **rooftops.** This is not a
cutesy tourist town, but a no-nonsense working community. For
centuries, no more than a few hundred people lived here. But the
island boomed between 1900 and 1920 with the rise of motorized fishing, and much of the downtown zone dates from that era.
Today, the 4,300 islanders still live off fishing, plus a little tourism.
Living out on the islands comes with some compromises: Many
errands require a trip to the mainland, and most expectant moth-
ers travel to Reykjavík to give birth there rather than in the tiny
hospital here. If the houses look a little ragtag, keep in mind that
maintaining real estate on a little island is a challenge. Despite the
islands' volcanic activity, there's no hot water source, so this is one
of the parts of Iceland where homes and water are heated with electricity and oil.

Look farther left, and find the two looming **volcanic peaks** on
the horizon. The one on the right, with the classic volcanic dome

WESTMAN ISLANDS

shape, is the dormant Helgafell, which last erupted 6,000 years ago. The lower-lying one to the left, Eldfell, is the one that blew its top in 1973—and for six months, the slow and steady flow of lava gradually consumed this corner of the island.

Continue looking left, across a **rocky landscape.** The entire "hill" upon which you stand—all the land between here and that volcano—is less than 50 years old. You're standing on a now-solidified molten glacier of liquid rock that's 50 feet deep. (Remember that staircase you climbed up?) All around you, notice the wood-carved "street signs," bearing the names of streets that now lie deep underfoot. Keep an eye out for plaques memorializing former landmarks (Kiwanis club, electrical plant, and so on). The low-lying, rust-colored, boxy building that sits between the V formed by the two volcanoes is the excellent Volcano Museum, called Eldheimar; a visit here is an essential Westman Islands experience (described later).

It's fun to wander around the **lava rocks,** which are blanketed in fuzzy moss and (in early summer) enlivened by colorful wildflowers. Hiking paths and gravel roads crisscross this area. If you have time and energy, you can hike all the way up to the volcano summit (see "Climbing up Eldfell Volcano" later).

• *Now continue along the gravel path, with the lava on your right and the harbor on your left. When the path reaches an asphalt road, cross it to the bench and look down over historic* **Skansinn Cove.** *Hike down the steep slope to the remaining walls of an old fortress with a lone cannon.*

Fortress (Virkið): In 1586, the Danish king built this to enforce Danish power against the British, who wanted to trade with the islands. The fortress saw action only once, during perhaps the only dramatic event in local history until the 1973 eruption: In 1627, pirates (often misidentified as "Turkish") raided the island and carried off most of its inhabitants to slavery in Algeria. The island's priest, Ólafur Egilsson, was one of the few who managed to return. He wrote a book about his experiences, which you can buy in English translation.

Just downhill from the fortress, embedded in the cliff on the right, look for the white, semicircular **water tank**—or what's left of it, as more than half of the structure was consumed by lava. Built in 1932, this was a seawater tank that helped local fishermen keep their catch fresh. It also fed a big swimming pool—which is now under the lava (see photos of happy swimmers on the nearby infor-

mation boards). For centuries, the Westman Islands suffered from a lack of fresh water, with just two wells and the rainwater that residents collected from their roofs. In 1968, a pipeline was completed that brought water from the mainland, which is now stored in the huge white tanks between here and the harbor.

• *Walk down toward the waterline, past the big mast mounted in the ground, to the old house.*

Landlyst: This is the oldest residence on the island and the former home of Iceland's first maternity hospital. Information boards explain how neonatal tetanus killed three-quarters of all babies born on the Westman Islands in the mid-19th century...a problem solved only when an islander went to Copenhagen to train as a midwife. Today the building houses a modest medical museum.

Just past the old house, you can't miss the small **wooden church,** donated by Norway in 2000 to mark a millennium of Christianity in Iceland (free to enter). While lacking a tall steeple, it's typical of humble Norwegian village churches (and designed as a replica of a c. 1170 church in Trondheim).

• *Walk out to the end of the stubby...*

Jetty (Hringskersgarður): This helps protect the harbor from the churning sea. Looking right, you'll see the narrow passage ships use to access Vestmannaeyjar's port—and you can clearly see how the harbor became even more protected by the 1973 lava flow, which came as far as this jetty. Islanders were terrified that the lava would seal off the harbor entirely, which would have turned Vestmannaeyjar into a ghost town with no industry. With the help of the US military, locals pumped seawater on the lava to try to cool sections of it and divert the flow away from the town and harbor. Opinions are divided about whether this had any real effect, but the islanders like to think it did. American writer John McPhee wrote a good account of this effort (*The Control of Nature,* 1989).

Now gaze up at the 930-foot-tall cliff that rockets up across the harbor—called **Heimaklettur.** Seabirds love to nest in the

WESTMAN ISLANDS

The Westman Islands Eruption of 1973

In the middle of the night on January 21-22, 1973, a volcanic eruption started along a fissure just above the town of Vestmannaeyjar. Most of the islanders were immediately evacuated, but the eruption went on for months—destroying a third of the town. This event is still fresh in the islanders' minds, and tourists usually spend part of their visit understanding it and seeing its consequences—including the  many bits of buried homes still sticking out of the lava all around the eastern side of town.

Lava gradually encroached on local homes, even as it expanded the island's footprint by about 20 percent. Meanwhile, the volcano ejected massive volumes of tephra (volcanic particles) into the air, blanketing much of the island's northern half under a thick layer of ash and rock. A small crew stayed on the island to observe the eruption and wrap up the evacuation, and when possible, they retrieved valuables from houses before they were buried by ash or set alight by hot lava bombs. Ultimately the eruption destroyed 400 homes, displacing 1,500 residents. One person died (from toxic gases that built up where he was sleeping).

By June, after six terrifying months, the eruption was finally over. Some islanders moved back home, but about a third never returned—they'd forged new lives on the mainland, or they didn't want to live in fear of another eruption.

Although the volcano caused great disruption, it also had some positive effects. Geothermal heat from the earth allowed the islanders to heat their water for a few years, with pipes running underneath the new lava (these days, they're back to electricity and oil). Tephra from the eruption was useful for road building and paving. Most importantly, the eruption didn't close off the island's harbor, but did helpfully narrow the harbor mouth enough to make it a much more sheltered anchorage. For better or for worse, the 1973 eruption shaped the Westman Islands that you're visiting today.

craggy horizontal walls, and you may spot some surefooted sheep grazing at the top. Hardy islanders race each other to the top of this cliff, using specially placed ladders; the record is 13 minutes. For us mortals, it's more like 45 minutes up, 25 minutes down...but only if you're in great shape—it's fearsomely steep and only for adventurous, dedicated climbers.

• *Let's head back into town. Retrace your steps back up to and through the fortress, then take the stairs down to the path on the water side of the big, white water tanks. Walk around the tanks and then keep going to...*

Vestmannaeyjar's Harbor: Stroll along the busy waterfront, peering into warehouses and onto ship decks. You'll bear left, then

right, to circle around the inner harbor, where smaller boats moor. This area, called Bæjarbryggjan ("Town Wharf"), was built in 1907, around the time motorized fishing arrived in the Westman Islands. It was later expanded, and eventually modern docks were built on the far side of the harbor.

Soon you'll reach a little skate park under a mural, with WCs nearby. Straight ahead are the sales kiosks for the various bus and boat tours (see "Helpful Hints," earlier). The ferry dock back to the mainland is just a couple minutes' walk past the ticket offices.

• *Our walk has come nearly full-circle. From here, you can browse tour options or head back up into town for lunch. Before leaving town, be sure to visit your choice of Vestmannaeyjar's three museums, described in the next section.*

Sights on Heimaey Island

Vestmannaeyjar's three museums collaborate on a 3,200-ISK combination ticket, which basically gives you the third museum for free if you visit the Volcano Museum (Eldheimar) plus one of the others. Save walking by seeing the town museum (Sagnheimar) and the Volcano Museum consecutively; extend this trip farther by walking from the Volcano Museum up the path to the summit of Eldfell volcano. Note that specific opening hours tend to change slightly from year to year; ask at the TI for the latest.

▲▲▲Volcano Museum (Eldheimar)

This museum tells the story of the 1973 Eldfell eruption, which destroyed half the town and has been an inseparable part of the islands' image ever since. The vivid exhibits are well-described by the included audioguide. The centerpiece of the museum is an actual house, half-immersed in lava rock.

Cost and Hours: 2,300 ISK; daily 10:30-18:00; mid-Oct-April Wed-Sun 13:00-17:00, closed Mon-Tue, or by arrangement; Gerðisbraut 10, tel. 488-2700, www.eldheimar.is.

Getting There: The museum is about a 20-minute, moderately uphill walk from the harbor; follow the red lampposts, and look for the boxy, rust-colored building on the hillside. It's about 10 min-

WESTMAN ISLANDS

utes uphill from Sagnheimar, the town museum; to walk between the two, take the street called Birkihlíð.

Visiting the Museum: The museum is built over the excavated remains of a house that was buried (but didn't burn) in the eruption. Guðni Ólafsson and Gerður Sigurðardóttir and their three young sons lived in the one-story, ranch-style house, which had just been finished two years before. Their home—now windowless, with its roof propped up by steel supports, and its contents left in disarray as they were found—is the highlight of the museum. You can't go in the ruin, but joysticks and monitors allow you to control cameras and investigate remotely. The oft-heard label "Pompeii of the North" is a bit of an exaggeration, but it's definitely a one-of-a-kind sight.

From there, the audioguide takes you around the seven stages of the exhibit in about 20 minutes. You'll learn about the town be-

fore, during, and after the eruption, with striking photographs and gripping (if grainy) television footage. In one exhibit, you can turn a giant wheel to watch the eruption slowly progress on a virtual map of the island. In another, you'll learn about the exhausting excavation of the town—as mountains of tephra had to be shoveled and trucked away. If you have time, there's also a 50-minute documentary film. And upstairs, you'll find good views over the house stuck in lava, a café, and a less engaging exhibit on the Surtsey eruption of 1963-1967 (also explained by the audioguide).

▲▲Aquarium (Sæheimar)

The island's lively little aquarium and natural history museum (called Sæheimar) has three rooms of exhibits. The first has stuffed birds and fish. The second room has a dozen tanks with changing local fish on display, and a touch tank with crabs, starfish, and shellfish. The third room has a rock collection and a replica of a bird cliff. But the star attraction is the opportunity to meet the town mascot, a real-life puffin named Tóti.

Cost and Hours: 1,200 ISK; daily 10:00-17:00; Oct-April Sat only 13:00-16:00, closed Sun-Fri; Heiðarvegur 12, tel. 481-1997, mobile tel. 863-8228, www.saeheimar.is.

Visiting the Museum: The museum's accidental celebrity is **Tóti**, a tame puffin who has lived here since August 2011. (Puffins usually live for 20-30 years.) He roams the aquarium freely, usually followed by a staff member who ensures his safety and cleans up after him. Visitors are welcome to take photos of him (no flash), but only the museum staff are allowed to hold him—due partly to the sensitive oils in his feathers. Tóti sometimes takes a midday rest, so there's no guarantee you'll see him, but it's likely.

Tóti is just one of many puffins who have passed through this museum. Puffins nest in burrows on the steep grassy slopes just above cliff edges. Every August, when the baby puffins raised on the island that summer are ready to take flight for the South Atlantic, some of them are distracted by the lights of the town and land in the streets. Traditionally, the island children collect the pufflings and bring them to the museum, which keeps them overnight and then releases them at an appropriate spot by the sea. Cute photographs all over the museum show local kids with the baby birds they brought in. Tóti himself was once one of these birds, but the museum staff judged him too small and weak to survive if released—so he was allowed to stay.

▲Town Museum (Sagnheimar)

This endearing museum has an eclectic array of exhibits about various facets of local history and culture. While a bit less engaging than the Volcano Museum or Tóti the puffin, it's well-done, insightful, and worth visiting if you have time.

Cost and Hours: 1,000 ISK; daily 10:00-17:00, Oct-April Sat only 13:00-16:00, closed Sun-Fri, or by appointment—don't hesitate to e-mail; Ráðhúströð, at the upper end of the Bárustígur main drag, on the second floor in the same building as the town library; tel. 488-2045, www.sagnheimar.is.

Visiting the Museum: Head upstairs, buy your ticket, and take a counterclockwise loop through the circular floor plan. First you'll learn about the 1973 eruption, including video interviews with local residents (English subtitles). The next section has photos of the roughly 200 islanders who converted to the Mormon Church in the mid-1800s and emigrated to Utah, and an illustrated retelling of the 1627 "Turkish Raid" on the islands (in which pirates kidnapped over 200 islanders and took them away to slavery in Algeria). Next you'll learn about the Danish governor who started a local militia in the 1850s—in this country without an army—to defend the islands against further attacks.

The back of the museum features an exhibit about the history of the annual Þjóðhátíð National Festival held in August, including some of the outrageous costumes the revelers wear. Then you'll loop around to a long exhibit about the fishing industry that is at the heart of Westman Island life, with a reconstructed 1924 town pier, a 1970s fishermen's dorm (with pinup girls and vintage rock 'n' roll), a poignant "in memoriam" wall honoring fishermen who have been lost at sea, and a seasickness-inducing video showing a fishing trawler navigating insanely rough seas, practically going airborne as the crew struggle to haul in their catch.

Climbing Up Eldfell Volcano

It's relatively straightforward to walk up to the summit of Eldfell (ELD-fehtl), the volcano that emerged in the 1973 eruption. The

simplest way is to follow the short path that starts a bit above the Volcano Museum (20-30 minutes up), by a small parking lot. You can also walk directly through the lava from downtown, starting at the stairway up into the lava from the end of Miðstræti (at the corner of Kirjustræti; this area is also de-scribed on my self-guided walk). The ground at the summit gets a bit cooler every year, and it has become difficult to boil an egg or bake bread or potatoes right on the lava. However, locals report that you can still make a chocolate or a cheese fondue. Via a different path, it's also easy to reach the center of the crater, which is marked by a large cross.

Driving Tour of the Island

With a car, you can take an easy spin around the island of Heimaey. The entire loop takes about a half-hour with no stops, but allow an hour or two at a leisurely pace, with plenty of photo stops for views of Westman islets and happy, roaming sheep grazing on scrubby groundcover. Once you leave town, you won't see much civilization. Heimaey once had several farms, but they have not been worked since the eruption, except for a bit of hobby farming.

• *From town, loop west to...*

Herjólfsdalur: This val-ley, surrounded by a cirque of mountains, is the site of the Þjóðhátíð (National Festival) held each August. There's not much to do at other times, but it's a dramatic setting. Look for the stage (which benefits from the acoustics of the mountain bowl) and the pulpit-like spot where bonfires are lit. The area also has a golf course and a campsite. The cliffs over the little, jagged inlet on the western side of the meadow is a good place to look for puffins in the summer. If you have time, a lovely walking path leads south from Herjólfsdalur along the island's western shore.

• *Drive south toward the island's southern point, Stórhöfði. Along the way are some prime...*

Offshore Island Views: The best views of the other (uninhabited) Westman Islands, worth ▲, are from the road that runs

south between Herjólfsdalur and Stórhöfði. Nobody lives on any of these islands full-time, but island men join together in fraternity-like clubs that own them. Each club builds and maintains a hut on its island—and some huts are quite elaborate. Locals go to the outer islands mostly to harvest seabird eggs.

The most distant of the smaller islands—which you can just barely see on the horizon, on very clear days—is Surtsey, which rose from the sea in a long eruption, lasting from 1963 to 1967, that attracted attention from around the world. Surtsey has been left alone and landing is forbidden, although scientists visit it regularly to follow along with the plants that colonize it and the wave erosion that makes it a little smaller each year.

• *About 10 minutes after leaving Herjólfsdalur, you'll reach...*

Stórhöfði: This hilly knob of land was a separate island before the isthmus was created by the Helgafell eruption several thou-

sand years ago. The light-house has a weather station that regularly records the strongest winds in Iceland...and that's really saying something. Along the road up to the light-house is a bird-watching blind where you can get a good view of the cliffs

where puffins nest in the summer (not visible from the road, just a two-minute walk over a ridge—the path out to it is marked, and starts by signs at a hairpin bend; be sure to close the windows when you're finished).

• *From here it's another 10 minutes back to town.*

Sleeping on Heimaey Island

All of these options are within a 10-minute walk of the harbor. Hotel prices on the island are low by Icelandic standards.

$$ Hótel Vestmannaeyjar is the big, well-established hotel in town, a few short blocks away from the harbor, with 43 predictable rooms, an onsite restaurant, an elevator, and an indoor sauna and hot tubs in the basement that are free for guests (Vestmannabraut 28, tel. 481-2900, www.hotelvestmannaeyjar.is, booking@hotelvestmannaeyjar.is).

$$ Hótel Eyjar ("Islands") is loosely run, but has a great location steps from the harbor, at the beginning of the shopping street. More of a guesthouse than a true hotel, it fills the two floors above the Eymundsson bookstore with 20 rooms with private baths (lots of stairs, Bárustígur 2, tel. 481-3636, www.hoteleyjar.is, info@hoteleyjar.is).

$-$$ Guesthouse Hamar, also close to the harbor, has 14 rooms with private bath at reasonable prices. It's also home to the "Puffin Nest"—40 capsule-like dormitory pods in a cavernous room with shared bath, which offers a little extra privacy over a hostel dorm (Herjólfsgata 4, 481-3400, www.guesthousehamar.is, info@guesthousehamar.is).

¢ The official **Sunnuhóll Youth Hostel,** with 25 beds, is actually the back wing of the Hótel Vestmannaeyjar. The six rooms share two sets of bathroom facilities and a kitchen (laundry facilities, Vestmannabraut 28, tel. 481-2900, www.hostel.is, vestmannaeyjar@hostel.is).

¢ Aska Hostel, with 33 beds in rooms of two to eight beds each, is situated on the little shopping street, in the same building as the recommended Gott restaurant (Bárustígur 11, mobile tel. 662 7266, www.askahostel.is, info@askahostel.is).

Eating on Heimaey Island

The Westman Islands are a good place to eat. Most mid-priced restaurants generally charge the same prices at lunch and dinner, and you can easily get a good, square meal for 2,500-3,000 ISK at any time of day. At nicer restaurants, it's smart to reserve for dinner. The island's restaurants don't serve puffin (breeding populations are low) or other seabirds.

$$$ Slippurinn ("The Shipyard") is the town's top restaurant and a mecca for foodies—offering Reykjavík quality at Reykjavík prices. Run by a respected chef who prides himself on mingling authentic traditions with modern cookery, it has a tempting menu of perfectly executed classic dishes. Its long, well-worn tables and other funky mismatched furniture fill a big, open, industrial-mod space a block above the harbor. It's most affordable at lunch, with a fish of the day for under 3,000 ISK, but prices rise substantially at dinner—when you might want to splurge on a blowout fixed-price dinner. Reservations are recommended (May-mid-Sept daily 12:00-14:30 & 17:00-22:00, Strandvegur 76, tel. 481-1515, www. slippurinn.com).

$$ Gott ("Good"), on the little shopping street, is small, tasteful, and casual (but with table service). They do fish, chicken, burgers, and sandwiches at competitive prices (Sun-Thu 11:30-21:00, Fri-Sat until 22:00, Bárustígur 11, tel. 481-3060).

$$ Tanginn ("The Spit"), at the harbor, has a great view of the cliffs and the fishing boats. Choose between the fish of the day, ribs, a whale steak, or—for the budget-conscious—burgers, soup, or salad (kitchen open Sun-Wed 11:30-14:00 & 18:00-21:00, Thu-Sat until 22:00, Básaskersbryggja 8, tel. 414-4420).

$$ Fiskibarinn ("Fish Bar") is a casual fish place, which doubles as a fresh fish shop. Go to the counter and choose your fish, which will be cooked up with vegetables and potatoes or rice and served in the pan (daily 11:00-22:00, Oct-April until 21:00, Skólavegur 1, a couple blocks up from the harbor at the corner of Vestmannabraut, tel. 414-3999).

Local Craft Beer: The Brothers Brewery, which makes their own microbrews right here on Heimaey, also runs a taphouse on the main street (Tue-Wed 16:00-21:00, Thu-Sat until 23:00, closed Sun-Mon, in the strip mall at Vesturvegur 5, tel. 571-5510).

Cheap Eats: There's a **Subway** on Bárustígur downtown with cheap fresh sandwiches. The **Bónus supermarket** is at Miðstræti 20, near the harbor (open daily until about 18:00). The **Krónan supermarket** right along the harbor has slightly longer hours.

Breakfast: Most planes from Reykjavík land before restaurants open. For a breakfast on arrival, **Stofan Bakhús** ("Living Room Bakery")—right along the main street—serves coffee and good pastries (daily until 18:00, Bárustígur 7, tel. 481-2424).

WESTMAN ISLANDS

WEST ICELAND

Vesturland

To round out your look at Iceland without straying too far from the capital region, head north from Reykjavík to West Iceland (Vesturland). A day trip here is more low-key than to the Golden Circle or the South Coast. The area is farming country—more sedate, thinly settled, and a bit more refined. There are fewer tourists, partly because the sights are less spectacular. But there are definitely some exciting natural wonders, as well as enjoyable attractions for those with a healthy interest in the early Icelandic sagas. And if you're heading around the Ring Road, you'll pass through this area regardless; consider pausing to take in the sights.

The heart of the region, called Borgarfjörður (BOR-gar-FYUR-thur), stretches from the waters of its namesake estuary up past thousand-year-old lava flows to Iceland's second-largest glacier, Langjökull. I've organized this chapter into four sections: a driving tour of the region; Borgarnes, the main town, with a striking setting on a peninsula in the middle of the fjord; a hike up the volcanic Grábrók crater; and the area around Reykholt, with sights and accommodations scattered across a broad valley a 45-minute drive east of Borgarnes.

As a Day Trip: You can visit West Iceland on your own by car (following the driving tour outlined in this chapter), or with a bus excursion. The major excursion bus companies offer day trips to the Víðgelmir lava-tube cave that include some, but not all, of the sights listed in this chapter (see list of tour companies on page 160).

As an Overnight: Accommodations in this area tend to be reasonably priced. In this chapter, I recommend staying in one of three areas: in Borgarnes, near Grábrók crater, or in and near Reykholt.

Sleeping here is particularly smart if you're continuing farther north along the Ring Road and want to see the region in depth. Some people stay in West Iceland on their first night in Iceland—bypassing Reykjavík and getting a head start on their trip around the Ring. (Borgarnes is less than two hours' drive from Keflavík Airport.)

Name Note: Pay attention if you are using GPS to navigate: Iceland has two towns that go by the name of Reykholt—one here in West Iceland, and the other about 100 miles away, near the Golden Circle.

West Iceland Driving Tour

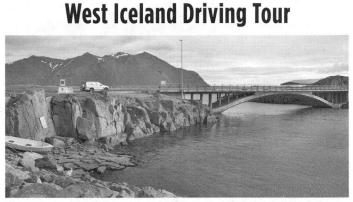

This self-guided itinerary assumes you're seeing West Iceland's highlights as a day trip from Reykjavík. Budget about 10 hours (about half of that is driving). Start by driving an hour along highway 1 to the town of Borgarnes for some sightseeing, detour up to Grábrók crater, then continue over to the area around Reykholt, where you'll do a circuit of the area's sights, before heading back to Reykjavík along highways 520 and 47 (a slower but more scenic return).

PLANNING YOUR DRIVE

The following plan is minimalistic; it assumes that you'll just visit the town of Borgarnes, Grábrók crater, and a few easy sights in and around Reykholt. To adjust this plan, see the tips on the next page.

9:00   Drive north from Reykjavík to the town of Borgarnes on highway 1 (1 hour)

10:00   Walk around Borgarnes; tour the Settlement Centre

11:30   Head to Grábrók crater (30 minutes) and climb to the top and back; have a picnic lunch there or eat at the Hreðavatnsskáli roadhouse café

13:30   Drive to Deildartunguhver hot springs (30 minutes) for a quick look

14:15   Drive from the hot springs to Hraunfossar and
        Barnafoss waterfalls (20 minutes); see the falls
15:00   Take scenic highways 520 and 47 back to Reykjavík,
        arriving back a little after 17:00

West Iceland Tips

Other Sights in the Area: There's plenty more to see beyond my suggested plan above. You can mix and match, depending on your interests, and the weather and road conditions. Historians can focus on the good museums in Borgarnes as well as the modestly interesting church complex at Reykholt. Outdoorsy travelers can spelunk through an underground lava-tube cave at Víðgelmir (it's best to book ahead). Hot-spring enthusiasts may want to check out the new premium thermal bath (Krauma) at Deildartunguhver. Families can add a visit to the Háafell Goat Farm (fun for kids and livestock lovers). Note: To add more sights—especially the Víðgelmir lava tube—you'll need to set out earlier, return later, skip something else, or stay overnight. You can shave off a half-hour by returning on highway 1 instead of the scenic route.

Doing the Route in Reverse: It's worth considering driving the route in the reverse direction from what I've described. Indoor sights here open at 10:00; if you're getting an early start (i.e., leaving Reykjavík around 8:00), you might as well take the scenic route on your way up, while you're fresh.

Weather and Road Conditions: As elsewhere in Iceland, check the weather forecast and road conditions before you head out—strong winds occasionally close highway 1 between Reykjavík and Borgarnes. Note that the scenic route from the Reykholt area back to Reykjavík (highways 520/47) is more difficult to drive, with long stretches curling around dramatic fjords, and short stretches on rough, unpaved roads—including one over a low mountain pass. Faint-hearted drivers should stick to highway 1. Before you go, double-check road conditions at Road.is.

West Iceland Route Overview

This section outlines the driving directions and various route options for your West Iceland drive. Recommended sights, restaurants, and hotels along this driving route are described later in the chapter.

FROM REYKJAVÍK TO BORGARNES

This route takes you north via highway 1 and the Hvalfjörður tunnel. It's a bit over an hour's drive to Borgarnes.

• *Leave Reykjavík on highway 1 to the north, following signs for* Borgarnes, Akureyri, *and* 1n.

As you leave the city, you pass under **Esja,** the mountain that shadows the city to the north, and you'll see the parking lot for hikers climbing the peak. As you round the mountain, you'll see some of the city's chicken hatcheries to your left. A little farther on, an intriguing stone structure is actually just the retaining wall for a pig farm. You'll pass Kjalarnes, a small suburban community. Strong winds are frequent along the road here. Soon after, you'll enter the two-lane, 3.5-mile-long tunnel that passes beneath the fjord. (If you prefer to take the scenic route around the fjord—highways 47 and 520—on your way up, turn off on the right just before the tunnel entrance.)

Finished in 1998, **Hvalfjörður tunnel** cut the travel time from Reykjavík to Borgarnes and Akureyri by almost two hours. Before that, you had to drive all the way around the fjord (on what is now highway 47). While the tunnel area is not actively volcanic, the undersea rock is warm (up to 135°F near its south end). If your car's controls show the outside temperature, notice how the south end of the tunnel is several degrees warmer than the north end. Watch your speed in the tunnel: The speed limit is 70 km/h, and monitored by cameras. You'll pay the tunnel toll on the north side, as you exit (1,000 ISK; for tunnel info see www.spolur.is).

• *At the roundabout just after the tunnel, go right, continuing to follow signs for* Borgarnes *and* Akureyri. *(Going left would bring you to Akranes, a relatively large but skippable town of 6,000 people, many of whom work in the fish processing industry or in the nearby metal smelters.)*

In a few minutes, you'll pass two huge **metal smelters** at Grundartangi. The green-and-brown one produces ferrosilicon, the blue one aluminum. A third smelter, producing silicon for the solar power industry, may be operational by the time of your visit. Smelters need to be along the coast, as ships bring in the raw ore (such as bauxite for making aluminum) and carry the finished product to market. This is an efficient way of putting Iceland's electricity surplus to use, and the smelters do create jobs (though they require a relatively small crew).

You'll now cross a low-lying, thinly settled plain between two mountains: **Akrafjall** on your left, and **Hafnarfjall** (HAHP-nahr-FYAHTL) to your right. On a clear day, you might be able to see the mountains of the Snæfellsnes Peninsula far ahead of you. Farther right past Hafnarfjall is another mountain, **Skarðsheiði,**

West Iceland

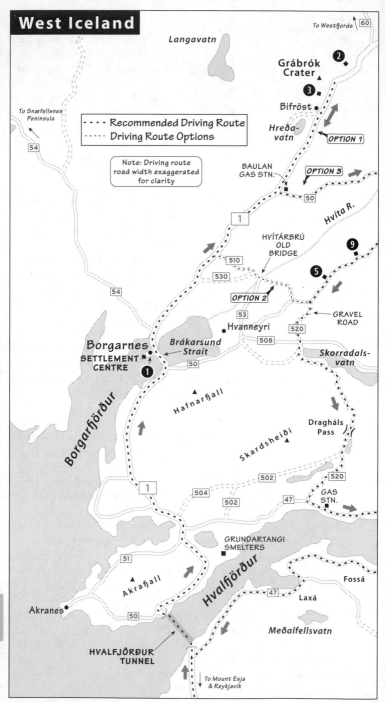

To Westfjords 60

Langavatn

Grábrók Crater ❷

❸

Bifröst

Hreða-vatn

OPTION 1

- - - - Recommended Driving Route

- - - - Driving Route Options

Note: Driving route road width exaggerated for clarity

To Snæfellsnes Peninsula

54

BAULAN GAS STN.

OPTION 3

50

Hvíta R.

1

HVÍTÁRBRÚ OLD BRIDGE

510

530

❾

❺

OPTION 2

GRAVEL ROAD

54

53

Hvanneyri

520

508

Skorradals-vatn

Borgarnes

Brákarsund Strait

SETTLEMENT CENTRE ❶

50

Borgarfjörður

▲ Hafnarfjall

▲ Skardsheiði

Dragháls Pass

502

520

504

502

47

GAS STN.

1

Hvalfjörður

51

GRUNDARTANGI SMELTERS

Fossá

▲ Akrafjall

47

Laxá

Akranes

50

Meðalfellsvatn

HVALFJÖRÐUR TUNNEL

To Mount Esja & Reykjavík

WEST ICELAND

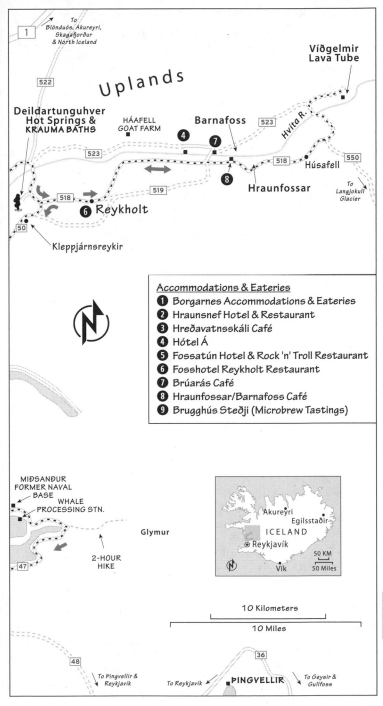

To Blönduós, Akureyri, Skagafjörður & North Iceland

1

522

U p l a n d s

Víðgelmir Lava Tube

Deildartunguhver Hot Springs & KRAUMA BATHS

HÁAFELL GOAT FARM

Barnafoss

523

Hvíta R.

4

7

523

518

Húsafell

550

8

To Langjökull Glacier

518

519

Hraunfossar

6 Reykholt

50

Kleppjárnsreykir

N

Accommodations & Eateries

1 Borgarnes Accommodations & Eateries
2 Hraunsnef Hotel & Restaurant
3 Hreðavatnsskáli Café
4 Hótel Á
5 Fossatún Hotel & Rock 'n' Troll Restaurant
6 Fosshotel Reykholt Restaurant
7 Brúarás Café
8 Hraunfossar/Barnafoss Café
9 Brugghús Steðji (Microbrew Tastings)

MIÐSANDUR FORMER NAVAL BASE

WHALE PROCESSING STN.

Glymur

47

2-HOUR HIKE

ICELAND

Akureyri

Egilsstaðir

⊕ Reykjavík

N

50 KM

Vík

50 Miles

10 Kilometers

10 Miles

48

To Þingvellir & Reykjavík

To Reykjavík

36

ÞINGVELLIR

To Geysir & Gullfoss

WEST ICELAND

More of West Iceland

There's more to West Iceland than what's covered here, including the heavily marketed Snæfellsnes Peninsula and the Westfjords—both of which are scenic but farther afield from Reykjavík and the Ring Road. If you want to visit either, here are some tips:

The **Snæfellsnes Peninsula** (the middle of the three peninsulas extending west off the coast of Iceland) is too far from Reykjavík for an easy day trip by car. It is picturesque in parts, but doesn't quite make it into the "best of Iceland." If you're set on seeing it, wait for good weather and relax on a 12-hour bus tour of the peninsula from Reykjavík, most of which will be spent on board. Or go by rental car and build in an overnight (Stykkishólmur is the most interesting town). The peninsula is notable for several pretty mountains: Kirkjufell, near Grundarfjörður, is a much-photographed mountain peak. Snæfellsjökull, the mountain at the end of the peninsula, is capped by a tiny glacier. On clear days, you can see Snæfellsjökull from Reykjavík by looking to the northwest, past the tip of the peninsula. The mountain rises mirage-like from the Atlantic—Reykjavík's answer to Seattle's Mount Rainier.

Farther north, the **Westfjords** are interesting but cumbersome to visit on a short trip. The largest town in the Westfjords, Ísafjörður, is about a six-hour drive from Reykjavík. Other worthwhile spots include the half-deserted town of Flateyri (now protected by a huge earthen berm after a deadly avalanche in 1995), the bird cliffs at Látrabjarg, and the island of Flatey (between Snæfellsnes and the Westfjords). Some roads here are unsurfaced. There's plenty to do and see, but the area is just too far out of the way unless you're spending at least a couple of weeks in Iceland.

---

which under snow cover looks like a meringue chopped into great wavy peaks.

The road curls around the left side of Hafnarfjall; this stretch is subject to frequent high winds. Soon you're driving along the base of vast gravel slopes that tumble down from Hafnarfjall. You'll see many small islands in Borgarfjörður, the fjord to your left.

Eventually the town of **Borgarnes** will come into view, and the road will bend left and cross a causeway and bridge into the town.

FROM BORGARNES TO THE REYKHOLT AREA

When you're ready to continue toward the Reykholt area, you have three options: In good weather, hikers will want to head up to the Grábrók volcanic crater, then loop back down toward Reykholt. (All together, Grábrók adds about 1.5 hours, including the drive and time to hike up to the crater, but not lunch.) If the weather's too cold or windy to hike to the crater, you could skip Grábrók and take the scenic route to the Reykholt area over the old bridge called Hvítárbrú. Or take the quicker route through Baulan.

Each of these options takes you to Deildartunguhver hot springs—the first of the Reykholt-area sights described later in this chapter. Notice that no single route connects all of your choices in the Reykholt area; you'll make one or more loops to connect them, via paved highway 518 and unpaved highways 519, 523, and 550. The recommended Brúarás Café, more or less at the center of the Reykholt sights, is a great all-purpose stop for a snack, drink, or meal; they're also happy to answer questions about this area.

For any of these, you'll begin by heading north from Borgarnes on highway 1, following signs toward *Akureyri*.

Option 1, Recommended Detour to Grábrók Crater (50 minutes): From Borgarnes, head up highway 1 about 30 minutes; you can't miss the crater, on the left side of the road. After visiting, return south and backtrack on highway 1 about 10 minutes; look for a small ÓB gas station (called Baulan). Turn left here onto highway 50, then drive another 15 minutes until you see a small turnoff to the right marked *Deildartunguhver*. (If you get to the junction with highway 518, you've gone a half-mile too far.)

Option 2, Skipping Grábrók, via Hvítárbrú Bridge (40 minutes): This pleasant route crosses bridges that don't allow trucks or buses. From Borgarnes, drive north along highway 1 for about 10 minutes, turning right on highway 510 (signposted *Hvanneyri)*, a potholed gravel road. (If you're using Google Maps, note that it mislabels this road as highway 53.) Drive slowly. Soon you'll cross a stream on wooden bridges and pass a farm called Ferjukot.

Then the old bridge called **Hvítárbrú** comes into view. This arched concrete bridge was built in 1928. The main route between Reykjavík and Borgarnes passed over it until the Borgarfjörður causeway was finished in 1983. The bridge has one narrow lane; before driving over, scan the far bank to make sure no one is coming toward you.

After crossing, follow signs for *Reykholt,* continuing along highway 510 and then turning north onto highway 50. Along the way, you'll pass **Fossatún** (with the recommended Rock 'n' Troll restaurant; described later) and the **Brugghús Steðji** ("Anvil") microbrewery (no meals, Mon-Sat 13:00-17:00, closed Sun, tel. 896-5001). Just after the greenhouse village of **Kleppjárnsreykir,** near the junction of highways 50 and

518, turn left to stay on highway 50. After a minute or two, turn left at the sign for *Deildartunguhver*.

Option 3, Easier Route, via Highway 1 and Highway 50 (30 minutes): If crossing antique one-lane bridges makes you faint of heart, you can just drive north from Borgarnes about 20 minutes along highway 1 to the junction with highway 50, at the Baulan ÓB gas station; turn right here and drive 15 minutes until you see the small turnoff to the right marked *Deildartunguhver*.

FROM REYKHOLT TO REYKJAVÍK

To head back south to Reykjavík, you have two choices. Off-season, or in doubtful weather, play it safe and loop back south along highway 50 to return the way you came: on highway 1, past Hafnarfjall and Akrafjall mountains, and through the tunnel (about 1.5 hours).

In decent weather (generally May-Sept), I'd take the scenic route via the Draghals pass and Hvalfjörður. From Reykholt, this adds about 30 minutes to your trip (2 hours to Reykjavík). It comes with some unpaved stretches (including a gravel pass that rises to several hundred feet above sea level). But the payoff is that Hvalfjörður feels more off-the-beaten-track than other day-trip destinations from Reykjavík, and comes with many fine views.

• *From Reykholt, drive south on highway 50, then turn off onto gravel highway 520.*

This road parallels **Skorradalsvatn,** a good fishing lake where you'll see many summer cottages. Then it climbs over the low **Draghals** pass to the east of the Hafnarfjall mountain system. Drive slowly and carefully, watching for potholes. Skirting a couple of small lakes, the road ultimately descends to **Hvalfjörður** ("Whale Fjord"), which you earlier traversed by undersea tunnel.

• *Where the road tees, you'll hit paved highway 47. Turn left, passing a tiny gas station (called Ferstikla) with a café that may be open in summer.*

Take Highway 47 all the way around the fjord (a pretty drive that also saves you the tunnel toll). After about five minutes, you'll pass the old Allied naval installation at **Miðsandur** (the only signpost you'll see reads *Hjálmsstaðir*). The Nissen huts and camp here are Iceland's best-preserved WWII-era buildings. The fjord here is quite deep. As the oil tanks on the far hillside suggest, this was a refueling station for ships, especially those traveling from North America to Murmansk in northern Russia. They could dock at two piers on either side of the camp.

After the war, the naval station was converted into a whale-processing facility. Today, slaughtered whales are still brought ashore at the eastern pier and processed in the buildings against the hillside. Iceland's whaling company also owns the camp area. Everything is fenced off and signs make it clear that they don't want you poking around (the station has been a target of animal-rights activists).

Highway 47 reaches the east end of the fjord (a small road here leads to the beginning of a challenging, two-hour hike to a high, pretty waterfall called Glymur). Next, the road doubles back along the south shore of the fjord. It crosses two rivers with fine waterfalls: **Fossá** (with a tiny, old, stone sheep pen next to the falls) and—farther along (next to the turnoff for road 48 to Þingvellir)—the low and beautiful **Laxá**. Unless it's fogged in, you'll be able to spot the metal smelters at Grundartangi on the far side of the fjord.

Ponder that until 1998, when the tunnel under Hvalfjörður was finished, this was the main road from Reykjavík to the north.

• *After about 35 minutes, you'll wind back to highway 1 near the south tunnel entrance, and turn toward Reykjavík, another 30 minutes away.*

Borgarnes

A pleasant town of approximately 2,000 people about an hour from Reykjavík, Borgarnes (BOHR-gahr-NESS) is the main hub of

West Iceland. The town is set on a rocky peninsula jutting out into the estuary formed by the region's several rivers, which merge near here (calling it a "fjord" is generous). A bridge and causeway, built in the early 1980s, cross the mouth of the estuary. Across the water from town, Hafnarfjall mountain—with its steep scree slopes—is an impressive sight.

Borgarnes was an important spot in the earliest days of Icelandic settlement. According to the sagas, this area was home to the early settler Skalla-Grímur Kveldúlfsson ("Grímur the Bald"; for background on the sagas, see page 106). After a bloody feud with Norwegian King Harald Fairhair, Skalla-Grímur fled Norway and sailed to Iceland. His father died on the journey, and—following

Viking Age custom—Skalla-Grímur dropped his casket in the sea, then built his settlement where it washed ashore...at a place now called Borg, on the outskirts of Borgarnes. Skalla-Grímur lived out his days here, where he raised his son Egill Skallagrímsson (pronounced AY-ihtl). An even more dynamic figure than his father, Egill was ugly and passionate—equal parts battler and bard—and the protagonist of some of Iceland's most colorful Settlement Age stories (now recounted in the town's Settlement Centre). For those intrigued by the sagas, Borgarnes is a fun place to visit.

Arrival in Borgarnes: As you cross the causeway, you'll pass the recommended Geirabakarí bakery (on the left). Just beyond, at the town's main road junction, the N1 gas station also houses a free WC, the town's bus station, and an expensive café and convenience store (long hours daily). Next door to the N1 complex is a Nettó supermarket, with the town **TI** inside (open daily in summer, off-season closed Sat-Sun; tel. 437-2214).

Turn left off the main road to reach the old part of town. The small park on your right has a few parking spaces where you can leave your car. Better yet, drive another couple of minutes down the main road to the Settlement Centre, which has a parking lot.

Sights in Borgarnes

▲Borgarnes Town Orientation

Get your bearings with this town orientation, either on foot or as you drive through. Start from the small park called **Skallagríms-garður** ("Park of Grímur the Bald")—with a few picnic tables—just off the main road from the top of the old town. The park is on the site of a burial mound thought to be Skalla-Grímur's tomb. Down the side street next to the park (to the right from the main road) is Borgarnes' good, large, outdoor **swimming pool,** which has fine sea views.

Continue a little farther down the main road. If you were to veer a couple of blocks to the left (down Bjarnarbraut), you'd find Borgarnes' **local museum,** which tells the 20th-century history of Iceland from a child's perspective (1,200 ISK, daily 13:00-17:00, likely closed off-season—but ask at the library upstairs if they'll open it for you, Bjarnarbraut 4—look for a big red building marked *museum,* tel. 433-7200, www.safnahus.is).

At the end of town—just before the bridge—is the **Settlement Centre** (described on the next page).

Capping the hill above the Settlement Centre, look for a monument called **Brákin,** which resembles a giant wheel with wings. It's an easy hike up to the monument, which offers nice views over the town, estuary, and Hafnarfjall mountain. The monument honors Egill's nanny and de facto mother, a Celtic woman named

Þorgerður Brák. According to the sagas, when an adolescent Egill angered his father during a game, Skalla-Grímur was about to beat the boy...likely to death. Brák stood up to Skalla-Grímur, who—now completely forgetting his son and furious with his servant—chased her to the top of this hill, where she leapt into the bay. Skalla-Grímur threw a giant stone at Brák, killing her in the water. Today the strait between Borgarnes and the mountain is still known as Brákarsund.

From the Settlement Centre, you can cross a bridge to the little island called **Brákarey,** home to Borgarnes's tiny, not-very-good harbor. Borgarnes is one of a very few coastal towns in Iceland that did not form as a fishing center, and remains home to a mix of services and light industry.

Between the Settlement Centre and the Brákarey bridge, a little parking lot offers access to a pleasant waterfront trail. The path arcs around **Englishmen's Cove** (Englendingavík) on the sleepy back side of the peninsula, where Englishmen reportedly lived during the Settlement Age. After passing a nice beach (and a recommended restaurant), the trail eventually leads to the town's playing fields and swimming pool. From here, you'll enjoy glorious views of the island and the mountains beyond.

▲Settlement Centre (Landnámssetur)

This modest yet thoughtfully presented sight is Borgarnes' best-known attraction and one of the prime places in Iceland to learn about the Settlement Age; for history buffs, it's worth ▲▲. The center has two exhibits: one (upstairs) explaining how Iceland was discovered and settled, and the other (downstairs) retelling the grisly Egill's Saga, which took place in and around Borgarnes. Each takes 30 minutes to see with the good, included audioguide.

Cost and Hours: Both exhibits-2,500 ISK, one exhibit-1,900 ISK, daily 10:00-21:00, Brákarbraut 13, Borgarnes, tel. 437-1600, www.landnam.is.

Visiting the Museum: The upstairs exhibit ponders the questions of why and how Viking Age **settlers** first came to Iceland.

The exhibit is interactive: You can press buttons to light up the locations where various settlers first arrived, and stand on a Viking ship's prow as it rocks back and forth on the waves.

The downstairs exhibition on **Egill's Saga** illustrates that story, step by step, with interesting wooden figures and carvings by a local artist. Egill (c. 904-995) was a poet-warrior, mixing brutishness and sensitivity, who got into all sorts of trouble in both Iceland and Norway. He feuded with the king of Norway, wrangled with a witch, and married his foster sister (and brother's widow). After two of his sons died, Egill composed *Sonatorrek,* a moving lament that is among the most famous examples of Old Norse poetry. By the age of 80, Egill—now a sour old man—toyed with the idea of throwing his wealth of silver pieces into the assembled crowds at Þingvellir, simply to start a riot. Instead, like his father before him, he buried his treasure somewhere in the Borgarnes area...where today, some people still look for it. For more on Egill's story—and the rest of the sagas—see page 106.

Sleeping in Borgarnes

Borgarnes has a big, pricey hotel, but I prefer these more affordable B&Bs. Borgarnes Bed & Breakfast and Kría Guesthouse are conveniently located on a bluff overlooking Englishmen's Cove, on the quiet back edge of town. Egils Guesthouse and the hostel are right in the center.

$$ Borgarnes Bed & Breakfast, conscientiously run by Bertha and Ohioan Jay, rents eight modern, comfortable, bovine-themed rooms (most share bathrooms), and has an inviting breakfast room/lounge (Skúlagata 21, tel. 848-1129, www.borgarnesbb. is, info@borgarnesbb.is).

$$ Egils Guesthouse, less personal, rents rooms around town. Their Guesthouse Kaupangur, with a wonderfully central location above a café just up the stairs from the Settlement Centre, has five rooms—some with private bath. Across the street, tucked in a residential area, are a variety of studio apartments (breakfast extra, Brákarbraut 11, tel. 860-6655, www.egilsguesthouse.is, info@egilsguesthouse.is).

$ Kría Guesthouse has two spacious rooms that share a bathroom behind a beauty parlor (Kveldúlfsgata 310, tel. 437-1159, www.kriaguesthouse.is, info@kriaguesthouse.is).

¢ The **Borgarnes Hostel** is in the old town center, not far from the Settlement Centre (Borgarbraut 9, mobile tel. 695-3366, www. hostel.is, borgarnes@hostel.is).

Eating in Borgarnes

$$ The Settlement Centre has the most appealing restaurant in town (just upstairs from the exhibit). You can eat here even if you don't visit the museum itself. At lunch, they offer a good-value vegetarian buffet (daily until 15:00). It's a substantial spread—soup, salads, pasta and potato dishes, and fresh fruit—and worth planning ahead for. At dinner, the restaurant has affordable main courses and expensive three-course fixed-price meals (restaurant open daily 12:00-21:00, same phone and hours as museum).

$ Geirabakarí bakery, the first building on the Borgarnes side of the causeway, serves budget lunches—soup with bread, sandwiches, and the like—and has tables with great views of Hafnarfjall and the water (Mon-Fri 7:00-18:00, Sat-Sun 8:30-17:00, Digranesgata 6—look for the gray-and-orange building marked *HAGKAUP*, tel. 437-2020, www.geirabakari.is).

$$ Englendingavík ("Englishmen's Cove") is a classy-feeling place that overlooks a beachy cove, with a few outdoor tables. It's pricey by local standards, but scenic (daily 12:00-21:00, Skúlagata 17, tel. 840-0314, www.englendingavik.is).

Grábrók Crater

A half-hour north of Borgarnes, highway 1 curls around the pint-sized volcanic cone of Grábrók (GRAU-broke, literally "Gray-pants"). In good weather, hiking up to its rim is easy, fun, and worth ▲▲.

Watch for the parking lot on the left, just after you pass the crater. From here, a well-marked path leads up into the rim. You can climb to the top in about 15 minutes, and—if it's not too windy—stroll a path that circles the crater rim, which takes less than 10 minutes.

Grábrók was formed in an eruption about 2,000 to 3,000 years ago—around the time of the ancient Greeks and Romans—but there was no one here to see it. The beautiful lava field that you drive through just before reaching Grábrók flowed out in the same eruption. A thick layer of moss has grown on top of the lava, and changes color with the seasons.

From the top, enjoy stunning panoramas of the crater and the surrounding area. The classically conical mountain to the north is called Baula (BOY-la, which means "to moo"). Closer in, to the northwest, is a sinister, heavy-browed ridge called Hraunsnefsöxl. To the west, away from the road, is a second, similar-sized crater called Grábrókarfell. To the south (toward Borgarnes) is the campus of Bifröst, a small college originally founded to train managers for Iceland's network of cooperative stores (and here I was hoping to find the Bifröst of the sagas: the rainbow bridge leading to Asgard, home to Óðinn (Odin) and other gods).

Just past Bifröst is Hreðavatn, a pretty lake with a managed forest at the far end. In the valley around you are both working farms and summer houses, some of them quite lavish.

As you descend Grábrók, look down along the slope to your left. You'll see an odd stone structure with many compartments, which looks at first glance like it might be a prehistoric ruin. It's actually a set of crudely built pens for rounding up sheep each fall, and it's still in occasional use (it's called Brekkurétt; *rétt* is the word for a sheep pen). You can walk through it if you'd like. If you continue farther north on the Ring Road, you'll pass more elaborate, modern pens.

Sleeping and Eating near Grábrók: About five minutes past Grábrók crater, **$$ Hraunsnef** ("Lava Nose") country hotel is a classy compound with cottages, a restaurant, and 15 straightforward rooms in various buildings. As it's located just before the pass to the north, this place works well for those headed around the Ring Road (breakfast extra). The hotel's fancy **$$$ restaurant** offers pricey main dishes and more affordable burgers (daily 12:00-21:00, lunch served mid-May-Aug only, tel. 435-0111, www.hraunsnef.is, hraunsnef@hraunsnef.is).

Other eating options include **picnicking** at Grábrók, or the roadhouse café called **$ Hreðavatnsskáli,** run by an Icelandic-Swiss chef who makes his own pasta (nice, casual atmosphere, daily 8:00-22:00, just beneath Grábrók on the Reykjavík side, tel. 421-1939, www.grabrok.is).

Reykholt and Nearby

These sights fill the broad, sparsely populated valley of the Hvítá ("White River"), which flows from the Eiríksjökull glacier and empties into the estuary near Borgarnes. I've listed these roughly in order from west to east. Fitting all of these into a single day is doable but challenging; you're better off being selective.

▲Deildartunguhver Hot Springs

Stop for a few minutes at Europe's most powerful hot spring, which gushes out almost 50 gallons of boiling water per second. Located

off Highway 50 near Reykholt, here you'll see steaming fountains of hot water spurting up next to a colorful rock face. Signs warn you not to touch the water. The beige concrete building is a pumping station that sends the water through a big pipe to Borgarnes and Akranes for home heating and bathing.

You might find tomatoes from nearby greenhouses for sale from an honor box.

Deildartunguhver is the site of a brand-new premium thermal pool and bathing facility called **Krauma;** it's open year-round (tel. 555-6066, www.krauma.is).

Continuing to Reykholt: From Deildartunguhver, return to the main road, head a half-mile downhill on highway 50, and turn left on highway 518, following signs five minutes to *Reykholt*.

Reykholt

Reykholt, set bucolically in the center of the valley, is home to a religious and scholarly complex devoted to medieval studies. While

it's boring for some, those excited about medieval Iceland and the sagas rate it ▲ for the chance to see its historic church and tour its museum. Scholars come on retreats here to write and use the fine library.

For 35 years, Reykholt was the home of **Snorri Sturluson** (1179-1241)—one of the most prominent figures of Iceland's post-Settlement Age. A poet, historian, and politician, Snorri wrote some of the famous sagas,

WEST ICELAND

including—possibly—the locally set Egill's Saga. Snorri was also a chronicler for all of medieval Scandinavia: He wrote *Gylfaginning,* a tale about the pantheon of Norse gods, and *Heimskringla,* the earliest and definitive history of Norwegian kings. Snorri was successful in the political realm, as well, serving two terms as the Alþingi's law speaker and hobnobbing with the king of Norway. In fact, his support of continued union with Norway made him plenty of enemies back home—enemies who killed him in a surprise attack, right here at Reykholt. To this day, Snorri is arguably more popular among Norwegians (whose history he chronicled) than among Icelanders; the statue of him in Reykholt was done by Norway's top sculptor, Gustav Vigeland.

Reykholt has two handsome **churches,** one small and traditional from the 1880s, the other large and modern from the 1990s (free). Underneath the modern church is the **"Snorri's Saga" Museum.** It's one large room, and is a bit dry (basically just posters), but modern and with good English—worth considering on a rainy day (1,200 ISK, daily 10:00-18:00, Oct-March until 17:00 and closed Sat-Sun, pay WCs, tel. 433-8000, www.snorrastofa.is).

The little outdoor hot pool, **Snorralaug** (Snorri's Pool), has been here for hundreds of years (it's mentioned in the sagas). Look for it behind the old school building, and unlatch the wooden door in the hillside behind the pool to see the first few feet of a tunnel. This once led to the cellar of a now-vanished building that was part of the complex in Snorri's time. (Such tunnels were typical at the time, and there's a similar one at Skálholt, along the Golden Circle.) Bathing in the pool is not allowed.

Sleeping near Reykholt: $$ Hótel Á ("River"), a five-minute drive past the recommended Brúarás café at the valley's crossroads, is an endearingly rural option run by a local farmer's family. Perched on a ridge overlooking the broad valley are 25 rooms with private bath (pricey dinner available to guests, Kirkjuból, Reykholt, tel. 435-1430, www.hotela.is, hotela@hotela.is).

$$ Fossatún ("Waterfall Field") is a fun little compound along highway 50 between Borgarnes and Reykholt, just where the road crosses a small river, with a nice view over "Troll Falls." They have 12 modern rooms with private bath in the hotel; six older, more rustic rooms with shared bath and kitchen in the guesthouse; and eight "camping pods" peppered throughout the property that share bathrooms and a kitchen (15 minutes from Reykholt, on-site

Rock 'n' Troll restaurant—see later, tel. 433-5800, www.fossatun. is, info@fossatun.is).

Eating in and near Reykholt: Several tree-sheltered picnic benches beckon on a nice day. At the back of the Snorralaug complex is the sleek, modern Fosshotel Reykholt, with a pricey **$$$ restaurant**—but I'd rather carry on just a few minutes to the excellent **$ Brúarás Café,** the best place to eat around here. In an angular, modern structure at the bridge where highways 518, 519, and 523 meet (between Reykholt and the waterfalls), it offers a brief but thoughtful menu of mostly locally sourced dishes, including lamb soup, burgers, and big salads. The café also serve as the area's unofficial TI (restaurant open daily 11:00-17:00, mid-June-Aug until 20:00, closed off-season, tel. 435-1270, www.facebook. com/bruaras).

Toward Borgarnes from Reykholt, the Fossatún, listed earlier, also runs the **$$ Rock 'n' Troll** restaurant, where the owner sometimes performs with his rock band (daily 18:30-21:00, in summer also 12:00-14:00).

▲▲Hraunfossar and Barnafoss Waterfalls

These two waterfalls are a 20-minute drive up the valley from Reykholt along highway 518. They're free and easy to see—just a few minutes' walk from your car (free parking, pay WCs).

The main river running through the valley here is called the Hvítá ("White River," the same name—but not the same river—as the one that flows over Gullfoss waterfall on the Golden Circle). As you approach the falls, you'll see that the upper part of the valley is covered by relatively new lava. New lava is porous, and streams often sink into lava fields, flowing underneath the surface for considerable distances. At **Hraunfossar** ("Lava Waterfalls"), you'll look across the river and see rivulets of groundwater pouring out from under the striped layers of lava on the other side and falling into the stream, like so many bridal veils.

A hundred yards upstream is **Barnafoss,** a more typical waterfall on the main stream. The name means "Children's Waterfall," and you can see what looks like the remains of a natural bridge spanning the falls here. According to legend, two children who were supposed to stay home while their parents were at church went out to play instead and drowned when they fell off the bridge; the mother destroyed the bridge so no other children would meet such a tragic fate. A pedestrian bridge over the river lets you get a closer look at the falls.

Eating at the Falls: By the waterfall parking lot is a small, basic **$ café,** with soup, snacks, ice cream, and coffee.

Húsafell

About 10 minutes past Barnafoss and the Hraunfossar, this hamlet is a service center for the union-owned cottages in the area that many Icelanders frequent. The area is anchored by a fancy hotel, with a variety of eateries (from a swanky dining room to a basic café/shop), and is the departure point for the "Into the Glacier" tours to Langjökull (described later). The main reason to stop here is to enjoy Húsafell's surprisingly extensive **thermal swimming pool,** with multiple outdoor pools and a waterslide. Aside from the premium Krauma bath at Deildartunguhver, this is your best option in this part of West Iceland—and the most affordable (1,300 ISK, www.husafell.is).

▲Víðgelmir Lava Tube

Víðgelmir (VEETHE-GHELL-meer)—marketed as simply "The Cave"—is a lava tube formed about a thousand years ago during an eruption in the Langjökull volcano system. The top of a river of lava crusted over, enclosing the molten part underground. When the lava stopped flowing, it left behind a hollow, tube-like, mile-long corridor, now below ground level. Today visitors can take a guided walk through the lava tube and ogle its unusual

lava formations: tubular lava stalactites shaped like strands of spaghetti, and formations that look like melted chocolate. While Víðgelmir requires a substantial commitment of time and money—and

I've toured far more impressive caves in Europe—the volcanic spin makes this worth considering for rock nerds. Dress warmly—wear a jacket, hat, and gloves at any time of year; underground, the temperature hovers right around freezing.

Cost and Hours: 6,500 ISK, daily tours run hourly 9:00-18:00, fewer tours mid-Sept–mid-May—generally 4-5/day, confirm times before you go, mobile 783-3600, www.thecave.is. They prefer that you book and pay in advance online, rather than just showing up. If you're running late for your tour time, they can normally switch you to a later tour on the same day.

Getting There: From Reykholt, it's a 30-minute drive down a mostly unpaved road. Cross the bridge at highway 519, then head east along highway 523. You'll drive to the end of a rough gravel road in the middle of a lava field.

Visiting the Cave: When you arrive, check in at a little shed, where you'll be issued a helmet and a headlamp. Then you'll walk across a petrified lava flow 300 yards to a hole formed centuries ago when part of the tube's roof collapsed. Here you'll climb down a wooden staircase and follow boardwalks through about a half-mile of the mile-long cave. You'll see multicolored layers of basalt lava, which built up over the course of the long eruption, and get a good, up-close look at some remarkable lava formations. Remember, this is a lava cave, rather than a limestone cave: The "stalactites" and "stalagmites" weren't formed over eons by dripping water, but all at once, a thousand years ago, as the liquid lava cooled and hardened. Your guide will point out where they found evidence of humans living here (perhaps a Viking Age outlaw); let you (gently) handle a few samples of the delicate lava formations; and flip off the lights so you can experience total darkness.

▲Háafell Goat Farm

This is a one-family project by Jóhanna Þorvaldsdóttir and her clan, who idealistically set out a few years ago to breed Iceland's nearly

extinct goat stock—descended from animals brought by the first settlers. Now the family invites travelers to visit their farm, meet (and, if you like, cuddle) some adorable baby goats, learn about their work, watch the goats butt heads playfully, and sample (and buy) the wide variety of products they make from their goats: feta cheese, ice cream, soap and lotions (from tallow), and goat-hide carpets and insoles. This is a fun, hands-on activity for kids. I consider the cost of admission worthwhile just to keep this Icelandic tradition alive.

Cost and Hours: 1,500 ISK, June-Aug daily 13:00-18:00, Sept-May by appointment only, mobile tel. 845-2331, www.geitur. is, haafell@gmail.com.

Getting There: The farm is on gravel highway 523, about midway between the junctions with highways 522 and 519, on the north side of the river Hvítá. It's about 20-25 minutes' drive from Reykholt, depending on which way you circle around.

Langjökull Glacier

At the far upper end of the valley, a four-wheel-drive track leads up to the Langjökull glacier—Iceland's second-largest. If you're in the area (particularly if you're overnighting and have extra time), consider paying for a pricey tour that gets you close to all that ice. Note, though, that the tours are time-consuming, there's a lot to do in the valley on your own, and you can get close to glaciers more easily and cheaply in other parts of Iceland (such as Sólheimajökull, on the South Coast).

One popular experience is **"Into the Glacier,"** a tour that takes you into a cave that has been bored in the snow and ice. You'll meet your tour at Húsafell and board an eight-wheel-drive super truck for the 30-minute transfer to the cave, where a guide will lead you around the tunnels. Bundle up—the temperature hovers right around freezing (20,000 ISK, 2,000 ISK extra for four-wheel drive shuttle, generally 6-7/day June-mid-Oct 10:00-15:30, fewer departures off-season, 2-3 hours total, also possible to combine with snowmobile trip or as an all-day excursion from Reykjavík, tel. 578-2550, www.intotheglacier.is).

THE RING ROAD

THE RING ROAD

Hringvegurinn

Circling the Ring Road is the ultimate Icelandic road trip. You will see the country in all its moods: the deep valleys and fjordside hamlets of the north, the not-quite-bustling second city of Akureyri, the volcanic landscape around Mývatn, the desolate Eastfjords, the glacial landscape of the southeast, and the gentle, green South Coast. Be prepared for long days behind the wheel, but they'll deliver a marvelous payoff: all of Iceland's scenic highlights, in one big loop.

In this chapter, I outline the best five- to seven-day self-guided drive around the Ring, with plenty of suggestions for those with more time. Note that two of the day trips described earlier in this book (South Coast and West Iceland) are basically part of the Ring Road, and two others (Golden Circle and Westman Islands) can easily be spliced into your Ring Road journey.

In theory, you could do the entire Ring and all the day trips in this book, and never set foot in Reykjavík: From the airport, you could drive a couple of hours to one of the day-trip zones, spend a night there, and then continue along the Ring (for example, land at Keflavík Airport, head straight to Borgarfjörður in West Iceland, and overnight there). However, most visitors stay in the Reykjavík area for a day or two before commencing the Ring.

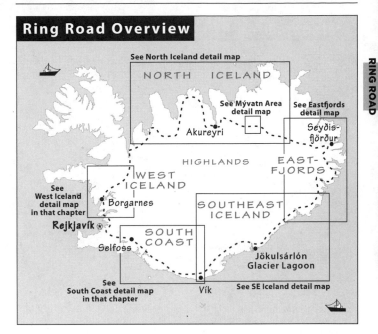

Ring Road Overview

See North Iceland detail map

NORTH ICELAND

See Mývatn Area detail map

See Eastfjords detail map

Akureyri

Seyðis-fjörður

HIGHLANDS

EAST-FJORDS

WEST ICELAND

See West Iceland detail map in that chapter

Borgarnes

SOUTHEAST ICELAND

Rejkjavík

SOUTH COAST

Selfoss

Jökulsárlón Glacier Lagoon

See South Coast detail map in that chapter

Vík

See SE Iceland detail map

RING ROAD

A week spent traveling Iceland's Ring Road is an epic journey unlike any other. Let's go!

Ring Road Driving Tour

Driving the Ring Road is a complex road trip that deserves serious planning. Use the day plans that follow as a guide as you customize your journey to match your interests, energy, and time. It's possible to do the loop in as few as five days (and four nights)—but that requires very long driving days. If you can, aim for seven leisurely days, even if they come at the expense of something else in Iceland.

PLANNING YOUR DRIVE

In the itinerary below, I've laid out a basic plan that takes you in five days—the absolute minimum—to the best-known sights, along with suggestions on where to overnight. With seven days or more, you can enjoy a saner pace, explore lesser-known destinations, avoid one-night stands, and really savor the trip. Be sure to read the Ring Road tips sprinkled throughout this chapter as you make your plans.

The Ring in Five Days or More

Note that this plan, and the closing times I list, are for summer

RING ROAD

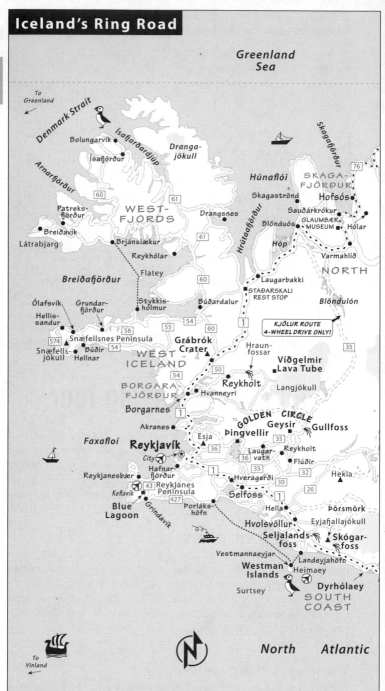

Iceland's Ring Road

Greenland Sea

To Greenland

Denmark Strait

Bolungarvík
Ísafjörður

Ísafjarðardjúp

Drangajökull

Arnarfjörður

Patreks-fjörður

WEST-FJORDS

Drangsnes

Húnaflói

Skagafjörður

SKAGA-FJÖRÐUR

76

Skagaströnd

Hofsós

Saudárkrókur

Breiðavík
Látrabjarg

Brjánslækur

60

Reykhólar

61

Hrútafjörður

Blönduós

GLAUMBÆR MUSEUM

Hólar

Breiðafjörður

Flatey

61

Hóp

Varmahlíð

NORTH

Ólafsvík

Grundar-fjörður

Stykkis-hólmur

60

Búðardalur

Laugarbakki

STADARSKALI REST STOP

Blöndulón

Hellis-sandur

56

574
Snæfells-jökull

55

Snæfellsnes Peninsula

54

WEST ICELAND

Búðir
Hellnar

54

60

1

Hraun-fossar

KJÖLUR ROUTE 4-WHEEL DRIVE ONLY!

Viðgelmir Lava Tube

35

Langjökull

Grábrók Crater

50

Reykholt

BORGAR-FJÖRÐUR

54

Hvanneyri

Borgarnes

1

GOLDEN CIRCLE

Geysir

Gullfoss

Faxaflói

Akranes

Esja

Þingvellir

35

Reykholt

Reykjavík

City

Laugar-vatn

36

Flúðir

32

Hekla

Hafnar-fjörður

36

1

Hveragerði

30

Reykjanesbær

Keflavík

43

Reykjanes Peninsula

Selfoss

1

26

Blue Lagoon

Grindavík

427

Þorláks-höfn

Hella

Hvolsvöllur

Þórsmörk

Eyjafjallajökull

Seljalands-foss

Skógar-foss

Vestmannaeyjar

Landeyjahöfn

Westman Islands

Heimaey

Surtsey

Dyrhólaey

SOUTH COAST

To Vinland

N

North Atlantic

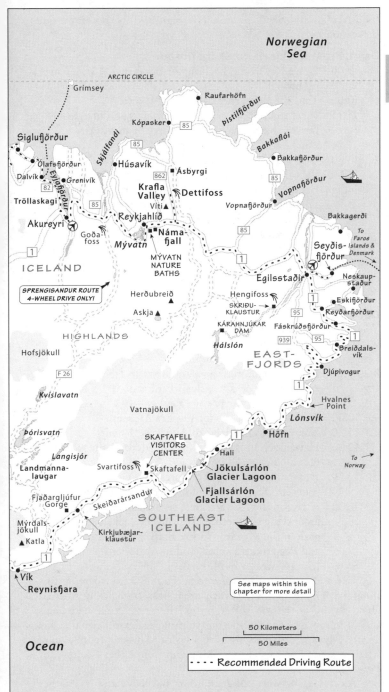

Norwegian Sea

ARCTIC CIRCLE

Grímsey

Raufarhöfn

Kópasker 85

Þistilfjörður

Bakkaflói

Siglufjörður

Ólafsfjörður

Dalvík

Grenivík

Húsavík

Ásbyrgi

Bakkafjörður

85

Vopnafjörður

Tröllaskagi

82

85

Eyjafjörður

Skjálfandi

Krafla Valley

Dettifoss

862

Bakkagerði

To Faroe Islands & Denmark

Akureyri

Goða foss

Reykjahlíð

Víti

Mývatn

Náma fjall

Vopnafjörður

85

Seyðis- fjörður

ICELAND

MÝVATN NATURE BATHS

1

Egilsstaðir

Neskaup- staður

SPRENGISANDUR ROUTE 4-WHEEL DRIVE ONLY!

Herðubreið

Hengifoss

SKRIÐU- KLAUSTUR

Eskifjörður

Reyðarfjörður

HIGHLANDS

Askja

KÁRAHNJÚKAR DAM

95

Fáskrúðsfjörður

EAST- FJORDS

939

95

1

Hofsjökull

Hálslón

Breiðdals- vík

Kvíslavatn

F 26

Vatnajökull

Djúpivogur

1

Þórisvatn

Langisjór

Hvalnes Point

Lónsvík

Landmanna- laugar

SKAFTAFELL VISITORS CENTER

1

Höfn

To Norway

Fjaðrárgljúfur Gorge

Svartifoss

Skaftafell

Hali

Jökulsárlón Glacier Lagoon

Fjallsárlón Glacier Lagoon

Myrdals- jökull

Skeiðarársandur

SOUTHEAST ICELAND

Katla

Kirkjubæjar- klaustur

1

Vík

Reynisfjara

Ocean

See maps within this chapter for more detail

50 Kilometers

50 Miles

· · · · Recommended Driving Route

(mid-May to mid-Sept); hours can be significantly shorter outside those months.

Day 1: From Reykjavík to Skagafjörður

9:00   Leave Reykjavík, heading for Borgarnes (1 hour) on highway 1

10:00   Tour the Borgarnes Settlement Centre

11:15   Head to Grábrók crater (30 minutes) and hike to the top; have a picnic lunch there or stop at the Hreðavatnsskáli roadside café

13:30   Continue north to Glaumbær (2.5 hours)

16:00   Visit the Glaumbær open-air museum (closes at 18:00)

Evening   Eat dinner in nearby Sauðárkrókur or in Hofsós (40 minutes from Glaumbær), and end your day with a soak at the Hofsós infinity pool (closes at 21:00)

Sleep   In the Skagafjörður countryside

Extra Overnight: Adding an overnight in the **Borgarnes area** lets you explore the sights in the West Iceland chapter (especially the area around Reykholt), and gives you a head start on the Skagafjörður and Tröllaskagi area.

Day 2: Around Tröllaskagi to Akureyri and Mývatn

You could make a beeline to Akureyri if you're in a rush (on highway 1); but it's worth the extra time to loop around the Tröllaskagi Peninsula and stop off in Siglufjörður.

8:30-9:00   Leave Skagafjörður area and drive to Siglufjörður, at the tip of the Tröllaskagi Peninsula (1-1.5 hours depending on where you sleep)

10:00   Tour Siglufjörður's Herring Era Museum

11:30   Enjoy the scenic drive to Akureyri (1 hour)

12:30   Have lunch in Akureyri (or in Dalvík on the way) and take a quick stroll downtown

14:30   Drive to Goðafoss (45 minutes) and view its grand waterfall, then press on to Mývatn lake (30 minutes)

16:30   Arrive in the Mývatn area, where you can sightsee around the southern end of the lake, take a restorative soak in the Mývatn Nature Baths (open until 24:00), and sleep like a log (oh, and have dinner)

Sleep   Mývatn area or in Húsavík

Extra Overnight: If I were to add a night anywhere on this itinerary, it'd be in the **Mývatn area.** It's strategically situated about a third of the way through the Ring; extra time here helps you fit in more of the fascinating volcanic and geothermal sights around Mývatn, and possibly even a visit to Húsavík (with a good whale museum) or a whale-watching trip from either Akureyri or Húsavík.

Akureyri, between Skagafjörður and Mývatn, is another

candidate for an extra overnight. This buys you more time for the Tröllaskagi area (including the Hofsós Emigration Center) and for Akureyri itself (great municipal swimming pool and a wide choice of restaurants).

Day 3: From Mývatn to the Eastfjords

Morning	See any Mývatn sights you missed yesterday, including the baths and the geothermal sights just east of the mountains (or consider driving 45 minutes each way to visit the charming port town of Húsavík and its whale museum); whatever you do, eat lunch before heading out, as there's virtually nowhere to eat between Mývatn and the Eastfjords (your next destination)
12:30	Begin your drive east to Dettifoss (about an hour), and explore that spectacular waterfall
14:30	Continue toward the Eastfjords, stopping in Egilsstaðir (2 hours) if you need to stock up on food or gas; then drive along one of Iceland's most scenic routes (45 minutes—including photo stops— over a breathtaking pass) to the appealing town of Seyðisfjörður
17:30	Arrive in Seyðisfjörður, enjoy dinner, and rest up for tomorrow's long Eastfjords drive
Sleep	In Seyðisfjörður (or Egilsstaðir, which saves some driving, but costs you spectacular scenery and a charming town)

Day 4: Along the Eastfjords to the Southeast

This is easily the hardest day of driving on this itinerary. Don't underestimate how long it takes to curve along all those beautiful fjords. Keep in mind that the most interesting sights are concentrated at the end of the day—you'll want enough time for them. Overnight options here span a two-hour stretch of road; the farther you go tonight, the less you'll have to drive tomorrow.

8:30	Leave Seyðisfjörður for the looooong drive along the Eastfjords to Höfn (nearly 4 hours without stops); break for WC/snacks in Djúpivogur (about 2.5 hours in)—your last chance before getting to Höfn
13:30	Late lunch in Höfn
15:00	Drive to the Jökulsárlón glacier lagoon (1 hour), ogle glaciers and nearby Diamond Beach, and consider a lagoon cruise (departures until 18:00)—or if sleeping nearby, do one first thing in the morning
Evening	With enough daylight and energy, consider an easy hike around Skaftafell National Park (45 minutes

from Jökulsárlón), or linger at the glacier lagoon and beach before driving to your evening accommodations

Sleep Near Höfn (better accommodations and restaurants), or near the Jökulsárlón glacier lagoon or Skaftafell (for outdoorsy types or those who want to shave off a bit of their Day 5 drive time); note that staying in Höfn adds about 1.5 hours to your Day 5 drive

Extra Overnight: Spending a second night in **Southeast Iceland** can help break up two long driving days. This is particularly tempting if you're interested in glacier activities or hiking at Skaftafell. But if you're *not* doing those things, you may prefer to overnight on the South Coast instead.

Day 5: Along the South Coast to Reykjavík

Before leaving—and if you're staying nearby—consider an easy nature hike at Skaftafell (or get up an hour earlier to hike all the way up to Svartifoss waterfall). Or, if you've slept near the glacier lagoons, do a cruise first thing this morning, before heading west.

Morning Drive west to the town of Vík, on the South Coast, aiming to get there by lunchtime (about 3.5 hours from Höfn, 2.5 hours from Jökulsárlón glacier lagoon, or 2 hours from Skaftafell, including a few brief photo stops)

13:00 Lunch in or near Vík, then go 10 minutes farther to view the black sand beach at Reynisfjara

14:30 Drive to Seljalandsfoss (1 hour) and enjoy the waterfall

16:00 Continue to Hvolsvöllur (20 minutes) and visit the Lava Centre (closes at 19:00)

Evening Drive to Reykjavík (1.5 hours), having dinner en route or in the city (late)

Sleep Collapse in Reykjavík. You did it!

Extra Overnight: Adding an overnight on the **South Coast** allows more time on the morning of Day 5 for glacier lagoon cruises and Skaftafell hikes, and lets you spread the South Coast sights over two days, breaking up the long drive back to Reykjavík. Other options include a Westman Islands side-trip (see Westman Islands chapter) or a Golden Circle loop (see Golden Circle chapter) on your way back to Reykjavík.

With More Time...

If you're adding time, and don't mind a series of one-night stays, I'd prioritize this way:

With a **sixth day,** add a second night in the Mývatn area.

With a **seventh day,** add a night on the South Coast.

With an **eighth day,** add an overnight in Akureyri.

With a **ninth day,** add an overnight in the Borgarnes area.

RING ROAD

With **even more time,** spend a second night in one (or more) of these areas, listed roughly in order of preference: Southeast Iceland; Seyðisfjörður, on the Eastfjords; or the charming North Iceland towns of Húsavík and Siglufjörður.

Ring Road Tips

Here are some important considerations as you plan your itinerary. For an overview on driving in Iceland—including common road hazards and a map with driving times, see the "Driving" section of the Practicalities chapter.

Time to Allow: The entire 800-mile circuit requires a minimum of about 20 hours of driving time—but that doesn't account for the many places along the way that sit on short spokes off the Ring. You may find yourself driving an extra hour or two to reach some of the top sights (such as the best towns—Siglufjörður and Húsavík in the north, and Seyðisfjörður in the Eastfjords—or the most impressive waterfall, Dettifoss). To get a sense of the pace you'll need to keep, figure on about 30 total hours of driving, and divide by the number of days you've allotted (with five days, you'll average six hours a day behind the wheel).

Remember that you'll be stopping frequently en route for sightseeing, and sometimes briefly hiking to reach a point of interest. Don't overdo it: The driving can be tedious in places, and challenging in others.

When to Go (and When Not to Go): The best time to drive the Ring Road is between mid-May and mid-September. Don't drive the full Ring anytime from November to March. April and October are chancy; if you're lucky, you'll dance between the snowstorms, but just as likely, an icy or closed mountain pass will block your progress and mess up your itinerary (in these months, prudent drivers should skip the Ring and stick within two or three hours of Reykjavík). Late September and early May along the Ring are fairly reliable, but you still could encounter slippery roads or a freak snowstorm at higher elevations. Regardless of when you travel, keep a close eye on the road conditions map at Road.is.

Two- or Four-Wheel Drive? In summer, rent a two-wheel drive car; you won't need four-wheel drive if you're circling the island in a week. Nearly the entire Ring is paved (except for some short stretches, mostly in the east), and the most rewarding detours are either paved or on gravel roads that are passable in a two-wheel drive. Although a four-wheel drive gives you a little more comfort and speed on unpaved roads, it's generally not worth the extra cost.

Clockwise or Counterclockwise? The Ring works well in either direction. I lean toward clockwise, which is how I've organized this chapter. The northwest quarter of the Ring is the least spectacular, so doing the trip clockwise lets you build to ever-greater highlights.

Sleeping Along the Ring: The trickiest part of your Ring itinerary is figuring out where to stay overnight. If plotting out an exact itinerary and **booking accommodations in advance,** you'll generally end up with a string of one-nighters. Be flexible on location; for example, when researching Mývatn accommodations, you might find better prices and availability in nearby Húsavík. Book well ahead—as far you can—as accommodations along the Ring fill up weeks (or even months) in advance during the summer. With Iceland's geography and dispersed settlement in mind, I've highlighted general areas that work well for an overnight and recommended a few reliable establishments that I've checked out and like. Still, it's smart to look around on Airbnb or Booking.com, and consider well-rated alternatives.

Another option is to **camp,** either with a campervan or tent. With a campervan, every parking lot becomes a potential hotel; with a tent, you just need a campsite to pitch it in, and Icelandic campsites practically never fill up. Both options leave you free to change your itinerary on the fly (for more on campervans and camping, see page 389).

WCs: Driving through the countryside, often your best (or only) WC option will be at a parking lot or café for a major sight. Some may be free, but most charge a fee (typically 100-200 ISK); some accept credit cards, but others require cash. Have a small amount of currency on hand for these situations. WCs at gas stations and at a café or restaurant where you are buying food are typically free.

Not Enough Time to Drive? If you don't want to drive the entire Ring Road but want to get a quick look at the north, a good plan is to fly from Reykjavík to Akureyri (frequent Air Iceland Connect flights take less than an hour) and home-base there for a few days, day-tripping by rental car, public bus, or excursion to places like Siglufjörður and Mývatn (each less than 1.5 hours away). Egilsstaðir, in the Eastfjords, is also reachable by plane from Reykjavík, with rental cars available at its airport.

Ring Road Excursions: If you want to do the Ring but don't want to drive it yourself, some boutique tour companies (including www.nicetravel.is and www.seasontours.is) offer seven-day excursions—for a very steep price.

West Iceland

Your Ring Road journey begins with a spin through West Iceland—the region called Borgarfjörður. This area has some fine sights and can be a satisfying side-trip from Reykjavík, but those doing the entire Ring Road will find more impactful sights, charming towns, and dramatic scenery farther along. For that reason, Ring Road through-trippers should feel free to make short work of West Iceland—stopping only at its two most worthwhile sights: the Settlement Centre in the beautifully set town of Borgarnes, and the fun-to-climb crater called Grábrók.

Planning Tips: If you're doing the Ring Road at a more leisurely pace (with more than a week), this area can be a convenient first stop, especially if you're setting out on the Ring right after your Iceland arrival. It's a fairly straightforward two-hour drive from the airport to the charming small town of Borgarnes, a fine place for your first night in Iceland before carrying on with the rest of the Ring.

Reykjavík to Skagafjörður Route Overview

For more on this region—including a map, specific driving instructions from Reykjavík, and a complete rundown of the area's sights—see the West Iceland chapter. This leg takes about 4.5 hours without stopping.

• *Drive north from Reykjavík along highway 1, following signs for* Borgarnes, Akureyri, *and* 1n. *About one hour from Reykjavík, a bridge crosses into...*

Borgarnes

This fine town of 2,000 people perches on a little peninsula facing sheer scree cliffs. Borgarnes (BOHR-gahr-NESS) has some historical ties to the early Icelandic sagas (especially the colorful warrior-poet Egill); you can learn more about him and the earliest days of Iceland's habitation in the **Settlement Centre,** which is well worth an hour (described on page 259).

Additional sights cluster about a half-hour east of Borgarnes, in the area near Reykholt (thermal springs and waterfalls, family-friendly goat farm, busy thermal-pool complex, lava cave, important early Icelandic Christian sights—all described in the West Iceland chapter). But for those blitzing the Ring, all are skippable.
• *To continue directly along the Ring Road, head north from Borgarnes on highway 1. After about 30 minutes, along the road on your left, you can't miss the towering crater called Grábrók. The parking lot is also on the left, immediately after the crater.*

Grábrók Crater
Climbing to the top of Grábrók takes about 30-45 minutes round-trip and offers grand views over the region (for details on the crater and the lunch spots listed next, see page 261).

Lunch Options: Consider getting lunch near Grábrók before heading north over the mountains. Options include the **$ Hreðavatnsskáli** roadhouse café, and the more upscale **$$$ Hraunsnef**. Otherwise, two basic, roadside restaurants lie between here and Skagafjörður (described in the North Iceland section, later).
• *After visiting the crater, get back on highway 1 north.*

From Grábrók to Blönduós
As you approach the pass over **Holtavörðuheiði** ("Hill-Cairn Heath"), the farms thin out and the road climbs, finally cresting the pass at almost 1,400 feet.

Coming back down, you'll see the small Hrútafjörður ("Ram Fjord") spread out before you. Just before the road meets the fjord, you'll hit **$ Staðarskáli,** a big rest-stop complex (free WC, burgers, Wi-Fi, long hours daily, tel. 440-1336, www.n1.is).

Another hour of driving on highway 1 across a relatively flat, dull landscape brings you to Blönduós, a small town along the Blanda river known to most Icelanders for its speed traps. There are a few restaurants here, including **$$ B&S** (daily 11:00-21:00, next to the big N1 gas station at the top of town, tel. 453-5060, www.pot.is).

From Blönduós to the Skagafjörður Area
As you make the trip over the mountain range from Blönduós to

the Skagafjörður area, you'll be crossing into North Iceland (covered in the next section). For this leg of the trip, you have a couple of route options.

Highway 744 to Sauðárkrókur or Hofsós (40 minutes/1 hour): If you're in a hurry to reach either of these towns, highway 744 is faster, lower in altitude, recently upgraded, and nicely scenic.

Highway 1 Bypass to Varmahlíð (40 minutes): This equally scenic road crosses the Vatnsskarð pass to the hamlet of Varmahlíð (VAR-mah-HLEETHE, "Warm Slope," pop. 140), with a gas station, hotel, school, swimming pool, and shop. Just before town is a turnoff to Víðimýrarkirkja, an 1834 sod-wrapped timber-frame church (small entry fee, open daily in summer).

From Varmahlíð, you have several options. Turning left on highway 75 takes you to the area's most interesting sight, Glaumbær Museum (less than 10 minutes) and the town of Sauðárkrókur (20 minutes); the road eventually connects with highway 76, which runs through Hofsós (45 minutes from Varmahlíð) and the Tröllaskagi Peninsula. All of these are described in the next section.

Continuing along highway 1 from Varmahlíð leads to the bigger city of Akureyri (1 hour). Note that if you stay on highway 1 straight through, you'll bypass the Skagafjörður fjord altogether and miss its most interesting sight, the Glaumbær Museum. Unless you're in a huge rush, be sure to turn off and enjoy the Skagafjörður area.

North Iceland

North Iceland is a delight, with beautiful fjords, the scenic Tröllaskagi Peninsula, Iceland's pleasant second city of Akureyri, and the country's most fascinating volcanic area at Mývatn. If this area were a bit closer to Reykjavík, it would be swamped with tourists. But it isn't...so it's not.

Planning Tips: Those without enough time to do the entire Ring could consider spending just a few nights in this area. But by car it's a long, six-plus hours one-way. A more efficient plan is to fly from Reykjavík to Akureyri, rent a car there (or do excursions) for two or three days of side-tripping, then drive or fly back to the capital.

Skagafjörður Area

Skagafjörður (SKAH-gah-FYUR-thur, "Peninsula Fjord") is the name of this broad fjord and of the valley at its head. The

Skagafjörður area has a picturesque seaside setting, a few humble towns (Hofsós is the most interesting), and several intriguing islands just offshore.

There are enough attractions here to keep you busy for several hours—including one of Iceland's most interesting folk museums, at Glaumbær; the evocative Icelandic Emigration Center, in Hofsós; and a tranquil valley that was an important site in the early days of Icelandic Christianity, at Hólar. The area also has several horseback riding options, and a rare Icelandic river suitable for rafting.

Planning Tips: The Skagafjörður area is sparsely populated—and not well-developed for tourism. Compared to some of the country's more mainstream destinations, you may need to lower your standards somewhat. If you make good time getting to this area, a possible late-afternoon plan is to close down the Icelandic Emigration Center in Hofsós (open until 18:00 in summer); take a dip in that town's relaxing, thermally fed infinity pool overlooking the fjord (open until 21:00 in summer); then grab dinner on your way back to your accommodations.

Sights in the Skagafjörður Area

These sights are listed in the order you'll approach them on highways 75 and 76 from the main Ring Road. For directions, see "From Blönduós to the Skagafjörður Area," earlier.

▲▲Glaumbær Museum

Inhabited until 1947 and a museum since 1952, this classic turf farm (pronounced GLOYM-bire) shows how Icelanders lived for

centuries, with limited access to timber for building and fuel. It's larger and better preserved than other similar farm-museums in Iceland, and offers perhaps the country's most informative and intimate look at traditional Icelandic lifestyles. It rates ▲▲▲ for those interested in Icelandic history.

Cost and Hours: Free to wander the grounds, but well worth paying 1,600 ISK to enter the farmhouse complex; late May-late Sept daily 9:00-18:00; April-late May and late Sept-late Oct Mon-Fri 10:00-16:00, closed Sat-Sun; late Oct-March by appointment only; on highway 75 (less than 10 minutes north of highway 1 at Varmahlið), tel. 453-6173, www.glaumbaer.is.

Eating: The sod houses sit between a modern church and two late-19th-century timber houses that were moved here in recent decades. In one of them, the cozy **$ Áskaffi** café serves soup, sandwiches, cakes, and a tasting plate of traditional Icelandic smoked and preserved foods (closed late Sept-April; tel. 453-8855, www.askaffi.is).

Visiting the Museum: The walls of the farm are made of sod and driftwood, with timber fronts and stone foundations. Study the alternating diagonal pattern used to pile up the layers of sod.

RING ROAD

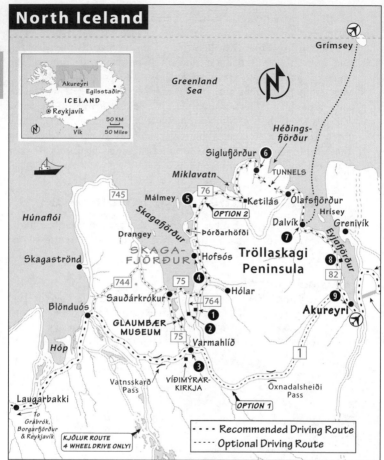

North Iceland

ICELAND
Akureyri
Egilsstaðir
Reykjavík
Vík
50 KM
50 Miles

Grímsey

Greenland
Sea

Hédings-
fjörður

Siglufjörður **6**

Miklavatn

TUNNELS

Ólafsfjörður

745

Málmey **5**

76

Ketilás

OPTION 2

Dalvík

Hrísey

Grenivík

Húnaflói

Skagafjörður

Drangey

Þórðarhöfði

7

SKAGA-
FJÖRÐUR

Tröllaskagi
Peninsula

Skagaströnd

Hofsós

8

82

744

Sauðárkrókur

75

4

Hólar

9

Akureyri

Blönduós

GLAUMBÆR
MUSEUM

764

1

2

Hóp

75

Varmahlíð

1

Laugarbakki

Vatnsskarð
Pass

3

VÍÐIMÝRAR-
KIRKJA

Öxnadalsheiði
Pass

To
Grábrók,
Borgarfjörður
& Reykjavík

OPTION 1

KJÖLUR ROUTE
4 WHEEL DRIVE ONLY!

- - - - Recommended Driving Route

----- Optional Driving Route

The tops of the houses are covered with grass—the original roof garden. While the facades give the impression of separate buildings, inside the rooms are all connected.

Each room is explained by an English leaflet. At the front of the house is the nicest (and least troglodyte-style) room, reserved for guests. From there, a long, claustrophobic sod hallway connects the kitchen (with a fire fed by peat or dried sheep dung) with various pantries and storage rooms, where you'll see big barrels of animal innards and *skyr*—now a trendy yogurt-like snack, but back then a well-preserved staple.

At the back of the complex, you'll pop into the fascinating *baðstofa*—the communal living and sleeping room, lined with dorm-like beds where workers slept, two to a bed. The women—who did delicate spinning and knitting work—got the bunks with better light, near the windows. The smaller, more genteel room on

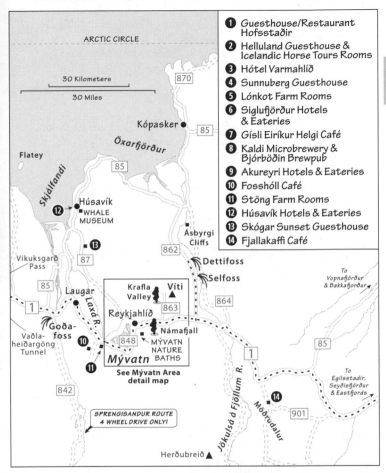

1 Guesthouse/Restaurant Hofsstaðir
2 Helluland Guesthouse & Icelandic Horse Tours Rooms
3 Hótel Varmahlíð
4 Sunnuberg Guesthouse
5 Lónkot Farm Rooms
6 Siglufjörður Hotels & Eateries
7 Gísli Eiríkur Helgi Café
8 Kaldi Microbrewery & Björböðin Brewpub
9 Akureyri Hotels & Eateries
10 Fosshóll Café
11 Stöng Farm Rooms
12 Húsavík Hotels & Eateries
13 Skógar Sunset Guesthouse
14 Fjallakaffi Café

the left was for the farmer and his wife; the one on the right was for children (notice the loft bed, with a step for easier access).

Here you can understand why the Scandinavian words for "bed" come from the same word as the English "room." Each bed's opening is blocked off by a wooden panel (called a *rúmfjöl*) engraved with prayers. Also look for the little, lidded pot above each bed; every person had their own personal pot *(askur)* from which they ate every meal. Imagine spending a long, dark, cold winter in here, huddled around the dim light of a candle.

People stored personal items under their pillows—the only place that was strictly off-limits to everyone else.

Back outside, you can peek into a few more rooms that held farming tools. The complex even had its own little blacksmith's workshop.

Sauðárkrókur Town

The provincial center of Sauðárkrókur (SOY-thour-kroh-kur, "Sheep River Bend," pop. 2,500) enjoys a spectacular fjordside setting about 15 minutes north of Glaumbær, but the town itself is dreary. It's convenient for gassing up, grabbing a meal, or setting up bird-watching or sea-cruise excursions—but otherwise, I'd give it a miss.

Eating in Sauðárkrókur: Most of the limited options line up within a block or so along the main street, Aðalgata (a couple of blocks inland from the main highway). **$$ KK Restaurant** (a.k.a. **Kaffi Krókur**) has a big, bright interior and a typical burgers-and-pasta menu (daily 12:00-22:00, Aðalgata 16, tel. 453-6454, www.kkrestaurant.is). **$$ Hard Wok Café** serves an acceptable approximation of Asian and Mexican dishes, plus pizza, in a pleasant setting (June-Aug daily 11:30-21:30, off-season closed 14:00-18:00 Mon-Fri, Aðalgata 8). **$ Sauðárkróksbakarí** is a popular main-street bakery with pastries and basic sandwiches, and inviting indoor seating (Mon-Fri 7:00-18:00, Sat-Sun 9:00-16:00, Aðalgata 5, www.saudarkroksbakari.net). There's also a supermarket in town.

Hólar Village

Hólar (HOE-lar, "Hills"), a pretty settlement at the upper end of a small valley, is a scenic detour if you have an hour to spare and

an interest in Iceland's history (from highway 76, turn off on highway 767 for about 15 minutes/8 miles).

The center of Iceland's northern bishopric up until 1800, Hólar had one of the country's first printing presses and is now home to a small college (Hólaskóli), a historic church, a trio of little turf-roofed houses (not open to the public), and an exhibit on Icelandic horses (only in Icelandic; open June-Aug Tue-Sun).

Hólar was home to a colorful and important bishop, Guðmundur Arason (1161-1237). An orphaned, disabled ascetic, Guðmundur devoted himself to the poor and needy. After he became bishop of Hólar, Guðmundur gathered a motley crew of desperately needy people, whom he sustained with church wealth. He became known as "Guðmundur the Good." However, his unusual ways—and his assertion of the judicial powers of the church—drew attention from the chieftains. The two factions came to blows, and Guðmundur was at various times imprisoned or sent into exile.

About 300 years later, another Hólar bishop—Jón Arason—was the main holdout of the Protestant Reformation. Jón was eventually executed at the headquarters of the other old Icelandic bishopric, Skálholt (on the Golden Circle).

Hofsós Village

On the east side of the fjord—about 40 minutes from Glaumbær, or 30 minutes from Sauðárkrókur—the village of Hofsós (HOFF-sose, "Temple Estuary," pop. 200) merits a stop, especially for anyone of Icelandic descent. A one-time summer trading center, it got its start in the 18th century, but never developed into a large town. Today it's a functional village with a fine location perched on a bluff overlooking the fjord. (The late Icelandic-Minnesotan author Bill Holm, who some will remember from his appearances on *A Prairie Home Companion*, spent summers in Hofsós and wrote about the town in *The Windows of Brimnes*.)

The core of the village (with the swimming pool and recommended guesthouse) is separated from its old port by a big river. To reach the port area—with the main buildings of the Emigration Center—you'll either have to loop all the way around on the road, or park by the Sólvík restaurant and take the footbridge.

Icelandic Emigration Center (Vesturfarasetrið): This is the main sight in town—worth ▲, or ▲▲▲ if you have Icelandic

ancestry. It fills three historic buildings on the old port. The low-tech but thorough exhibits tell the story of the 20,000-some Icelanders who emigrated to the Americas from 1870 to 1914—a time when a series of volcanic eruptions, lower temperatures, and a general lack of prospects conspired to make life

very difficult, particularly in the northern parts of the island. In 1860, more Icelanders died than were born. Those who fled went mainly to Canada, where part of Manitoba became known as "New Iceland"; others wound up in the Dakotas, and a handful went to Brazil.

To see the museum, first tour the overview exhibit in the light green house (including a peek into a typical fishing shack—*burrabúð*, or "dry house," and in the basement, a glimpse at life at sea and what the émigrés found when they reached the New World). In the big, black house, a touching exhibit of photographs (made in 1890) lets you look into the brave faces of an Icelandic immigrant community in Manitoba. And across the footbridge, you'll learn about an Icelandic settlement in North Dakota. Visitors can also use the genealogy library (1,700 ISK, June-Aug daily 11:00-18:00, Sept-May by appointment, tel. 453-7935, www.hofsos.is).

Thermal Swimming Pool: Hofsós sports a fine, large municipal pool, which opened in 2010 as a gift to the village by two very wealthy Icelandic business-women. Entirely outdoors, the complex has both a big, warm infinity pool (with unobstructed views over the icy waters of the fjord) and a smaller hot pool. If you only have time for one thermal pool on your Ring drive, this is a good choice—small, user-friendly, scenic, reason-

ably priced, and in an area with few other evening diversions (900 ISK, generally daily in summer 9:00-21:00, tel. 455-6070, www.facebook.com/sundlauginhofsosi).

Eating in Hofsós: The only real eating option is the casual **$ Sólvík** restaurant, filling a cozy house down near the footbridge, with a short but appealing menu of fish, lamb, and burgers (daily 10:00-21:00, mobile 961-3463).

Sleeping in the Skagafjörður Area

Skagafjörður is a good place to spend the night. While accommodations in the fjord's main town, Sauðárkrókur, are gloomy, several fine countryside options are more appealing. Another option is to carry on about 1.5 hours farther to sleep in Siglufjörður, near the tip of the Tröllaskagi Peninsula (with some excellent accommodations—see recommendations later in this chapter).

Overlooking the Skagafjörður Valley: $$$ Guesthouse Hofsstaðir is a cozy oasis perched on a ridge, with cut-glass peaks in one direction and the broad estuary of the Skagafjörður valley in the other. Well-run by Rósa María, they have 20 rooms (all with private bath and views) and a relaxing upscale-log-cabin vibe (tel. 453-7300, www.hofsstadir.is, info@hofsstadir.is). Their good **$$$ restaurant,** open to all, has an appealing menu and sells homemade syrups and jams (daily 18:00-22:00, reserve ahead off-season). Coming from Sauðárkrókur on highway 75, turn right at the T-intersection with highway 76 (signed for *Reykjavík* and *Akureyri*); the guesthouse is a few minutes south.

Islands in North Iceland

As you drive through North Iceland—if the visibility is good—you'll see a number of small islands scattered offshore. Ring travelers who aren't in a rush might consider a visit.

Drangey rises up like a tabletop in the waters of the Skagafjörður. The steep cliffs of this uninhabited island are summer nesting grounds for seabirds (including puffins)—and a draw for birders.. It's well-known to saga readers as the refuge of the outlaw Grettir. You can visit the island with a tour from Sauðárkrókur (see www.drangey.net). Farther north is **Málmey,** the fjord's other island, which was farmed until 1950 and is now home to a lighthouse.

Hrísey ("Brushwood Island") sits in Eyjafjörður (near Akureyri). This was once Iceland's quarantine island for cats and dogs imported here from abroad (a more convenient quarantine has now been built near Keflavík Airport). A 15-minute ferry ride from Árskógssandur (near Dalvík) takes you to a small village (pop. 150) with a café and some pleasant, short hikes (www.hrisey.is).

Grímsey, the northernmost inhabited point in Iceland (pop. under 100), has two big draws: Its northern tip is *just* over the Arctic Circle, as if designed for people who want to say they've been there. And it's a good place to see puffins in summer. The island itself is pleasant (not stunning), and the small village with its little harbor is typically Icelandic. You can either take a ferry from Dalvík (3 hours one-way); an excursion boat from Akureyri (6 hours round-trip including 2 hours on the island); or fly (30 minutes from Akureyri). Various North Iceland companies offer excursion packages. As flights and ferries run at most once daily, stay overnight if you really want to experience the island.

You can't visit **Kolbeinsey,** Iceland's northernmost point, which lies far beyond Grímsey. Now basically a sea rock, waves have eroded it to the point where it barely sticks up above the surface of the sea, and it's too small for a lighthouse. Not far back in the geological past, it was the top of an active volcano, probably similar to Surtsey in the Westman Islands. As it's important for establishing the bounds of Iceland's fishing zone, the government recently shored up the island with concrete to keep it from disappearing altogether.

Flatey is a pancake-shaped island in Skjálfandi bay. It was inhabited until the late 1960s, and some landowners still spend time there in the warmer months. There are occasional bird-watching tours to the island in summer.

$ Helluland Guesthouse has five simple but tidy, modern, and nicely appointed rooms, all with shared bath, plus a bright and cheery breakfast room and a mod lounge. High on a ridge overlooking the valley, it's a winner (tel. 853-3220, www.helluland.is, info@helluland.is). If you're in a pinch, their neighbor, **$ Icelandic Horse Tours,** has three even simpler rooms (tel. 847-8577, www.icelandhorsetours.com, info@icelandhorsetours.com). To reach either, head east from Sauðárkrókur on highway 75. After crossing the bridge, immediately turn right on highway 764 (marked *Hegranes*); the guesthouses are on the left after two miles (about 5 minutes on the unpaved road).

Practical Hotel in Varmahlíð: At the junction of highway 1 and highway 75—a short drive south of Glaumbær and the fjord—sits **$$$ Hótel Varmahlíð.** It's overpriced but convenient and relatively large (with 19 spacious rooms)—so it may have beds when others are full. It also works well if you're skipping the Skagafjörður sights, and just need a place to sleep before continuing east on highway 1 (tel. 453-8170, www.hotelvarmahlid.is, info@hotelvarmahlid.is).

In Hofsós: The simple **$ Sunnuberg Guesthouse** fills a modern house right in the heart of the village (facing the little grocery/gas station). Its five practical rooms are nothing fancy—no frills and no breakfast, though you can use the kitchen to make coffee—but the rooms all have private bathrooms, and the price is reasonable (Suðurbraut 8, tel. 893-0220, www.sunnuberg.is, gisting@hofsos.is).

Just North of Hofsós: **$$ Lónkot,** a remote waterfront farm with six basic rooms about 15 minutes north of Hofsós along the coast, is handy for those continuing around the tip of the Tröllaskagi Peninsula (cheaper rooms with shared bath, restaurant, Lónkot 76, tel. 453-7432, www.lonkot.is, lonkot@lonkot.is).

Skagafjörður to Akureyri Route Overview

When you're ready to proceed from the Skagafjörður area to Akureyri, you have two choices: Drive inland on highway 1, over a mountain pass, to Akureyri; or—my preference—invest a little extra time to take one of Iceland's classic scenic drives: north around the tip of Tröllaskagi Peninsula ("Troll Peninsula").

Option 1, Tröllaskagi (about 115 miles, 2.5 hours): This route stays at lower altitudes as it hugs the northern coast through the towns of Hofsós, Siglufjörður (an appealing small town), Ólafsfjörður, and Dalvík, before heading south along Eyjafjörður to Akureyri. The road is very scenic the entire way around and well worth the extra time. (For a detailed description of the Tröllaskagi route, see below.)

Option 2, Straight Shot on Highway 1 (about 60 miles, 1 hour): From Varmahlíð, highway 1 heads southeast over the Öxnadalsheiði pass (1,800 feet). The road is good, fast, scenic, and fun to drive, but can easily get snow in April and October (or even May and September). Near Akureyri, it broadens out into a fine green valley under jagged mountain peaks.

Which Route to Take?: The decision depends largely on how much time you can spare. The faster inland route buys more time in Akureyri, and—if continuing onward the same day—gets you into the Mývatn area earlier (you'll be glad to have more time for its many wonderful sights). The attractive coastal route runs along the sea (and Siglufjörður will tempt you to stop), but you'll sacrifice some time in Akureyri and Mývatn. If you have a night in Akureyri, or a second night near Mývatn, the Tröllaskagi detour is easier to justify.

The choice also depends on your departure point in Skagafjörður. If you sleep as far north as Hofsós, continuing north around the coastal route is only about 30 minutes slower than backtracking to highway 1 (not counting sightseeing stops).

Tröllaskagi Peninsula

The mountainous Tröllaskagi (TREW-tlah-sky-ee)—"Troll Peninsula"—is flanked by two fjords, Skagafjörður and Eyjafjörður.

Drivers who opt for the scenic route around the peninsula's tip will curve high above the sea and skirt deep glacial valleys. Along the way, you'll be tempted to stop for photographs (use the strategically placed, scenic picnic pullouts), and two of the towns—Hofsós and Siglufjörður—have good museums that merit an hour or two of your time. The drive around the peninsula—from the heart of the Skagafjörður area to Akureyri—takes about 2.5 hours.

• *From Varmahlíð or nearby, head north to highway 76.*

Hofsós North to Siglufjörður

About 15 miles from the base of the fjord is the tiny village of **Hofsós,** with its fine Icelandic Emigration Center and small but tempting thermal swimming pool, overlooking the fjord. (For more on Hofsós, see earlier in this chapter.)

Continuing north, look out to the dramatic offshore islands: In good weather, you'll be able to see the more distant **Drangey** island, a popular destination for birders. If it's socked in, you might pick out a pair of closer-in islands: the table-like **Þórðarhöfði** (technically a peninsula, connected to the mainland by a sandy causeway), then **Málmey.**

As the road curves right—heading around one of the peninsula's fingers—it alternates abruptly between paved and unpaved stretches. Steady as you go, carrying on through desolate, spectacular scenery.

• *As you approach the Miklavatn lagoon, at the junction called Ketilás (with an N1 gas station), you hit a T-intersection; turn left to stay on highway 76 (marked* Siglufjörður*).*

Curl up along the far side of the water, with nice views back on the mountainous coastline. As you reach the topmost part of the peninsula, look out to sea and realize that the next stop is the Arctic Circle. This is the northernmost point of this drive—and perhaps the farthest north you'll ever be in your life.

• *About 45 minutes after leaving Hofsós, the road winds along high bluffs over the sea before taking you through a short tunnel that deposits you in the adorable town of Siglufjörður.*

▲▲Siglufjörður

The town of Siglufjörður (SIG-loo-FYUR-thur, "Mast Fjord," pop. 1,200) is reason enough to tour Tröllaskagi. Tucked away from the sea at the end of a short fjord, and dramatically flanked by high peaks, it has a tidy charm and a pioneer spirit. The harborfront provides a lovely stroll, and colorful homes scamper up the hillside above town. There's a free parking lot right at the old harbor downtown, next to the landmark Sigló Hótel and a  short walk from the Herring Era Museum. There are public WCs at the adjacent campground.

Fish is what put the town on the map. Practically no one lived here until the mid-19th century, when locals started to use the good harbor as a trading post and shark-fishing base. Later, herring took over, and the town boomed from about 1900 until mid-century, when herring stocks began to collapse.

At its peak, Siglufjörður's harborfront was jammed with piers, bristling with boats, and fragrant with fish-processing stations; the population swelled to over 3,000. Salted herring—nutritious and well-preserved—was prized in many countries during the world wars, and for a time represented up to half of Iceland's total export income. In fact, the wealth generated by the herring operation here helped make Iceland financially independent—and, soon after, politically independent—from Denmark. But by the late 1960s, the herring shoals had disappeared for good, and Siglufjörður's population crashed. Today this burg is sleepy, with a little fishing and more and more tourism.

Herring Era Museum (Síldarminjasafn): One of Iceland's most engaging, this museum (worth ▲▲) has exhibits filling three large, historic buildings, right along the main road (just past Sigló Hótel toward Akureyri). It's well worth an hour (or more) of your time. I never knew the herring industry could be so fascinating (1,800 ISK, June-Aug daily 10:00-18:00, May and Sept 13:00-17:00, Oct-April by appointment, Snorragata 10, tel. 467-1604, www.sild.is).

Begin at the red building at the far end of the row—the **Salting Station** (a.k.a. "Róaldsbrakki," from 1907). At the entrance,

notice the panoramic photograph of the embankment out front—now so sleepy—lined with hundreds upon hundreds of herring-filled barrels. This Norwegian-owned factory (one of 23 salting stations in town) could crank out 30,000 barrels of salted herring in a year. On the main level, peek into the offices of a typical herring company. Don't miss the creaky upstairs, with the living quarters for the "herring girls" who lived and worked here, 50 at a time, through the herring season. All summer long, the girls worked outdoors, rain or shine, cutting and salting herring. You'll see rows of dorm-like beds, with clothes still hanging from hooks and music playing on the wireless. At the very top of the attic, equipment hangs from the rafters. Exiting this building, find the warehouse down below, where the salting line and storage areas were.

Then head to the multicolor-fronted building next door, the **Fish Factory**—a jumble of heavy machinery where some of the catch was processed into oil or fishmeal (for animal feed). You'll see everything from an old hand press to motorized equipment powered by a huge diesel engine. The exhibits upstairs help tell the story.

Finally, enter the yellow **Boathouse,** where you can stroll through a re-creation of the jammed harbor at its peak. Step into shacks decorated with antique pulleys, lanterns, nets, buoys, and other tools. Walk around on the decks of the largest boat (the *Týr*), imagining this scene multiplied a hundredfold on the harbor out front.

Sleeping in Siglufjörður: One of Iceland's most appealing high-end, fjordside hotels, **$$$$ Sigló Hótel** fills a picture-perfect building on the waterfront in the middle of town. Everything is done with class in its 68 harbor-view rooms and its stay-a-while atrium bar/lounge. If you're going to splurge on an Icelandic fjord, do it here (private hot tub and sauna, Snorragata 3, tel. 461-7730, www.siglohotel.is).

$$ Siglunes Guesthouse, a few short blocks away in a residential zone, is a homey place (well-run by proud Hálfdán) with 19 rooms above a dark, retro-feeling lounge. It's a nice mix of antiques, modern features, and local artists' work. About half the rooms have private bathrooms (breakfast extra, Lækjargata 10, tel. 467-1222, mobile 659-9699, www.hotelsiglunes.is).

Eating in Siglufjörður: Sigló Hótel runs several eateries in the colorful sheds around the harbor. Of these, **$ Kaffi Rauðka** (in the red building) serves basic but good fish, burger, and soup lunches, and has outdoor seating (daily 12:00-17:00, Fri-Sat until 22:00, tel. 461-7730, www.kaffiraudka.is). A block north is the little main square (directly under the church) and another good eatery: **$ Torgið** ("The Square"), a popular, casual bar/café with international cuisine (lunch and dinner served daily, likely closed for lunch off-season, tel. 467-2323, www.torgid.net). If you're around at dinnertime, venture a block farther to the recommended **$$ Siglunes** guesthouse, which serves an interesting Moroccan-fusion cuisine (closed Mon).

• *As you leave Siglufjörður, head south.*

South to Dalvík

From Siglufjörður, you'll drive up on a headland (scenic pullout on the left), then disappear into a **long tunnel.** After 2.5 miles, you'll pop out at a virgin lake, **Héðinsfjarðarvatn,** a good picnic spot.

From here, you'll immediately enter an even **longer tunnel** (4.5 miles), eventually surfacing above the town of Ólafsfjörður.

• *Passing through Ólafsfjörður, the road becomes highway 82 and follows alongside the fjord.*

Leaving Ólafsfjörður (picnic pullout on the left), you'll begin to gain altitude, and go through an older one-lane tunnel with passing places. Signs explain who has to pull over (there's even an instructional YouTube video—search "Ólafsfjarðargöng"). You'll emerge along the shore of Eyjafjörður ("Island Fjord")—whose name is inspired by its resident island, Hrísey, which you can't miss ahead of you, just offshore.

• *Next stop, Dalvík.*

RING ROAD

From Dalvík to Akureyri

Pulling into the town of Dalvík ("Valley Bay"), you'll drive along its busy harbor. Where the road bends right and heads inland, consider stopping at the **$ Gísli Eiríkur Helgi café.** This relaxed and inviting coffeehouse has great view seating upstairs; sells good coffee, cakes, and sandwiches; and puts on an excellent lunchtime soup-and-bread buffet (daily 12:00-22:00, Grundargata 1, mobile 666-3399).

• *Continue south on highway 82.*

Beer pilgrims might consider a short detour at **Árskógssan-dur** ("Riverwood Sands," about 7 miles/10 minutes past Dalvík). This is home to **Kaldi,** Iceland's oldest microbrewery (since 2006), which offers tours of its factory (2,000 ISK, hourly tours Mon-Fri 11:00-15:00, call ahead at other times, tel. 466-2505, www.bruggsmidjan.is). A short drive away is their brewpub, **Bjórböðin,** with locally produced beers, food, and even a beer spa—where you can immerse yourself in the hoppy stuff (reserve ahead for the spa, www.bjorbodin.com).

• *Highway 82 dead-ends at highway 1 (the Ring Road proper), about 20 miles beyond Dalvík. From the T-intersection where highways 82 and 1 meet, it's six more miles to Akureyri.*

Akureyri

Akureyri (AH-kuh-RAY-ree; "Field Spit"), with just 18,000 people, still qualifies as Iceland's second city and the unofficial capital of North Iceland. In many ways, Akureyri is a mini Reykjavík. Its pint-sized, pedestrian-friendly old town has an artfully graffitied vibe and small outposts of big Reykjavík shops. There's a mini church designed by Guðjón Samúelsson (architect of Reykjavík's Hallgrímskirkja), a mini *Sun Voyager* statue along its waterfront, and even its own mini Pond (south of town, near the airport).

But, like any second city, Akureyri has its own proud identity. The town is a jolt of prosperity and commerce wedged between the many sleepy Ring Road villages. And its setting, right along

the deep Eyjafjörður, easily one-ups Reykjavík's. The city's history is very short, as there was little settlement here until the late 19th century. Fishing is the mainstay of the economy, and there's also a small university and a hospital.

Though a perfectly pleasant place, Akureyri doesn't have a lot of sightseeing. On a quick trip around the Ring Road, it's best as a handy stop for a meal and a short stroll. With a little more time, poke into its striking church, wander its botanical gardens, or enjoy its large thermal swimming pool complex (both the botanic gardens and the pool are open late). And if you're interested in whale watching, this is one of the places in Iceland to do it (though it's arguably better in Húsavík, a bit farther along the Ring, and easier in Reykjavík).

Orientation to Akureyri

Whether you're coming directly across the mountains from Skagafjörður, or around the top of Tröllaskagi, you'll approach Akureyri on southbound high-way 1. This main road carries you right through the center of town, and then turns to cross the fjord just by Akureyri's air-port.

Tourist Information: You'll find Akureyri's TI in the Hof conference and cultural center, a striking, round, brown build-ing—you can't miss it as you drive in. The staff is helpful and well-informed, and you can pick up brochures for all of Iceland (June-late Sept daily 8:00-18:30, late-Sept-May until 16:00, closed Sat-Sun in winter, Strandgata 12, tel. 450-1050, www.visitakureyri.is).

Parking: Lots in downtown Akureyri require that you put a little blue cardboard clock (called a *bifreiðastæðaklukka*, or *klukka* for short) on your dashboard showing the time you arrived (signs clearly indicate the maximum stay; enforced Mon-Fri 10:00-16:00). If you need a clock, ask at the TI, a local gas station, or a bank.

Sights in Akureyri

Town Walk

Begin by exploring the vest-pocket town center, a pleasant grid of not quite traffic-free streets lined with good restaurants and touristy shops (including branches of Eymundsson bookstore, Rammagerðin gift shop, and clothing stores 66° North and Geysir). It takes just a few enjoyable minutes to wander here and get your bearings. With ample time and a desire to go for a long, level stroll, head right (as you face the fjord) and walk along the water, past

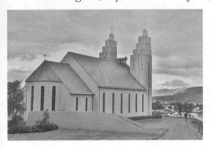

some traditional architecture, all the way to Akureyri's mini Pond and sports arena, then loop back.

With less time, head up rather than out: In the town center, with your back to the water, you'll see steps leading up to the hill-capping Lutheran Akureyri church (Akureyrarkirkja), with Art Deco lines and a crushed-volcanic-rock facade.

Akureyri Botanical Garden (Lystigarður Akureyrar)

Akureyri's top attraction is its botanical garden. This city park—compact but smartly designed and impeccably maintained—showcases northern plants (all labeled). Its pleasant, recommended café, in the middle of the park, is a handy landmark. Uphill (away from the waterfront) and to the left, you'll find a little alpine gar-

den, with mountain flora planted in a pretty rockery. Downhill from the café is planted with lusher Icelandic and Arctic flora.

Cost and Hours: Free, open daily June-Sept, between Eyrarlandsvegur and Þórunnarstræti, free parking by the east (main) and west entrances, tel. 462-7487, www.lystigardur.akureyri.is.

Akureyri Thermal Pool (Sundlaug Akereyrar)

Akureyri's fine thermal swimming pool has extensive outdoor areas, including an ambitious waterslide. If you have yet to try an Icelandic pool, this sprawling complex is a fun place to start.

Cost and Hours: 900 ISK, June-Aug Mon-Fri 6:45-21:00, Sat-Sun 8:00-19:30, shorter hours off-season, corner of Þingvallastræti and Þórunnarstræti at the top of town (east of the botanical garden), parking lot just south on Hrafnagilsstræti, tel. 461-4455.

Akureyri Museums

If you have the time, consider one of Akureyri's many good museums. Top of the list is the **aviation museum** (Flugsafn Íslands), in a building at the airport (June-Sept daily 11:00-17:00, Oct-May by appointment, tel. 461-4400, www.flugsafn.is). There's also a city history museum, an engineering museum, and a motorcycle museum. For details, ask at the TI.

Whale Watching, Island Hopping, and Other Excursions

Whale watching and other excursion boats line up at the waterfront. It's best to book ahead—well-established companies include Elding (www.elding.is) and Ambassador (www.ambassador.is). Expect to pay around $100 for a classic three-hour cruise (double that for a high-speed RIB trip).

Akureyri is also a hub for day trips (by boat or plane) to the little island of Grímsey, just north of the Arctic Circle (see the "Islands in North Iceland" sidebar, earlier).

An excursion can make it easier to link up Akureyri with the worthwhile sights around Mývatn. Star Travel (www.startravel.is), The Traveling Viking (www.ttv.is), and Saga Travel (www.sagatravel.is) all run day tours (around $200).

Sleeping in Akureyri

You could do worse than sleeping in Akureyri, which feels like a return to civilization for Ring drivers. The town is also a good base for day trips: Head to lake Mývatn one day, to Siglufjörður the next, and so on.

In the Center: $$$$ Hótel Kea is a classic address with 104 business-class rooms right downtown, putting all of Akureyri at your doorstep...but you'll pay royally for the privilege (very slushy rates, elevator, Hafnarstræti 87, tel. 460-2000, www.keahotels.is, kea@keahotels.is). **$$$ Icelandair Hótel Akureyri,** with 100 well-designed rooms, offers big-hotel comfort at more reasonable prices. It's in a residential zone up at the top of town, across from the swimming pool (breakfast extra, Þingvallastræti 23, tel. 518-1000, www.icelandairhotels.com, akureyri@icehotels.is). ¢ Akureyri's **official**

youth hostel has 49 beds (Stórholt 1, tel. 462-3657, www.hostel.is, akureyri@hostel.is).

Cheaper Options Outside Town: In the idyllic countryside 10 minutes south of Akureyri, **$$ Lamb Inn** is on a working family farm called Öngulsstaðir. It rents 24 straightforward rooms in a converted cowshed, most with simple, prefab-like bathrooms (but some cheaper rooms with shared bath). They have a hot tub for guests, and a good dinner-only restaurant serving lamb raised right here (Öngulsstaðir 3, tel. 463-1500, www.lambinn.is, lambinn@lambinn.is). **$ Lónsá,** a suburban farm on the northern edge of town, is a 13-room guesthouse with shared bath, a guest kitchen, lounge, and laundry facilities. The lodgings are quite basic, but clean. In old-fashioned Icelandic style, you get a better rate if you bring your sleeping bag—you get a pillow, pillowcase, and bottom sheet, and can pay extra for a towel (tel. 462-5037, www.lonsa.is, lonsa@simnet.is).

Eating in Akureyri

In the Town Center: To get a taste of Akureyri, window-shop menus at the dozen or so eateries—ranging from a hot-dog wagon or fish-and-chips to Tex-Mex or curry.

For a cozy, casual space, look for **$$ Kaffi Ilmur** ("Aroma Café"), filling an old house on a hillside a few steps above the main grid of streets (daily 8:00-23:00 in summer, lunch-only in Oct-May, Hafnarstræti 107b, tel. 571-6444, www.kaffiilmur.com).

$ Berlín, with a cozy, tight, hipster vibe, is popular for breakfast and lunch (cheap salads and sandwiches, daily 8:00-18:00, Skipagata 4, tel. 547-2226).

Nearby, you can ride an elevator to the top floor of a downtown high-rise (which, here in Akureyri, means just five stories) to **$$$ Strikið,** a modern Nordic bistro with an eclectic menu. While quite pricey at dinner, they offer good lunch specials with a view (daily 11:30-22:30, Skipagata 14, tel. 462-7100, www.strikid.is).

And for top-end dining, **$$$$ Rub 23** has a reputation even among Reykjavík urbanites for its grill-focused Asian-fusion food (Mon-Fri 11:00-14:00 & 17:30-22:00, dinner-only Sat-Sun, across the street from the church steps at Kaupvangsstræti 6, tel. 462-2223, www.rub23.is).

In the Botanical Garden: At the center of the gardens is **$ Café Laut,** serving sandwiches, salads, and soup in a striking picture-windowed building (late May-late Sept daily 10:00-20:00, closed off-season, Eyrarlandsvegur 30, tel. 461-4601).

Supermarket: Bónus is along the main road as you drive into town from the west (Langholt 1). There's also **Nettó,** in the Glerártorg mall, also along the main road.

Akureyri Connections

Akureyri is a transportation hub for the north and is well-connected to **Reykjavík** by bus (2/day, 1/day on Sat, 6.5 hours, www. straeto.is). You can also fly from Reykjavík into the Akureyri airport, which is about two miles from the center (car rental and taxis available; look for flights at www.airicelandconnect.com).

In summer (June-mid-Aug), other bus connections may be useful, but they don't work for a same-day round-trip: Once daily, a bus leaves in the afternoon for **Mývatn** (3.5 hours), then continues on to **Egilsstaðir** (a hub for the Eastfjords, 5.5 hours).

To reach the fun little fjordside town of **Siglufjörður** and its Herring Era Museum, in summer three daily buses allow for a same-day return (1.5 hours each way; for the best views, sit on the right on the way up, and the left on the way back).

Off-season, all bus schedules are reduced. Long-distance buses stop at the Hof conference and cultural center, by the TI.

Akureyri to Mývatn Route Overview

It's about 60 miles/75 minutes from Akureyri to Mývatn.

Leaving Akureyri: From Akureyri, highway 1 crosses the fjord by the airport and turns north along the opposite shore (pull-outs offer views across the fjord to the city). After about 20 minutes, the road climbs steeply away from the fjord and crosses the first pass of the day, **Víkurskarð** (1,100 feet). Víkurskarð is treacherous in snow; a toll tunnel called Vaðlaheiðargöng, which barrels straight under the mountain, is under construction. It may be open by the time you read this, but in good weather, I'd take the scenic pass rather than paying for the tunnel, which only saves a few minutes.

• *After about 45 minutes, you'll reach...*

Goðafoss Waterfall: This ▲ pretty, horseshoe-shaped waterfall is not so high (only 40 feet), but it is quite broad (30 yards). It's right along the main road, there's free parking (as well as a big shop with the uninspired **$ Fosshóll Café**), and it takes just a couple of minutes to walk to the best views. The pedestrian bridge here was once the main road. People enjoy scram-bling across the tidepool-like rocks at the top of the falls.

This waterfall plays a role in the sagas. In A.D. 1000, the law speaker of the Alþingi made a momentous decision: Þorgeir Ljósvetningagoði, whose home farm (Ljósavatn) was in this area, was assigned to choose whether Iceland would remain pagan or (under great pressure from Norway) become Christian. Þorgeir chose to have Iceland convert, and to fully own up to his decision, he became a Christian, came home, and threw his carved pagan statues into this waterfall—giving it the name "Waterfall of the Gods" (Goða-foss). For more on Þorgeir, see page 188.

• *From Goðafoss, the road climbs over a low pass called **Fljótsheiði** (800 feet) and drops down to the small settlement of Laugar, with hot springs and a high school.*

Laugar to Mývatn: There's not too much to see in this sparsely populated countryside. You'll pass a few farms and drive along the shore of a desolate lake, then along a small river, **Laxá**. The river is famous as the site where, in 1970, almost two hundred locals took matters into their own hands and blew up a small, controversial dam they had opposed. Over a hundred individuals "confessed" to the crime and refused to say who did what, making prosecution difficult.

• *About an hour from Akureyri, you'll reach the junction of highways 1 and 848. Carry straight along on highway 848.*

You're just west of lake **Mývatn**. From here, follow highway 848 counterclockwise as it loops around the south and east shore of the lake, with several attractions (described next).

From Mývatn, it's a 45-minute detour north on highway 87 to the bayside town of **Húsavík** (described on page 312).

Mývatn

Mývatn (MEE-vaht; *n* almost silent—literally "Midge Lake," after the tiny gnats that thrive here) is one of Iceland's most impressive natural areas. The lake itself—about 14 square miles, broad and shallow—has an intriguingly ragged coastline, with lots of bays and islets. Better still, it's ringed by a delightful array of volcanic features, from bubbly pseudocraters to otherworldly pillars to a climbable volcanic cone.

RING ROAD

Mývatn Area

Leirhnjúkur · Víti

Krafla Geothermal Valley

KRAFLA GEOTHERMAL POWER PLANT · Krafla

ICELAND
Akureyri · Egilsstaðir
⊗ Reykjavík
Vík

50 KM
50 Miles

3 Kilometers
3 Miles

To Húsavík 87

To Dettifoss, Egilsstaðir & Eastfjords

Reykjahlíð 1

Námaskarð Pass 863

SIGURGEIR'S BIRD MUSEUM

848 860

Námafjall

❼ MÝVATN NATURE BATHS

Grjótagjá Cave

Lake Mývatn

To Akureyri, Goðafoss & ❺

Höfði Promontory ❷

Hverfjall Crater

❻ Dimmuborgir Lava Formations

Skútustaðir Pseudocraters

1 848

Skútustaðir ❸ 848

849

Note: Driving route road width exaggerated for clarity

- - - - Recommended Driving Route

❶ Vogafjós Guesthouse & Cowshed Café
❷ Dimmuborgir Guesthouse
❸ Sel-Hótel Mývatn, Skútustaðir Guesthouse & Kaffi Sel
❹ Icelandair Hótel Reynihlíð
❺ To Stöng Farm Rooms
❻ Kaffi Borgir
❼ Kaffi Kvika

A short drive away are even more sights, including a geothermally active valley and one of Iceland's best premium thermal baths. The entire area is ringed by striking flat-topped mountains, making it feel like the setting for an interplanetary science fiction epic. With its accessible size, remote location, and diversity of easy nature hikes, Mývatn feels like Iceland's Yellowstone; many visitors hail it as their favorite area of all.

Note that the Mývatn area lacks a real town, but the appealing small town of Húsavík is just a 45-minute drive north. Húsavík is worth a detour (and can be a good place to stay, if Mývatn is full or if you're interested in whale watching; see page 313).

The Geology, Flora, Fauna (and Midges) of Mývatn

Because Mývatn sits along the gap between the Eurasian and North American tectonic plates, the area is very active geothermally. Relatively recent volcanic eruptions—about 2,300 years ago—shaped the landscape here: A volcanic eruption created the Hverfjall crater, and vast amounts of lava from a fissure (vent) eruption poured out over the area and flowed down the valley toward Akureyri.

The lake is protected, and boating is restricted. The water is shallow and calm; ducks and other water birds breed around the lake and its surrounding wetlands. Far from the sea, the area has slightly warmer, drier, and less windy summers than other parts of the country.

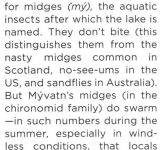

Unfortunately, these conditions make it a perfect home for midges *(mý)*, the aquatic insects after which the lake is named. They don't bite (this distinguishes them from the nasty midges common in Scotland, no-see-ums in the US, and sandflies in Australia). But Mývatn's midges (in the chironomid family) do swarm —in such numbers during the summer, especially in windless conditions, that locals often wear nets over their heads to stop the little things from getting into their ears, mouths, and noses.

Mývatn is also home to black flies *(Simulium vittatum)*, which do bite. Fortunately, these are mostly concentrated in the less touristed western end of the lake and the Laxá river, and with luck, you won't encounter them at all. (They're also found elsewhere in Iceland.)

Mývatn has plenty of biodiversity beyond its bugs and birds. The lake itself is rich in nutrients and has an abundance of aquatic life. For example, Mývatn once supported an unusual algae that forms into lovable green, softball-size spheres. Unfortunately, the balls have mostly disappeared from Mývatn in the last few years—no one knows exactly why.

Orientation to Mývatn

"Mývatn" is the name of the lake, but also refers to the entire area (which Icelanders call Mývatnssveit). Sights are scattered around the lake, which is ringed by two roads. Highway 1 runs along the east and north side, with few sights other than Sigurgeir's Bird Museum. Highway 848, on the south and east sides, is more interesting, especially along the 10-mile stretch between the hamlets of Skútustaðir and Reykjahlíð. Another cluster of sights lines the stretch of highway 1 that runs east away from the lake, toward the Eastfjords.

Most settlement around the lake is on dispersed farms. **Reykjahlíð** (RAKE-ya-HLEETHE, "Smoky Hills"), at the lake's northeast corner, is the closest Mývatn comes to having a village. It has a small supermarket and fast-food stand, bank, gas station, health center, and a few streets of houses. **Skútustaðir** (SKOO-tu-STAH-theer), on the southern shore, is just a church, hotel, convenience store, and gas pumps, next to a farm.

Tourist Information: Locals are generous with tips, and the website VisitMyvatn.is is helpful.

Navigation Note: Google Maps makes some errors in this area; supplement with printed maps or the local website Ja.is.

Tours and Activities: In the parking lot of Icelandair Hótel Reynihlíð, **Mývatn Activity** rents bikes and can arrange bike, hiking, and jeep tours as well as other activities (tel. 899-4845, www.myvatnactivity.is). **Mýflug Air** runs sightseeing flights over the region (www.myflug.is). Various local companies offer **horseback riding** (Saltvík: www.saltvik.is; Safari Horse Rental: http://safarihorserental.com). If you stay longer in the region, several operators offer day trips to the giant **Askja** volcanic caldera, deep in the Highlands south of Mývatn, which you can reach only in a 4x4 vehicle (Fjallasýn: www.fjallasyn.is; Mývatn Tours: www.myvatntours.is).

Eating: This area has no real "destination" restaurants, but I've listed a few practical choices mixed in with the sights. Try to sample two local products that are often served together: sweet, dark-rye bread that's buried underground and baked with natural thermal heat, then topped with decadent, smoked lake trout.

Dealing with Midges: You may want to wear a net to protect yourself from midges flying into your nose, ears, or mouth (see sidebar, previous page). You can bring one from home or buy one locally (sold at area supermarkets). Don't bother using insect repellent: The bugs aren't out to bite you—they're just a nuisance.

Sights near Mývatn

AROUND THE SOUTH AND EAST SHORE

These attractions ring the lakefront. I've listed them in the order you'll encounter them driving counterclockwise from Skútustaðir (southwest) to Reykjahlíð (northeast) along highway 848.

▲Skútustaðir Pseudocraters

At the tiny settlement called Skútustaðir, you reach the first of many striking volcanic sights at the lake. Park at the lot (across from the big Sel-Hótel Mývatn) and spend 20 minutes walking the half-mile "Crater Trail," between the road and the lake, through

the pseudocraters (also called "rootless cones"). These are not real volcanic craters. They're all that's left of what had been giant bubbles in molten lava: Water under the lava boiled into steam, rose to the surface, and popped. Metal stairs lead up to the rims of several of the craters. A longer path here ("Bird Trail," 1.5 miles) takes an hour.

Eating at Skútustaðir: Located in the hotel's parking lot, **$ Kaffi Sel** serves cheap, simple grill meals and a handy, lunchtime soup-and-bread buffet (daily, tel. 464-4164, www.myvatn.is). The restaurant inside **$$ Sel-Hótel Mývatn** has a more substantial lunch buffet for about double the price (daily).

• *To continue around the lake, follow the lakeside road counterclockwise. Within a few miles you'll leave grassy rolling hills and enter a lunar landscape covered by a petrified lava flow. Watch on the left for a pullout overlooking a lagoon that's filled with serrated lava islands. As you look out over the water, notice the wooded peninsula to the north (on your right). This is...*

Höfði Promontory

For years, a local couple worked to reforest this small peninsula, and laid out sheltered walking trails with views of the lake and the lava columns that rise up from it. It has its own parking lot (just beyond the pullout mentioned above) and makes a nice 30-minute stop on a pleasant day. If you come on a calm summer day, you may see more insects than you ever have in your life. Wear a net, or prepare to spit midges; they don't bite, and the swarms are actually kind of impressive.

• *On the land side of the road, a little farther north (toward Reykjahlíð), is the next stop.*

▲▲Dimmuborgir Lava Formations

Literally the "Dark Castles," this area is a fantasyland of spectacular pillars and crenellated formations. It's the most satisfying place around the lake for an easy nature walk, and it's fun for kids. The Dimmuborgir (DIM-moo-BOR-geer) formations originated when everything here was underwater. From the lake bed, magma leaked upward and solidified, forming spiky, stalagmite-like columns. Well-marked, paved trails lead through Dimmuborgir; study the

posted map to plan a route for
the amount of time you have.
The shortest walk takes only 15
minutes, but you could easily
spend two hours here. Entrance
and parking is free (pay WC at
the café), and if you visit early or
late, it will be less crowded.

Eating at Dimmuborgir:
In the Dimmuborgir parking
lot, **$$ Kaffi Borgir** has a soup-and-bread lunch buffet and a short
menu of main dishes. If you can handle the midges, their outdoor
seating is atmospheric (daily 10:00-21:30, closed off-season, tel.
461-1144, www.kaffiborgir.is).

▲▲Hverfjall Crater

This vast, dry volcanic crater (HVER-fyahtl, sometimes spelled
Hverfell) rises just east of the lake—you can't miss it. A short gravel
road (watch for *Hverfjall* signs) leads 1.5 miles along a rutted gravel
road off highway 848 to a free parking lot (pay WCs, credit card
only). From the parking lot, a path leads up the side of the moun-
tain to the rim, where there's an excellent view down into the broad
crater and back toward the lake. The hike up is a good workout,
but isn't too steep and takes about 20 minutes one-way. In strong
winds, the walk up isn't much fun, and the loose soil can start to fly
around; otherwise, it'll reward your effort.

Eating near Hverfjall: Just north along the road toward
Reykjahlíð is **$$$ Cowshed Café,** with a country-kitschy vibe and
tasty homemade cooking; it's my favorite choice for a meal in the
area (it's part of the recommended Vogafjós Guesthouse). It's in a
barn, with views of the lakeshore and mooing cows—you can ask
to see the milking area (daily 11:00-22:00 in summer, may close
earlier off-season, tel. 464-3800, www.vogafjos.is).

• *The next stop is best reached from highway 1 (see complete directions
below).*

Grjótagjá Thermal Cave

Tucked in the middle of nowhere a few minutes' drive from the lake
is a hidden cave filled with natural thermal waters. It gets more
attention than it deserves for being a filming location for *Game of
Thrones* (the romantic retreat where Jon Snow and Ygritte, ahem,
violated the oath of the Night's Watch). While skippable for most,
curious *GoT* fans may find the brief detour justifiable. You'll walk
to a crevasse, where extremely uneven, rocky footing leads down to
a steaming pool. Watch your step—this is at your own risk, with
no guardrails or barriers—and actually getting in the water is for-

bidden. While this feels impossibly remote, you'll likely see a steady stream of bus tours stopping here.

Getting There: Even though it's on road 860, Grjótagjá is most easily accessed from highway 1, just east of the lake but before the turnoff for Mývatn Thermal Baths; watch for the small *Grjótagjá* sign. From the turnoff, it's a quick 1.5-mile drive. Note that road 860 continues (unpaved) from the cave all the way to Mývatn's east shore (near Vogafjós Guesthouse); this can be a handy shortcut, but you'll need to let yourself through a gate.

ON THE NORTHWEST SHORE
▲Sigurgeir's Bird Museum (Fuglasafn Sigurgeirs)

Mývatn is famous among birders, who have observed more than 115 species here (including 30 different types of ducks)—making it one of the richest birding areas in the world. This museum offers an opportunity to examine hundreds of taxidermied specimens up close (as well as an extensive egg collection). Display cases show off a striking diversity of birds, including nearly every bird found in Iceland and many who migrate here to breed. Webcams and telescopes let you observe living birds on the lake, and the staff loves to advise visiting birders. A second, smaller building displays artifacts from the Mývatn area, including a boat once used to ferry passengers across the lake.

The collection is named for avid birder Sigurgeir Stefánsson, who lived on this farm and collected most of the specimens you see (usually birds that were already dead). Nature did not return his kindness, as at age 37, Sigurgeir drowned during a freak storm on the lake. But his legacy—and his passion—live on here.

Cost and Hours: 1,200 ISK, June-late Aug daily 9:00-18:00, late May and late Aug-Oct daily 12:00-17:00, shorter hours off-season, on-site café, on road 8735 at the farm called Ytri-Neslönd—signposted off highway 1, tel. 464-4477, www.fuglasafn.is.

GEOTHERMAL SIGHTS JUST EAST OF MÝVATN

On and near highway 1 going east from the lake are several other worthwhile attractions—most of them related to the geothermally alive landscape. You might find it simplest to fit these in on your way from Mývatn to the Eastfjords, but it'd be a shame to rush them. Since they're all within 10 miles of the lake, you can easily double back if you're staying nearby.

RING ROAD

• *Just off highway 1, five minutes from Reykjahlíð (and before Námaskarð pass), you'll come to...*

▲▲▲Mývatn Nature Baths (Jarðböðin við Mývatn)

This premium swimming pool is one of Iceland's most appealing thermal bath experiences. Imagine the Blue Lagoon, but a bit more modest, less crowded, and about half the price. The baths' outdoor lagoon is beautifully designed: two big pools with natural contours, rocky walls, pebbly bottoms, and fine views over the volcanic countryside (black rock, steaming vents, and distant lake views). Like the Blue Lagoon, the water here is naturally heated excess from a nearby geothermal power station (at Bjarnarflag); unlike the Blue Lagoon, the water here isn't salty, has no silica suspended in it, is more white than blue, and has a slightly sulfurous odor. The nature baths are open late, making it an ideal way to unwind after a long day driving the Ring or exploring Mývatn. It's not quite luxurious or spa-like (no swim-up bar, no mud masks, no private shower cabins), but for many, these baths are a just-right Goldilocks compromise between the expense and pretense of the Blue Lagoon and the austere functionality of standard municipal pools. Locals enjoy it, too.

Cost and Hours: 4,300 ISK, towel rental-700 ISK, daily late May-Sept 9:00-24:00, off-season 12:00-22:00, they don't take reservations, often referred to as *Jarðbaðshólar* on maps and signs, tel. 464-4411, www.myvatnnaturebaths.is.

Visiting the Baths: The modern entry building has free parking, a nice café, free WCs even for nonbathers, and a view deck overlooking the pool. Buy your ticket (prepay for a drink, if you like), find your way to the simple locker room, shower, and stow your clothes. It's best to remove easily tarnished jewelry and glasses or other delicate lenses, which can be damaged by the water's minerals (for more on best practices at thermal pools, see page 42). Then head outside and lower yourself into the steaming water, which is highly alkaline and slightly milky. Temperatures range from 34°C to 41°C (93-105°F), with hot and cool spots around the pool. Explore, float, and relax. If you bought a drink, flag down an attendant to bring it to you. The two steam baths, in little sheds around the pools' perimeter, vent natural geothermal steam through the floor at a temperature of about 50°C (122°F).

Eating at the Baths: The complex has a good cafeteria, **$ Kaffi Kvika** ("Magma Café"), with indoor and outdoor seating overlooking the lively lagoon (no bath ticket required). As this is essentially your "last-chance lunch" (other than picnicking) between here and the Eastfjords, consider stopping on your way out of the area (open same hours as pool). You're not allowed to eat your own food on the premises.

• *Just five minutes beyond the baths, you'll crest the small Námaskarð pass. Watch on the right (after the steep initial climb) for a pullout with a commanding panoramic view over the entire Mývatn area. Coming down the other side of the pass, a turnoff on the right leads in a couple hundred yards to a parking lot for the...*

▲▲▲Námafjall Geothermal Area

The steaming, bubbling, brightly colored landscape of Námafjall (NOW-mah-fyahtl)—which is also sometimes called Hverir ("Hot Springs") or Hverarönd— is one of Iceland's most accessible and impressive geothermal areas. While it lacks a spouting geyser, it's more colorful and more interesting (and in a more impressive setting, ringed by mountains) than Geysir on the Golden Circle—and it's far less crowded, with very few ropes and signs (be careful and stay on the trodden paths).

Park and step outside—getting slapped in the face with pungent hydrogen sulfide fumes. Then plug your nose and explore this compact, astonishingly diverse landscape. You'll see fumaroles (like little stacked-rock ovens spitting steam), bubbling pools, and a terrain brushed in a rainbow of vivid colors. The mountainside just beyond the plain also has steaming vents; with extra time, you can hike up the trail for a closer look and for views back over this landscape. The sulfur deposits in this area were once mined for gunpowder (*náma* means "mine").

• *A quarter-mile farther on, detour onto paved highway 863 (to the north). This five-mile-long road passes through a steaming landscape, linking several worthwhile attractions.*

▲▲Krafla Geothermal Valley

The volcano Krafla (KRAH-plah), at the end of this valley, was active as recently as the 1980s; now the valley is the site of a geothermal power plant (notice the pipeline and electric cables on your left).

• *As you head up the valley, keep an eye out on the right for a...*

Showerhead: Sticking up from the ground, a single showerhead stands lonely in the middle of a volcanic plain. It appeared overnight several years ago—perhaps as a prank or art installation—but it really is hooked up to natural thermal water; you may see it being used by campers and hikers who can't afford the pricey thermal-baths complex.

• *Continuing up the valley, you can't miss the simmering...*

Krafla Geothermal Power Plant: This plant taps into su-

perheated liquid deep underground. Its modest, summer-only visitors center has exhibits and a brief film about Iceland's geothermal plants (free entry, WCs, and coffee; June–mid-Sept daily 10:00-17:00, closed off-season).

• *After leaving the power station, there's a parking lot on the left at the head of a marked path that takes you across a lava field to the...*

Leirhnjúkur Volcanic Cone: Meaning literally "Clay Peak," this low volcanic cone formed recently in eruptions around 1980. Volcano buffs enjoy the full hiking circuit here—all the way around the mountain. It takes about three hours and includes colorful pools, still-steaming lava formations, and more. To get a quick feel for the place, walk out to the mountain and back (about 15 minutes each way, partly on boardwalks); you'll see some mud pots and fumaroles. The footing can be slippery—if you value your shoes (and feet), stay on the marked paths.

• *Continuing on the main road past the Leirhnjúkur parking lot, look for a pullout on the right with a stunning view back over the valley. Then drive to the end of the road and the...*

Víti Crater: This unearthly

volcanic crater with a lake inside was formed during eruptions in the 1720s. You'll park virtually next to the rim, with fantastic views over the colorful walls and water. From here, a path leads all the way around the crater. Víti ("Hell") is big, wild, and an altogether powerful and forbidding sight. Don't go down to the water, which is hot.

Sleeping near Mývatn

The sparsely populated communities that ring the lake have a handful of accommodations, but not enough to cater to the increasing summertime crowds. While this is a delightful area to spend the night, reserve your rooms well ahead, as hotels can book up very quickly. If things are booked solid, stay in Húsavík—a pleasant waterfront town a 45-minute drive north (described later). You can also try checking back to see if you can fill a cancellation. Camping is allowed only at designated sites.

On the Eastern Shore: Near all the major attractions, **$$$$ Vogafjós Guesthouse** is a family-run working farm with 26 good, tidy rooms in three new prefab wooden buildings. Reception is at the recommended Cowshed Café restaurant (tel. 464-3800, www.vogafjos.is, vogafjos@vogafjos.is). **$$ Dimmuborgir Guesthouse** has eight simple rooms (with private bathrooms and a shared kitchen) in a main building, as well as prefab wooden cottages (all with private bath and kitchen). It's loosely run but family-friendly, and they catch and smoke their own fish (2-night minimum in summer, Geiteyjarströnd 1, tel. 464-4210, www.dimmuborgir.is, dimmuborgir@emax.is).

On the Southern Shore, at Skútustaðir: Family-run but characterless, **$$$$ Sel-Hótel Mývatn** has 58 expensive rooms that feel designed for tour groups and conferences. It's right next to the pseudocraters, with a shop, café, and restaurant on-site (elevator, tel. 464-4164, www.myvatn.is, myvatn@myvatn.is). **$$ Skútustaðir Guesthouse,** tucked behind the Sel-Hótel complex, rents 15 modern rooms (10 of which share bathrooms, 5 with private bathrooms) in a mix of old and new buildings, plus a standalone cottage (tel. 464-4212, www.skutustadir.is, info@skutustadir.is).

On the Northern Shore, at Reykjahlíð: Bragging that it's the "oldest country hotel in Iceland," **$$$ Icelandair Hótel Reynihlíð** has 41 modern, hardwood rooms, along with a restaurant, comfy lounge with piano, and sauna for guests (tel. 464-4170, www. icelandairhotels.com). Note: This is different from the Hótel Reykjahlíð, an older option nearby.

In the Countryside to the West: An authentic farm, **$$ Stöng** is a couple of miles down an unpaved side road, on the way from Goðafoss to Mývatn. Their two dozen rooms are spread among a main building (from the 1920s), a motel, and cottage-style outbuildings. It's not as spiffy as other options, but it's less expensive and guests can use the hot tub. Older rooms in the main building have a shared bath; private-bath rooms are more modern but still basic (closed Nov-March, restaurant with pricey traditional dinners, tel. 464-4252, mobile 896-6074, www.stong.is, stongmy@stong.is).

Húsavík

Húsavík (HOOS-ah-VEEK, pop. 2,200), north of Mývatn, is a pretty town with a nice harbor facing the fjordlike Skjálfandi bay. For visitors with time to linger, Húsavík offers a pleasant real-town vibe, appealing restaurants, a good swimming pool, a colorful town church, a good whale museum, and some of Iceland's best whale watching. If you're enjoying long summer days and want to take a dinnertime side-trip, Húsavík

is pleasant enough to warrant the drive from Mývatn. Húsavík is also a good fallback home-base when rooms around Mývatn are all booked up.

Getting There: Húsavík is about a 45-minute drive (35 miles) from Mývatn, north on highway 87 from near Reykjahlíð. As you leave the lake area, you'll pass through a bulging volcanic landscape; you can see clearly where the undulating lava buckled and bubbled as it cooled. Then you'll traverse a stark, desolate terrain,

The Other Circle

In the Mývatn and Húsavík area, you may notice references to the "Diamond Circle." This recently coined tourist route—a would-be competitor to the Golden Circle closer to Reykjavík—is a suggested sightseeing route through northeast Iceland that connects Mývatn, Húsavík, the Tjörnes Peninsula, Ásbyrgi (a stunning set of cliffs and canyons formed by massive glacial flooding a few thousand years ago), and Dettifoss waterfall (for specifics, see www.diamondcircle.is).

Note that from Ásbyrgi (50 minutes north Húsavík), gravel roads 862 and 864 (open in summer only) lead along either side of the Jökulsá á Fjöllum river to Dettifoss; from there you can continue back to the Ring without backtracking through Mývatn. You'll probably need four-wheel drive for these rough roads, though (check conditions at www.road.is and with locals before proceeding). While striking, Ásbyrgi is, for most visitors, a long and challenging drive. But if roads improve in this area, Ásbyrgi could become easier to build into a Ring Road trip.

with little settlement and several stretches of unpaved road. Eventually you run into the picturesque Skjálfandi bay, turn right onto highway 85, and carry on into town.

Orientation to Húsavík: This little town is simple. The main road coasts downhill to the town center and a handy parking lot on the harbor. Everything I mention is within a five-minute stroll. The Húsavík Whale Museum ticket desk serves as a basic town **TI,** with maps and brochures (see www.visithusavik.com).

Sights in Húsavík

▲▲Whale Watching

Facing the Greenland Sea and about as far north as you can get in Iceland (next stop: Arctic Circle), Húsavík is one of Iceland's

top whale watching destinations, with the best likelihood of actually seeing a whale. Several well-established companies have sales kiosks overlooking the hardworking harbor. Options range from classic old wooden boats to high-speed RIBs (rigid

inflatable boats). A standard three-hour trip costs around 10,000 ISK. The main operators include North Sailing (www.northsailing. is), Gentle Giants (www.gentlegiants.is), and Salka Whale Watching (www.salkawhalewatching.is). If your time in this area is limited, consider whale watching from Reykjavík or Akureyri.

▲Húsavík Whale Museum (Hvalasafnið á Húsavík)

This thoughtful museum offers an informative look at the whales that fill the waters around Iceland. Though fairly dry and scientif-

ic, the exhibits are good, with miniature models of whales, an actual jawbone of a sperm whale, a display on seabirds, a one-hour *Giants of the Deep* film, and several good children's areas. But the museum's highlight is hanging from the rafters

upstairs: the skeletons of 11 different whale species, including narwhal, sperm, humpback, orca, and pilot. The biggest skeleton—in the side hall on the main floor—is an 80-foot-long blue whale. These specimens were not hunted, but washed up on beaches, then

Whaling in Iceland

While early Icelanders did occasionally catch whales, using Moby Dick-style harpoons, they lacked the technology to exploit the sea mammals at any commercial scale. Whalers in the seas around Iceland came mostly from Europe: Basque sailors began whaling in the Atlantic in the 11th century, reaching Icelandic waters in the 17th century. They occasionally clashed with locals, and in 1615, Icelanders massacred 30 Basque castaways in the Westfjords in an event called the "Slaying of the Spaniards." In the late 17th century, Dutch whalers arrived, and Norwegians dominated the industry from about 1883 until overhunting led to a ban in 1915. Whaling resumed in 1935, with another ban in 1983. In 2006, Iceland controversially decided to permit commercial whale hunting, both of relatively abundant minke whales and of threatened fin and sei whales.

removed and processed by the museum. (Anytime a beached whale corpse appears around Iceland, locals call the museum to come cart it away.) Rounding out the exhibits are art installations related to whales and an unapologetic overview of the history of whaling in Iceland, including a film with archival footage of workers processing and rendering slabs of blubber.

Cost and Hours: 1,900 ISK; generally daily May-Sept 8:30-18:30, Oct-April 10:00-16:00, closed Sat-Sun in Nov-March; Hafnarstétt 1, tel. 414-2800, www.whalemuseum.is.

Húsavík Church (Húsavíkurkirkja)

Húsavík's unusually colorful and interesting town church dates from 1907 (you can't miss it along the main street as you come into town). Stepping inside, it's clear this church was designed by shipbuilders: Stout beams intersect in the middle of the ceiling, like perpendicular boat hulls, all painted in cheery colors. Rather than a pulpit, there's a simple lectern, shaped like an open book. Notice the c. 1930 painting over the altar depicting the resurrection of Lazarus...but set in Iceland (see the backdrop of lava rock).

Sleeping and Eating in Húsavík

Sleeping in Town: Youthful but accessible, **$$ Port Guesthouse** fills a renovated former fish factory with 10 rooms (all with shared bathrooms). It has shipshape wood-pallet furniture, a cozy lounge, and amazing views over the busy port and mountains across the fjord—you'll pay a bit extra for a view (breakfast extra, Garðarsbraut 14, tel. 464-0255, www.port-guesthouse.com). **$$ Árból Guesthouse,** a couple of blocks up from the harborfront, has 10 contemporary rooms with shared bathrooms in a fine, creaky old house (Ásgarðsveguri 2, tel. 464-2220, www.arbol.is, arbol@arbol. is); they also have six studio apartments across the street.

Sleeping Outside Town: $ Kaldbaks-Kot is a lovely little country-cutesy compound of 17 simple wooden cottages (sleeping 2-10 people, all with private bathrooms and kitchenettes). It's in a gorgeous setting, perched just above the bay a few minutes' drive outside Húsavík (breakfast extra, tel. 892-1744, www.cottages.is, cottages@cottages.is). **$$ Skógar Sunset Guesthouse,** on a remote ridge along highway 87 (about 15 minutes south of Húsavík and 30 minutes north of Mývatn), has four tidy, well-constructed prefab rooms (with private bathrooms and kitchenettes) on a sleepy family farm (no breakfast, tel. 845-3757, ornsig66@simnet.is or book on Airbnb).

Eating in Húsavík: Overlooking the pier at the town's main harborfront, **$$$ Salka** is a good all-around choice for high-end Icelandic cooking in a bright setting (daily 11:30-21:00, Garðarsbraut 6, tel. 464-2551). **$$ Naustið,** a block up in town, fills a bright yellow house and has inviting outdoor seating, but no views (daily 12:00-22:00, Ásgarðsvegur 1, tel. 464-1520).

Mývatn to Eastfjords Route Overview

It takes about two hours, nonstop, to drive the 110 miles from Mývatn to Egilsstaðir, the gateway to the Eastfjords. Though relatively short in terms of driving distance, this stretch takes you over a wild, uninhabited highland (at 1,700 feet) that can be snowy well into spring. The worthwhile detour to the impressive Dettifoss waterfall adds two more hours (one for driving, and another to hike around the falls). Coastal Seyðisfjörður, a more interesting place to overnight than Egilsstaðir, adds yet another 30-45 minutes of driving. So all told, expect about five hours en route from the shores of Mývatn to the shores of Seyðisfjörður.

Avoid the temptation to spend several extra hours taking the longer northern route (along highway 85) from Mývatn to Seyðisfjörður via Kópasker. Devote time to Iceland's far northeast corner only if you're spending several weeks here.

Be aware that blowing sand can sometimes kick up between Mývatn and Egilsstaðir; check the forecast before setting out.

Sights near Mývatn

• *From the lakefront settlements around Mývatn (last chance for gas!), head east, passing Mývatn Nature Baths (last chance for food!). Then head over Námaskarð pass. Once you leave the Krafla Valley, there are no services (and virtually no civilization) along highway 1 for nearly two hours (though there are portable toilets at the Dettifoss parking lot).*

If you haven't yet, consider stopping off at the fascinating **Ná-mafjall** geothermal area (easy to see quickly) or drive up the **Krafla Valley** to see the geothermal sights there (takes longer)—both are described earlier in this chapter, under "Mývatn."

• *About 12 miles (15 minutes) east of Krafla, watch for the turnoff on the left for paved highway 862. The parking lot for the Dettifoss falls sits about 15 miles (20 minutes) off the main road. (Note that there's a second turnoff to Dettifoss a bit farther east—highway 864—which heads up the opposite, east side of the river and falls. This affords a slightly better view, but is accessed via a slow-to-drive gravel road. There's no bridge across the river near the falls.)*

▲▲Dettifoss Waterfall

Iceland's most powerful waterfall, Dettifoss (DEH-tih-foss) is both broad (340 feet) and high (150 feet). Like Gullfoss on the Golden Circle, you'll view it from above.

From the parking lot (free, always open, portable toilets), you'll walk 15 minutes (about a mile) along a well-marked path to the overlook. The walk in—through a stony plain with basalt columns—is part of the fun. Finally you reach the falls, which thunder into their canyon, spitting up a misty cloud (often with a rainbow). There are two viewpoints: The lower one, on slippery rocks, gets you fairly close to the top of the falls. Then you can follow the trail up to the upper viewpoint, for the big-picture view.

A few hundred yards upstream from Dettifoss, on the same river, is a smaller waterfall called **Selfoss.** You'll see the trail fork

off on the left as you walk back toward your car. It's about two-thirds of a mile—10 minutes—to the falls. The walk rewards you with epic views of the milky, strikingly wide Jökulsá á Fjöllum ("Glacial River in the Mountains") as it flows between the two falls. The riverbanks are striped with bold, vertical basalt ledges—some of which are sloughing off—and a few black sand beaches are tucked between the rapids. This river flows 130 miles from the northern edge of the Vatnajökull glacier—Iceland's largest—to the Greenland Sea.

Downstream from Dettifoss is yet another waterfall, **Hafragilsfoss,** which is almost as broad and high as Dettifoss itself; it's difficult to reach without a 4x4 vehicle, and best skipped.

From Dettifoss to Egilsstaðir

• *Leaving Dettifoss, return to the main road and continue east. After a few miles, you'll cross a scenic white suspension bridge across Jökulsá á Fjöllum—the river that flows over the Dettifoss waterfall.*

From here, it's about 80 miles (1.5 hours) through a stark, almost lunar landscape, essentially Iceland's "Big Sky Country." This is a real Highland experience.

• *As you proceed, keep an eye on your right for the tabletop mountain called...*

Herðubreið: Iceland's answer to Norway's Pulpit Rock is a tuya—a steep, flat-topped volcano created when molten rock pushed up through a glacier. Just behind Herðubreið—but not visible from here—is Askja, a volcanic crater lake buried deep in Iceland's interior, and one of the country's most famous remote and scenic destinations.

If you're in a pinch, there is one place for refreshment between Mývatn and Egilsstaðir, but it's not directly on highway 1: About 24 miles (30 minutes) after the Dettifoss turnoff, watch on the right for road 901 to *Möðrudalur.* About five miles down this road is Fjalladýrð, a working farm with a campsite, guest rooms, a shop, views of Herðubreið, and the café **$$ Fjallakaffi** (tel. 471-1858, www.fjalladyrd.is).

• *Continue along the desolate plain, with very little vegetation save for some parched, scrubby grasses.*

Jökulsá á Dal Valley: Finally you wind your way down a picturesque, lush-green valley of Jökulsá á Dal ("Glacial River in the Valley"). Enjoy the scenery, following the turquoise river with waterfalls all around, as you drop down from the Highlands into the Eastfjords.

• *Where the road bends and crosses the river, stay on highway 1 and drive toward the panorama of snowcapped peaks, eventually crossing the wide Lagarfljót river to the large town of...*

Egilsstaðir ("Egill's Farm"): This functional hub and gateway to the Eastfjords has gas stations and some decent places to eat or spend the night in a pinch. But for even better scenery and a legitimately charming town, continue on to **Seyðisfjörður.**

From Egilsstaðir to Seyðisfjörður

Your drive is not quite over—you're 30-45 minutes from Seyðisfjörður. (For more on both towns and a map of the area, see the next section, "Eastfjords.")

• *From Egilsstaðir's main intersection (at the N1 gas station), take highway 1 (marked* Reyðarfjörður*) and drive up through the residential part of town. After just a half-mile—as you crest the hill and leave town—turn left onto highway 93, marked* Seyðisfj *(with a ferry icon); almost immediately, be ready to turn right to stay on highway 93.*

Over the Fjarðarheiði Pass: Here begins one of Iceland's most scenic drives—the stunning road that summits Fjarðarheiði ("Fjord Heath"), the pass leading to Seyðisfjörður. (Note: This road is frequently snow-covered and sometimes closed in April and October.) You'll curve up switchback after switchback, gaining altitude (and gasping at the lack of guardrails) before disappearing into an otherworldly landscape of mountaintop ponds. Icebergs bob in the big Heiðarvatn ("Heath Lake"), even well into summer. You'll crest the pass at 2,030 feet, and then begin the slow, stunning switchbacks down to the fjord. The road wraps around on itself several times, tying neat little bows around craggy cliffs and gushing waterfalls. It's often socked in, but when clear, this route offers breathtaking fjord-and-waterfalls views.

• *Returning to sea level, you pull into artsy* **Seyðisfjörður**—*ready to explore.*

Eastfjords

Iceland's remote, sparsely populated east is as scenic as it is lonesome. Its coast is slashed with a dozen deep, steep fjords, with very few tunnels and no bridges to speed your progress. Wrapping around fjords is very slow-going, making this the most tedious (albeit scenic) stretch of the Ring Road. You can easily drive for miles and miles without ever seeing another car.

The main tourist draw here is the charming fjordside town of Seyðisfjörður—the most interesting stop, by far, in eastern Iceland, and the no-brainer choice for an overnight. To get there, you'll pass through the practical population center of Egilsstaðir (lots of services and a possible place to sleep). The nearby long, skinny lake called Lagarfljót, with a few mediocre sights, may also be worth a stop. But with limited time, don't linger here: From this area, you'll turn south, tracing the long, jagged shoreline to Southeast Iceland and glorious glacier country.

Planning Tips: Seyðisfjörður, with its striking setting and excellent assortment of hotels and restaurants, is the best place to spend the night. Egilsstaðir is a good backup—and it cuts down on driving. Accommodations can be tough to find the night before the weekly Norröna ferry to Denmark departs from Seyðisfjörður (schedules at www.smyrilline.com)—but if you're here that night, you'll find these towns (especially Seyðisfjörður) particularly lively.

Egilsstaðir

The workaday community of Egilsstaðir (AY-ill-STAHTH-ear, pop. 2,500) lacks Seyðisfjörður's creative charm, but it enjoys a fine setting along the lovely Lagarfljót lake. It's the largest community in the east, with a big swimming pool, supermarkets, and other services—making it a good place to stock up before your long onward journey.

RING ROAD

Eastfjords

To Bakkafjörður

85

Vopnafjörður

Vopnafjörður

Norwegian Sea

917

To Dettifoss, Mývatn & Akureyri

85

94

Bakkagerði

To Faroe Islands & Denmark

901

2 Fjarðarheiði Pass

Egilsstaðir

4 Seyðisfjörður

93

Lagarfljót

1

Neskaupstaður

931

92

Hengifoss

Hallorms-staður

Eskifjörður

3

Reyðarfjörður

SKRIÐUKLAUSTUR

933

Fáskrúðsfjörður

TUNNEL

KÁRAHNJÚKAR DAM

910

95

OPTION

WILDERNESS CENTER

939

Stöðvarfjörður

95

Öxi Pass

1

Breiðdalsvík & **5**

Snæfell

6

Blábjörg Cliffs

Berufjörður

Djúpivogur & **7**

Vatnajökull

Hamarsfjörður

To Norway

Þvottá Point

1

Note: Driving route road width exaggerated for clarity

Hvalnes Point

Lónsvík

To Jökulsárlón Glacier Lagoon & Vík

1

Höfn

North Atlantic Ocean

Akureyri

Egilsstaðir

ICELAND

Reykjavík

Vík

50 KM

50 Miles

● Hali

- - - Recommended Driving Route

---- Optional Driving Route

1 Egilsstaðir Hotels & Eateries

2 Hótel Eyvindará

3 Klausturkaffi

4 Seyðisfjörður Hotels & Eateries

5 Kaupfjélagið Café/Store

6 Havarí Organic Farm

7 Við Voginn Diner & Langabúð Café

20 Kilometers

20 Miles

Tourist Information: Right along highway 1, you'll find a regional TI (Mon-Fri 8:30-18:00, Sat 10:00-16:00, Sun 13:00-18:00, shorter hours and closed Sun off-season, shares a storefront with Hús Handanna art shop right at the town's main intersection, www.visitegilsstadir.is).

Sights near Egilsstaðir

Lagarfljót

This deep lake is so long and skinny that it can be thought of as a broad river—as reflected by its name (LAH-gar-flyoht, "Lake River"). Lagarfljót feels like Iceland's answer to Loch Ness. It even comes with its own Nessie-style legend: The Lagarfljót Wyrm. The story goes that a young girl placed a slug in a box with a golden ring, hoping it would increase her gold. But when the slug grew instead of the ring, she threw it into the water—where it got bigger and bigger, wreaking havoc on lakeside settlements. Finally the Wyrm was chained to the bottom of the lake, where it (supposedly) still sits.

For most travelers, glimpsing Lagarfljót as you drive through Egilsstaðir is enough. If you're on your way south along the Ring Road and have lots of driving ahead of you, I'd take a quick glance and move along. But if you're spending the night in Egilsstaðir, consider a drive along Lagarfljót.

Driving Along the Lake: It's about a 35-minute drive from Egilsstaðir to Skriðuklaustur, the settlement near the lake's south end. A few sights cluster here, but most are closed off-season—call or check in Egilsstaðir before heading out. From Egilsstaðir, drive seven miles south along highway 95, then split off on highway 931, which runs along the lake's east bank. You'll eventually drop down along the lakeshore, pass the national forest at Hallormsstaður, then cross a bridge over the lake, where you can choose among several sights.

To reach the **Hengifoss waterfall,** turn right after the bridge (still on highway 931); you'll soon see the Hengifoss parking lot (free WCs). It's a steep, 1.5-mile hike (about an hour one-way) up a gorge to reach the 390-foot waterfall; if the flow is light, you

can walk around behind the fall (www.hengifoss.is).

To reach the little settlement of **Skriðuklaustur** ("Landslide Monastery"), turn left after the bridge (onto highway 933) and drive five minutes. The sights here are a bit underwhelming: **Gunnarshús,** the home of author Gunnar Gunnarsson (1881-1975), who made a name for himself in Denmark and Germany writing popular books about Iceland (www.skriduklastur.is); the **Snæfellsstofa visitors center,** run by the nearby national park, with advice on hiking and other activities (look for boxy building on the left at the Skriðuk-laustur turnoff, tel. 470-0840, www.vjp.is); and the scant remains of the **Skriðuklaustur monastery,** the final Catholic monastery built in Iceland before the Reformation (c. 1493). It's been excavated in recent years (look for information panels at the site)...but there's not much to see.

For lunch consider the top-notch **$$$ Klausturkaffi,** downstairs in the Gunnarshús. This wonderful little spot is run by a mother-and-daughter team, who lay out a buffet of traditional, homemade Icelandic dishes. It's a filling, delicious, and memorable meal (April-mid-Oct daily 12:00-14:30, they also have a coffee-and-cake buffet daily 15:00-17:00, tel. 471-2992).

South from Skriðuklaustur: With even more time, you could continue south of town and up the valley, where there are some natural thermal pools, a museum about Iceland's Highlands, an abandoned farm with a crank-it-yourself cableway bridge, a closer look at Snæfell (Iceland's tallest mountain not covered by a glacier), and plenty of hiking options. For details, ask at the Snæfellsstofa visitors center or stop in at the Wilderness Center, a 20-minute (10-mile) drive, on partly unpaved roads, past Skriðuklaustur (tel. 440-8822, www.wilderness.is).

Other Day Trips from Egilsstaðir

If you stay an extra night in Egilsstaðir and are interested in environmental issues or dams, you could take a day to drive south to the big dam at **Kárahnjúkar,** in Iceland's reindeer country (though the animals don't always show themselves). The tiny coastal village of **Bakkagerði** (also called Borgarfjörður Eystri), a good hour to the northeast by car, is another interesting destination for those not in a rush.

Sleeping and Eating in Egilsstaðir

Sleep here only if Seyðisfjörður is full, you're in a rush, or the roads are questionable; Egilsstaðir spares you the challenging drive over Fjarðarheiði pass. **$$$ Gistihúsið Egilsstaðir,** on the site of the original Egilsstaðir farm, is a big, functional, group-oriented, country-style hotel renting 52 rooms (near the lakefront just off the town's main intersection, tel. 471-1114, www.egilsstadir.com, egilsstadir@isholf.is). Up above town—just before you head up the road to Seyðisfjörður—is **$$$ Hótel Eyvindará,** with 35 rooms and seven cottages in a rustic, forested setting (tel. 471-1200, www. eyvindara.is, eyvindara2@simnet.is).

Eating in Egilsstaðir: For an easy roadside meal, **$ Bóka-kaffi**—in Fellabær, right along highway 1, is a cozy, old-timey bookshop/café that serves an inviting weekday lunch of soups and savory crêpes. In the late afternoon, they have a coffee-and-cake buffet (Mon-Fri 11:00-18:00, closed Sat-Sun, watch for it on the right immediately before crossing the bridge into Egilsstaðir, www. bokakaffi.is). The recommended Gistihúsið Egilsstaðir hotel also has a pricey but good restaurant, **$$$ Eldhúsið,** that's open to nonguests. You'll find a **Bónus supermarket** on highway 1, near the town's main junction (open daily).

Seyðisfjörður

The most appealing town in eastern Iceland, Seyðisfjörður (SAY-this-FYUR-thur, pop. 700) is a strange hybrid. It's a gritty, worka-

day port, where the Norröna car ferry from Denmark injects Iceland with a weekly fix of international car-trippers. But it's also, per capita, Iceland's most artistic corner, with a youthful, creative spirit. Fortunately, these two factions wear their peeling paint and rust equally well. Postindustrial decay just looks right in Seyðisfjörður.

The town—with a fine harbor at the innermost point of a 10-mile-long fjord—was built up by Danish merchants in the mid-19th century; it boomed around the turn of the 20th century thanks to Norwegian-run herring fisheries. Many fine buildings survive from this time, when Seyðisfjörður also became the terminus for the telegraph cable connecting Iceland to Europe. As herring stocks collapsed, the town went into slow decline.

Fortunately, the town took an artistic turn—largely thanks to German artist Dieter Roth (1930-1998), who moved to Iceland in 1957 and later founded an art academy here. Today Seyðisfjörður's art programs attract young people from across Iceland and abroad, giving this tiny, remote community an unexpectedly cosmopolitan vibe. A top-notch sushi restaurant and a bustling microbrew pub face each other across the rainbow-painted main drag.

While light on "sights," per se, Seyðisfjörður is an enjoyable place to simply wander and explore. The town has more than its share of services for travelers, thanks to the regular ferry traffic.

Tourist Information: The TI is inside the ferry terminal, but save yourself a trip by checking their excellent website (tel. 472-1551, www.visitseydisfjordur.com).

Sights in Seyðisfjörður

Town Walk

Get your bearings in this little burg with this brief spin-tour and stroll. Begin just across the bridge from the supermarket and Hótel Aldan, by the black obelisk honoring Otto Andreas Wathne—a Norwegian entrepreneur who helped develop the town.

Spin Tour: Look out over the little lagoon (Lónið), and find the white tower and glass gangway for the Norröna car ferry, which runs weekly to the Faroe Islands and Denmark. The ferry, the town's main industry, is an important plot point for the popular Icelandic TV series *Ófærð (Trapped)*, which is set in Seyðisfjörður.

Look farther right and up the road, which runs along the fjord past the Hótel Snæfell and below a pretty waterfall. For some remote seaside beauty, you can walk (or drive) as far as you like along this road, which extends 10 miles to the end of the fjord.

Next, spin right to look up into the little town center. The gray-and-red blocky building is the town's fine thermal swimming pool. Standing out front is an abstract sculpture, called *Útlínur,* that represents the outline of the fjord. This sculpture, and the murals adorning the school building at the corner, are reminders of the importance of art in this remote hamlet. Uphill and just to the right of the swimming pool, the classic old red building, once the town hospital, is now its youth hostel. Notice the little rust-colored half-pillar across the street from you (by the river), which identifies area peaks.

Stroll: Now let's stretch our legs. Cross the bridge, turn right at Hótel Aldan, and walk up the pretty "rainbow street" toward the town church. This colorful stretch captures Seyðisfjörður's creative spirit. On the left you'll pass the local pub, which is *the* place in town to sample Icelandic microbrews. The next house, slathered in black-and-white graffiti, is a local art boutique called Gullabúið. At the end of the street is the photogenic, but  often closed, Blue Church (Bláa Kirkjan), which hosts weekly concerts in summer (www.blaakirkjan.is). A block behind the church is *Snjóflóð (Avalanche),* a monument made with the mangled girders of a factory that was swept away by an avalanche in 1996. Scenic as they are, the steep mountain walls around Seyðisfjörður come with a steep price: the danger of being buried by snow.

From here, if the weather's decent, it's an enjoyable 15-minute stroll around the lagoon—offering enjoyable looks at local homes and backyards.

Artistic Sights and Museums

If you're lingering here, you can explore a variety of artistic sights. For example, a 15-minute hike up a steep hillside (above the Brimberg seafood factory) is **Tvísöngur,** a "sound sculpture" made of interconnected concrete huts that resonate in a five-tone harmony. The **Skaftfell Center for Visual Art** often has free exhibitions on view. They also guide tours through the **House of Geiri,** the former home of a local artist (summer only, www.skaftfell.is/the-house-of-geiri).

The town is also home to the **Technical Museum of East Iceland,** housed in a machine shop, where you can learn about everything from town history to that original telegraph (www.seydisfjordur.org).

Hikes

Avid hikers can attempt to climb the **Bjólfur** mountain, with stunning views over the fjord (1,970 feet; you can hike steeply up from the avalanche barriers on the Fjarðarheiði road), or the **Seven Peaks** that surround the fjord.

Sleeping in Seyðisfjörður

Remember, Seyðisfjörður can fill up on the night before the weekly ferry leaves—book well ahead on those days. Hótel Aldan is the only of these listings to serve breakfast (a buffet for which they charge a hefty fee). It's open to nonguests and is where virtually every tourist in town winds up each morning. You can also buy breakfast items at the supermarket.

Hótel Aldan offers the town's only real hotel rooms, divided between two historic buildings. Check in at their reception building in the heart of town (can't miss it, by the bridge), and they'll take you to one of two annexes: **$$ Hótel Snæfell,** a creaky old house on the waterfront with 12 contemporary-style rooms; or **$$$ The Old Bank,** with 9 bigger rooms and more amenities, in a residential area (breakfast extra, served at the reception building at Norðurgata 2, tel. 472-1277, www.hotelaldan.is, booking@hotelaldan.com).

$$ Við Lónið ("By the Lagoon"), well run by Maggý, has eight beautifully appointed, modern-minimalist rooms (all with private bath, half with view balconies for extra). It's right along the main street facing the lagoon and fjord (fjord-facing rooms are

RING ROAD

quieter and have a balcony for a bit more, mobile 899-9429, www.
vidlonidguesthouse.com, email through website to reserve).

$ The Old Apothecary rents three rooms with private bath in
a c. 1885 house right at the main bridge in the town center. There's
no reception—you'll check yourself in—but it's a good value,
and owner Oliver is available if needed (no telephone, website, or
email—book on Airbnb or Booking.com).

¢ Hafaldan Hostel, part of the Hostelling International network, runs a tight ship at its two branches: They have 34 beds in the
wonderfully creaky old hospital building, and 18 more across the
fjord near the old harbor. They also rent private rooms (reception at
old hospital location at Suðurgata 8, tel. 611-4410, www.hafaldan.
is, seydisfjordur@hostels.is).

Eating in Seyðisfjörður

Hótel Aldan has two pricey but excellent eateries in its reception
building (at Norðurgata 2) in the heart of town: **$$$ Nordic Res-
taurant,** on the main floor, has a nicely rustic, casual atmosphere
and modern Icelandic fare, including good salads (May-Sept daily
12:00-22:00, tel. 472-1277). Upstairs, **$$$$ Norð Austur** ("North
East") has exceptional sushi and other Japanese-Icelandic fusion
dishes in a cozy setting. The ingredients are fresh, the chefs are tal-
ented, and the ambience is delightful. Let this place tempt you into
a splurge (dinner only, June-Sept daily 17:00-22:00, tel. 787-4000,
www.nordaustur.is).

$$ Bistro Skaftfell is a casual cellar bar below an art gallery,
a short walk around the fjord from downtown. They have afford-
able pizzas at lunch or dinner, as well as a small, changing menu of
main courses at dinner, always with a vegan option. Order at the
counter, then find a seat; feel free to head upstairs to see what's on
in the gallery (daily 12:00-21:00, Austurvegur 42, tel. 472-1633).

$ Kaffi Lára (named for the house's former resident)—also
called **"El Grillo"** for the local beer on tap—is a boisterous bar
right along the little main street, serving 20 types of beer and basic
pub grub. On weekends, it's open very late and rollicking, with
occasional live music (daily 12:00-22:00, Norðurgata 3, www.
elgrillobrew.com).

Supermarket: Stock up on picnic or breakfast supplies at
Samkaup Strax (marked *Kjörbúðin*), right at the bridge in the
center of town (open daily).

Eastfjords to the Southeast Route Overview

Driving along the Eastfjords (from Seyðisfjörður) to Southeast Iceland is a long but scenic day. Following my recommended route, it's about 145 miles (3.5 hours nonstop) to the lighthouse at Hvalnes point (which marks the shift to the southeast landscape) and 175 miles/4 hours to Höfn (the biggest town in the southeast region).

As you plan your day, note that you may want to continue beyond Höfn before stopping for the night. It's another 45 minutes to accommodations near the glacier lagoon at Jökulsárlón, and 45 minutes beyond Jökulsárlón to Skaftafell National Park. The farther you get tonight, the shorter tomorrow's drive will be.

Before leaving Egilsstaðir, it's smart to stock up on supplies, use the WCs, and get gas. Services are extremely sparse for the rest of the day. From Egilsstaðir, you have two options for continuing south:

Option 1, Highway 95 (summer only): This inland route is shorter but less scenic than option 2 (my recommended route). It climbs up to 1,500 feet over an unpaved pass, descending to the coast near Breiðdalsvík. You could then take the shortcut along highway 939, called Öxi—a sometimes-steep gravel road with no guardrails that climbs even higher, to 1,800 feet. Taking Öxi shaves about 30 miles off the trip, but only a little time, as you'll need to drive slowly. (If you're weighing the choice, check out videos of driving Öxi on YouTube, and look at current road conditions at www.road.is.)

Option 2, Highway 1: The main route hugs the coast and is more scenic, paved all the way, adds about 30-45 minutes to your drive, and is the route I recommend (and detail next). From Egilsstaðir, highway 1 runs down to the sea at Reyðarfjörður; from there, the highway continues through a tunnel and along the coast.

From Egilsstaðir to Reyðarfjörður

• *From Egilsstaðir's main intersection (at the N1 gas station), take highway 1 (marked* Reyðarfjörður*) southeast. (Coming from Seyðisfjörður, you can bypass Egilsstaðir as you drop down from the pass.) You'll curve down a long, grooved valley, framed by craggy mountains rutted with waterfalls. Finally you hit your first fjord at...*

Reyðarfjörður ("Baleen-Whale Fjord"): The fjord is home to an industrial town of the same name (pop. 1,100). When you're still a mile or so outside of town, watch on the right for the turnoff to stay on highway 1 (marked *Fáskrúðsfjörður* and *Höfn*). You'll cut across a few thin rivers, and enjoy views across the fjord on your left of the town of Reyðarfjörður. The aluminum smelter located

RING ROAD

here gives Reyðarfjörður a more diverse economic base than usual in a small Icelandic village, and more jobs—a key to keeping young people here.

• *From Reyðarfjörður, you'll go through a nearly four-mile tunnel, then drive down toward—but not through—the village of Fáskrúðsfjörður.*

Fjordside Villages

Long ago, **Fáskrúðsfjörður** ("Austere Fjord," pop. 660) was a supply center for French boats fishing off Iceland, and honors its history with both Icelandic and French on its street signs.

• *At the fork as you approach town, turn right to stay on highway 1 (marked* Stöðvarfjörður*).*

Now settle in for a lo-o-o-ong drive—a couple of hours, at least, cutting in and out of deep fjords and passing scattered farms. Highway 1 goes up and down and up and down, as you cross the various finger foothills of the mountains, then drops down into deep ravines formed by receding glaciers. Each fjord is anchored by a sparsely populated little village. These hardscrabble communities debate whether to keep schools open and services alive. Pull over as you like for photo ops—there are ample roadside waterfall views. If it's sunny, you'll be in heaven. If it's socked in...pretend.

First, dramatic **Stöðvarfjörður** (pop. 200) has a handy little Saxa guesthouse/café/gas station. The town also has a little museum (Steinasafn Petru) that displays the rock collection and garden of a dearly departed local woman (www.steinapetra.is).

Next, **Breiðdalsvík** ("Wide-Valley Bay," pop. 140) is wider and less scenic—notice it's a *vík* (bay) rather than a *fjörður* (fjord). The cozy, artsy **$ Kaupfélagið** café/general store is a good pit stop here. This town is better developed for tourism than some, and even has some accommodations and a spiffy website (www.breiddalsvik. is). (Note that at Breiðdalsvík, highway 95 rejoins highway 1.)

Berufjörður, a long, skinny fjord, has virtually no settlement at all. Just as you've rounded the bend from Breiðdalsvík, watch on your right for the blink-and-you'll-miss-it organic farm **$ Havarí.** Tucked in the back of the barn is a little café run by a local artist/musician couple. They serve a vegetarian menu and host live music events every other week though the summer (daily, shorter hours off-season, they also rent a few hostel beds, www.havari.is). A bit farther along on the left (just after Þiljuvellir farm), watch for **Blábjörg**—naturally "blue cliffs" that rise above a black-pebble beach.

At the far end of Berufjörður, you'll pass the towering, pyramid-shaped Búlandstindur mountain, then reach **Djúpivogur** (DYOOP-ih-VOE-ur, "Deep Cove," pop. 500)—considered the last town of the Eastfjords. With its harbor huddling under beautiful views of grand peaks, Djúpivogur is a natural place to take a break. **$ Við Voginn** is a diner-style eatery perched on a little hill with views over the harbor (burgers, fish-and-chips, tel. 478-8860). Nearby, **$ Langabúð** is a historic log building from 1790, housing a museum and a café. If you're desperate to recharge, there's a fine little municipal swimming pool at the top of town.

• *From Djúpivogur, you'll leave the fjords in your rearview mirror. It's another 45 minutes to Hvalnes point.*

From the Fjords to the Southeast

With the fjords behind you, you'll curl around two more bays— **Hamarsfjörður** ("Crag Fjord"), then **Álftafjörður** ("Swan Fjord," speckled with islands)— with stunning views of cascading mountains receding to the horizon.

Near the end of Álftafjörður, you'll pass the little point called **Þvottá** where, in the tenth century, a missionary sent by the king of Norway first arrived to Christianize the Icelanders. This "Washing River" (as its name means) is where the missionary baptized his first Icelander.

Just after, you'll round the bend of the last of the Eastfjords, pass the Stapinn sea stack, then reach the point of land marked by the **Hvalnes lighthouse.** Here the landscape changes unmistakably. You're no longer in fjord country, but in Southeast Iceland.

To continue your drive to **Höfn**—the biggest population center for about 300 miles (about 30 minutes away)—and through the rest of the southeast, see the next section.

Southeast Iceland

The rugged, 200-mile-long coastline of Southeast Iceland is shaped by Vatnajökull, Iceland's (and Europe's) biggest glacier. It is massive: By volume, Vatnajökull (VAHT-nah-YUR-kutl, "Lakes Glacier") contains more water than Africa's Lake Victoria, and by area, it's larger than the state of Delaware. Greedy with its superlatives, Vatnajökull is also home to Iceland's tallest mountain (Hvannadalshnúkur, 6,900 feet). This is one big chunk of ice.

Throughout Southeast Iceland, the Ring Road tightropes between Vatnajökull and the open Atlantic. You'll cross many broad beaches of pebbles, ground up and washed out by glaciers, and get a good look at several glacier tongues, stretching down from the top of the big ice monster and lapping at the lowland valleys.

Southeast Iceland has a few widely scattered sights, including some spectacular natural wonders. The highlights are glacier lagoons, where icebergs bob in dreamy pools: the famous (and quite touristy) Jökulsárlón, and the lesser-known and smaller Fjallsárlón. Near Jökulsárlón is the so-called Diamond Beach, where glittering chunks of ice wash up on a velvety black sand beach.

To get up close to all that glacial scenery, the Skaftafell wilderness area offers hikes, from easy to strenuous. And the main town of this area, Höfn, is a practical, peninsular little burg whose restaurants specialize in the delectable local specialty, *humar* (langoustine).

Planning Tips: You'll likely want to spend a night in this area, to rest up between two long days of driving. Accommodations are sparse, so book well ahead. While Höfn is the only real town in Southeast Iceland—and has some good accommodations—it's at the region's easternmost end, so sleeping there makes the next day's onward drive that much longer. From a practical point of view, you may be better off dining in Höfn, then continuing farther west to your hotel. You'll find accommodations around Hali and Jökulsárlón, 45 minutes past Höfn (allowing you both a late-evening and early-morning look at the glacier lagoon), and in the Skaftafell area, another 45 minutes beyond that.

Glacier Activities: It's best to reserve ahead for many activities in this area, including boat trips on the glacier lagoons; hiking or snowmobiling across a glacier; or visiting an ice cave. For details on your options, see the Icelandic Experiences chapter. Do some homework and book your activity a few days ahead (as soon as weather reports become reliable), but before they sell out (most attractions have online calendars that count down available slots). Consider booking your activity for the morning after you overnight in the southeast (avoiding a stressful drive to make a late-afternoon appointment). If you're especially interested in glacier activities, add a second overnight—either in this area, or along the South Coast.

Southeast to South Coast Route Overview

Driving from where Southeast Iceland begins (at Hvalnes point) to Vík (which kicks off the South Coast) is about 200 miles—or about four hours of driving, nonstop. Some of Iceland's most impressive natural sights are here, but they're spread out, with long stretches of road in between. In this section I describe the drive between Hvalnes point and Vík. For detailed descriptions of the towns and sights recommended along this route, see the "Southeast Iceland Towns and Sights" section later in this chapter.

Sandstorm Alert: The most dangerous area for potentially car-damaging sandstorms along the Ring Road is the section between Skaftafell and Vík, where you'll pass through wide stretches of sand. If windy conditions are forecast, try to avoid this area.

Hvalnes Lighthouse: The first stretch—as you round the bend from the Eastfjords, at Hvalnes point—offers a glorious introduction to the glacial scenery of the southeast. The simple orange tower of Hvalnes lighthouse, barely visible from the road, welcomes visitors to this area. Notice the more intense surf here— crashing on the rocks—rather than the gentle lapping of Eastfjord waves.

Lónsvík Bay: Immediately after the lighthouse, there's a pullout at the end of an astonishingly long, far-as-the-eye-can-see, natural causeway along the bay of Lónsvík. Scrambling

RING ROAD

Southeast Iceland

Kvíslavatn

Vatnajökull

26

Þórisvatn

26

Langisjór

Skaftafells-
jökull

Svartifoss

▲Hekla

Landmanna-
laugar

SKAFTAFELL
VISITORS
CENTER

Lómagnúpur▲

12

MANGLED
BRIDGE
GIRDERS

F-210

Fjaðrárgljúfur
Gorge

Skeiðarársandur

Kirkjubæjar-
klaustur

6

Mýrdals-
jökull

208

5

To
Skógarfoss,
Hvolsvöllur
& Reykjavík

▲ Katla

204

1

North

Mýrdalssandur

Vík

Dyrhólaey
Promontory

Reynisfjara
Black Sand Beach

out on the pebbly footing provides a nice stretch-your-legs-after-
the-fjords, welcome-to-the-southeast moment.

Continuing around the bay, notice that the landscape has
shifted from mossy cliffs to massive, sloping mounds of loose pebbles. Keep an eye out for bunkers on the right side of the road,
which block rockslides. And notice the water changing colors, as
mineral-murky glacial runoff mixes in shades of green, blue, and
yellow.

Just past the settlement of **Stafafell,** you'll use a one-lane
bridge to cross the first of many glacial riverbeds. These distinctive
waterways—where centuries-old ice finally melts and runs off to
the ocean—are always shifting.

• *At the far end of Lónsvík bay, you'll go through a short tunnel. Pop-
ping out the other side, straight ahead you'll get your first glimpse of a
glacier: the Hoffellsjökull tongue of Vatnajökull. Soon after—about 30*

To Breiðdalsvík, Seyðisfjörður & Eastfjords

Djúpivogur

Stafafell

Hvalnes Point
LIGHTHOUSE

Lónsvík

To Norway

Jökulsárlón Glacier Lagoon

Höfn

Hali

Öræfa-jökull

Diamond Beach

Fjallsárlón Glacier Lagoon

Akureyri

Egilsstaðir

ICELAND

Reykjavík

Vík

50 KM

50 Miles

30 Kilometers

30 Miles

Atlantic Ocean

Eating & Sleeping
1. Höfn Hotels & Eateries
2. Seljavellir Guesthouse
3. Guesthouse Skálafell
4. Hali Country Hótel
5. Hrífunes Guesthouse
6. Icelandair Hótel Klaustur & Fosshótel Núpar
7. Fosshótel Glacier Lagoon
8. Fosshótel Vatnajökull
9. Brunnhóll Restaurant
10. Jón Ríki Restaurant
11. Fjallsárlón Bistro
12. Skaftafell Cafeteria

- - - - Recommended Driving Route

minutes later—you reach the turnoff (on the left, highway 99) for the town of Höfn.

From Höfn to Hali: As it's the biggest population center for more than a hundred miles in either direction, **Höfn** is good for a break—gas up, use the WC, and have a meal. For suggestions on places to eat in Höfn, see page 336. Otherwise, there are a couple of options past town.

Beyond Höfn, the roadside restaurant **Brunnhóll** has a popular ice-cream counter. But for a better meal, carry on about a mile farther to the recommended **$$ Jón Ríki** brewery/restaurant (on the right, at Hólmur farm).

About 35 miles (45 minutes) past the Höfn turnoff, on the left, is a building shaped like a long bookshelf, at the little settlement of **Hali,** with a hotel, no-frills café, and museum honoring a local author.

• *About 10 minutes beyond Hali, glacial views open up on your right.*

Glacier Lagoons and Tongues: Watch for the big parking lot (on the right, immediately before a white suspension bridge) for the stunning **Jökulsárlón glacier lagoon**—a must-stop to gape at the icebergs. Getting back on highway 1, cross the bridge and immediately turn left on the unmarked gravel road to reach the just-as-dramatic (and often overlooked) **Diamond Beach,** where small icebergs wash up on a black sand shoreline.

About 10 minutes farther, and easy to miss (since it's not visible from the road), is another glacier lagoon, **Fjallsárlón.** This quieter and smaller lagoon has a better view of the glacier itself.

• *Back on highway 1, cut across the flats between glacier-topped mountains and coastline.*

Take turns spotting the glacial tongues filling grooves in the mountains on your right. About 20 minutes past the lagoons, on the right (just past Hótel Skaftafell), you'll enjoy ideal views of glacial tongues flowing around a jagged rock face.

In this area, you'll pass vast **purple fields** of Nootka lupine. In 1945, this flowering plant was introduced (from North America) to Iceland to combat erosion and to fertilize the soil. It's now becoming invasive in some areas, and threatens delicate native species —particularly certain mosses. Just down the road, locals are actively destroying fields of lupine to protect what lies beneath.

• *About 30 miles (45 minutes) past the glacier lagoons, on the right, is the easy-to-miss turnoff for highway 998 and...*

Skaftafell National Park: About 1.5 miles off the main road, you'll reach the park's visitors center (with WCs and a cafeteria; for more on the park, see later in this chapter).

Almost immediately after the Skaftafell turnoff, on the left, watch for a pullout next to a pair of **mangled girders.** They're all that's left of a bridge that washed out in the fall of 1996: A volcanic eruption heated up a mountaintop lagoon of glacier water, which came rushing down the mountainside in a days-long flood that peaked at more than 10 million gallons per second. Such floods, called a *jökulhlaup,* are relatively common along Iceland's southern coast. That's partly why many of the bridges you'll cross on this drive are wimpy one-lane ones, which can be easily replaced.

• *Continuing west, you'll cross the extremely broad outwash plain called...*

Skeiðarársandur ("Spoon-River Sands"): The majority of meltwater from Vatnajökull drains to the Atlantic from this delta, which covers 500 square miles—the largest such glacial drainage delta in the world. (Geologists worldwide sometimes call an outwash plain a *sandur*—borrowing the Icelandic word). To cross Skeiðarársandur, you'll go over an extremely long one-lane bridge (take turns with oncoming traffic on the strategically placed pull-outs).

Approaching the end of the sands, you'll spot the beefy peak called **Lómagnúpur.** Here the landscape shifts to jagged lava chunks—striking, sharp-edge cliffs with lots of waterfalls.

• *Eventually, about 45 miles (nearly an hour) past the Skaftafell turnoff, you'll pull into...*

Kirkjubæjarklaustur: The lone point of civilization between Höfn and Vík, Kirkjubæjarklaustur (KEERK-yoo-bay-yahr-KLOY-stur; "Church-Farm Monastery," pop. 120) is the place to gas up and grab some food. Turn off at the main roundabout and follow the main street; you'll reach a little building housing the busy **$$ Systrakaffi café,** a little grocery store, and a liquor store.

• *A few minutes past Kirkjubæjarklaustur, there's a fine little natural area good for stretching your legs. To reach it, just after leaving town, watch for the turnoff marked* Holt/206.

Fjaðrárgljúfur ("Feather-River Canyon"): An unpaved road takes you in about 10 minutes to this gently scenic gorge of soft,

rounded hills grooved by a deep river (parking lot with WCs and picnic tables). From here you can hike up along the upper rim of the 1.5-mile-long, 300-foot-deep canyon, peering down into its unique formations.

• *From Kirkjubæjarklaustur, it's about an hour (45 miles) to the next town, Vík.*

The Road to Vík: You'll pass through an otherworldly volcanic landscape of lava rock blanketed with yellow moss—a world of molehills with pointy tops, alternating with purple lupine. Somewhere in there, you'll see a pointy-ridged mountain that looks like a sleeping stegosaurus. And soon you'll begin to catch glimpses of the **Mýrdalsjökull** glacier on the horizon to your right.

Before long, you're crossing another broad *sandur* (Mýrdalssandur). The row of cliffs on the left marks your next stop: the town of Vík, the gateway to the South Coast area.

Southeast Iceland Towns and Sights

You'll reach the following towns and sights as you drive south from Hvalnes to Vík via the route above.

▲Höfn

Höfn ("hurpp," with a nearly silent *n;* pop. 2,200) is the only real town in Southeast Iceland. This fishing-harbor town doesn't have much to see, but it offers easy access to the Vatnajökull glacier, a supermarket, a good swimming pool, and some enticing places to eat. The harborfront, more practical than quaint, serves as a local tourism hub, with lots of restaurants and tour operators offering trips to the glacier. In this area is a handy national-park visitors center called Gamlabúð.

Eating in Höfn: Höfn is a good, if expensive, place for a meal, with several seafood restaurants clustered around the harbor. Most menus are dominated by the local delicacy, *humar* (langoustine—a smaller cousin of the American lobster). While you'll pay royally to sample it, foodies consider it a justifiable investment. **$$$$ Pakk-hús Restaurant** has a lively dining room, a cozy pub downstairs, and a menu of *humar* and other specialties. If you really want to settle in for a memorable meal at the end of a long day's drive, do it here (daily 12:00-22:00, Krosseyjarvegi 3, tel. 478-2280, www. pakkhus.is). For something simpler and cheaper, try the diner-style **$ Hafnarbuðin,** which sits in a little shack farther around the harbor. Order at the counter, then try to find a seat in the cramped interior. Their "langoustine baguette" is Iceland's answer to a lobster roll (they also serve fish-and-chips and other basic meals, daily 9:00-22:00, Ránarslóð 12, tel. 478-1095). **$$ Íshúsið** is a good, high-end pizzeria right on the harbor (daily 12:00-22:30, Heppuvegur 2a, tel. 478-1230, www.ishusidpizzeria.is). Farther out, along the road toward highway 1, **$$$ Kaffi Hornið** is a convivial, reliable choice for comfort food in a log-cabin shed (daily 11:30-23:00, Hafnarbraut 42, www.kaffihornid.is).

Eating near Höfn: **$$ Jón Ríki** ("Jón the Rich") is tucked in a nondescript farming settlement called Hólmur, right along the Ring Road (about 20 minutes/17 miles west of the Höfn turnoff). This sociable, casual microbrewery/restaurant, in an artistically decorated barn, serves pizzas and local dishes. Reserve ahead in peak season (daily June-Aug 11:30-14:00 & 18:00-21:30, closed off-season, tel. 478-2063, www.jonriki.is).

Sleeping in and near Höfn: See the "Sleeping in Southeast Iceland" section, later in this chapter.

Hali Farm

The 20th-century Icelandic author Þórbergur Þórðarson was born on this farm in 1888. Þórbergur is most remembered for his humorous, self-deprecating essays and *The Stones Speak,* a memoir of his childhood in this isolated place, where the glacial rivers weren't bridged until the 1970s.

The farm is now home to the **Þórbergssetur museum,** which is designed to look like a giant bookshelf containing Þórbergur's works. Inside, you'll learn about the history of the property and its famous resident, and you can step into a re-created *baðstofa* (main room of a traditional farmhouse) and bedroom. The exhibit makes Þórbergur and his writings meaningful to outsiders—and it's a good break from driving. (The building is also the reception for the recommended Hali Country Hótel—see "Sleeping in Southeast Iceland," later.)

Cost and Hours: 1,000 ISK, if they're not busy an attendant can show you around, daily 7:30-21:00, café, tel. 478-1078, www.thorbergur.is.

Glacier Lagoons
▲▲▲Jökulsárlón

This glorious sight is one of Iceland's best: a lagoon where giant, bobbing chunks of centuries-old ice float in dreamy tranquility, in front of a glacier backdrop. The lagoon called Jökulsárlón (YUR-kurls-OUR-lohn, "Glacier-River Lagoon") first appeared around 1935, gouged out by the receding Breiðamerkurjökull glacial tongue (which continues to retreat about a foot per day,

a pace that has increased dramatically over the last decades). The lagoon covers seven square miles and reaches a depth of up to 800 feet; the water temperature hovers just above freezing. Salt water backing up the river into the lagoon helps prevent it from freezing over. (The nearby Atlantic rarely goes above about 45°F.)

Spot any wildlife? Occasionally seals swim up the river and can be seen basking on the ice chunks. And various seabirds, including Arctic terns, nest nearby in the early summer. If you happen to wander too close to a nest, you could get dive-bombed.

Glacier Lagoon Boat Trips: At Jökulsárlón, you have two options for getting out on the frigid water—a large, slow-moving "amphibian boat" (5,500 ISK for 45 minutes) or a smaller, faster RIB/zodiac boat (9,500 ISK for an hour). You'll be provided with

Visiting Glacier Lagoons in the Southeast

The glacier lagoon at Jökulsárlón is big and impressive, but for many visitors, it feels touristy and crowded. With multiple boats cruising its waters at once, the experience can lose some magic. I'd stop off to ogle the dramatic lagoon (and the nearby Diamond Beach), then carry on 10 minutes for a more intimate boat trip at Fjallsárlón. This often-over-looked lagoon is just as spectacular.

Whichever lagoon you visit, be extremely careful. Tempting as it might seem, trying to step out onto an iceberg that drifts near the shore is a terrible idea. The ice chunks can flip over, trapping you underneath, immersed in near-freezing water.

Icebergs crack off the glacier with a sharp bang, like a gunshot. When they first calve off, the ice is a brilliant, deep blue. After just a few hours in the sun, the outer layer begins to melt, trapping tiny air bubbles and turning the surface white. Darker patches show where the ice dredges up sediments while grinding along the glacier bed. Because the grit stays put when the ice melts, icebergs grow darker as they age. All that sediment is what makes the lagoon's water murky.

Like icebergs at sea, these chunks of ice extend far beneath the surface. Occasionally the melting patterns make an iceberg unbalanced, until it suddenly flips over with a thundering splash. Like a living organism, the lagoon is always changing, with icebergs bobbing and drifting around the still water. They slowly decrease in size until they're finally small enough for the current to carry them up the short Jökulsá river and out to the Atlantic.

warm coveralls and lifejackets, but bundle up before heading out. Ideally, check the schedule and book online once you're fairly confident that the weather will justify the trip (tours run daily July-Aug 9:00-18:00, shorter hours off-season, no trips Nov-April, tel. 478-2222, www.icelagoon.is).

▲▲▲Diamond Beach

This dramatic sight hides down an unmarked gravel road (see page 334 for directions), but don't miss it. Glittering icebergs both large and small lay stranded on a fine black-powder beach...like so many diamonds on display. By the time they reach these sands, many of the icebergs have been tumbled by currents and waves, leaving them shiny and smooth. The beach changes constantly: Sometimes the "diamonds" are many, other times they're sparse. Sometimes they're transparent, other times white, occasionally blue, and often there's a mix of colors and sizes. Photographers can occupy themselves for hours.

Be extremely careful exploring this area. The Atlantic coastline here is notorious for its sneaker waves, and if you wade into the (frigid) water here, you're taking your life in your hands. But even from a safe distance, Diamond Beach takes your breath away.

▲▲Fjallsárlón

Fjallsárlón (FYATL-sour-lohn, "Mountain-River Lagoon")—the Back Door alternative to the crowded Jökulsárlón—is just seven miles farther down the main road (10 minutes), but tucked out of sight (watch for easy-to-miss red *Fjallsárlón* sign). From the parking lot—with a modern services building, including WCs, a good café, and boat-trip ticket offices—you can hike up onto a little ridge for great views of the Fjallsjökull glacial tongue, with the lagoon in the foreground. This lagoon started to form about 20 years ago as the glacier receded up the slope. It's smaller than Jökulsárlón (about one-fifth the size and one-third the depth), but that means you're up closer to the glacier itself.

Boat Trips: With Fjallsárlón's smaller size, the 45-minute RIB cruises here feel more personal and intimate. Boat trips run

nearly hourly through the summer (6,800 ISK, April-mid-Oct daily 10:00-17:00, hourly except 12:00, www.fjallsarlon.is). You can just show up and hope for an available slot, but it's more reliable to book online a day or two ahead.

Eating at Fjallsárlón: The modern, inviting **$ Fjallsárlón Bistro** offers a soup-and-bread buffet and reasonably priced entrées (daily in summer from 11:30 to end of last boat trip).

Skaftafell National Park

Skaftafell (SKAFF-tah-fehtl) is part of the Vatnajökull national park (watch for the turnoff for highway 998 from the Ring Road).

This area is named for the Skaftafellsjökull glacial tongue, which pokes down from Vatnajökull near the sprawling parking lot (which teems with hikers on nice summer days). The **visitors center** has some small exhibits about the area and plenty of advice about local hikes (maps for sale, typically open daily 8:00-19:00 in summer, shorter hours off-season, free WCs, tel. 470-8300, www.vjp.is).

Eating at Skaftafell: A big, basic **$ cafeteria** serves uninspired salads, sandwiches, and main courses (daily 9:00-21:00 in summer, 10:00-19:00 in off-season).

▲▲Hiking at Skaftafell

Some people spend days hiking in this area, but even if you're just passing through, it's worth sampling one of the trails. Here are some popular choices, all of which begin from the Skaftafell parking lot (time and distance estimates are round-trip). Before heading out, be sure to get the hiking pamphlet (or ideas for other hikes) from the visitors center, and be aware of local weather conditions. The last three hikes require a stiff uphill climb to the ridge called Skaftafellsheiði, which looms above the visitors center.

"Geology Trail" to Skaftafellsjökull (easy, 2.3 miles, 1 hour): The easiest and most popular choice, this loop hike (mostly over even and flat terrain, blue trail S1) takes you to the glacier tongue that runs off Vatnajökull. This is perhaps your best chance to get up close to a glacier without taking a lagoon cruise. (If you're planning to hike at Sólheimajökull farther along the South Coast, this trail may be somewhat redundant.)

To start, you'll cut through a field, walk along the base of a cliff, and go up the valley cut by the receding glacier. Finally you approach the glacier itself. Conditions may allow you to walk up and touch the glacier (though, more likely, your path will be impeded by a pool of water). Don't attempt to climb the glacier without proper equipment, and don't be surprised by the glacier's brown or black appearance—it picks up a lot of grit as it grinds along its valley.

Svartifoss (moderate, 2-2.5 miles, 1.5-2 hours): While only about 60 feet tall, Svartifoss ("Black Waterfall") enjoys one of Iceland's most dramatic waterfall settings, gushing over a cliff of basalt columns. While utterly spectacular, a visit requires a sturdy uphill hike (elevation gain of about 850 feet). Note that there are two routes to Svartifoss: Short and steep (red trail S2), or longer and more gradual (blue trail M3/S2). Sort out your options at the visitors center and take your pick.

Svartifoss-Sjónarsker-Sel (moderate, 3.5 miles, 3 hours): From Svartifoss, further hikes tempt those with more time and energy. One popular, moderate option links the waterfall to the fine viewpoint at Sjónarsker—overlooking the astonishingly broad Skeiðarársandur glacial river delta—and a traditional turf house at Sel (blue trail S2).

Svartifoss-Sjónarnípa (challenging, 4.5 miles, 4-5 hours): More ambitious is the hardy trail across to the hillside to Sjónarnípa, which rewards the effort with stunning views over Skaftafellsjökull. From Svartifoss, you'll take red trail S5/S6.

Glacier Walks and Ice Cave Tours

For these up-close glacier experiences you'll need to book ahead with a private company. The following offer one or both activities: Glacier Journey (www.glacierjourney.is), Arctic Adventures (www.adventures.is), and Extreme Iceland (www.extremeiceland.is). For glacier walks, these companies are more specialized: Icelandic Mountain Guides (www.mountainguides.is) and Glacier Guides (www.glacierguides.is). For more on glacier activities, see the Icelandic Experiences chapter.

Sleeping in Southeast Iceland

For locations, see the map on page 332.

In Höfn: The guesthouse called the **$$$ Milk Factory,** along the road between Höfn and highway 1 (a long walk or short drive from the harbor), is a fun choice, renting 17 rooms with clean, tidy, modern style (Dalbraut 2, tel. 478-8900, www.milkfactory.is, reception@milkfactory.is). **$$$ Hótel Edda Höfn** is your big-hotel option in town, with a large, modern lobby and 36 rooms in a characterless building just off the harbor (breakfast extra, Ránarslóð, tel. 444-4850, www.hoteledda.is, edda@hoteledda.is). **$$ Guesthouse Dyngja** is a reliable, simple, traditional place with seven rooms (some with shared bath) a few steps above the harbor (tel. 866-0702, www.dyngja.com, fanney@dyngja.com).

In the Countryside near Höfn: In a modern motel-style building, **$$$ Seljavellir Guesthouse** is practical with 20 rooms in a farm valley just off highway 1 a few minutes north of Höfn (tel. 845-5801, www.seljavellir.com, info@seljavellir.is).

Between Höfn and the Glacier Lagoons: Tucked beneath a huge mountain about a half-hour from Höfn or Jökulsárlón, **$$ Guesthouse Skálafell** is a cozy, family-run compound with nine rooms (some with private bath) and two cottages (tel. 478-1041, www.skalafell.net, info@skalafell.net). **$$$ Hali Country**

Hótel is big and functional, just a 10-minute drive east of the Jökulsárlón glacier lagoon by the Hali farm. It has 39 rooms scattered through three buildings (tel. 867-2900, www.hali.is, hali@hali.is). They also have a restaurant and a museum about the writer Þórbergur Þórðarson, who grew up here (described on page 337).

Between Skaftafell and Vík: Cozy and well-run, **$$$ Hrífunes Guesthouse** is almost to the South Coast; some rooms have views, and some have private bathrooms (tel. 863-5540, www.hrifunesguesthouse.is).

Big Chain Hotels: For less personality but plenty of beds, you'll find big branches of well-established Icelandic chains that cater mainly to tour groups. **$$ Icelandair Hótel Klaustur** has 57 rooms in the village of Kirkjubæjarklaustur (tel. 487-4900, www.icelandairhotels.com, klaustur@icehotels.is), while the Fosshotel chain has multiple branches (www.fosshotel.is): **$$ Fosshótel Núpar,** with 60 rooms in Kirkjubæjarklaustur (tel. 517-3060); **$$$$ Fosshótel Glacier Lagoon,** a newer splurge with 104 rooms between Skaftafell and Jökulsárlón (tel. 514-8300, glacier@fosshotel.is); and **$$ Fosshótel Vatnajökull,** with 66 rooms just outside of Höfn (tel. 478-2555, vatnajokull@fosshotel.is).

South Coast

Iceland's South Coast—stretching from Vík about 40 miles west to the Markárfljót river and Seljalandsfoss waterfall—is one of Iceland's most enjoyable corners. Within this hour-long stretch you'll encounter black sand beaches, scenic promontories, hikeable and touchable glaciers, a pleasant folk museum, and two spectacular waterfalls. On the way back to Reykjavík, there's less to see, though the Lava Centre is a good stop to learn more about volcanoes.

Planning Tips: If you're rushing the Ring, you'll have a busy day of sightseeing and a late drive back to Reykjavík. Spending a night here allows you to linger at the area's attractions before returning to Reykjavík (or side-trip to the Westman Islands, an easy ferry ride from here, if the weather cooperates).

Vík to Reykjavík Route Overview

For more specifics on the South Coast—including a map, sightseeing details, recommended eateries and accommodations, and strategic tips—see the South Coast chapter. Since that chapter is designed for day trips from Reykjavík, the sights are presented there in "backwards" order for those completing a clockwise Ring tour. Below is a rough outline for visiting these sights, traveling from east to west.

The first part of the drive—from Vík to Seljalandsfoss waterfall—takes only about an hour (about 40 miles), but contains many hours' worth of sightseeing. (If you're very selective, you can have a satisfying visit to this stretch in about 3-4 hours.)

Once you leave Hvolsvöllur (and its Lava Centre), it's a fairly straightforward 1.5-hour, 70-mile drive to Reykjavík, with fewer temptations en route.

From **Vík** (where you'll find gas stations and eateries), you'll twist up and over a mountain pass. As you descend, watch on the left for the turnoff to the **Reynisfjara black sand beach,** with striking basalt formations, scenic sea stacks, handy beach café, and dangerous sneaker waves (10-minute drive from the main road on highway 215).

Just a bit farther along on highway 1, the turnoff for highway 218 leads five minutes to **Dyrhólaey promontory,** with fine views and a lighthouse hike (skippable for those in a rush).

Continuing 25 more minutes, you'll reach the turnoff for **Sólheimajökull glacier** (a five-minute drive from the Ring Road on highway 221). From the parking lot, it's a 15-minute hike to the glacier itself; depending on conditions (and your own surefootedness), you can often walk right up and touch the glacier. But if you've already visited the glacier lagoons in the southeast, this is skippable.

Just past the Sólheimajökull turnoff, also on the right, is the settlement called **Skógar,** which has a striking waterfall (Skógafoss) and a folk museum.

From here, the road continues west in the shadow of **Eyjafjallajökull,** the volcano whose 2010 eruption famously disrupted European air travel. A small, roadside Iceland Erupts exhibit tells the story (but the Lava Centre—coming up soon—relates it more professionally). You'll enjoy great views of the **Westman Islands,** with teeth-like cliffs hovering just offshore (for details, see Westman Islands chapter).

Around 25 minutes (18 miles) after leaving Skógar, turn off on the right to highway 249 and the parking lot for the dramatic **Seljalandsfoss waterfall**—you can actually walk behind the tumbling torrent.

Back on highway 1, you'll cross the Markárfljót river and curve inland—going through the humble communities of **Hvolsvöllur** (with its excellent Lava Centre—a state-of-the-art volcano exhibit), **Hella,** and **Selfoss** (with the grave of chess legend Bobby Fischer). Highway 1 cuts north past **Hveragerði** (with an excellent pizzeria/brewery—see page 201), then switchbacks up and across the volcanic, desolate **Hellisheiði** plateau. Before you know it, you're approaching the Reykjavík suburbs.

Your epic Ring Road odyssey is finally at its end. Well done!

ICELAND WITH CHILDREN

With relatively few museums and plenty of stunning natural wonders and other outdoor activities, Iceland is practically made for
kids. Icelandic culture prizes kids. You'll find many restaurants and
museums have designated play areas, and every neighborhood has
a playground. And its mind-blowing landscapes make for a road
trip that rivals the great national parks of the US. Encourage your
kids to learn about exciting geological features like volcanoes and
glaciers so they can play tour guide. Figure out what their friends'
names would be using the Icelandic naming system (I'd be "Rick
Dicksson"). And challenge them to master the pronunciation of
"Eyjafjallajökull."

Trip Tips

PLAN AHEAD
Involve your kids in trip planning. Have them read about the places
that you may include in your itinerary (even the hotels you're considering), and let them help with your decisions.

Where to Stay
- Accommodation selection is critical. In Reykjavík, hotels are
  pricey and can be cramped; renting an apartment or house
  (such as through Airbnb) can be cheaper and gives you more
  space. Particularly with a family, the advantages of renting a
  home in Reykjavík's suburbs are substantial—you'll have more
  space and a better look at real Icelandic life than tight downtown hotels near rowdy nightlife streets. But be warned that
  short-term rentals might not be childproofed or fully equipped
  for small kids (unlike hotels, which are likely to have a loan-

er crib available). Search carefully for the specific amenities you'll need—or, if necessary, bring them along.

- Outside of the capital area, you'll find fun farmstay opportunities that are ideal for families. For more on farmstays, see the "Sleeping" section of the Practicalities chaper.

- Minimize changes by planning longer stays. From the Reykjavík area, you can spend days side-tripping to many of Iceland's highlights: Golden Circle, South Coast, Blue Lagoon/Reykjanes Peninsula, West Iceland, and more. If doing the entire Ring Road, budget plenty of time to minimize one-night stays; spend multiple nights in places like Mývatn, Southeast Iceland, or the South Coast.

- Aim to stay at places with restaurants (on-site or nearby), so older kids can go back to the room while you finish a pleasant dinner.

- In most of Iceland, hot water is piped directly from geothermal sources. It can be scalding right out of the tap. Show your kids how to carefully test the water temperature before washing their hands or getting in a shower or bathtub. (Also reassure them that the sometimes-sulfurous odor of the hot water is perfectly natural and safe.)

What to Bring (or Not)

- Don't bother bringing a car seat—car-rental agencies usually rent them (but reserve in advance).

- Bring your own drawing supplies and English-language picture books, as these are pricey in Iceland.

- Pack a swimsuit, towel, and maybe goggles for fun in Iceland's many thermal swimming pools.

- With the unpredictable weather (even in summer), bring a waterproof jacket and plenty of layers to bundle up your child if the wind starts howling.

- If you're flying Icelandair, ask for the nice, complimentary box of items that kids under 10 will appreciate. And there's a wide variety of video entertainment showcasing Iceland's many attractions that may help get your child excited about what lies ahead.

EATING

Iceland offers plenty of food options for children.

What to Eat (and Drink)

- Icelandic soups (especially the staple lamb soup, called *kjötsúpa*) are hearty, nourishing, and plenty accessible for kids.
- Iceland's wide variety of yogurt-like treats (*þykkmjólk, jógurt,* and *skyr*) are tasty for kids and grown-ups alike.
- Most accommodations provide a hearty buffet-style breakfast (including cereals, breads, cheeses, juices, yogurts, etc.) with enough options for kids to fortify themselves for a busy day of sightseeing.

CHILDREN

- While certain Icelandic dishes might challenge less adventurous young eaters, plenty of familiar American-style food is available—and many restaurants offer a children's menu. Hot dogs are a mainstay even for Icelandic families; you'll find Subway sandwich shops all over the country; burgers and fries are easy to find (and taste more or less like their American counterparts); and fish-and-chips is readily available. In the Reykjavík area, Domino's, the IKEA cafeteria, and other international chains are good fallbacks.
- Most kids will enjoy sampling local sweets. Icelandic candy is tasty and unique. Licorice encased in chocolate is a specialty. Note, though, that a lot of Icelandic licorice is stronger than a kid's palate is used to. And Icelanders love soft-serve ice cream. For a special treat, ask at an ice-cream store for a *bragðarefur*—an overflowing cup of soft serve with candy or sauces mixed in. Also look for familiar sweets in new packaging—for example, *Rís Buff* (puffed rice and marshmallow covered in chocolate). Kids also might like to try the local orange soda, Egils Appelsín.
- Adventurous older kids might get a kick out of trying some of Iceland's more exotic foods, such as whale, the infamous fermented shark, or other "hardship meats."

When and Where to Eat

- Eat dinner early, when restaurants are less crowded.
- Skip romantic or super-traditional eateries. Try relaxed cafés (or fast-food restaurants) where kids can move around without bothering others. Many eateries around the country have play areas.

- Picnics work well. Stock up on supplies at one of Iceland's budget supermarkets, Bónus and Krónan.

SIGHTSEEING

The key to a successful Iceland family vacation is to slow down. Tackle one or two key sights each day, mix in a healthy dose of pure fun at a park or natural area, and take extended breaks when needed.

Planning Your Time

- Lower your sightseeing ambitions and let kids help choose daily activities. Plan longer stays at fewer stops—you won't regret it.
- To make your trip fun for everyone in the family, mix heavy-duty sights with kids' activities—such as having a picnic after tackling a museum.
- Keep in mind that museums in Iceland can be very expensive. Even a fairly modest exhibit that takes less than an hour to see can cost $20 or more per person; younger children may get discounts. To avoid blowing through a lot of money, carefully weigh your sightseeing options and consider the investment each place requires... and remember that, for families with a car, most of Iceland's best attractions—in the great outdoors—are free.

Successful Sightseeing

- Older kids and teens can help plan the details of a sightseeing visit, such as what to see, how to get there, and ticketing details.

- Audioguides are great for older children. Many exhibits—like the Museum of Icelandic Natural Wonders at the Pearl in Reykjavík, or the Lava Centre near the South Coast—offer interactive exhibits that will keep kids of all ages engaged. For younger children, hit the gift shop first so they can buy postcards and have a scavenger hunt to find the pictured items. When boredom sets in, try "I spy" games.
- Bring a sketchbook and encourage kids to select an object or

landscape to draw. It's a great way for them to slow down and observe.

Making or Finding Quality Souvenirs

- Souvenirs tend to be extremely expensive. Parents may find it wise to give kids a budget and advise them to choose their souvenir carefully. You'll soon realize that many of the same items are available (and are the same price) at multiple locations; it seems there's a finite number of souvenirs, and most stores stock the same items.

- One of my favorite suggestions is to buy your child a trip journal where he or she can record observations, thoughts, and favorite sights and memories. This journal could end up being your child's favorite souvenir.

- For a group project, keep a family journal. Pack a small diary and a glue stick. While relaxing at a café, take turns writing about the day's events and include mementos such as ticket stubs from museums, postcards, or pinches of black sand from volcanic beaches.

- Younger kids may enjoy a typically Icelandic stuffed animal, like a cuddly puffin. An Icelandic flag is simple, colorful, and low-cost. T-shirts with unique Icelandic words or sayings are fun.

MONEY, SAFETY, AND STAYING CONNECTED

Before your trip gets underway, talk to your kids about safety and money.

- Give your child a money belt and an expanded allowance; you are on vacation, after all. Let your kids budget their funds by comparing and contrasting the dollar and the *króna*.

- If you allow older kids to explore a museum or neighborhood on their own, be sure to establish a clear meeting time and place.

- It's good to have a "what if" procedure in place in case something goes wrong. Give your kids your hotel's business card (or write down the address of your rental apartment), your phone number (if you brought a mobile phone), and emergency taxi fare. Let them know to ask to use the phone at a hotel if they are lost. And if they have mobile phones, show them how to make calls in Iceland (see the "Staying Connected" section of the Practicalities chapter).

- If traveling with older kids, you can help them keep in touch with friends at home with cheap texting plans and by email. Hotel guest computers and Wi-Fi hotspots are a godsend. Readily available Wi-Fi (at just about every business in Iceland) makes bringing a mobile device worthwhile. Most parents find it worth the peace of mind to buy a supplemental messaging plan for the whole family: Adults can stay connected to teenagers while allowing them maximum independence.

Top Kids' Sights and Activities

ATTRACTIONS AROUND REYKJAVÍK

For specifics, see the individual listings under "Sights in Reykjavík," page 89.

Reykjavík City Hall

The large 3-D map of Iceland (on display some, but not all, days) will fascinate many kids and can be a nice prelude or postscript to your Iceland visit.

Laugardalur

This valley, just east of downtown, is where Icelanders spend time with their kids. It has a "family park" (including the city's biggest jungle gym and a few amusement-park rides), a zoo (with mostly farm animals), botanic gardens, and an indoor ice rink.

Árbær Open-Air Museum

Not far from Laugardalur, this very kid-friendly exhibit lets you walk through historic buildings from around Iceland.

Whales of Iceland

While this attraction is very expensive, kids love wandering among the life-size models of majestic giants. Actual **whale-watching cruises** may bore kids; read my description in the Icelandic Experiences chapter before assuming yours will enjoy one.

Kolaportið Flea Market

Open weekends only, this downtown flea market is fun for the whole family to explore.

Hallgrímskirkja Lutheran Church

This architecturally distinct church is an eye-catching symbol of the capital, which kids might enjoy seeing inside and out. If the line isn't too long, ascending its tower offers a fine view over the city's colorful rooftops. The statue of **Leifur Eiríksson** out front is a fun photo-op landmark (with a dramatic story).

Perlan (The Pearl)

The viewpoint here offers a farther-out, big-picture view of Reykjavík, and the **Museum of Icelandic Natural Wonders** downstairs makes Icelandic nature fun for kids, especially the ice tunnel and interactive exhibits. Enjoy an ice cream with a 360-degree view of the city and surroundings.

The Pond

The small lake in the heart of Reykjavík has walking paths and ducks to feed—and if it's cold enough in winter, they may have a skating rink. At the northeast corner of the lake, find the sweet little "Mother's Garden" (Mæðragarðurinn)—  designed in 1925 for moms to bring their kids to play (notice the touching statue, called *Motherly Love).*

Walking Paths

On a nice day, the paths along the south side of the Reykjavík Peninsula make for a nice stroll and have lots of diversions. At low tide, you can walk down onto the rocks and sand (in the bay, there are no giant ocean waves to worry about). Start near the streets called Ægisíða and Faxaskjól (take bus #11).

Indoor Play Areas

Kids can spend an afternoon on bouncy castles and doing other tumbly activities at several indoor facilities. Both major shopping malls have supervised play zones where parents can pay to leave kids for an hour or two (ages 3-9). These include Ævintýraland in Kringlan, (www.kringlan.is/aevintyraland) and Smáratívolí in Smáralind (www.smarativoli.is). The giant IKEA has a small, supervised play area, called Smáland, for kids ages 3-7 (free for up to an hour or so, may be a line to get in, www.ikea.is).

Saga Museum

Life-size mannequins enacting great moments of early Icelandic history help bring those tales to life. But some of the mannequins

CHILDREN

may be too graphic (violence and a little nudity) for certain kids; before buying tickets, flip through the picture book at the entrance to help you decide. At the end of the visit, kids have a chance to dress up like a Viking. Skip the audioguide—it's too dry for younger kids.

Harpa Concert Hall

Kids enjoy walking around the lobby of this bold concert hall—with its many multicolored windows—and walking out on the jetty just beyond it for views back on the sailboat harbor in front of the building. The nearby *Sun Voyager* sculpture is a fun spot to take photos.

The Settlement Exhibition

Older kids might enjoy seeing the actual remains of this Viking Age longhouse from the 10th century, well-explained by interactive exhibits.

Icelandic Phallological Museum

Jaded, older teenagers (bored with every other museum in town) may show a spark of interest at this collection of preserved animal phalluses. In some ways, 12-year-old boys are the most fitting audience possible for this collection.

Viking World

Near the international airport in the town of Keflavík, this museum features a replica Viking boat and some interactive exhibits. For younger kids, the highlight is across the parking lot, in the Settlement Age petting zoo (summer only). While mostly underwhelming, this exhibit is a handy place to kill some time near the airport and Blue Lagoon (see page 174).

OUTDOOR AND WATER FUN

There are many remarkable things for kids to see in nature—from glaciers to volcanoes, and from puffins to horses. Most of these are equally suitable for kids as for adults, though some do have age restrictions. Below I've called out a few highlights for families. For an overview of these activities, see the Icelandic Experiences chapter.

Important Safety Warning: Particularly outside of the

capital area, Iceland's nature is untamed and can be quite dangerous. Anytime you're near the open ocean (especially along the South Coast), be aware of the risk of sneaker waves—which can suddenly deluge a beach, pulling people out to the open ocean. At any geothermal area (such as at Geysir on the Golden Circle), keep children very close at hand and ensure that they understand the extreme danger of straying from marked paths and into scalding springs. (Impress on your kids that the water is extremely *hot*, not just warm...they shouldn't try to "test" the temperature with their finger.) And if you're walking up close to a glacier, don't go on top of the ice unless you are properly outfitted and with a guide. For a complete rundown about safe travel, see the sidebar on page 34.

CHILDREN

Waterfalls

Iceland offers many opportunities to get up close to waterfalls, from Gullfoss (on the Golden Circle) to Seljalandsfoss and Skógafoss (on the South Coast) to Dettifoss (in the North). Each one's a bit different, but they're all thrilling. Surefooted kids particularly enjoy **Seljalandsfoss,** where they can walk behind the falls (see page 210). Be very careful at any waterfall when it's cold—the mist can make footing icy and slippery.

Basalt Columns

The black sand beach at **Reynisfjara,** on the South Coast, has sea-

side caves and stair-step basalt columns that kids enjoy climbing on (see page 219). But be very careful with kids at this beach, as this is one of the places prone to sneaker waves (see safety warning above).

Glaciers and Glacier Lagoons

All along the South Coast, you'll spot glacial tongues lapping down from giant, slow-motion rivers of ice. If you're doing a long road trip, the best place to see these is from the glacier lagoons in Southeast Iceland: **Jökulsárlón** and **Fjallsárlón** (see page 339). You can also walk right up to a glacier at **Skaftafell National Park** (see page 339) and at **Sólheimajökull,** which is a bit closer to Reykjavík (see page 216). Older kids might enjoy walking (or snowmobiling) on top of a glacier, or touring an ice cave, both of which you can experience by joining an excursion. For more on these options, see the "Glaciers" sections in the Icelandic Experiences chapter.

Volcanoes and Other Geothermal Areas

Iceland's volcanic landscape is fascinating to see and learn about. For some tips, see the "Volcanoes" section of the Icelandic Experiences chapter.

Grábrók (in West Iceland, see page 261) and **Hverfjall** (by Mývatn, see page 306) are comparatively easy and safe crater experiences for small kids (they'll still need a bit of hand-holding at the top). The most kid-friendly volcano museum is the **Lava Centre** in Hvolsvöllur, which you'll drive right by on a South Coast day trip (see page 209). And the best all-around volcanic sight is the **Westman Islands,** where you can walk up onto a lava flow that partly covered the town in 1973, visit the excellent Volcano Museum (called Eldheimar), and hike up to the still-warm summit of Eldfell (see the Westman Islands chapter).

At places like **Geysir Geothermal Field** (on the Golden Circle), it's mind-blowing for kids to walk through a bubbling, steaming, spurting landscape of hot water (see page 193). But—again—stay on the trail!

The **Mývatn** volcanic area in North Iceland—with its many unique land formations, steaming geothermal landscapes, and easy nature walks—is Iceland's Yellowstone. The lava castles at Dimmuborgir are fun for kids and relatively safe. If you're setting up for a few days of nature trips anywhere outside of the capital, Mývatn is a good choice (see page 301).

Historic Sights

While its historical importance may be lost on younger kids, Þingvellir, on the Golden Circle route, can still be fun. Although

the rocky outcrops and rushing river may make parents nervous, children like the boardwalks and paths. Near the P2 parking lot are picnic benches, woods, and a grassy area that's suitable for games (see page 183).

In the northern town of Skagafjörður, the open-air **Glaum- bær Museum** does a fine job re-creating the lifestyles of medieval Icelanders. You can actually walk through several sod-walled homes and really understand how people lived. While the museum is not specifically aimed at kids, older children interested in local folk culture enjoy it (see page 283).

Zoos, Farms, and Animal Activities

Slakki Zoo, just off the Golden Circle route, is a combination petting zoo and indoor minigolf complex that's aimed at kids under eight. Families could make this their main target for a Golden Circle day trip and manage to glimpse some of the better-known sights on the way (see page 199).

In the summer, try to find a place to look for **puffins.** You can spot these adorable seabirds all over—you're likely to have luck on a short cruise from Reykjavík or on the Westman Islands (where you can usually meet a real, live puffin in the feathers, at the local aquarium).

Icelandic farms are getting into the tourism game. Many have horseback riding experiences, accommodations, restaurants, or areas where visitors can see animals and learn a bit about the workings of Icelandic farm life. Many of my accommodations outside of Reykjavík are on working farms. Good restaurants on farms include Efstidalur II and Friðheimar on the Golden Circle, and Fjósið on the South Coast (see those chapters for details). There's also Cowshed Café near Mývatn and Jón Ríki in Southeast Iceland (see the Ring Road chapter).

The unique Icelandic horse—typically small and mighty—offers an enjoyable **horseback riding** experience for visitors old and young. Riding opportunities are plentiful at any one of dozens of horse farms around Iceland, including some near Reykjavík (for details, see page 47). In West Iceland, kids love the family-run **Háafell Goat Farm,** which is working hard to revive the nearly extinct Icelandic goat. It's a fun visit for families—with hands-on goat encounters (page 267).

Thermal Swimming Pools

Iceland's thermal bathing scene is extremely kid-friendly—particularly at the municipal swimming pools, which you'll find around the capital area and throughout the country. Many of the larger pools have colorful waterslides and other activities that are designed just for kids, and there's usually a shallow wading section for tiny tots. For tips on thermal pools—including the procedure for entering a pool complex—see the Icelandic Experiences chapter.

Note that Iceland's upscale premium baths are less suitable for kids. For example, families may want to steer clear of the famous and expensive Blue Lagoon, as it doesn't have any areas or activities designated for children, the mellow and spa-like atmosphere feels very grown-up, and its opaque water makes anything that slips under next to impossible to find. I also wouldn't take younger kids to the rugged natural thermal bathing experiences (like Reykjadalur); those landscapes are quite volatile, and it's easy to absent-mindedly step into too-hot water. It's best to stick with the many municipal pools around Iceland.

Sledding

If you're in Reykjavík on a snowy winter day, you can borrow sleds and drive to the slope at Ártúnsbrekka in the eastern part of the city. It's off the street called Rafstöðvarvegur, near the Elliðaá River.

ICELAND: PAST & PRESENT

On the far northern fringe of Europe, surrounded by the open Atlantic, Iceland has an epic history that's been shaped by the sea. Here's a brief overview.

PREHISTORY

As the North American and Eurasian tectonic plates pulled apart, lava welled up between them. Over many millions of years of eruptions, Iceland was formed. Eruptions continue today in the middle of the island, along a belt running roughly from the north to the south and southwest. This belt, which passes close to (but not through) Reykjavík, contains Iceland's active volcanoes, as well as its hot springs and geothermal energy sources. The older lava has been pulled east and northwest by the spreading plates, meaning the western and eastern fjords are volcano-free (good) but also have little or no underground hot water for heating (bad). The sea's waves have eroded the rock to form steep cliffs in some parts of the island, while in others, glaciers flowing down from the Highlands have carved deep valleys and fjords.

For most of human history, Iceland was uninhabited. Egypt, Greece, and Rome rose and fell, but the only creatures here were birds, fish, foxes, and an occasional confused polar bear who drifted over on an iceberg from Greenland.

700-900: THE SETTLEMENT AGE

During the Viking Age, Celtic monks and Scandinavian seafarers began to explore the North Atlantic: first the Faroe Islands, and then Iceland. The innovation of a sturdier keel—spanning the entire length of a ship—allowed the early Scandinavians to sail with confidence on the open ocean. They pickled their foods in

Iceland Almanac

Official Name: The Republic of Iceland (Lýðveldið Ísland), but locals just say "Ísland" (EES-lond).

Population: With about 340,000 people, Iceland is the least-populated country in Europe. About 13 percent of Icelandic residents were born outside Iceland, and about 8 percent are foreign citizens. Almost half of the foreign citizens are from Poland.

Religion: Over two-thirds of Icelanders (238,000) are registered members of the state-supported Lutheran church, and more than 20,000 belong to other Protestant denominations. There are 12,000 Catholics, 3,000 members of the revived Old Norse religion (called Ásatrú), 3,000 Zuists (a made-up religion which reimburses its members for the $80 annual church tax), and 1,500 members of the atheist Humanist Association.

Latitude and Longitude: Between 63° and 66°N and 13° and 25°W (similar latitude to Fairbanks, Alaska). The island is located between the Greenland Sea, the Norwegian Sea, and the open North Atlantic Ocean.

Area: 39,682 square miles, a little larger than the state of Maine. The country is sparsely populated, with about eight inhabitants per square mile.

Geography: Iceland is oval-shaped, with three peninsulas extending from the west side. The coastal regions are green and grassy. The interior uplands are mostly wasteland—cold and snowy in winter—with glaciers and swift-flowing rivers. Iceland is located on a geological hotspot and is home to over 130 active and inactive volcanoes. There are more glaciers in Iceland than in all of continental Europe.

Rivers: The two largest rivers are both in the south of the country: Ölfusá (which flows into the Atlantic by Selfoss), and Þjórsá, the next major river to the east. There are also powerful rivers in the northeast, such as Jökulsá á Fjöllum, which flows over the Dettifoss waterfall.

Mountains: Hvannadalshnúkur, at 6,921 feet, is Iceland's highest point. It's one of the summits around the crater of the Öræfajökull volcano, in the southeast of the country, which last erupted in 1727. The Öræfajökull glacier is a branch of Vatnajökull, the country's largest glacier.

Biggest Cities and Towns: Nearly two-thirds of the population resides in Reykjavík (the capital, made up of six separate munic-

fermented whey (to preserve valuable nourishment when far from home) and used birds and whales to help them navigate the seas.

No one knows exactly how, when, or where the first arrivals came to Iceland. Much of the country's early history was passed down orally over the centuries, then finally recorded for the first time in the "sagas"—a series of tales mixing historical fact and fan-

ipalities with a total of 220,000 people). Other "cities" include Akureyri (in North Iceland, pop. 18,000), Keflavík (15,000, including its sister town of Njarðvík), and Selfoss (7,000).

Economy: The Gross Domestic Product is about $20 billion, and the GDP per capita is around $47,000. The major money-makers for Iceland are tourism, fishing (representing 40 percent of exports), and hydropower (from dams that generate electricity used for metal smelting). Over three-quarters of Iceland's exports go to European countries, while 8 percent go to the United States and Canada. Iceland's unemployment hovers around 4 percent. About 2 percent of Icelanders work in agriculture, 4 percent in fishing and fish processing, 1 percent in metal processing, 15 percent in other industries, and 78 percent in services.

Government: The prime minister is the chief executive, and typically the head of the leading vote-getting party. The president has a mostly ceremonial role, but helps to form parliamentary coalitions and can refer legislation to a referendum. There are 63 legislators in the single-house parliament (the Alþingi), who sit for four years unless early elections are called. Iceland is divided into 74 municipalities.

Flag: The flag is a red-and-white Scandinavian cross on a blue field. Blue represents the skies, white represents glaciers and ice, and red represents volcanic fire.

Soccer: The Icelandic national team has a strong following, gaining worldwide attention with a surprising quarterfinals appearance in the 2016 European Championships. Many Icelanders root for one of the English Premier League teams as well.

The Average Icelander: The average Icelander will live 83 years. He or she has two children and goes through 18 pounds of coffee beans per year. Legend has it that 1 in 10 Icelanders will publish a book.

ciful legend. While the sagas can't be taken as literal history, they are loaded with stories (rooted in who-knows-how-much truth) that are deeply ingrained in the Icelandic national identity. For more on the sagas, see the sidebar on page 106.

According to the sagas, the discoverer of Iceland was Hrafna-Flóki Vilgerðarson, who released three ravens when he was under

sail; the first two turned back to
Norway, but the third flew in
the opposite direction—eventually leading him to Iceland. He
became known by the nickname
Hrafna-Flóki—"Raven Flóki."
The sagas say that Ingólfur Ár-
narson was the first permanent
settler in Iceland, near today's
Reykjavík, around A.D. 874.
But archaeologists have found
evidence of settlement dating
much earlier than that.

Whoever came first, these settlers grew in number around
the middle of the ninth century. Once they established a course
they could follow with confidence, it took these early Scandinavians just 72 hours to cross from Norway to Iceland. Influenced by
political events in Norway and Ireland, a mix of people from both
lands brought their livestock and took up permanent residence in
Iceland. Most were pagan, following the old Germanic religion of
Thor (Þórr) and Odin (Oðinn), and spoke Old Norse.

Interestingly, geneticists believe that many of the female settlers were Celts, while more of the men were Scandinavian. It
seems that Ireland and Scotland were good places for Scandinavian
men to find wives (willing or unwilling) to bring on the journey.
Today, Icelandic history is dominated by the Scandinavian narrative; only faint traces of Celtic culture survive.

Settlement Age Iceland had no towns; everyone lived on
farms. The newcomers appreciated Iceland's abundant fresh water
and grazing land for sheep. It was a challenging existence, but early
Icelanders tamed the land and made it their own.

900-1300: THE ICELANDIC COMMONWEALTH

The settlers established a primitive government, in which several
dozen local chieftains *(goðar)* held power. The chieftainships could
be inherited or sold. As in other Germanic lands, they held regular courts and legislative assemblies (called a *þing*, like the English
"thing"). Beginning around A.D. 930, an island-wide assembly—
called the Alþingi ("all-thing")—convened once a year, at Þingvellir. (For more on this great gathering, see the Þingvellir listing on
page 183.)

Meanwhile, Icelanders began to explore farther and farther
into the chilly North Atlantic. Around the 980s, led by an exiled
outlaw named Eiríkur Þorvaldsson ("Erik the Red"), Icelanders settled on the west coast of Greenland, and eventually established over 300 farms there. These communities would last until

Iceland's Neighbors: Greenland and the Faroe Islands

Iceland is just a short flight (1.5-2 hours) from east Greenland and the Faroe Islands, making it possible for travelers to combine a trip to Iceland with one of these two destinations.

Iceland, Greenland, and the Faroes share a history of medieval Norse settlement and later, Danish colonial rule. Greenland and the Faroes have much smaller modern populations—both about 50,000 people—and were not large enough to declare independence as easily as Iceland.

Today, both remain part of Denmark, but manage some of their own affairs. Locals learn Danish in school and use it in some contexts, but prefer their own tongues (two related Inuit languages in Greenland; Faroese, which is somewhat similar to Icelandic, in the Faroes).

The Faroes are a relatively wealthy Scandinavian society with rich fishing grounds, like Iceland. In Greenland, the original Norse settlement was abandoned in the 1400s, and the population today is Inuit with some later Danish intermarriage. Greenland has great potential wealth, but also a legacy of social problems (similar to that experienced by native communities in Canada and the US).

It's easy to fly round-trip from Iceland to either Greenland or the Faroes, although fares are high. You can also travel from Iceland to the Faroes on the Norröna car ferry from Seyðisfjörður in eastern Iceland, which continues on to Denmark. Both Greenland and the Faroes are spectacular destinations—Greenland is icy, barren, and majestic; the Faroes green, wet, and steep.

The easiest way to visit Greenland from Iceland is to fly from Reykjavík to Kulusuk (pop. 250) in east Greenland. In summer, regional airline Air Iceland Connect offers a day-trip to Kulusuk, with four hours on the ground. Kulusuk is on a small island of the same name, and anyone staying overnight usually takes a 10-minute helicopter flight to the main town of Tasiilaq (pop. 2,000) on the larger island of Ammassalik.

Air Iceland Connect also flies via Akureyri to a less practical destination, the east Greenlandic airport at Nerlerit Inaat (also known as Constable Point), which serves the village of Ittoqqortoormiit (pop. 500, also known as Scoresbysund). Bear in mind that east Greenland is a world away from the capital of Nuuk (pop. 18,000), on the west coast facing Canada. The east and west coasts even have their own languages, about as different as Italian and Spanish. Flights from Iceland to Nuuk and other west coast destinations take about three hours.

the 1400s, when the weather turned colder. A few years after the settlement of Greenland, an Icelander named Bjarni Herjólfsson was blown off course on his way to Greenland, and sighted the coast of northeastern Canada. Leifur Eiríksson (son of Erik the Red) bought Bjarni's ship and explored the unknown continent. Another man, Þorfinnur Þórðarson, settled there, possibly at L'Anse aux Meadows in Newfoundland, but the Icelanders' North American settlements did not last. (For more on "Leif Erikson," as he's known stateside, see page 87.)

Iceland maintained a diplomatic and trading relationship with Norway, whose King Ólafur Tryggvason (r. 995-1000) tried to introduce Christianity to his subjects. He also sent missionaries to Iceland, who succeeded in making some converts, but failed in Christianizing the entire island. To nudge the Icelanders further, the king detained some Icelandic traders. This kicked off a furious debate at the assembly in Þingvellir in the year A.D. 1000. The assembly chose to convert rather than engage in a devastating trade war with Norway, and the entire country accepted Christianity in one fell swoop. (For more on the legend surrounding this mass conversion, see page 188.) Privately, however, Icelanders continued to follow their pagan faith. Icelandic culture features a blending of Christianity and Old Norse ways, and to this day, many Icelanders have two given names—one with Christian roots, and the other pagan.

Skálholt (near Geysir and Gullfoss) became the religious center of south Iceland, and Hólar (in Skagafjörður) the religious center of the north. Small communities grew up at each place. Otherwise, there were still no towns in Iceland. Farmers who were rich enough built small churches on their property.

All told, there were about 4,000 farms in Iceland during this period. The weather was warmer then, allowing grain to grow. At first there were large stretches of woodland, and the grassy areas (not yet destroyed by overgrazing) extended far inland. The settlers were pastoralists, living off their animals' meat, milk, and wool. They kept cattle, sheep, and pigs, and used horses for transport and herding. They also did some fishing at certain times of the year.

Although you'll often hear this period described as a golden age that was later "restored," and Iceland's Alþingi is sometimes described as "the world's oldest parliament," the commonwealth period was no modern democracy. Society was stratified, with property owners on top, tenant farmers a step down, then landless laborers and slaves at the bottom. Women kept to the home and were mostly shut out of the realms of power, politics, and frontier justice.

The sagas were first written down around the end of this period, in the 12th through 14th century. No one knows exactly why Iceland became such a center of literary activity. Some scholars have suggested that the Celtic element of Icelandic society brought a talent for storytelling.

During these years, the language spoken in Iceland was about the same as in mainland Scandinavia. The archbishop of Iceland was in Norway. Icelanders sometimes thought of themselves as Norwegian, but in some ways emphasized their distinctness. At first, they were not formally subjects of the king of Norway. This changed in the 1200s, as chieftains from different families and parts of Iceland warred against each other inconclusively for control of the country. After decades of fighting, they resolved their differences by swearing allegiance to the king, who was just then trying to consolidate Norwegian power over Greenland and Scotland as well. In 1262, at the annual assembly in Þingvellir, Icelanders agreed to what became known as the "Old Covenant"—unilaterally declaring themselves to be subjects of Norway. The esteemed Alþingi was reduced from a primitive "parliament" to, essentially, an appeals court.

1300-1600: MEDIEVAL TIMES

Although Iceland was part of Norway, it retained its own laws. Aside from a single Norwegian governor (who lived at the farm called Bessastaðir, near Reykjavík), local officials were all Icelanders. Norway, preoccupied by its relations with Sweden and Denmark, showed little interest in Iceland or Greenland. In 1397, Norway joined with Sweden and Denmark in the Kalmar Union. Sweden left the union in the 1520s; meanwhile, Norway (suffering from the cooling climate) effectively became a dependency of Denmark. Thus, it became faraway Copenhagen—rather than Trondheim, Bergen, or Oslo—that Iceland answered to.

During the 1300s, Icelanders began to export fish and set up fishing stations on the coast, where they lived temporarily in the springtime. Christianity, which allowed eating fish on fast days, created a strong market for dried cod in Europe.

But Icelanders were not allowed to live permanently on the coast. Icelandic law required any landless person to live on a farm, for one-year periods starting each May. The farmer had to provide food and shelter in return for labor. If the farmer sent the laborer fishing in the spring, he got all their catch. Landless laborers were not allowed to marry. It was possible for them to buy or lease a farm, but not always easy. This system, called the *vistarband*—similar in some ways to Russian-style serfdom (if less harsh)—persisted all the way up until the 1890s.

The plague known as the Black Death reached Iceland in 1402, about 50 years after it decimated Europe. Approximately one-third of the island's inhabitants perished. Scholars and printers turned their attention to more pressing matters—effectively bringing the age of the sagas to an abrupt end. But, because Icelandic society was rural and isolated (rather than urban and interconnected), the country was not as disrupted as many in Europe. In fact, the plague opened up more opportunities for upwardly mobile peasants to buy their own land.

In the 1400s and 1500s, English and German merchants began to fish in Icelandic waters and trade with Icelanders, and they tried to set up permanent settlements on the Icelandic coast. They were, however, kicked out by the Danish government, which slowly began to see Iceland as an economic asset...and wanted its trade for themselves.

Around 1540, the Protestant Reformation reached Iceland by royal decree. The only real resistance came from the bishop of the northern diocese at Hólar, Jón Arason, who saw the Lutheran faith as an unwelcome Danish imposition. He was captured, brought to Skálholt, and executed.

It was during these centuries that the mainland Scandinavian languages developed away from Old Norse, while Icelanders' speech remained the same. By the end of this time, mainlanders could no longer understand Icelandic—and Icelanders felt themselves more and more separate. After the Reformation, the Bible was translated into Icelandic for the first time and printed in Denmark.

1600-1800: DANISH MONOPOLY

In 1602, King Christian IV of Denmark decreed that only a few specific merchants from Copenhagen and nearby towns would be allowed to trade with Iceland. Twenty harbors around the Icelandic coast were set up as trading points, where these merchants would come each summer to sell grain, timber, fine cloth, and other goods in return for Icelandic fish and woolens, all at fixed prices. Icelanders who had something to sell had no choice but to deal with the local merchant, a similar relationship to the one between the Hudson's Bay Company and native Canadians.

During these years, Iceland had about 50,000 people—the number rising and falling with famines and epidemics. Since only property-owning men could marry, the rate of marriage was low, and illegitimacy was common—prefiguring Scandinavia's loose attitude toward marriage today. Infant mortality was high, partly due to the odd belief—prevalent in northern Scandinavia—that

(side margin) PAST & PRESENT

babies should be given cow's milk instead of being breast-fed. Iceland still had no towns and no schools. Children were supposed to learn to read the Bible from others on the farm, under the watchful eye of the local pastor. In the mid-1700s, about half the population was literate. Dancing was banned, and there were very few musical instruments. Pirate raids along the coast were a problem, and the authorities often suspected witchcraft among the population—and meted out punishments as stiff as those in Salem.

Up until the 1700s, Reykjavík was just a large farm, like many others around the country. But around mid-century, Skúli Magnússon, a high Icelandic official, got support from Denmark to set up several businesses in Iceland, including textile manufacturing. He chose Reykjavík as the location, as it was close to the country's administrative seat at Bessastaðir. A row of workers' houses built in what is now downtown Reykjavík, and although Skúli's enterprises failed, they were enough to seed settlement at what became Iceland's capital.

Unfortunately, the late 1700s also brought natural catastrophes that demonstrated how fragile settlement on this volcanic island can be. In 1783, on the heels of several cold winters, a huge eruption started along a fissure running southwest from Vatnajökull glacier, creating a set of craters now called Lakagígar. Strong earthquakes destroyed most of the buildings of the southern bishop's seat at Skálholt. The ash from the eruption was loaded with toxic gases and blocked the summer sunlight. Livestock died and famine struck the land, killing one-fifth of the population.

One bright consequence of the eruption was a loosening of the trade monopoly in 1787. Now any Dane (not just certain merchants with a license) could trade with Iceland. (Germans and English were still excluded.) As part of these reforms, in 1786 the Danish crown selected six Icelandic harbors, including Reykjavík, as official trading locations. That same year, Reykjavík received "town" status. With the decline of Skálholt, Reykjavík emerged as the logical seat of Iceland's religion (becoming home to both bishops), government (the annual Alþingi gathering), and education system. As Reykjavík took over as Iceland's administrative center, the Alþingi was abolished in 1800 (it was restored in 1844). Even as Denmark extended more rights to Iceland, change was in the air.

1800-1900: A NATION EMERGES

In the 19th century, Icelanders redefined their relationship with Denmark. They wanted to restart their own legislative assembly and have control over their own affairs, though within the Danish realm. They also wanted the freedom to trade with whomever they wanted—not just Danes—and at whatever price the market would bear. The leader of the fight for these reforms was Jón Sigurðs-

son, an Icelandic scholar who lived in Copenhagen (now honored by a statue facing Iceland's parliament). Through persistence, they reached both goals in the 1840s and 1850s. In 1874, the king of Denmark approved a written constitution for Iceland. Icelanders thus gained much more autonomy than their neighbors in the Faroe Islands and Greenland, which are still part of Denmark today.

Iceland remained very poor. As the century drew to a close, most Icelanders still lived in houses made with thick turf walls and a grassy sod roof. The nicer rooms were paneled with timber. The houses often backed up against a hillside for support and insulation. You can see these sod houses today at Árbær

Open-Air Museum, just outside Reykjavík; at Skógar, on the South Coast; and—best of all—at Glaumbær near Skagafjörður in North Iceland.

In the late 1800s, about 20,000 Icelanders emigrated to North America (principally Manitoba, Canada; for more on this story, visit the Iceland Emigration Center in Hofsós). Among those who stayed, about a quarter suffered from a debilitating tapeworm called echinococcus, acquired from living in proximity to dogs and sheep. Only in the 20th century was the parasite eliminated by banning meat processing on farms, and limiting contact between people and dogs. Laws against dog ownership in Icelandic towns have only recently been relaxed.

Fishing technology improved, and by the 1870s, Icelanders exported more fish than agricultural products. Defying age-old custom, Icelanders began to settle along the coast and gather into towns, where they built wood-frame homes with corrugated iron roofs.

In the 1880s, Icelandic farmers banded together in cooperatives to challenge the Danish merchants who still dominated Icelandic commerce. Together, they had enough negotiating power to buy consumer goods and sell wool and lamb abroad on better terms than before. Up until about 1990, many of Iceland's shops still belonged to farmer's cooperatives.

1900-2000: INDEPENDENCE AND MODERNIZATION

In 1902, the first boat motor came to Iceland—and within a couple of decades, the fishing industry was revolutionized. The country kept urbanizing, and by the 1930s, two-thirds of Icelanders lived in towns (including one-third in Reykjavík). But while the country slowly modernized, it remained poor. Roads were few and bad. Housing in towns was cramped, chilly, and heated with coal. Icelanders, accurately, saw themselves as country cousins to their Scandinavian relatives, who lived in cities with grand architecture, museums, and fine universities. The Great Depression hit hard, and at the outbreak of World War II, Iceland was one of the poorest parts of northern Europe.

Icelanders continued to chip away at Danish control. They created their own flag and currency, and developed their own political parties. In 1918, they negotiated a 25-year agreement to become a separate state under the Danish crown.

One morning in 1940, British soldiers landed in Iceland without asking permission—knowing that Germany would act if they didn't. The next year, the American and Canadian military relieved the British. Sixty thousand corn-fed North Americans arrived on the island, outnumbering the local men, who naturally saw them as a threat. (Meanwhile, some local women saw them as an opportunity, and started new lives and families behind the white picket fences of American towns with soldier husbands.) Iceland didn't participate actively in World War II, but 230 Icelanders were killed—mostly on merchant ships sunk at sea. While that sounds minimal, it's almost the same loss of life, per capita, as in the United States.

For the most part, Icelanders didn't mind the wartime Allied "occupation," which left them with improved roads, bridges, and other infrastructure. For example, the Allies built Keflavík Airport and an adjoining base, which American troops ran until 2006.

In 1943 (while Denmark was occupied by the Nazis, and Iceland by the Allies), Iceland declared its complete independence. After the war, Iceland joined NATO (in 1949). The US base at Keflavík, though mostly walled off from Icelandic society, provided income and employment to Icelanders and influenced Iceland culturally. Only after Icelanders started tuning into the base's TV station in the 1960s did the Icelandic state broadcasting service finally start a local television station of its own.

Icelanders had begun tapping geothermal sources for home heating with hot water in the 1930s. Slowly, coal disappeared as a fuel, and by the 1960s, all of Reykjavík was heated with water piped from underground sources in the countryside. This meant very low energy costs, still today one of the saving graces of living in Iceland. Meanwhile, rivers were dammed for power generation—and soon Iceland had an electricity surplus.

In the 1970s, the first metal smelters were built to make use of the electricity. The fishing industry prospered; each small town had a fishing fleet and freezing plant. The political parties in Iceland dispensed jobs and mortgages to members in return for their fidelity to the cause.

Icelanders maintained close ties to the Nordic countries through the 20th century. In the 1990s, Denmark, Sweden, and Finland chose to join the European Union. Iceland and Norway stayed out of the EU—but they did join the European Economic Area (EEA), a looser alliance that makes Iceland subject to most EU regulations, but keeps local control over fishing, agriculture, and customs policy. Since then, Icelanders have started to see themselves more as Europeans than as Scandinavians.

THE 21ST CENTURY AND ICELAND TODAY

In the first decade and a half of the 2000s, it seemed like Iceland—so long ignored by the rest of the world—was constantly in the international news: First came its financial boom-and-bust cycle, culminating in the 2008 crisis; then the eruption of Eyjafjallajökull in 2010, which left European air travelers cursing this remote island; and most recently its unprecedented tourism boom.

Starting around 2000, Iceland privatized its publicly owned banks. The banks grew tremendously, taking advantage of European rules to accept deposits from other countries. Icelanders flocked to work for the banks, and society prospered. Skeptics were silenced: When a politician questioned some of the government's banking policies on the floor of parliament, the then-finance minister, a trained veterinarian, famously quipped, "Guys, can't you see the party?" Driving their Lexuses around Reykjavík, Icelanders finally felt they had arrived; they were Scandinavia's hillbillies no more.

But the "party" was an illusion. The banks didn't have enough assets to cover their debts, and collapsed in 2008 in one of history's largest bankruptcies—a cold shower for the entire country. The Icelandic *króna* crashed in value, and many people lost their jobs, savings, and homes. Some bankers, exposed as charlatans, received brief prison terms.

Tourism was a saving grace. A relatively minor player in Iceland's economy for many decades, after 2010 it started to boom

and is now the country's largest source of income. In 2015, tourism surpassed fishing as Iceland's top industry. In 2016, for the first time, more Americans visited Iceland than the number of people who live in Iceland. And it continues. Icelanders are scrambling to deal with the huge demand by improving infrastructure and discussing what limits they might need to place on visits to their natural wonders—which have always been free and open to all. And while all that tourism may seem like easy money, it's very seasonal, and jobs in tourism are not lucrative (immigrants hold many of them).

Iceland today is a secure, peaceful, and fairly well-off country, but still lags behind mainland Scandinavia in indicators such as educational achievement, press freedom, government transparency, and health care. Icelanders work longer hours but are less productive per hour than their Scandinavian cousins. It's difficult to attract businesses to the country, and like any small community, many educated Icelanders leave for jobs in Europe's big urban centers (where they are free to settle due to Iceland's EEA membership).

Perhaps the most controversial issue for Icelanders today is the question of control over natural resources. Iceland's neighbor, Norway, has channeled much of its oil wealth into a fund that the country draws on for everyone's benefit, and that secures Norway's prosperity into the future. In contrast, Icelandic fishing "quota" (the right to harvest fish from the sea) is in the hands of private investors who pay society little or no rent for it. Similarly, profits from Iceland's energy surplus go largely to multinational companies who buy electricity at cut-rate prices. Many Icelanders believe that more of this wealth should be channeled to the public good, and that more investment in health and education would finally bring the country's standard of living up to a mainland level. Fishing-quota owners have also concentrated fish processing in fewer and fewer places. This is efficient, but has decimated jobs in some formerly flourishing small towns.

The control of retail trade is also a key issue for Iceland today, just as it was in the 1700s and 1800s. Many of Iceland's wholesale companies are still run by the descendants of those original Danish merchant families. Visitors often assume that the country's high prices are due to transport costs or the small size of the market. In fact, they have more to do with weak competition, protectionism, inefficient businesses, and the difficulties of keeping the Icelan-

Who Are the Icelanders?

Iceland is the most sparsely populated country in Europe, with only about eight people per square mile. And yet, it has a seat in the United Nations, ambassadors, a flag, its own currency, and a president—who governs only about 340,000 people, but nevertheless hobnobs with the likes of Justin Trudeau, Angela Merkel, and Vladimir Putin.

Icelanders are sensitive to this irony. They know their nation's small size can bring them disproportionate (and some would say undeserved) prominence on the world stage. (Consider that Icelanders get their own Eurovision contestant, while similar-sized communities in Norway compete for the privilege.) Exaggerated tales of Iceland's small scale persist: You may hear that the president's home number is listed in the phone book, but that hasn't been true for years.

In some ways, Iceland is the most Scandinavian country, where the old common Scandinavian language survives best, and where historical narratives were first written down. In other ways, Iceland is the least Scandinavian—physically and linguistically distinct from the others, considerably influenced by American culture, and the least progressive in its education, health, and welfare systems.

Icelanders frequently criticize themselves as *kærulaus* (a

dic *króna* stable (some favor pegging it to another currency). Also, local retailers have successfully lobbied to make it hard for Icelanders to order from online retailers like Amazon. Many Icelanders, frustrated with the poor selection and high prices in local stores, fly abroad to shop, and bring home clothes and toys in their suitcases. Sensing opportunity, multinational cost-cutters like IKEA, Costco, H&M, and the German DIY chain Bauhaus have recently opened stores in Reykjavík.

There are also unresolved political issues. Iceland's voting system over-represents rural interests in parliament, and farmers have used their disproportionate power to lobby for import restrictions that inflate the price of meat and dairy products. The Icelandic constitution is outdated—much of it dates from 1874. A committee elected by referendum drafted a new constitution in 2013, but beneficiaries of the status quo blocked any change.

Locals and foreigners alike used to see Iceland as a very honest, transparent country. But since the banking mania ended, Iceland-

word which means negligent, careless, inconsiderate, or flippant). *Kærulaus* suggests that there are no rules; and even when there are rules, no one knows them; even when people know the rules, they don't follow them; when people break the rules, no one cares; and if anyone tries to enforce the rules, they will be laughed at. This doesn't apply in all situations (and doesn't mean you can start driving off-road or stealing from your hotel), but it does accurately describe the country's opportunistic, frontier mentality.

Another, more hopeful phrase that Icelanders like to use is *Þetta reddast* ("It'll work out"); this represents a conviction that your special needs can be accommodated, and that no one will be left behind in the end. Icelanders are quick to make special exceptions, and expect others to do the same for them.

Icelanders often project an image of unity and Mayberry-like innocence to outsiders, and visitors sometimes come away with an idealized picture of the country, focusing on things like renewable energy and the low crime rate. But if you take the time to read and understand Iceland's complex political, social, and environmental issues, you'll find that beneath the sheen, the country is as contentious and competitive as any other.

One impressive thing about Icelanders is how gracefully they have handled the enormous influx of tourism to their sparsely populated homeland. Of course, there are plenty of grumbles and thoughtful criticism—including those who, quite justifiably, worry that so many people passing through could spoil what's so special about this country. Few countries could manage such a drastic spike in tourism as well as Iceland has. One way or another... *Þetta reddast.*

ers have realized that what they once thought of as "keeping wealth in the family" or "helping out friends and political allies" could also be described as "corruption." Some would like Iceland to become a full member of the European Union, seeing regulation from Brussels as a professional, stabilizing influence on a small country that has limited local expertise. Others value Iceland's partial autonomy, and see the EU as burdensome, bureaucratic baggage.

Environmentally, Icelanders struggle with the effects of hundreds of years of soil erosion and deforestation. The government has worked to increase forest cover and reseed barren land (recently using lupine, whose purple flowers you'll see along roadsides in early summer). Another perennial environmental debate is whether to build more dams to harvest the country's remaining hydroelectric potential.

Even as it becomes popular among tourists, Iceland struggles to keep its young people interested in making lives here, rather than going to more dynamic European cities that are better connected with the rest of the world. You may notice that many of the young people you meet in the tourist trade are not Icelandic, but rather recently arrived Eastern Europeans seeking adventure and higher wages. Some politicians say the way forward is to lower the cost of living, improve schools and health care, raise public-sector salaries for jobs like teaching and nursing, and make shopping easier. The vision is to make living in Iceland as appealing as living in Norway or Denmark or Germany (although these priorities often threaten the deeply ingrained interests of the agricultural and fishing lobbies).

Despite the unique challenges this remote island grapples with, one thing remains steady: the ability to impress its many visitors. Icelanders have come a long way from the millennium they spent as hardscrabble peasants on isolated farms. Against all odds, their plucky little country is prosperous, known and respected around the world, and enjoying a moment as everyone's favorite transcontinental layover.

PAST & PRESENT

PRACTICALITIES

This chapter covers the practical skills of Icelandic travel: how to get tourist information, pay for things, sightsee efficiently, find good-value accommodations, eat affordably but well, use technology wisely, and get between destinations smoothly. For more information on these topics, see www.ricksteves.com/travel-tips.

Tourist Information

Iceland's **national tourist office** offers practical information and trip-planning ideas on their website (www.visiticeland.com), which also links to good regional information.

In Iceland, a good first stop is generally the tourist information office—abbreviated **TI** in this book. While you can get plenty of information online, I still make a point to swing by the local TI to confirm sightseeing plans, pick up maps, and get information on transit (including excursion bus schedules), walking tours, special events, and nightlife.

Prepare a list of questions and a proposed plan to double-check. Some TIs have information on the entire country or at least the region, so try to pick up maps and printed information for destinations you'll be visiting later in your trip.

Two thick, **free booklets** are especially useful for travelers in Iceland. *Áning—Accommodation in Iceland* lists swimming pools and campgrounds around the island (as well as hotels, guesthouses, and bus routes). *Around Iceland* is a directory of sights and services around the whole country, including useful maps. Both are advertising-supported, but comprehensive and fairly neutral. Download them at www.icelandreview.com/publications, or pick up paper copies once you arrive.

Travel Tips

Emergency and Medical Help: In Iceland, dial 112 for all emergencies (police, fire, or ambulance).

For simple illnesses, go to a pharmacist for advice. For more complicated problems, ask at your hotel for help—they'll know the nearest medical and emergency services. Or dial 1770 to reach the efficient after-hours medical service called Læknavakt (www.laeknavaktin.is), available for phone consults at no charge weekdays from 17:00 to 8:00 and around-the-clock on weekends. Non-Europeans can pay a reasonable fee to visit any of Iceland's state-run primary care centers *(heilsugæslustöð)* during business hours.

Theft or Loss: To replace a passport, you'll need to go in person to an embassy or consulate (see page 425). If your credit and debit cards disappear, cancel and replace them (see "Damage Control for Lost Cards" on page 379).

File a police report either on the spot or within a day or two; you'll need it to submit an insurance claim for lost or stolen travel gear, and it can help with replacing your passport or credit and debit cards. For more information, see www.ricksteves.com/help.

Avoiding Theft: While Iceland is generally safe, if there are thieves or crooks about, they'll target tourists. Keep a close eye on your suitcase and daypack, and don't set valuables down absent-mindedly.

Time Zones: Iceland doesn't observe Daylight Savings Time (due to its far-north location, it's already often either light or dark). In summer, Iceland is one hour behind Great Britain and four/seven hours ahead of the East/West coasts of the US. In winter, Iceland is on par with Great Britain and five/eight hours ahead of the East/West coasts of the US. The exceptions are the beginning and end of Daylight Saving Time: Europe "springs forward" the last Sunday in March (two weeks after most of North America) and "falls back" the last Sunday in October (one week before North America). During those weeks, Iceland is even with Great Britain and four/seven hours ahead of the East/West coasts of the US.

For a handy online time converter, see www.timeanddate.com/worldclock.

As Iceland's clocks are set closer to Europe than the island's geography justifies, the sun doesn't reach its zenith in the sky until after 13:00, and rises and sets later in the day than you might expect. This is especially noticeable in winter.

Business Hours: Shops in Iceland are usually open from 10:00 or 11:00 until at least 18:00, with no lunch break. Supermarkets, other large retailers, and tourist-oriented shops are mostly open long hours daily, with slightly reduced weekend hours. Small shops often close early on Saturday. Banks are generally open Monday through Friday from 9:00 to 16:00.

Sundays have the same pros and cons as they do for travelers in the US: Sightseeing attractions are generally open, banks and smaller shops are closed, and public transportation options are fewer (for example, city buses may run only every 30-60 minutes). Friday and Saturday evenings are lively; Sunday evenings are quiet.

Watt's Up? Like continental Europe, Iceland's electrical system is 220 volts, instead of North America's 110 volts. Most newer electronics (such as laptops, battery chargers, and hair dryers) convert automatically, so you won't need a converter, but you will need an adapter plug with two round prongs, sold inexpensively at travel stores in the US.

Discounts: Discounts for sights are generally not listed in this book. However, seniors (age 60 and over), youths under 18, and students and teachers with proper identification cards (www.isic.org) can get discounts at many sights. Always ask.

Online Translation Tips: Google's Chrome browser instantly translates websites. You can also paste text or the URL of a foreign website into the translation window at Translate.google.com. The Google Translate app converts spoken English into most European languages (and vice versa) and can also translate text it "reads" with your smartphone's camera.

Money

Here's my basic strategy for using money in Iceland:
- Upon arrival, head for a cash machine (ATM) at the airport and withdraw a small amount of local currency, using a debit card with low international transaction fees.
- Keep your cash safe in a money belt.
- Pay for most purchases with a credit card with low (or no) international fees.

Exchange Rate

100 Icelandic krónur (ISK) = about $1

Iceland uses the *króna* (meaning "crown"; plural *krónur*). To very roughly convert prices from Icelandic *krónur* to dollars, simply lop off the last two zeros: 2,000 ISK = about $20, 6,000 ISK = about $60. Coins range from 1 to 100 ISK, and bills from 500 to 10,000 ISK. (Check www.oanda.com for the latest exchange rates.)

PLASTIC VERSUS CASH

Icelanders rarely use cash; they pay with plastic even for small purchases such as parking meters and hot dogs. It's possible to get through an entire Icelandic trip without ever using local cash.

In Iceland, I use my credit card nearly exclusively, for everything from hotel reservations and car rentals to everyday expenses such as meals and sightseeing. While you could use your debit card for some of these expenses, keep in mind that you have greater fraud protection with your credit card. The card you use may depend on which one charges the lowest international transaction fees.

Exceptions to Iceland's all-plastic system are in-city buses, some coin-operated parking meters, and unstaffed pay WCs at countryside sights—where you're asked, usually on the honor system, to put 100-200 ISK in a box (or the equivalent in US dollars). You could withdraw a couple thousand crowns and change them into 100 ISK coins for these WCs. Or just bring a handful of dollar bills to save a trip to the bank.

Don't withdraw or exchange more Icelandic currency than you need. Most merchants prefer plastic, and you'll scramble to spend unused crowns at the end of your trip. Whatever you do, don't bring *krónur* home with you: It's bothersome to exchange crowns back to dollars even in Iceland, and impossible (or possible only at punishing rates) outside the country.

WHAT TO BRING

I pack the following and keep it all safe in my money belt.

Credit Card: Use this to pay for most items (at hotels, larger shops and restaurants, travel agencies, car-rental agencies, and so on).

Debit Card: Use this at ATMs to withdraw local cash as needed (you'll use your credit card more than cash).

Backup Card: Some travelers carry a third card (debit or credit; ideally from a different bank), in case one gets lost, demagnetized, eaten by a temperamental machine, or simply doesn't work.

US Dollars: I carry $100-200 US as a backup. While you

won't use it for day-to-day purchases, American cash in your money belt comes in handy for emergencies, such as if your ATM card stops working.

What NOT to Bring: Resist the urge to buy *krónur* before your trip (you'll pay the price in bad stateside exchange rates). Wait until you arrive to withdraw money. I've yet to see an airport that didn't have plenty of ATMs.

BEFORE YOU GO
Use this pre-trip checklist.

Know your cards. For credit cards, Visa and MasterCard are universal, American Express and Diners Club are less common, and Discover is unknown. Debit cards from any major US bank will work in any standard Icelandic bank's ATM (ideally, use a debit card with a Visa or MasterCard logo).

Newer credit and debit cards have chips that authenticate and secure transactions. In Iceland, as in much of Europe, the cardholder inserts the chip card into the payment machine slot, then enters a PIN. (In the US, you provide a signature to verify your identity.)

Any American card, whether with a chip or an old-fashioned magnetic stripe, will work at Iceland's hotels, restaurants, and shops. I've been inconvenienced a few times by self-service payment machines that wouldn't accept my card, but it's never caused me serious trouble.

If you're concerned, ask if your bank offers a true chip-and-PIN card. Cards with low fees and chip-and-PIN technology include those from Andrews Federal Credit Union (www.andrewsfcu.org) and the State Department Federal Credit Union (www.sdfcu.org).

Report your travel dates. Let your bank know that you'll be using your debit and credit cards overseas, and when and where you're headed.

Know your PIN. Make sure you know the numeric, four-digit PIN for each of your cards, both credit and debit. Request it if you don't have one and allow time to receive the information by mail.

Adjust your ATM withdrawal limit. Find out how much you can take out daily and ask for a higher daily withdrawal limit if you want to get more cash at once. Note that international ATMs will withdraw funds only from checking accounts; you're unlikely to have access to your savings account.

Ask about fees. For any purchase or withdrawal made with a card, you may be charged a currency conversion fee (1-3 percent), a Visa or MasterCard international transaction fee (1 percent), and—for debit cards—a $2-5 transaction fee each time you use a foreign ATM (some US banks partner with European banks, allowing you to use those ATMs with no fees).

PRACTICALITIES

If you're getting a bad deal, consider getting a new credit or debit card. Reputable no-fee cards include those from Capital One, as well as Charles Schwab debit cards. Most credit unions and some airline loyalty cards have low-to-no international transaction fees.

USING CREDIT CARDS

European cards use chip-and-PIN technology, while most cards issued in the US use a chip-and-signature system. But most Icelandic card readers can automatically generate a receipt for you to sign, just as you would at home. Some card readers will prompt you to enter your PIN (so it's important to know the code for each of your cards). If a cashier is present, you generally should have no problem. At self-service payment machines (transit-ticket kiosks, parking garages, etc.), results are mixed, as US chip-and-signature cards aren't configured for unattended transactions. If your card won't work, look for a cashier who can process your card manually.

Drivers Beware: Be aware of potential problems using a credit card to fill up at Icelandic gas stations. Know your PIN, fuel up often, and be prepared to move on to the next gas station if necessary. For more tips on paying for fuel, see the "Driving" section, later in this chapter.

Dynamic Currency Conversion

Some merchants and hoteliers cheerfully charge you for converting your purchase price into dollars. If it's offered, refuse this "service" (called dynamic currency conversion, or DCC). If, when you insert your chip card into a reader, you get a message asking whether you want to pay in dollars or Icelandic *krónur,* always choose *krónur*— you'll pay extra for the expensive convenience of seeing your charge in dollars.

Using Cash Machines

Icelandic cash machines (labled *Hraðbanki*) have English-language instructions and work just like they do at home—except they spit out local currency instead of dollars, calculated at the day's standard bank-to-bank rate. When possible, withdraw cash from a bank-run ATM located just outside that bank. If your debit card doesn't work, try a lower amount—your request may have exceeded your withdrawal limit or the ATM's limit. If you still have a problem, try a different ATM or come back later—your bank's network may be temporarily down.

Avoid "independent" ATMs, such as Travelex, Euronet, Moneybox, Cardpoint, and Cashzone, which have high fees.

Security Tips

Pickpockets target tourists. To safeguard your valuables, wear a money belt—a pouch with a strap that you buckle around your waist like a belt and tuck under your clothes. For convenience, you can carry a wallet with one credit card and a little cash in your front pocket, but it's wise to secure your backup cards, passport, and bills in your money belt.

Before inserting your card into a payment machine, inspect the front. If anything looks crooked, loose, or damaged, it could be a sign of a card-skimming device. When entering your PIN, carefully block other people's view of the keypad.

To access your accounts online while traveling, be sure to use a secure connection (see the "Tips on Internet Security" sidebar, later in this chapter).

Damage Control for Lost Cards

If you lose your credit or debit card, report the loss immediately to the respective global customer-assistance centers. Call these 24-hour US numbers: Visa (tel. 303/967-1096), MasterCard (tel. 636/722-7111), and American Express (tel. 336/393-1111).

You'll need to provide the primary cardholder's identification-verification details (such as birth date, mother's maiden name, or Social Security number). You can generally receive a temporary card within two or three business days (see www.ricksteves.com/help for more).

If you report your loss within two days, you typically won't be responsible for unauthorized transactions on your account, although many banks charge a liability fee of $50.

TIPPING

Iceland is emphatically a no-tipping country. That means that you should not tip at restaurants, in taxis, in hotels, or anywhere else. Since you'll pay for almost everything with plastic—and most people carry little or no cash—it's difficult to tip even if you wanted to. A nice side effect of the tipless culture in Iceland is that waiters in Icelandic restaurants are usually happy to split the bill and let individual members of a group pay for their own order.

Despite the no-tipping culture, guides on bus tours and other excursions in Iceland will sometimes suggest that you tip them. While you're free to slip them a little extra money (in any currency) for a job especially well done, you are neither expected nor required to. Icelandic labor law requires that employees receive a full basic wage, independent of any expected gratuities.

GETTING A VAT REFUND

Wrapped into the purchase price of your Icelandic souvenirs is a Value-Added Tax (VAT, called VSK or *virðisaukaskattur* in Icelandic) of about 24 percent. You're entitled to get most of that tax back if you purchase more than 6,000 ISK (about $55) worth of goods at a store that participates in the VAT-refund scheme. You must ring up the minimum at a single retailer—you can't add up your purchases from various shops to reach the required amount. (If the store ships the goods to your US home, VAT is not assessed on your purchase.)

Getting your refund is straightforward...and worthwhile if you spend a significant amount on souvenirs.

Get the paperwork. Have the merchant completely fill out the necessary refund document. You may need to show ID. Get the paperwork done before you leave the store to ensure you'll have everything you need (including your original sales receipt).

Get your stamp at the border or airport. At your last stop in Iceland (most likely at Keflavík Airport), arrive an additional half-hour before you need to check in for your flight to allow time to find the customs office and process the paperwork. Before you check your luggage, find the tax refund desk (across from the car rental counters and marked with a large sign). Have your passport and ticket available, as well as the credit card you want the refund to go to. Show them your purchases, receipts, and forms, which they will stamp.

You're not supposed to use your purchased goods before you leave. If you show up at customs wearing your hand-knit Icelandic wool sweater, officials might look the other way—or deny you a refund.

Collect your refund. After getting your paperwork stamped, bring it to the bank in the airport's main hall; they are responsible for refunding VAT.

CUSTOMS FOR AMERICAN SHOPPERS

You can take home $800 worth of items per person duty-free, once every 31 days. Many processed and packaged foods are allowed, including vacuum-packed cheeses, dried herbs, jams, baked goods, candy, chocolate, oil, vinegar, mustard, and honey. Fresh fruits and vegetables and most meats are not allowed, with exceptions for some canned items. As for alcohol, you can bring in one liter duty-free (it can be packed securely in your checked luggage, along with any other liquid-containing items).

To bring alcohol (or liquid-packed foods) in your carry-on bag on your flight home, buy it at a duty-free shop at the airport. You'll increase your odds of getting it onto a connecting flight if it's packaged in a "STEB"—a secure, tamper-evident bag. But stay away from liquids in opaque, ceramic, or metallic containers, which usually cannot be successfully screened (STEB or no STEB).

For details on allowable goods, customs rules, and duty rates, visit http://help.cbp.gov.

Sightseeing

Sightseeing can be hard work. Use these tips to make your visits to Iceland's finest sights meaningful, fun, efficient, and painless.

MAPS AND NAVIGATION TOOLS

A good map is essential for efficient navigation while sightseeing. The maps in this book are concise and simple, designed to help

you locate recommended sights. Maps with more detail are available at local TIs and sold at bookstores.

You can also use a mapping app on your mobile device. Be aware that pulling up maps or looking up turn-by-turn walking directions on the fly requires an Internet connection: To use this feature, it's smart to get

an international data plan or to only connect with Wi-Fi. With Google Maps or City Maps2Go, it's possible to download a map while online, then go offline and navigate without incurring data-roaming charges, though you can't search for an address or get real-time walking directions. A handful of other apps—including City Maps 2Go and OffMaps—also allow you to use maps offline.

For advice about maps for drivers, see page 412.

PLAN AHEAD

Set up an itinerary that allows you to fit in all your top sights. Sight-seeing in Iceland is distinctive in that many of the things you'll want to see are natural wonders (volcanoes, geothermal areas, glaciers). Many are within striking distance of Reykjavík, but require a car or an excursion. You won't typically have to worry about opening hours or admission (see below), but you will need to plan how you'll get there. For advice, see the Near Reykjavík chapter.

For a one-stop look at opening hours in Reykjavík, see the "At a Glance" sidebar in that chapter. Many sights keep stable hours, but things change. It's smart to confirm the latest by checking with the TI or individual sights' websites.

Don't put off visiting a must-see sight—you never know when a place will close unexpectedly due to bad weather, a holiday, or restoration. Some sights are closed or have reduced hours at least a few days a year, especially on holidays such as Christmas, New Year's, and Labor Day (May 1). A list of holidays is on page 425; check online for possible closures during your trip. In summer, some sights may stay open late; in the off-season, hours may be shorter or sights may be closed completely.

If you plan to hire a local guide, reserve ahead. Popular guides can get booked up.

Study up. To get the most out of the sight descriptions in this book, read them before you visit.

AT SIGHTS

Much of the sightseeing you'll do in Iceland is outdoors—and almost all of that is free (there may be a charge for parking and WCs).

Icelanders have lately been debating if this can endure, given rising tourist numbers and the cost of upkeep. Tickets, passes, or local taxes may figure in the future for some popular natural sights.

At Outdoor Sights: Usually you'll park in a big, free parking lot (a few charge a fee). Near the parking lot, you'll often find WCs (some pay, some free); a small café or snack stand; and orientation panels with a helpful introduction to the sight. Bigger sights might have a staffed visitors center where you can get more information.

For some natural attractions, expect a walk (5-15 minutes each way) to reach the sight itself from the parking lot. Always stay on marked trails—both for your own safety and to avoid disrupting the beauty you came to see.

In general, be aware that Iceland's raw nature is as potentially dangerous as it is gorgeous. Read the "The Many Ways Iceland Can Kill You" sidebar in the Icelandic Experiences chapter; carefully review sight-specific details in this book; and heed any warning signs posted at the sight itself.

At Museums and Other Indoor Sights: You may not be allowed to enter if you arrive too close to closing time. Guards start ushering people out well before the actual closing time, so don't save the best for last. If the museum's photo policy isn't clearly posted, ask. Pick up a floor plan as you enter, and ask museum staff if you can't find a particular item.

Audioguides and Apps: Many sights use audioguides, which generally offer useful recorded descriptions in English. Often, you'll download the audioguide for free to your own mobile phone, using on-site Wi-Fi; if you want to rent an audioguide device (where available), you'll pay a token amount.

Sleeping

Extensive and opinionated listings of good-value rooms are a major feature of this book's Sleeping sections. I like places that are clean, central, relatively quiet at night, reasonably priced, friendly, small enough to have a hands-on owner or manager and stable staff, and run with a respect for Icelandic traditions. I'm more impressed by a convenient location and a fun-loving philosophy than flat-screen TVs and a fancy gym. Most places I recommend fall short of perfection. But if I can find a place with most of these features, it's a keeper. My recommendations run the gamut, from dorm beds to fancy rooms with all the comforts. You can also consider a short-term rental, or camping your way around Iceland in a campervan.

Book your accommodations as soon as your itinerary is set, especially for Reykjavík and on the Ring Road (where there aren't enough rooms to meet demand in the areas around Mývatn and Höfn). For the peak summer months, rooms can be completely booked up many months ahead. See the appendix for a list of major holidays and festivals in Iceland: Some—like Þjóðhátíð in the Westman Islands—merit reserving far in advance. For tips on making reservations, see the "Making Hotel Reservations" sidebar later in this chapter.

Icelandic homes and smaller hotels rely on geothermal energy for heat. There's usually no central thermostat, just individual controls on each radiator. Typically, if it gets too warm, Icelanders will open a window before they turn down the radiator.

Be aware that if you visit Iceland in June or early July, it will never get fully dark. Accommodations come with blackout curtains that try to darken your sleeping quarters, but some travelers still find it hard to sleep. Light sleepers will want to bring a nighttime eye mask.

RATES AND DEALS

I've categorized my recommended accommodations based on price, indicated with a dollar-sign rating (see sidebar). The price ranges suggest an estimated cost for a one-night stay in a standard dou-

PRACTICALITIES

Sleep Code

Hotels are classified based on the average price of a standard double room with breakfast in high season.

$$$$	**Splurge:**	Most rooms over 35,000 ISK
$$$	**Pricier:**	28,000-35,000 ISK
$$	**Moderate:**	20,000-28,000 ISK
$	**Budget:**	15,000-20,000 ISK
¢	**Backpacker:**	Under 15,000 ISK

Unless otherwise noted, credit cards are accepted, and free Wi-Fi is available. Comparison-shop by checking prices at several hotels (on each hotel's own website, on a booking site, or by email). For the best deal, always book directly with the hotel.

PRACTICALITIES

ble room with a private toilet and shower in high season, include breakfast, and assume you're booking directly with the accommodation (not through a booking site, which extracts a commission). Room prices can fluctuate significantly with demand and amenities (size, views, room class, and so on), but these relative price categories remain constant.

Room rates are especially volatile at large hotels that use "dynamic pricing" to set rates. Prices can skyrocket during periods of peak demand, and discounted deeply on weekends when demand plummets. Of the many hotels I recommend, it's difficult to say which will be the best value on a given day—until you do your homework.

Once your dates are set, check the specific price for your preferred stay at several places. You can do this either by comparing prices on Hotels.com or Booking.com, or by checking hotel websites. To get the best deal, contact family-run hotels directly by phone or email. When you go direct, the owner avoids the 20 percent commission, giving them wiggle room to offer you a discount, a nicer room, or free breakfast if it's not already included. If you prefer to book online or are considering a hotel chain, it's to your advantage to use the hotel's website.

Some places offer a discount to those who stay longer than three nights. To cut costs further, try asking for a cheaper room (for example, with a shared bathroom or no window) or offer to skip breakfast.

TYPES OF ACCOMMODATIONS
Hotels
Double rooms listed in this book range from $100 (very simple, toilet and shower down the hall) to $400 suites (maximum plumbing and more), with most clustering around $200-250. Most hotels

also offer single rooms, and some offer larger rooms for four or more people (I call these "family rooms" in the listings). If there's space for an extra cot, they'll cram it in for you. In general, a triple room is cheaper than the cost of a double and a single. Three or four people can economize by requesting one big room.

In Iceland, hotels are usually large (big enough for groups), impersonal, and corporate-owned. If you want a more mom-and-pop feeling, look for guesthouses and farmstays (described below). An ample breakfast buffet is generally included.

Arrival and Check-In: If you're arriving in the morning, your room probably won't be ready. Check your bag safely at the hotel and dive right into sightseeing.

In Your Room: More pillows and blankets are usually in the closet or available on request. Towels and linens aren't always replaced every day. Hang your towel up to dry.

Most hotel rooms have a TV, telephone, and free Wi-Fi. Simpler places rarely have a room phone, but usually have free Wi-Fi.

To guard against theft in your room, keep valuables out of sight. Some rooms come with a safe, and other hotels have safes at the front desk. I've never bothered using one, and in a lifetime of travel I've never had anything stolen from my room.

Checking Out: While it's customary to pay for your room upon departure, it can be a good idea to settle your bill the day before, when you're not in a hurry and while the manager's in. That way you'll have time to discuss and address any points of contention.

Hotelier Help: Hoteliers can be a good source of advice. Most know their town well, and can assist you with everything from route tips to finding a good restaurant or the nearest launderette.

Hotel Hassles: Even at the best places, mechanical breakdowns occur: Sinks leak, toilets may gurgle or smell, or the Wi-Fi goes out. Report your concerns clearly and calmly at the front desk. For more complicated problems, don't expect instant results.

In downtown Reykjavík, street noise on Friday and Saturday nights can be high. If you find that noise is a problem (if, for instance, your room is over a nightclub), ask for a quieter room in the back or on an upper floor.

Above all, keep a positive attitude. Remember, you're on vacation. If your hotel is a disappointment, spend more time out enjoying the place you came to see.

PRACTICALITIES

Making Hotel Reservations

Reserve your rooms as soon as you've pinned down your travel dates, particularly for Reykjavík and some places on the Ring Road (Mývatn and Höfn). For busy national holidays and some festivals, it's wise to reserve far in advance (see page 425).

Requesting a Reservation: For family-run hotels, it's generally cheaper to book your room directly via email or a phone call. For business-class hotels, or if you'd rather book online, reserve directly through the hotel's official website (not a booking agency's site). For complicated requests, send an email. Remember to ask for the hotel's best price—some offer discounts. Almost all of my recommended hotels take reservations in English.

Here's what the hotelier wants to know:
- type(s) of rooms you need and size of your party
- number of nights you'll stay
- your arrival and departure dates, written European-style as day/month/year (for example, 18/06/19 or 18 June 2019)
- special requests (such as en suite bathroom vs. down the hall, cheapest room, twin beds vs. double bed, quiet room)

Confirming a Reservation: Most places will request a credit-card number to hold your room. If you're using an online reservation form, look for the *https* or a lock icon at the top of your browser. If you book directly, you can email, call, or fax this information.

Canceling a Reservation: If you must cancel, it's courteous-and smart—to do so with as much notice as possible, especially for smaller, family-run places. Cancellation policies can be strict;

Small Guesthouses and Farmstays

In the countryside, $150-200 buys you a simple room with a shared bathroom in a small guesthouse or rural farm accommodation. For a private bathroom, you'll step up to the $250-300 range—and that often means a bigger property that's less personal and charming. Even if you're disinclined to share a bathroom, consider compromising from time to time—not only to save money, but also to land at a better place.

While becoming less common, at guesthouses and farmstays you may see separate prices for "made-up beds" and "sleeping-bag space." Sleeping-bag space means that the guesthouse provides a mattress with sheet and pillow (no pillowcase); you bring your own sleeping bag. A made-up bed includes a comforter and duvet cover.

Guesthouses: Especially in Reykjavík and other towns, you'll find plenty of small guesthouses with 5 to 10 rooms and shared bathrooms (some offer private bathrooms). Guesthouses are usually cozier, cheaper, and have more character than hotels, but tend to come with simpler amenities and smaller breakfasts.

From:	rick@ricksteves.com
Sent:	Today
To:	info@hotelcentral.com
Subject:	Reservation request for 19-22 July

Dear Hotel Central,

I would like to stay at your hotel. Please let me know if you have a room available and the price for:
- 2 people
- Double bed and en suite bathroom in a quiet room
- Arriving 19 July, departing 22 July (3 nights)

Thank you!
Rick Steves

PRACTICALITIES

read the fine print or ask about these *before* you book. Many discount deals require prepayment, with no cancellation refunds.

Reconfirming Your Reservation: Call to reconfirm your room reservation a few days in advance. For guesthouses or very small hotels, I call again on my day of arrival to tell my host what time I expect to get there (especially important if arriving late—after 17:00).

Phoning: For tips on calling hotels overseas, see page 404.

Farmstays: Many Icelandic farms rent space to travelers, ranging from a room or two in the main farmhouse to a string of prefab cabins set up elsewhere on the property. Aside from Reykjavík, Iceland had practically no towns until the late 1800s—staying in the countryside lets you experience Iceland as it was for centuries. Sheep are the most common livestock (they're up in the mountains during the summer), and some farms keep cows or horses; hay is the main crop. While farm families offer a cordial welcome, Icelanders tend to be reserved and you should mostly expect to be left alone. The Icelandic farm tourism association, cleverly branded as **Hey Iceland,** has a helpful interactive map on their website that lets you pick a spot (www.heyiceland.is, tel. 570-2700). Member farms also tend to list at Airbnb, Booking.com, and similar sites (described next).

Short-Term Rentals

A short-term rental—whether an apartment, house, or room in a local's home—is an increasingly popular alternative, especially in expensive Iceland. Particularly in peak season, you can often find an apartment that costs approximately half what you'd pay at a hotel—likely with more space, a kitchen, and other features. You trade away the convenience of a staffed reception desk, a ready-made breakfast option, and other hotel amenities, but the savings are substantial. And, while it varies dramatically, some short-term hosts are more helpful than any hotel receptionist. If you're willing to stay in a room in someone's home (rather than have an entire property to yourself), you can save even more.

Apartments: Icelandic apartments, like hotel rooms, tend to be small by US standards. But they often come with laundry facilities; a balcony, patio, or a private garden; and a small, equipped kitchen, making it easier and cheaper to dine in. If you make good use of the kitchen, you'll save on your meal budget.

Private and Shared Rooms: Renting a room in someone's home is a good option for those traveling alone, as you're more likely to find true single rooms—with just one single bed, and a price to match. Some places allow you to book for a single night; if staying for several nights, you can buy groceries just as you would in a rental house.

Other Options: Swapping homes with a local works for people with an appealing place to offer and who can live with the idea of having strangers in their home (don't assume where you live is not interesting to Icelanders). A good place to start is HomeExchange. Icelanders, who are the world's heaviest per-capita users of this site, like traveling to North America and typically vacation abroad around the same time of year that Americans do (June-Aug). To sleep for free, Couchsurfing.com is a vagabond's alternative to Airbnb. It lists millions of outgoing members, who host fellow "surfers" in their homes.

Finding Short-Term Accommodations: Aggregator websites such as Airbnb, FlipKey, Booking.com, and the HomeAway family of sites (HomeAway, VRBO, and VacationRentals) let you browse properties and correspond directly with Icelandic property owners or managers. Of these, **Airbnb** is definitely the biggest name in the Iceland short-term rental market. However, Airbnb is controversial here, where critics say it has exacerbated the chronic housing shortage in Reykjavík, driven up real estate prices, and made it harder for young people to afford their first home (Iceland has traditionally been a country where even young adults own rather than rent). That shouldn't stop you from taking advantage of it, though.

Confirming and Paying: Before you commit to a rental, be clear on the details, location, and amenities. I like to virtually "explore" the neighborhood using the Street View feature on Google Maps. Also consider proximity to public transportation and how well-connected the property is to the rest of the city. Ask about amenities (elevator, air-conditioning, laundry, Wi-Fi, parking, etc.). Reviews from previous guests can help identify trouble spots.

Many places require you to pay the entire balance before your trip. It's easiest and safest to pay through the site where you found the listing. Be wary of owners who want to take your transaction offline to avoid fees; this gives you no recourse if things go awry. Never agree to wire money (a key indicator of a fraudulent transaction).

Hostels

A hostel provides cheap beds where you sleep alongside strangers for about $40-50 per night. Travelers of any age are welcome if they don't mind dorm-style accommodations and meeting other travelers. Most hostels offer kitchen facilities, guest computers, Wi-Fi, and a self-service laundry. Hostels almost always provide bedding, but the towel's up to you (though you can usually rent one for a small fee). Family and private rooms are often available.

Independent hostels tend to be easygoing, colorful, and informal (no membership required; www.hostelworld.com). You may pay slightly less by booking directly with the hostel.

Official hostels are part of Hostelling International (HI) and share an online booking site (www.hihostels.com or www.hostel.is). HI hostels typically require that you be a member or pay extra per night. Iceland has over 30 official hostels, more or less evenly distributed around the island. They're generally clean, well-run, and a great value for solo travelers on a budget. Many are open all year, though the more rural hostels typically close from November or December to February or March.

Campervans and Camping

In Iceland, you can rent a converted van or pickup outfitted with beds, which lets you drive around the island without needing to find a place to stay. Some campers even have four-wheel drive and high clearances that let you drive over the mountain roads in the interior. While a campervan rental isn't cheap, it can cost less than other forms of accommodation, and lets

you be more flexible with your itinerary.

Campervan Rentals: A two-bed, two-wheel-drive campervan outfitted with basic cooking gear and bedding will run you about $150/day in summer ($110/day in shoulder season). Larger vans and those with four-wheel drive are more expensive. Major campervan outfitters (all located near Reykjavík) include Kúkú Campers (tel. 415-5858, www.kukucampers.is), GO Campers (tel. 517-7900, www.gocampers.is), Cozy Campers (tel. 519-5131, www.cozycampers.is), and Happy Campers (near the Keflavík airport, tel. 578-7860, www.happycampers.is). You'll also find campervans advertised on Airbnb.

Arrange your rental period to cover only the dates when you'll be driving around the island: Begin and end your trip in the Reykjavík area—using public transportation or a rental car and sleeping in a regular bed—then pick up the camper from the Reykjavík suburbs.

Where to Camp: Once you're out in the countryside, it's generally OK to park discreetly overnight in any semipublic lot,

unless a sign specifically prohibits it. As for showering, that's what Iceland's municipal thermal pools are for: You'll pay a few extra dollars per day to clean up—and luxuriate—in endless hot water (an unofficial list of pools is at www.sundlaugar.is). Or pay to use the facilities at a campground along your route (see next).

If you prefer a more formal place to overnight, you'll find inexpensive campgrounds *(tjaldsvæði)* all around the island. Most don't require reservations and are open from about mid-May to mid-September. For an unofficial list, get the free *Áning—Accommodation in Iceland* booklet (downloadable from www.icelandreview.com/publications), or visit the unofficial website Tjalda.is. A 28-day pass that covers most campgrounds is sold at CampingCard.is.

Car Camping: Camping while driving a regular rental car has many of the same advantages as a campervan, and is cheaper. If you bring your own camping gear, make sure it's suited to Iceland's high winds and chilly temperatures. Or rent gear in Iceland: **Iceland Camping Equipment,** in downtown Reykjavík, rents everything you might need at fair prices (Barónsstígur 5, mobile tel. 647-0569, www.iceland-camping-equipment.com).

Eating

Traditional Icelandic cuisine isn't too far removed from its Viking Age roots—relying heavily on anything hardy enough to survive the harsh landscape (lamb, potatoes), caught in or near the sea (fish,

seabirds), or sturdy enough to withstand winter storage (dried and salted fish). Today's chefs have built on this heritage, introducing international flavors and new approaches to old-style dishes. In recent years, Reykjavík has emerged as a foodie destination—with both high-end, experimental "New Icelandic" cuisine and a renewed appreciation for the country's traditional, nose-to-tail "hardship" cuisines. The capital offers a wide variety of dining options, but even in the countryside, you're never far from a satisfying meal.

Food and drink prices in Iceland are strikingly high, but it is possible to eat well here without going broke. There's no tipping, taxes are built into prices, and restaurants cheerfully dispense free tap water, making eating out more reasonable than it might seem.

Icelanders eat three meals a day at about the same times as Americans. Breakfast *(morgunmatur)* in homes tends to be oatmeal, cereal with milk, or bread and cheese, but hotels and guesthouses will lay out a good spread with eggs and cold cuts. Lunch *(hádegismatur)* is served between about 11:30 and 13:00, while dinner *(kvöldmatur)* usually starts at 18:00.

RESTAURANT PRICING

I've categorized my recommended eateries based on price, indicated with a dollar-sign rating (see sidebar). The price ranges suggest the average price of a typical main course—but not necessarily a complete meal. Obviously, expensive specialties, fine wine, appetizers, and dessert can significantly increase your final bill.

The dollar-sign categories also indicate a place's overall personality: **Budget** eateries include street food, takeout places, basic cafeterias, bakeries, and soup-and-bread buffets. **Moderate** eateries are nice (but not fancy) sit-down restaurants, ideal for a straightforward, fill-the-tank meal. Many of my listings fall in this category.

Pricier eateries are a notch up, with more attention paid to the setting, presentation, and cuisine. These are ideal for a memorable meal that doesn't break the bank. And **splurge** eateries are dress-

The Good and Bad of Online Reviews

User-generated review sites and apps such as Yelp, Booking.com, and TripAdvisor can give you a consensus of opinions about everything from hotels and restaurants to sights and nightlife. If you scan reviews of a hotel and see several complaints about noise or a rotten location, it tells you something important that you'd never learn from the hotel's own website.

But as a guidebook writer, my sense is that there is a big difference between the uncurated information on a review site and a guidebook. A user-generated review is based on the experience of one person, who likely stayed at one hotel in a given city and ate at a few restaurants there (and who doesn't have much of a basis for comparison). A guidebook is the work of a trained researcher who, year after year, visits many alternatives to assess their relative value. I recently checked out some top-rated user-reviewed hotel and restaurant listings in various towns; when stacked up against their competitors, some were gems, while just as many were duds.

Both types of information have their place, and in many ways, they're complementary. If something is well-reviewed in a guidebook, and also gets good ratings on one of these sites, it's likely a winner.

up-for-a-special-occasion swanky—typically with an elegant setting, polished service, and pricey and intricate cuisine.

I haven't categorized places where you might assemble a picnic, snack, or graze: supermarkets, delis, ice-cream stands, cafés or bars specializing in drinks, and so on.

RESTAURANT AND CAFÉ DINING

Not very long ago, it was unusual for Icelanders to eat outside the home or a workplace cafeteria, except on special occasions. But with the country's increasing wealth (and the influx of tourism) over the last decade or two, restaurants have become much more popular. All restaurants are smoke-free, and all restaurant staff speak English.

In Reykjavík, lunches are a particularly good value, as many places offer the same quality and similar selections for far less than at dinner. Make lunch your main meal, then have a lighter evening meal at a café. Many places offer a lunch special—typically a plate of fish, vegetables, and a starch (rice or potatoes) for 2,000-3,000 ISK.

Outside Reykjavík, the easiest lunch spots are roadside grills—often connected to a gas station and serving hamburgers, hot dogs, and fries, and possibly breaded fish. Any decent-sized town will also have a real (if small) café or restaurant with better food.

Restaurant Code

I've assigned each eatery a price category, based on the average cost of a typical main course. Drinks, desserts, and splurge items (steak and seafood) can raise the price considerably.

$$$$ **Splurge:** Most main courses over 5,500 ISK
$$$ **Pricier:** 4,000-5,500 ISK
$$ **Moderate:** 2,500-4,000 ISK
$ **Budget:** Under 2,500 ISK

In Iceland, a takeout place or soup-and-bread buffet is **$**; a sit-down café is **$$**; a casual but more upscale restaurant is **$$$**; and a swanky splurge is **$$$$**.

The best and healthiest lunch option at a small café or bakery is often an all-you-can-eat soup buffet, which includes unlimited bread and butter. For about 1,500-2,000 ISK, this can make for a satisfying meal. Look for thick, homemade soups (such as lamb soup, *kjötsúpa*).

Paying: Icelandic restaurants are often very flexible about splitting the bill between several guests, and waiters will ask each person to recall what they ate. There really is no tipping at Icelandic restaurants, and credit cards are accepted everywhere. Perhaps because of the lack of tipping, it's common even at quite respectable restaurants in Iceland to order and pay at the counter and then sit down, or to stand up and pay at the counter after your meal.

ICELANDIC CUISINE
Seafood

In this island nation, you'll see fish *(fiskur)* on every menu, prepared just about every way you can think of—and some ways that might not have occurred to you. Look for fish-and-chips, smoked salmon, fried balls o' cod, shrimp-on-a-sandwich, sushi, and hearty fish stew.

Icelandic fish is almost always very good. Don't get hung up on fresh versus frozen—here, both are fine (fish that's frozen at sea, right after it's netted, often tastes the freshest, although never-frozen fish has better texture). Deboned fish filets are the mainstay of the Icelandic diet. Haddock *(ýsa)* is by far the most common, followed by cod *(þorskur)* and plaice *(rauðspretta,* a small flatfish like flounder or sole). You'll also see more expensive salmon *(lax)* and arctic char *(bleikja),* both of which are farm-raised in pens.

Plokkfiskur ("mashed fish") was traditionally made with whatever fish scraps were at hand. Today this fish gratin or hash is made from haddock or cod cooked with milk, butter, and chopped potatoes; it's a comfort food, often eaten with sweet rye bread. You'll sometimes see cod cheeks *(gellur)*, and Icelanders eat the roe (eggs) of both cod and lumpfish. Lately, Icelanders have started to make fish chips, which look a bit like potato chips but are much more expensive.

One favorite Icelandic splurge is *humar*, which is typically translated on menus as "lobster" but is actually a 10-inch-long crustacean that's somewhere be-

tween a prawn and a crayfish (a more precise name is "langoustine," "Norway lobster," or—in Britain—"scampi"). *Humar* is expensive and considered a delicacy; it's often made into soup, but you can pay royally to enjoy it baked or sautéed in butter and garlic. Tiny precooked and peeled Greenland shrimp *(rækjur)* are often added to sauces or eaten on open-face sandwiches.

More Icelandic Fish

Grásleppa: Lumpfish, small and, yes, lump-like. Its eggs are dyed red and black, and widely sold in Iceland as *kavíar.*

Karfi: Atlantic redfish, also known as ocean perch; can be served steamed or deep-fried

Keila: Cusk; mild and sweet-flavored, similar to cod

Langa or blálanga: Ling, a long, slim whitefish

Lúða: Halibut

Makríll: Mackerel, often smoked or canned

Saltfiskur: Cod preserved in salt, then rinsed before cooking

Síld: Herring, generally pickled and eaten with bread

Silungur: Trout, farm-raised and often smoked

Skötuselur: Monkfish or anglerfish; only the firm-textured tail is eaten

Steinbítur: Wolffish, also known as ocean catfish; mild and sweet-flavored

Ufsi: Pollock, a whitefish that's often fried

Meat *(Kjöt)*

Don't miss the chance to try the excellent Icelandic **lamb** *(lambakjöt)*. Icelandic sheep range free, grazing on wild grass, resulting in a lean and tender meat. You'll find leg of lamb, rack of lamb, and other top-notch preparations on menus. *Kjötsúpa*

(literally "meat soup"), an Icelandic staple made with chunks of lamb and root vegetables, is a more traditional way to eat lamb that warms you on cold days. *Hangikjöt,* smoked lamb, may be served warm or cold. *Svið,* an acquired taste, is a sheep's head that's been split down the middle; you eat the cheeks and, if you like, the eye and tongue.

Icelanders have traditionally eaten only modest amounts of **beef** *(nautakjöt),* and almost no **chicken** *(kjúklingur)* or **pork** *(svínakjöt)*—but today the latter two make up more than half of local meat consumption. Like some other European countries, Icelanders eat the meat of young horses (called *hrossakjöt* or *folaldakjöt),* but it's rare on menus.

Thanks to the Danes, **hot dogs** *(pylsur)* became a common snack in Iceland in the 20th century. Unlike the average Ameri-

can frankfurter, some Icelandic hot dogs contain lamb in addition to beef and pork—but you probably won't taste the difference. You'll find hot dogs sold at gas station grills and at stands around town, often near swimming pools and in shopping malls. Wieners come in a bun with your choice of condiments (mustard, ketchup, mayonnaise-based remoulade, chopped raw onions, and crispy fried onions are popular). To keep things simple, ask for "one with everything" *(eina með öllu).* At about 300 ISK, this makes for a good fill-me-up on the go.

Whale, Puffin, and Other Novelty Meats

Restaurants here market nonendangered **minke whale meat** to tourists as a special experience. You'll see it offered both raw (like sushi) or grilled as steaks or on skewers. Some say it resembles beef—or, because it's a bit gamey, perhaps deer or elk. Ahi tuna is perhaps the best comparison, in terms of flavor and texture. Whale isn't a traditional Icelandic dish, and while some travelers enjoy the chance to sample it, others raise ethical concerns (see sidebar on the next page).

A few restaurants offer relatively expensive **seabird** dishes. You'll be eating a member of the auk family *(svartfugl)*—more likely a guillemot or murre than a puffin, as Iceland's puffin populations are currently low. These birds were, and still are, netted on seaside cliffs at certain times of year.

Iceland's **reindeer** population, introduced from Sweden in the 1700s, isn't large enough to support a large commercial market.

Eating Whale in Iceland

Iceland is a rare country where you're likely to find whale offered in restaurants. Some travelers see this as an exciting tasting opportunity, but for others, it's offensive and unethical.

The whale on Icelandic menus is the relatively small minke whale (*hrefna*), which is not endangered. Historically, Icelanders rarely ate whales (although they did hunt whales for blubber). Antiwhaling groups point out that tourists, thinking they're doing something "local," consume most of the whale meat sold in Iceland today.

A sizable minority of Icelanders would like to see their countrymen stop whaling, arguing that the practice serves no valid commercial or scientific need. The safety of eating whale is also debated. Toothed whales, which feed higher on the food chain, have high concentrations of mercury. Baleen whales, like the minke, are considered safer to eat, as they are filter feeders—the baleen in their mouths acting as big strainers. Still, Iceland's food research institute recommends that pregnant and breastfeeding women limit their intake of minke whale meat.

More nationalistic Icelanders support whaling, seeing it as a symbol of their country's independence and power over its marine resources. It's fair to say that Iceland, Norway, and Japan continue to hunt whales more to make a political point than to supply a strong market for the meat (which, rumor has it, mostly winds up in Japanese school lunches).

But you may occasionally see it on the menu of a restaurant with a private source.

Hardship Meats (Þorramatur)

In deep winter, when food supplies ran low on the farm, Icelanders traditionally reached down to the bottom of the barrel and ate the least appetizing parts of their livestock, which they had preserved in sour whey. In the 20th century, nostalgic urban Icelanders started the custom of serving these dubious delicacies at parties and buffets in January and February. They're known as *þorramatur*, after the Old Norse winter month of *þorri*.

The most commonly served dishes are pressed ram's testicles (*hrútspungar*), which actually aren't bad; liver and blood sausage (*lifrapylsa*, *blóðmör*, and *slátur*), somewhat similar to Scottish haggis; sheep's head (described earlier); and fermented Greenland shark, cut up into smelly little cubes (*hákarl*). While a few restaurants sell (overpriced) tiny portions of "rotted shark" (as it's casually called), the most affordable way to sample this is to buy a tiny tub in the food section of Reykjavík's Kolaportið flea market.

Dairy Products

As well as regular **milk** *(mjólk)*, try thicker, fermented *súrmjólk* or *AB-mjólk* on your cereal. Protectionist policies make imported cheeses very expensive, and (perhaps because of the lack of competition) Icelandic **cheese** *(ostur)* is generally bland and undistinguished. The most flavorful hard cheeses are *Óðals Tindur* and *Óðals-ostur*. Like other Scandinavians, Icelanders enjoy brown "cheeses" that are made from boiled-down, slightly sweetened whey. The soft, spreadable version, called *mysingur* (similar to Swedish *messmör*) is much more popular in Iceland than the hard *mysuostur* (which resembles Norwegian *brunost*). Rice pudding *(grjónagrautur)* with cinnamon is a comfort food and common snack.

Icelanders eat **yogurts** and other curdled milk products in endless varieties (plain, sweetened, low-fat, high-fat, sold with folding plastic spoons and caps full of muesli, and so on). Of the sweetened, flavored yogurts, the richest is called *þykkmjólk* (a real treat); a close second are the flavors sold as *Húsavíkur jógúrt.*

At the other end of the spectrum—and an Icelandic staple—is *skyr* (pronounced "skeer"), a plain, no-fat product made from skim milk that's similar to Greek yogurt sold in the US. Though you'll hear *skyr* hailed as a magical low-fat discovery, Icelanders have long agreed that *skyr* tastes best mixed with cream and fruit. It's also good baked into cheesecakes.

Mysa is whey—the acidic liquid leftover from the cheese- or *skyr*-making process. Sold in cartons in the supermarket, it's become trendy as a probiotic beverage (think kombucha). The taste is a mix of sweet and sour.

Fruits and Vegetables

Icelanders have traditionally collected an edible lichen that grows wild here, called *fjallagras* ("mountain grass"). *Fjallagras* is added to breads and soups, and brewed into tea. The only fruits that grow easily in Iceland are berries—especially blueberries *(bláber)*, crowberries *(krækiber)*, and currants *(rifsber)*. Potatoes do well here, as do turnips (the main starchy root vegetable before potatoes arrived from the New World). Then there's rhubarb, often used in baking and jam.

Today, Icelanders also grow a range of vegetables—tomatoes, cucumbers, mushrooms—in massive, geothermally heated greenhouses, but even with the cheap energy here these are usually more expensive than imported equivalents.

Breads and Baked Goods

Most grain won't grow here, so all grains (except barley) are imported. Since rye was once the cheapest grain to buy, and lacking much wood or fuel, Icelanders learned to bake **rye bread** in makeshift ovens dug in hot spots in the ground, near geothermal springs. Today this dense, chocolate-brown bread, called *rúgbrauð*, is made with a little barley malt or other sugar, and baked slowly at a low temperature, making it slightly sweet and cake-like. It's often served with *plokkfiskur* (fish gratin) or just with butter for breakfast. Another traditional rye bread, *flatbrauð* is an unleavened, flat circle baked in a pan; it resembles a soft tortilla. It's typically buttered and topped with sliced smoked lamb.

The island's bakeries make several characteristic wheat-based **pastries,** many with Danish origins. *Vínarbrauð* (like a danish), sold at bakeries in long, wide strips, is usually filled with jam and topped with a stripe of sugary glaze. *Kleinur* are knots of deep-fried dough; sold fresh, singly, in bakeries or in bags in the supermarket, they go well with a cup of coffee.

A relic from earlier times is *laufabrauð* ("leafbread"), paper-thin circles of wheat-flour dough, which Icelanders, in the weeks before Christmas, inscribe with patterns and fry (traditionally in sheep tallow, these days more often in oil). You'll see round containers of factory-made *laufabrauð* on sale in supermarkets in December.

Sweets

Chocolate-covered **licorice** is the signature Icelandic candy. Supermarkets sell dozens of varieties on this theme, such as *Draumur* ("Dream") candy bars and bags of olive-shaped *Kúlu-súkk*—the name is a play on the words for ball *(kúla)*, chocolate *(súkkulaði)*, and the Greenlandic town of Kulusuk. By European standards, Icelandic licorice is very tame, with little salt and a mild flavor. Some like *fylltar reimar,* hollow ropes of licorice stuffed with a sugary filling. Iceland's thriving candy industry (the islanders are still making up for centuries of deprivation) also cranks out lots of licorice-free sweets and chocolates, such as the inexpensive *Hraun* ("Lava") bars, whose rocky surface resembles a lava field.

Like other Scandinavians, Icelanders prefer **soft-serve ice cream.** When you order your cone, prepare to say whether, for a few extra krónur, you'd like it *með dýfu* (dipped into a chocolate sauce that hardens over the cold ice cream), *með kurli* (rolled in little chocolate beads), or both. At better ice-cream shops, a *bragðarefur* (literally "flavor fox") is soft ice cream blended with your choice of chocolate chunks, crushed candy bars, nuts, or other goodies (basically like a gigantic McFlurry). Ask for two spoons.

INTERNATIONAL CUISINES

Perhaps because so much of the country's food is imported (and many native dishes are so unpalatable), Icelanders are very open to other cooking traditions. A wave of Thai, Vietnamese, and Filipino immigrants came to the country in the 1980s, and now you can buy coconut milk, tofu, and fish sauce at the discount supermarket Bónus. Icelanders love pizza (though Italians here are few), and the American military presence has left behind a taste for Cheerios and Doritos. And in the last couple of decades, Polish immigrants have opened a couple of good supermarkets and started to produce fine sausage.

SUPERMARKETS AND OTHER CHEAP EATS

Travelers can save money, especially at dinnertime, by assembling a picnic at one of Iceland's supermarkets. The two discount supermarket chains, **Bónus** and **Krónan,** are the names to know. **Hagkaup** is more expensive, but carries a wider range, and some Reykjavík branches are open daily 24 hours. **Samkaup** is common in the countryside (but not particularly cheap). Steer clear of the extremely high-priced **10-11** convenience stores when possible.

Hagkaup and other larger supermarkets sometimes have a hot food counter with grilled chickens or roasted meats sold by weight. Supermarkets also sell prepared sandwiches, soft cheeses, shrimp and tuna "salads" that can be spread on bread, and plenty of cold cuts.

Other than **Subway** and **Domino's,** major fast-food franchises have only a slight presence in Iceland. (That means no McDonald's...and no Starbucks. You'll survive.)

BEVERAGES
Water, Coffee, and Other Nonalcoholic Drinks

Restaurants dispense the country's excellent tap **water** *(vatn)* for free, sometimes from a help-yourself table with pitchers and a stack of glasses. Buying bottled water is a waste of money here, unless you want it with bubbles—in that case, look for *kolsýrt* (carbonated) *vatn* or *sódavatn*. Blueberry is the country's only native **juice** *(safi or djús)*, an expensive delicacy produced in small quantities in the fall.

Icelanders are among the world's biggest **coffee** *(kaffi)* drinkers. Many cafés and restaurants offer free refills. For other hot beverages, look for tea *(te)* or hot chocolate (*heitt súkkulaði* or *kakó*).

Icelanders love **malt soda** *(malt)*, a sweetened and carbonated beverage made from yeast, malt, and hops just like beer, but with little or no fermentation. Egils Maltextrakt is the best-loved brand.

Though thought of as nonalcoholic, Icelandic *malt* reportedly contains about 1 percent alcohol, which is not mentioned on the label. That means you'd need to drink practically a six-pack of *malt* to get the same effect as from one beer. At Christmas time, Icelanders like to mix *malt* fifty-fifty with orange soda; they call the result *jólaöl* (Yule ale).

Wine, Beer, and Spirits

All **wine** *(léttvín)* in Iceland is imported. Light **beer** *(bjór;* 2.25 percent alcohol) is sold in supermarkets, but for anything stronger you'll need a state-run Vínbúðin store (or a bar or restaurant). Prices are high, especially for wine and spirits. If you plan to seriously imbibe during your visit, make a point of stopping at the airport duty-free store on your way into the country, before you retrieve your luggage. Prices are 20-50 percent lower than in Reykjavík, and the limit is generous. (You can plan your purchases, and check the current allowances, at www.dutyfree.is.)

In recent years, many small craft breweries have sprung up in Iceland, offering interesting alternatives to the major Scandinavian and local beer brands like Tuborg and Viking. There's even a holiday dedicated to beer—Beer Day, on March 1, marks the 1989 end of the country's 74-year prohibition of beer.

The local hard **liquor** industry has also diversified, and produces a range of vodka, gin, and even local single-malt whiskey. You'll also see liqueurs made with local berries. Björk is a liqueur flavored with birch and even comes with a birch twig in the bottle. The most traditional strong spirit, called *brennivín* (and marketed as "Black Death"—you've been warned!) is an aquavit similar to vodka, made from fermented potatoes and flavored with caraway.

Staying Connected

One of the most common questions I hear from travelers is, "How can I stay connected?" The short answer is: more easily and cheaply than you might think.

The simplest solution is to bring your own device—mobile phone, tablet, or laptop—and use it just as you would at home (following the tips below, such as connecting to free Wi-Fi whenever possible). Another option is to buy an Icelandic SIM card for your mobile phone—either your US phone or one you buy abroad. Or you use Icelandic landlines and computers to connect. Each of these options is described below; more details are at www.

Tips on Internet Security

Make sure that your device is running the latest versions of its operating system, security software, and apps. Next, ensure that your device and key programs (like email) are password- or passcode-protected. On the road, use only secure, password-protected Wi-Fi hotspots. Ask the hotel or café staff for the specific name of their Wi-Fi network, and make sure you log on to that exact one.

If you must access your financial info online, use a banking app rather than accessing your account via a browser. A cellular connection is more secure than Wi-Fi. Avoid logging onto personal finance sites on a public computer.

Never share your credit-card number (or any other sensitive information) online unless you know that the site is secure. A secure site displays a little padlock icon, and the URL begins with *https* (instead of the usual *http*).

---

ricksteves.com/phoning. For a very practical one-hour talk covering tech issues for travelers, see www.ricksteves.com/travel-talks.

USING A MOBILE PHONE IN ICELAND
Here are some budget tips and options.

Sign up for an international plan. To stay connected at a lower cost, sign up for an international service plan through your carrier. Most providers offer a simple bundle that includes calling, messaging, and data. Your normal plan may already include international coverage (T-Mobile's does).

Before your trip, call your provider or check online to confirm that your phone will work in Iceland, and research your provider's international rates. Activate the plan a day or two before you leave, then remember to cancel it when your trip's over.

Use free Wi-Fi whenever possible. Unless you have an unlimited-data plan, you're best off saving most of your online tasks for Wi-Fi. You can access the Internet, send texts, and make voice calls over Wi-Fi.

Most accommodations offer free Wi-Fi, and many cafés have free hotspots for customers; look for signs offering it and ask for the Wi-Fi password when you buy something. You'll also often find Wi-Fi at TIs, major museums, public-transit hubs, airports, and aboard some buses.

Minimize the use of your cellular network. Even with an international data plan, wait until you're on Wi-Fi to Skype, download apps, stream videos, or do other megabyte-greedy tasks. Using a navigation app such as Google Maps over a cellular network can take lots of data, so do this sparingly or use it offline.

Limit automatic updates. By default, your device constantly

PRACTICALITIES

The Icelandic Language

Pretty much all Icelanders speak English comfortably, although usually not with the accent-less fluency typical of mainland Scandinavians. Locals will visibly brighten when you know and use some key Icelandic phrases (see "Icelandic Survival Phrases" on page 435). Don't try too hard, though; Icelandic pronunciation is easy to muff, and many of the tourism employees you'll encounter are immigrants who don't speak much Icelandic either.

If you know Norwegian, Danish, or Swedish, you'll be able to pick out some words on signs and menus, but Icelandic vocabulary and grammar are different enough that the other Scandinavian languages aren't of much practical help.

A thousand years ago, all Scandinavians—from Greenland to the Baltic—spoke the same language. In the Middle Ages, many Germans settled in Norway, Sweden, and Denmark. The residents of those countries borrowed many words, and their grammar and sound patterns changed. But isolated Icelandic changed far less over the centuries. Modern Icelanders can learn to read the sagas—recorded in the 13th and 14th centuries—with only a little more difficulty than English speakers learning to read Shakespearean English. Modern Icelandic, like English, preserved the original Germanic unvoiced and voiced "th" sounds (spelled þ and ð; capital Þ and Ð). And like German, Icelandic still has four cases and three genders.

The hardest thing about modern Icelandic is the pronunciation. Several Icelandic sounds are rare in the world's languages. Among these are the voiceless versions of *l, r,* and *n,* often spelled *hl, hr,* and *hn.* To make these sounds, put your tongue in position, then breathe out. Another unusual sound is a sort of breathy *h* that Icelanders make before the double consonants *pp, tt,* and *kk* (*stoppa,* "to stop," sounds like *stohpa*). Then there's the Icelandic *ll,* which is usually pronounced *tl.* Yet another quirk: you'll often hear Icelanders say "yes" (*já*) while breathing in, instead of breathing out. It sounds like a little gasp. (Try it yourself.)

Several common sounds are absent from Icelandic, notably those spelled *sh, ch, zh, j,* and *z* in English (they pronounce Cheerios "Sirius"). And a few exotic consonant clusters can create confusion: *fl* and *fn* are pronounced like *pl* and *pn* (so Keflavík and Hafnarfjörður come out sounding like "Keplavík" and "Hapnarfjörður"). But *pt* sounds like *ft,* and *kt* like *cht* (with the *ch* of "loch"), so the Icelandic names for the ninth and tenth months of the year sound like "Seftember" and "Ochtober." After a consonant at the end of a word, *l* and *n* turn into the sounds written *hl* and *hn*, so the *n* in the word *vatn* (water) sounds almost silent to foreign ears.

Like the other Scandinavian languages, Icelandic tacks the definite article onto the end of a word: it comes in several forms, including -*inn*, -*in*, and -*ið*, all of which mean "the." So *hús* means "house," and *húsið* means "the house."

Abstract and technical words, which in other languages tend to take an international form, are often unrecognizable in Icelandic. That's because 20th-century Icelanders put a lot of effort into creating old Norse-based words for new inventions: Today, all Icelanders call a telephone *sími*, a radio *útvarp,* and a computer *tölva*. But Icelanders completely rejected the invented word *flatbaka* in favor of the word *pítsa*—which, heresy of heresies, they tend to spell *pizza*.

If you'd like to try tackling Icelandic pronunciation, the list below shows the most common sounds. The stress is always on a word's first syllable, although longer words may have a secondary stress. For a breezy, humorous introduction to the language, pick up Alda Sigmundsdóttir's *The Little Book of Icelandic*.

Letter	Sounds like:
Þ	unvoiced th, like "breath"; the letter is called thorn (capital form: Þ)
Ð	voiced th, like "breathe"; the letter is called eth (capital form: Ð)
hl, hr, hn	unvoiced versions of *l, r, n* (blow the sound out)
J	*y* in *you*
Hj	*h* in *hue*
Hv	*kv* in *kvetch*
Ll	*tl* in *butler*
Á	*ow* in *how*
É	*ye* in *yet*
Í, ý	*ee* in *seen*
Ó	*oa* in *road*
Ú	*oo* in *soon*
A	*a* in *father*
E	*e* in *set*
i, y	*i* in *sit*
O	*o* in *not*
U	the German *ü* ("oo" with pursed lips)
Ö	the German *ö* ("oh" with pursed lips)
Au	*ö* followed by *i*
ei, ey	*ay* in *may*
Æ	*ie* in *pie*

How to Dial

International Calls

Whether phoning from a US landline or US mobile phone, or from a number in another European country, here's how to make an international call. I've used one of my recommended Reykjavík hotels as an example (tel. 514-6000). Note that Iceland does not use area codes.

Mobile Tip: With a mobile phone, the "+" sign can replace the access code (for a "+" sign, press and hold "0").

US/Canada to Europe

Dial 011 (US/Canada access code), country code (354 for Iceland), and phone number.

▸ To call the Reykjavík hotel from home, dial 011-354-514-6000.

Country to Country Within Europe

Dial 00 (Europe access code), country code, and phone number.

▸ To call the Reykjavík hotel from Germany, dial 00-354-514-6000.

Europe to the US/Canada

Dial 00, country code (1 for US/Canada), and phone number.

▸ To call from Europe to my office in Edmonds, Washington, dial 00-1-425-771-8303.

Domestic Calls

To call from one Icelandic landline or Icelandic mobile phone to another, simply dial the phone number.

▸ To call the Reykjavík hotel from Akureyri, dial 514-6000.

More Dialing Tips

Icelandic Phone Numbers: Icelandic phone numbers are all seven digits long (except for special services like weather and directory information). Iceland's land lines start with 4 and 5; mobile lines start with 6, 7, and 8 and cost substantially more to dial.

checks for a data connection and updates apps. It's smart to disable these features so your apps will only update when you're on Wi-Fi, and to change your device's email settings from "auto-retrieve" to "manual" (or from "push" to "fetch").

When you need to get online but can't find Wi-Fi, simply turn on your cellular network just long enough for the task at hand. When you're done, avoid further charges by manually turning off data roaming or cellular data (either works) in your device's Settings menu. Another way to make sure you're not accidentally using data roaming is to put your device in "airplane" mode (which also disables phone calls and texts), and then turn your Wi-Fi back on as needed.

It's also a good idea to keep track of your data usage. On your

Toll and Toll-Free Calls: Toll numbers start with 9. Rare toll-free numbers start with 800, and are only free from land lines, not mobile phones. International rates apply to US toll-free numbers dialed from Iceland—they're not free.

More Phoning Help: See www.howtocallabroad.com.

European Country Codes		Ireland & N. Ireland	353 / 44
Austria	43	Italy	39
Belgium	32	Latvia	371
Bosnia-Herzegovina	387	Montenegro	382
Croatia	385	Morocco	212
Czech Republic	420	Netherlands	31
Denmark	45	Norway	47
Estonia	372	Poland	48
Finland	358	Portugal	351
France	33	Russia	7
Germany	49	Slovakia	421
Gibraltar	350	Slovenia	386
Great Britain	44	Spain	34
Greece	30	Sweden	46
Hungary	36	Switzerland	41
Iceland	354	Turkey	90

Drop an initial zero when dialing a European phone number—except when calling Italy.

PRACTICALITIES

device's menu, look for "cellular data usage" or "mobile data" and reset the counter at the start of your trip.

Use Wi-Fi calling and messaging apps. Skype, Viber, Face-Time, and Google+ Hangouts are great for making free or low-cost voice and video calls over Wi-Fi. With an app installed on your phone, tablet, or laptop, you can log on to a Wi-Fi network and contact friends or family members who use the same service. If you buy credit in advance, with some of these services you can call any mobile phone or landline worldwide for just pennies per minute.

Many of these apps also allow you to send messages over Wi-Fi to any other person using that app. Be aware that some apps, such as Apple's iMessage, will use the cellular network if Wi-Fi isn't available: To avoid this possibility, turn off the "Send as SMS" feature.

USING AN ICELANDIC SIM CARD

With an Icelandic SIM card, you get an Icelandic mobile phone number and access to cheaper rates than you'll get through your US carrier. This option works well for those who want to make a lot of voice calls or need faster connection speeds than their US carrier provides. Fit the SIM card into a cheap phone you buy in Iceland, or swap out the SIM card in an "unlocked" US phone (check with your carrier about unlocking it).

A SIM card that also includes data (and roaming) will cost a little more than one that covers only voice calls. The most efficient way to buy an Icelandic SIM card is either on the plane (Icelandair flight attendants sell them) or at Keflavík Airport (before you claim your bags, detour into the duty-free store; after you exit, visit the 10-11 and Elko convenience stores in the arrivals hall). If you wait until you're in Reykjavík, you can find phone-company stores in the Kringlan and Smáralind shopping malls. The two companies to consider are Síminn (www.siminn.is) and Vodafone (www.vodafone.is); they offer comparable starter packages for about 2,000-3,000 ISK, depending on how much data is included. Ask a store clerk or friendly local to help you insert your SIM card, set it up, and show you how to use it. You can top it up with cards bought at gas stations, convenience stores, supermarkets, and phone-company stores.

PUBLIC PHONES AND COMPUTERS

It's less convenient but possible to travel in Iceland without a mobile device, using landlines and public computers. Most hotels charge a fee for placing calls—ask for rates before you dial. You can use a prepaid international phone card (one brand in Iceland is called AtlasFrelsi, sold at supermarkets, convenience stores, and gas stations). These cards offer a cheaper rate if you access the system by calling the landline, and a higher rate if you call the toll-free number.

Many hotels have a computer in their lobby for guests to use, and some may let you borrow a laptop. If typing on an Icelandic keyboard, use the "Alt Gr" key to the right of the space bar to insert the extra symbol that appears on some keys. For example, to insert an @ symbol, press the "Alt Gr" key and Q at the same time. If you can't locate a special character, simply copy and paste it from a web page.

MAIL

You can mail one package per day to yourself worth up to $200 duty-free from Europe to the US (mark it "personal purchases"). If you're sending a gift to someone, mark it "unsolicited gift." For details, visit www.cbp.gov, select "Travel," and then "Know Before You Visit." The Icelandic postal service works fine, but for quick transatlantic delivery (in either direction), consider services such as DHL (www.dhl.com).

Transportation

Your options for linking destinations in Iceland are tourist-oriented excursion buses, unguided do-it-yourself excursion buses, public buses, rental cars, and short-hop flights. (Iceland has no rail system.)

If you're staying in Reykjavík and plan only a few brief forays outside the city, you can get by without a car. But most visitors find that renting a car gives them maximum flexibility for getting out into the Icelandic countryside. You won't find convenient public transportation options for reaching some sights (including the biggies—the Golden Circle and South Coast); instead you'll likely need to rely on pricey excursions. For this reason, renting a car can be more cost-effective than it initially seems.

For general information on transportation throughout Europe, see www.ricksteves.com/transportation.

PRACTICALITIES

EXCURSION BUSES

Guided Excursion Buses

You can select from a full menu of guided bus tours to get into the countryside. You're paying a premium for a guide and a carefully designed experience, but these excursions take the guesswork out of your trip. For more on this option, see the Near Reykjavík chapter.

Do-It-Yourself Excursion Buses

In summer months, several private companies offer direct, regularly scheduled bus transport to many popular outdoor destinations, especially spots off the Ring Road and in the interior, such as

Þórsmörk and Landmannalaugar. These buses are unguided, with routes intended to get hikers and campers to popular outdoor destinations, but anyone can use them to reach some of Iceland's most spectacular sights.

For example, you can leave Reykjavík early in the morning, spend a couple of midday hours taking a short hike in Þórsmörk or Landmannalaugar, and return to the city for a late dinner; you could also overnight in a tent or cabin and get picked up the next day. These buses can come in handy for day-tripping from Akureyri to Dettifoss, or from Skaftafell to the Lakagígar craters.

Companies to consider include Reykjavík Excursions (under the name Iceland On Your Own, www.ioyo.is), Sterna Travel (www.icelandbybus.is or www.sternatravel.com), and Trex (www.trex.is). Confirm your departure location in Reykjavík; there may be several options. Reykjavík Excursions, Sterna, and Trex buses stop at the BSÍ bus terminal, which is within walking distance of downtown. Note that several of these companies also offer guided trips to some of the same destinations.

Highland Route to the North: An exciting bus journey is to travel from Reykjavík to the north (Skagafjörður, Akureyri, or Mývatn) through Iceland's interior Highlands, over either of two passes—Kjölur or Sprengisandur. The trips run only when the passes are clear—usually from late June to early September. The route, which can't be driven in a normal rental car, gives you a look at some of Iceland's most desolate and remote scenery. (The high-clearance buses have large tires that can cope with the rocky roads...be prepared for a very bumpy ride.)

East Iceland: Reykjavík Excursions and Sterna also run one daily bus in each direction around the east end of the island, between Akureyri and Höfn.

Circle Passes: The bus companies offer passes (about 40,000 ISK) that allow you to circle the island, stopping wherever you like (early June-early Sept only). If you're planning to loop through several parts of Iceland by bus, one of the "passport"-style fares can be handy—they're essentially hop-on, hop-off tickets covering a specific route and cheaper than paying for individual journeys.

PUBLIC BUSES

Iceland has a good network of scheduled public buses (painted yellow and blue and called *strætó*), run as a single system by city and local governments (www.straeto.is). The Strætó system doesn't cover the country's sparsely populated eastern edge (from Egilsstaðir to Höfn), but a privately run bus service fills in the gaps.

Although the Strætó network is more geared to locals than visitors, it can be useful to those traveling from one town to another, such as from Reykjavík to Selfoss or Akureyri. Reykjavík city buses are part of the Strætó network and use the same tickets and fare structure.

For long-distance trips, you can pay by credit card or through a Strætó app (see page 61). Strætó's buses also accept cash (although no one pays this way) and little brown paper tickets (sold only in 20-ticket strips). From Reykjavík, Strætó's long-distance buses leave from a terminal in the suburbs called Mjódd, which is linked to downtown by frequent city buses (ask driver for a free transfer ticket).

RENTING A CAR

Car rental makes a lot of sense in Iceland, unless you're traveling solo. Two people splitting the cost of a rental car and gas will save

a lot over the cost of bus excursions, while enjoying the flexibility of stopping whenever and wherever they want. The Ring Road is practically made for road trips with friends. (For a Ring Road trip, also consider a campervan rental—see page 390.)

Rental companies require you to be at least 21 years old and to have held your license for one year. Drivers under the age of 25 may incur a young-driver surcharge, and some rental companies do not rent to anyone 75 or older.

Research car rentals before you go. It's cheaper to arrange most car rentals from the US. Consider several companies to compare rates. Most of the major US rental agencies (including Avis, Budget, Enterprise, Hertz, and Thrifty) have offices in Iceland. Also consider the two major Europe-based agencies, Europcar and Sixt. Iceland's smaller, homegrown rental agencies may offer cheaper used vehicles (beware that some of these cars are real clunkers—read carefully before booking). Or consider using a consolidator, such as Auto Europe/Kemwel (www.autoeurope.com—or the often cheaper www.autoeurope.eu), which compares rates at several companies to get you the best deal—but because you're working with a middleman, it's especially important to ask in advance about add-on fees and restrictions.

Always read the fine print or query the agent carefully for add-on charges—such as one-way drop-off fees, airport surcharges, or mandatory insurance policies—that aren't included in the "total price."

For the best deal, rent by the week with unlimited mileage. To save money on fuel, request a diesel car. I normally rent the smallest, least-expensive model with a stick shift (generally cheaper than an automatic). Almost all rentals are manual by default, so if you need an automatic, request one in advance.

Many tourists think of a trip to Iceland as more of an "expedition" than it really is, and shell out for a high-clearance SUV when they would do just fine with a teeny two-wheel-drive car. You won't need four-wheel drive for the itineraries in this book in summer, or for a quick winter stopover if you stick to Reykjavík. A more rugged vehicle makes sense only if you're planning to traverse Iceland's interior Highlands (not covered in this book), drive outside the capital area in winter, ford unbridged rivers (such as on the road to Þórsmörk), or spend lots of time on mucky, rutted dirt roads in the countryside.

Air-conditioning isn't standard in all of Iceland's rental cars, but don't pay extra to get it. Although cars can heat up when parked on a sunny summer day, the outside air temperature is never that warm, so rolling down the window is enough to cool things down.

In Iceland, figure on paying roughly $350 for a one-week rental in summer, and $50-100 less in spring or fall. Allow extra for supplemental insurance, fuel, tolls, and parking.

Picking Up Your Car

Most visitors to Iceland pick up their rental car either at Keflavík Airport or at the rental company's Reykjavík office. It's generally easiest to pick up and drop off at the airport, which has the widest selection of on-site rental operators. It's also possible to pick up in Reykjavík and drop off at the airport (or vice-versa). This is considered a one-way rental, with a small extra charge (but often less than the airport bus fare).

Car rental in Akureyri and some smaller towns is also possible.

Always check the hours of the location you choose: Off-airport, many rental offices close from midday Saturday until Monday morning and, in smaller towns, at lunchtime.

When selecting a location, don't trust the agency's description of "downtown" or "city center." In Reykjavík, these locations are all either at the domestic airport or in industrial areas on the outskirts of the city—a long, costly taxi ride from the center. Before choosing, plug the addresses into a mapping website.

When you pick up the rental car, check it thoroughly and make sure any damage is noted on your rental agreement. Rental agencies in Europe tend to charge for even minor damage, so be sure to mark everything. Before driving off, find out how your car's gearshift, lights, turn signals, wipers, radio, and fuel cap function, and know what kind of fuel the car takes (diesel vs. unleaded). When you return the car, make sure the agent verifies its condition

with you. Some drivers take pictures of the returned vehicle as proof of its condition.

Off-Limit Roads: Be clear on where you can drive your rental car. Normal two-wheel-drive vehicles are fine for well-maintained unpaved roads. But rental cars can't be driven on roads in the interior, which cross unbridged rivers and can be very rough. (If you want to drive on these roads, rent a four-wheel-drive vehicle.) Consider any road designated with an "F" on maps or road signs to be off-limits. Highway 35 (over the Kjölur pass) and highway 550 (called Kaldidalur) are also off-limits even though they don't have an F—this should be stated on your rental agreement.

Car Insurance Options

When you rent a car, you are liable for a very high deductible, sometimes equal to the entire value of the car. Limit your financial risk with one of these options: Buy Collision Damage Waiver (CDW) coverage with a low or zero deductible from the car-rental company, get coverage through your credit card (free, if your card automatically includes zero-deductible coverage), or get collision insurance as part of a larger travel-insurance policy.

Basic **CDW** includes a very high deductible (typically $1,000-1,500), costs $15-30 a day (figure roughly 30-40 percent extra) and reduces your liability, but does not eliminate it. When you reserve or pick up the car, you'll be offered the chance to "buy down" the basic deductible to zero (for an additional $10-30/day; this is sometimes called "super CDW" or "zero-deductible coverage").

If you opt for **credit-card coverage,** you'll technically have to decline all coverage offered by the car-rental company, which means they can place a hold on your card (which can be up to the full value of the car). In case of damage, it can be time-consuming to resolve the charges with your credit-card company. Before you decide on this option, quiz your credit-card company about how it works.

If you're already purchasing a **travel-insurance policy** for your trip, adding collision coverage can be an economical option. For example, Travel Guard (www.travelguard.com) sells affordable renter's collision insurance as an add-on to its other policies; it's valid everywhere in Europe except the Republic of Ireland, and some Italian car-rental companies refuse to honor it, as it doesn't cover you in case of theft.

Car-rental agencies may encourage you to spend upwards of $25/day for supplemental insurance to cover damage from sandstorms (blowing sand can ruin a car's finish and gravel can break windows). Depending on where you're driving, this isn't always worthwhile (sandstorms are most likely to occur between Vík and Skaftafell on the Ring Road). You may also be offered insurance against damage from volcanic ash. Unless there's an active eruption, the risk from ash is very low.

For more on car-rental insurance, see www.ricksteves.com/cdw.

NAVIGATION OPTIONS

Navigating in the Icelandic countryside is fairly easy. Signage is good (though the lettering on signs can be quite small), there's only one Ring Road (though many side roads), and free paper maps and/or downloaded maps on the device of your choice are usually enough to get you around. If you'll be navigating using your phone or a GPS unit from home, remember to bring a car charger and device mount.

Your Mobile Device: The mapping app on your mobile phone works fine for navigation in Iceland, but for real-time turn-by-turn directions and traffic updates, you'll generally need Internet access. And driving all day while online can be very expensive if you are on a limited data plan. Helpful exceptions are Google Maps, Here WeGo, and Navmii, which provide turn-by-turn voice directions and recalibrate even when they're offline.

Download your map before you head out—it's smart to select a large region. Then turn off your cellular connection so you're not charged for data roaming. Call up the map, enter your destination, and you're on your way. View maps in standard view (not satellite view) to limit data demands.

GPS Devices: If you prefer the convenience of a dedicated GPS unit, consider renting one with your car ($10-30/day). These units offer real-time turn-by-turn directions and traffic without the data requirements of an app. Also make sure your device's language is set to English before you drive off.

A less-expensive option is to bring a GPS device from home. Be aware that you'll need to buy and download maps of Iceland before your trip.

Maps and Atlases: Even when navigating primarily with a mobile app or GPS, I always make it a point to have a paper map. It's invaluable for getting the big picture, understanding alternate routes, and filling in when my phone runs out of juice. The free maps you get from your car-rental company usually don't have enough detail. Look for the free *Big Map* (www.bigmap.is), which has a map of Reykjavík, including suburbs, on one side, and on the other, a serviceable map of the whole country. The free *Around Iceland* booklet includes maps of each region and of small towns. You could also buy a better map of the country in advance (they're cheaper in the US—Michelin #750 is good), or pick one up (for a hefty 3,000 ISK) at a gas station, convenience store, or bookshop in Iceland.

Websites: Google Maps covers Iceland about as well as Europe or the US (though it occasionally gets Icelandic street names wrong and, as anywhere, it sometimes lacks detail). The Icelandic telephone directory website, www.ja.is, has more precise maps, but it's less user-friendly; you can't download the data, and it sometimes expects you to search for place names in an unusual format.

The "Road Info Viewer" at the Icelandic Road Authority website (www.road.is) is up-to-date and shows at a glance which stretches of road are paved and which are gravel. Click on "Layers," then "Names" to show place names.

DRIVING

Exploring Iceland by car is a pleasure. Most of the main roads are paved and (outside Reykjavík) relatively uncrowded. But driving in Iceland does come with unique customs and hazards you should know about. A large percentage of serious car accidents in Iceland involve foreign tourists. The website www.drive.is has a helpful (if overlong) video introducing the basics. Remember to pack sunglasses for driving: The sun stays low in the Icelandic sky all year.

Road Rules: Be aware of typical European road rules; for example, Iceland requires headlights to be turned on at all times

(usually an automatic feature in Icelandic cars), and forbids using a mobile phone without a hands-free headset. In Iceland, you're not allowed to turn right on a red light, unless a sign or signal specifically authorizes it, and on expressways it's illegal to pass drivers on the right. Even major highways like Highway 1 are predominantly two-lane, so remember to pass with care. Seat belts are required by law in Iceland for all passengers. Ask your car-rental company about these rules, or check the US State Department website (www.travel.state.gov, search for your country in the "Learn about your destination" box, then click on "Travel and Transportation").

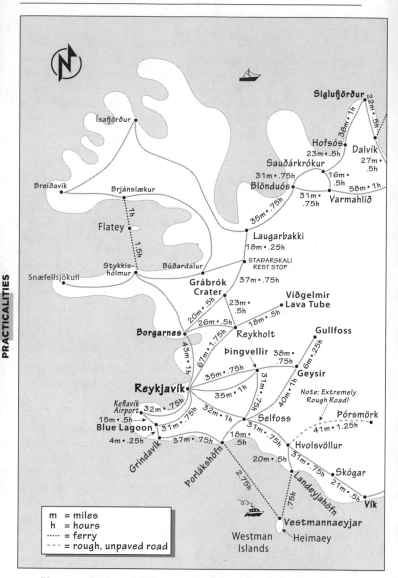

You may be stopped for a routine check by the police (be sure you have your rental paperwork close at hand).

Speed Limits: Speed limits are by road type and often aren't posted. Generally, the speed limit in rural Iceland is 90 km/hour (or about 55 mph) on paved roads and 80 km/hour (50 mph) on gravel roads. In towns, the limit is 50 km/hour (about 30 mph; often lower in residential neighborhoods). The tunnel under Hvalfjörður

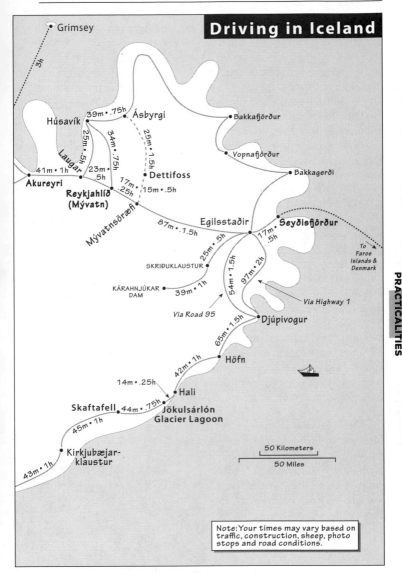

Driving in Iceland

Grimsey

3h

Húsavík — 39m • .75h — Ásbyrgi — Bakkafjörður

25m • .5h   34m • .75h   25m • 1.5h   Vopnafjörður

Laugar

Akureyri — 41m • 1h — 23m • .5h — Reykjahlíð (Mývatn)

Dettifoss — Bakkagerði

17m • .25h   15m • .5h

Mývatnsöræfi

87m • 1.5h — Egilsstaðir — Seyðisfjörður

17m • .5h

To Faroe Islands & Denmark

25m • .5h

SKRIÐUKLAUSTUR

54m • 1.5h   97m • 2h

KÁRAHNJÚKAR DAM — 39m • 1h

Via Highway 1

Via Road 95

Djúpivogur

65m • 1.5h

42m • 1h — Höfn

14m • .25h — Hali

Skaftafell — 44m • .75h — Jökulsárlón Glacier Lagoon

45m • 1h

50 Kilometers

50 Miles

Kirkjubæjar-klaustur

43m • 1h

Note: Your times may vary based on traffic, construction, sheep, photo stops and road conditions.

PRACTICALITIES

has a 70 km/h (45 mph) limit. Speed cameras are widely used and limits are enforced with high fines.

Roundabouts: The rules at double-lane roundabouts (traffic circles) in Iceland differ from those elsewhere in Europe. Here, the car in the *inner* lane of the circle has the right of way when exiting the roundabout. That means that cars in the outer lane who want to continue around the circle must yield to cars in the inner lane that want to exit. If you're in the inner lane, you have priority, but still use your right-turn signal when you want to exit.

Here's some good advice for double-lane roundabouts: If you're going straight through or left, stay to the left when approaching and enter the inner lane. If you're turning right at the roundabout, stay right and enter the outer lane, because you'll be exiting immediately anyway. If you're in the outer lane and don't want to take the next exit, put on your left-turn signal to show that you'll be continuing around. In all cases, drive defensively (keeping in mind that there may be a tourist in the outer lane who isn't used to the local rules).

The above advice applies only to double-lane roundabouts, which you'll find mostly in Reykjavík and larger towns. Once in the countryside, the vast majority of roundabouts are single-lane, which work the same as anywhere. Remember that at any roundabout, all cars already in the circle have priority over cars entering, in any lane.

Fuel: Gas is around $7 a gallon; diesel is a bit cheaper. Be careful to use the right fuel: Unleaded gas is called *bensín* and sometimes identified with the octane rating (95 *okt*); diesel is *dísel*.

Note that your US credit and debit cards may not work at some Icelandic gas pumps, even with a chip. Know your credit card's PIN, and be prepared to move on to another gas station. Especially in rural areas, don't let your tank get too low. If you have trouble buying gas at the pump, try asking inside the gas station for a prepaid gas card, which you should be able to purchase with any US card.

Navigation: Conveniently, street names in the same neighborhood in Icelandic cities and towns all end with the same element. For example, Faxaskjól, Sörlaskjól, Granaskjól, and other streets ending with *"skjól"* are all next to each other in Reykjavík; to find them, follow road signs reading *"Skjól."*

On highways, signage is less prevalent than other European countries. Yet when you turn off onto local roads, you'll often encounter almost comically detailed signs showing the location of every local sight and farmhouse.

Parking: Paid parking zones in Reykjavík are marked with a blue-and-white sign with a large "P" and the number of the zone (for a map, see www.bilastaedasjodur.is/gjaldskylda/gjaldsvaedin). Don't assume it's free—check around for meters or ticketing machines. In downtown Akureyri, you'll need to put a "parking clock"

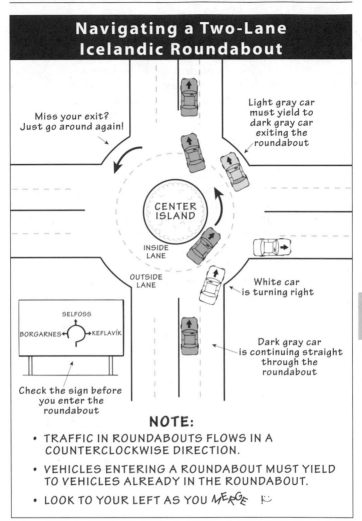

Navigating a Two-Lane Icelandic Roundabout

Miss your exit? Just go around again!

Light gray car must yield to dark gray car exiting the roundabout

CENTER ISLAND

INSIDE LANE

OUTSIDE LANE

SELFOSS
BORGARNES ← → KEFLAVÍK

Check the sign before you enter the roundabout

White car is turning right

Dark gray car is continuing straight through the roundabout

NOTE:

- TRAFFIC IN ROUNDABOUTS FLOWS IN A COUNTERCLOCKWISE DIRECTION.

- VEHICLES ENTERING A ROUNDABOUT MUST YIELD TO VEHICLES ALREADY IN THE ROUNDABOUT.

- LOOK TO YOUR LEFT AS YOU MERGE

PRACTICALITIES

(bifreiðastæðaklukka) in your car window showing the time you arrived; time limits are posted at each lot. For more specifics, see those chapters.

Tolls: Iceland does not have road tolls, with the exception of the tunnel under Hvalfjörður, on the Ring Road north of Reykjavík (see the West Iceland chapter).

Driving Hazards

Weather and Road Conditions: Always check the weather forecast and road conditions before you drive. The Icelandic Road Authority (Vegagerðin) website (www.road.is) shows up-to-date snow, ice, and wind conditions on all the major roads in the country. Visiting this site is a must before setting off on any car trip, even in summer. Learn the colors: Green means the road is totally clear, orange means there are a few icy patches, light blue means that the road is definitely slippery, and dark blue means that you should just stay home. White means snow cover. Closed roads are in red.

Regional maps let you click on weather stations to see a readout of the latest wind-speed measurements, so you know whether things are getting worse or dying down. Clicking on the individual measurement stations lets you see webcams, wind-speed data, and the number of cars that have passed by in the last ten minutes and since midnight. If no one else is driving a particular stretch of road, don't let yourself be the first. To speak to a real person about road conditions, call the Icelandic Road Authority's hotline at tel. 1777 or 522-1100 (daily in summer 8:00-16:00, in winter 6:30-22:00). They also have recorded information at tel. 1778.

Giant signs with information on temperature and wind conditions are set up along roads leading to high mountain passes and notoriously windy spots. These post the information you need to decide if winds are too strong or road conditions otherwise too dangerous to continue.

Wind: High winds occur all year and present real danger to drivers. Two notoriously windy spots are just north of Reykjavík along the Ring Road, at Kjalarnes (before the Hvalfjörður tunnel) and at Hafnarfjall (across the estuary from Borgarnes). An average sustained wind speed of 15 m/s (meters per second—that's about 35 mph) is enough to make you tighten your grip on the steering wheel, while anything from 20 m/s (45 mph) on up can get dangerous quickly. Gusts, measured separately, can be much stronger. The effect is worst if you're driving a long, high, or flat-sided vehicle, and slippery roads magnify the risk. In some parts of the country, high winds can damage your car by blowing sand and even gravel onto it (see "Sandstorms," later).

If you're caught in high winds, slow way down, keep two hands on the wheel, don't pass, and keep an extra-safe distance from other vehicles. If things turn very bad, pull over and stop—though ideally not somewhere with loose, blowing soil. When opening and closing car doors in windy weather, especially when parked next to other cars, never let go of the door.

In addition to the Icelandic Road Authority resources described earlier, the Icelandic weather service (http://en.vedur.is) can

PRACTICALITIES

give you a general sense of the expected wind conditions around the island.

Banked Roads: Many roads in Iceland have narrow to nonexistent shoulders and are banked up above the surrounding terrain to improve drainage. Be especially careful in icy or slippery conditions: If your car slips off the road, it will likely roll over. (Another good reason to wear your seatbelt.)

One-Lane Bridges: There are more than 30 of these on the Ring Road alone (most in the southeast), and many more on side roads. They're announced with an *Einbreið Brú* sign and an easy-to-understand picture. The car that reaches the bridge first has priority, but before dashing across, slow down and make sure the other driver has judged the situation in the same way.

Blind Summits: Signs saying *Blindhæð* warn you that you're about to crest a rise where you can't see oncoming traffic. Slow down and stay to the right. Blind summits are especially common on unsurfaced roads in the countryside.

Unsurfaced Roads: In rural areas, side roads and driveways are usually dirt or gravel, and in eastern Iceland, a few stretches of the Ring Road are still unsurfaced. The "Road info viewer" at www.road.is shows which roads are paved. Speed limits on unsurfaced roads (which can be pocked with deep potholes) are lower (80 km/hour—about 50 mph), and you'll usually want to go even slower than that. Be especially careful at the points where the pavement ends and gravel starts (marked with a *Malbik endar* sign). Driving on a good gravel road in a two-wheel-drive car is nothing to be afraid of, but don't try to force your car down a muddy road that's a mess of puddles and ruts.

Marshy Shoulders and Fields: In the spring, poorly drained, unpaved surfaces can be marshy. If visiting isolated sites in the countryside, think twice about where you park to avoid getting stuck.

Off-Road Driving: This is strictly forbidden and looked on very unfavorably. You can help protect Iceland's natural beauty and ecosystem by staying on official roads.

Sandstorms *(sandfok):* If you stay in the southwestern part of the country, there's very little danger of sand damage to your car, because there are no extensive sandy areas near roads. There are, however, several places along the Ring Road where blowing sand is common in windy weather: along the South Coast where the road crosses the Markárfljót river; between Vík and Skaftafell; and in northeast Iceland, between Mývatn and Egilsstaðir. Avoid these stretches when high winds are forecast.

Sheep: In early summer, stay alert for free-ranging sheep on countryside roads. Typically, a ewe and her lambs will be on opposite sides of a road, and as a car approaches, the lambs will run to their mother for safety. If you hit a sheep, you are liable for damage to both your car and the sheep. If you see sheep ahead, slow to a crawl, stop if needed, and wait for them to regroup before slowly continuing on.

Photo Stops: Many roads have no shoulders and few pullouts, so it's tempting to stop in the middle of a deserted road to take a photo. Even if it means missing a great shot, find a spot where you can pull over safely. The mouth of a farm driveway often works.

Other Drivers: Driver education standards in Iceland are lower than in other European countries, and aggressive driving and speeding is common. In addition, the many tourists on the road are sometimes inexperienced drivers or unfamiliar with local conditions; some come from countries where you can get a driver's license without any real-life driving experience. Drive defensively and watch out for distracted or confused motorists.

Winter Driving: I don't recommend driving outside Reykjavík and the airport area at all during the winter months (roughly Nov-March). In Reykjavík, winter snowfall tends to be fairly light, and when there is a storm, city streets are cleared fairly well. The road to the airport is also usually kept in decent shape.

Outside the city, though, roads can be a sheet of ice for weeks at a time, especially at higher elevations (for example, on parts of the popular Golden Circle daytrip from Reykjavík). In winter, Icelanders only navigate these roads with studded tires and all-wheel-drive cars, and that's what you should do, too, if you absolutely must drive in the countryside at this time of year.

FLIGHTS

The best comparison search engine for both international and intra-European flights is Kayak.com. An alternative is Google Flights, which has an easy-to-use system to track prices. For inexpensive flights within Europe, try Skyscanner.com.

To Iceland

International visitors to Iceland almost always arrive at **Keflavík Airport** (see page 149).

Flying from North America to Iceland: Start looking for international flights about four to six months before your trip, especially for peak-season travel. Off-season tickets can usually be purchased a month or so in advance. US routes are dominated by Icelandair, but you should also look into the Iceland-based low-cost carrier Wow Air (www.wowair.com). Delta also has a few flights to Keflavík.

Stopovers: Many people visit Iceland as a stopover on their way between North America and Europe. Icelandair's hub-and-spoke operation makes this easy, and the extra cost is negligible (usually just a few dollars in extra taxes).

Plan your visit to minimize jet lag: Visiting Iceland on the way from the US is doable, but tends to make jet lag tougher (landing in Iceland early in the morning after an overnight flight from the US, staying two or three days, then continuing on to mainland Europe on an early-morning flight). For a more relaxed stopover, visit Iceland on your way back (leave Europe on an afternoon flight to Iceland, stay for a few days, then continue to the US on a late-morning or afternoon flight).

Flying from Mainland Europe to Iceland: Especially in summer, Iceland is served by a huge range of flights from many different companies. These include legacy airlines, especially Icelandair, but also SAS, Lufthansa, and British Airways, as well as discount airlines such as Wow Air, Wizz Air, EasyJet, and Norwegian.

Within Iceland

Icelanders fly frequently within the country. Domestic flights are hassle-free (with no security checkpoints), reasonably priced (by Icelandic standards), and a good option for tourists—especially in winter (when roads are icy) or to make the best use of limited time. Purchased in advance, the 45-minute flight from Reykjavík to Akureyri is not that much more expensive than the much-longer bus ride. The 20-minute flight from Reykjavík to the Westman Islands is a great time-saver. Iceland is very scenic from the air on a clear day. But note that in very windy weather, flights are delayed or cancelled.

PRACTICALITIES

Most internal flights leave from the "domestic" **Reykjavík City Airport** (code: RKV), just south of downtown (for details, see page 154).

Air Iceland Connect (tel. 570-3000, www.airicelandconnect. com) serves Akureyri, as well as Egilsstaðir, Ísafjörður, some smaller towns, and the Faroe Islands and Greenland. Their terminal is on the west side of the domestic airport (city bus #15, Reykjavíkurflugvöllur stop).

Eagle Air (tel. 562-2640, www.eagleair.is) uses smaller planes and serves the Westman Islands, Höfn, and Húsavík. Their terminal is on the east side of the domestic airport, next to Icelandair's Hotel Natura (city bus #5, Nauthólsvegur stop).

From Keflavík Airport, there is also sparse service to Akureyri, restricted to passengers connecting to or from an international flight (at most one flight a day).

TO ICELAND BY SEA

Smyril Line's **Norröna car ferry** sails between Hirtshals in Denmark and Seyðisfjörður in eastern Iceland once a week (tel. +298 345 900, www.smyrilline.com), stopping at its home port of Tórshavn in the Faroe Islands en route. The trip takes from 48 to 60 hours, depending on the season. In summer you can add a two- to three-day stopover in the Faroe Islands. Consider this approach: Fly from the US to Europe, sail as a one-way foot passenger on the ferry from Denmark to Iceland, rent a car for your Iceland explorations (either in Seyðisfjörður or after flying or going by bus to Reykjavík), then fly home from Keflavík (this works fine in reverse, too).

Several **cruise lines** visit Iceland, often as part of North Atlantic sailings that include European and North American ports as well as Greenland, Svalbard, or the Faroe Islands—a scenic approach that links Iceland to other northern lands that share its maritime history.

Resources from Rick Steves

Begin your trip at www.ricksteves.com: My mobile-friendly **website** is *the* place to explore Europe. You'll find thousands of fun articles, videos, photos, and radio interviews organized by country; a wealth of money-saving tips for planning your dream trip; monthly travel news dispatches; a video library of my travel talks; my travel blog; and my latest guidebook updates (www.ricksteves. com/update).

Our **Travel Forum** is an immense yet well-groomed collection of message boards where our travel-savvy community answers questions and shares their personal travel experiences—and our well-traveled staff chimes in when they can be helpful (www.ricksteves.com/forums).

Our online **Travel Store** offers travel bags and accessories that I've designed specifically to help you travel smarter and lighter. These include my popular carry-on bags (which I live out of four months a year), money belts, totes, toiletries kits, adapters, other accessories, and a wide selection of guidebooks and planning maps (www.ricksteves.com/shop).

Choosing the right **rail pass** for your trip—amid hundreds of options—can drive you nutty. Our website will help you find the perfect fit for your itinerary and your budget: We offer easy, one-stop shopping for rail passes, seat reservations, and point-to-point tickets (www.ricksteves.com/rail).

Small Group Tours: Want to travel with greater efficiency and less stress? We offer more than 40 itineraries and have 900 departures annually reaching the best destinations in Europe. You'll enjoy great guides, a fun bunch of travel partners (with small groups of 24 to 28 travelers), and plenty of room to spread out in a big, comfy bus when touring between towns. You'll find European adventures to fit every vacation length. For all the details, and to get our Tour Catalog, visit www.ricksteves.com or call us at 425/608-4217.

Books: *Rick Steves Iceland* is one of many books in my series on European travel, which includes country guidebooks, city guidebooks (Rome, Florence, Paris, London, etc.), Snapshot guidebooks (excerpted chapters from my country guides), Pocket guidebooks (full-color little books on big cities), "Best Of" guidebooks (condensed country guides in a full-color, easy-to-scan format), and my budget-travel skills handbook, *Rick Steves Europe Through the Back Door*. Most of my titles are available as ebooks.

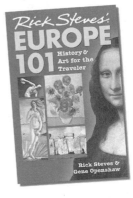

My phrase books—for German, French, Italian, Portuguese, and Spanish—are practical and budget-oriented. My other books include *Europe 101* (a crash course on art and history designed for travelers), *Mediterranean Cruise Ports* and *Northern European Cruise Ports* (how to make the most of your time in port), and *Travel as a Political Act* (a travelogue sprinkled with tips for bringing home a global perspective). A more complete list of my titles appears near the end of this book.

TV Shows: My public television series, *Rick Steves' Europe*, covers Europe from top to bottom with over 100 half-hour episodes, and we're working on new shows every year. To watch full episodes online for free, see www.ricksteves.com/tv.

Travel Talks on Video: You can raise your travel I.Q. with video versions of our popular classes, including talks on travel skills, packing smart, cruising, tech for travelers, European art for travelers, travel as a political act, and individual talks covering most European countries. See www.ricksteves.com/travel-talks.

Radio: My weekly public radio show, *Travel with Rick Steves*, features interviews with travel experts from around the world. It airs on 400 public radio stations across the US, and you can also listen to it as a podcast on iTunes, iHeartRadio, Stitcher, Tune In, and other platforms. A complete archive of programs (over 400 in all) is available at www.ricksteves.com/radio.

Audio: I've also produced dozens of free, self-guided audio tours of sights in Europe. My audio tours and other audio content are organized into handy geographic playlists and available for free through my **Rick Steves Audio Europe app.** You can download the app via Apple's App Store, Google Play, or Amazon's Appstore (or see www.ricksteves.com/audioeurope.

APPENDIX

Useful Contacts

Emergencies
Police, Fire, and Ambulance: Tel. 112 (Europe-wide in English)

Embassies
US Embassy in Reykjavík: By appointment only Mon-Fri 8:00-17:00, tel. 595-2200, after-hours line for emergencies only—595-2248, Laufásvegur 21, (may move to Engjateigur 7 by the time you visit) http://is.usembassy.gov.
Canadian Embassy in Reykjavík: Mon-Fri 9:00-12:00 and by appointment, Túngata 14, tel. 575-6500, www.canadainternational. gc.ca/iceland-islande.

Holidays and Festivals

This list includes selected festivals plus national holidays observed in Iceland. Many sights and banks close on national holidays—keep this in mind when planning your itinerary. Before planning a trip around a festival, verify the dates with the festival website, the national tourist office (www.visiticeland.com), or my "Upcoming Holidays and Festivals in Iceland" web page (www.ricksteves.com/europe/iceland/festivals).

Jan 1	New Year's Day
Jan 6	13th Day of Christmas (bonfires, fireworks)
Mid-Jan-mid-Feb	Þorri (Old Norse midwinter celebration)
Early-mid-Feb	Carnival Week: starts Feb 13 in 2018; Feb 4 in 2019 (special foods, costumes)
April	Easter: April 1, 2018; April 21, 2019
April	Aldrei Fór Ég Suður music festival in Ísafjörður, Westfjords (Easter weekend, www.aldrei.is)
Late April	Old Norse first day of summer: April 19, 2018; April 25, 2019 (parades, sports)
May 1	Labor Day
May	Ascension Day: May 10, 2018; May 30, 2019
May-June	Whitsunday and Whit Monday: May 20-21, 2018; June 9-10, 2019
Early June	Seaman's Day, Reykjavík (first Sun, www.hatidhafsins.is)
June 17	Icelandic National Day (parades, theater)
Mid-June	Viking Festival in Hafnarfjörður (www.fjorukrain.is)
Early July	Goslok festival in Vestmannaeyjar (commemorates end of 1973 volcanic eruption)
Early July	Icelandic horse convention (even years only, www.landsmot.is)
Early Aug	Commerce Day, a.k.a. "Shop Workers' Day Off" (first Mon)
Early Aug	Þjóðhátíð National Festival in Herjólfsdalur, Westman Islands (first weekend; fireworks, bonfires, and singing; www.dalurinn.is)
Late Aug	Culture Night in Reykjavík (free admission to museums; www.menningarnott.is)
Sept	Réttir—sheep roundups in the countryside
Late Sept-early Nov	Reykjavík International Film Festival (www.riff.is)
Oct 8	Lighting of Imagine Peace Tower, Viðey Island, Reykjavík (www.imaginepeacetower.com)
Late-Oct-early Nov	Iceland Airwaves music festival, Reykjavík (www.icelandairwaves.is)

Dec 23	St. Þorlákur's Day (Christmas shopping, evening strolling, traditional meals of skate)
Dec 25	Christmas
Dec 31	New Year's Eve (bonfires and fireworks)

Books and Films

To learn more about Iceland past and present, check out a few of these books and films. Some of these books may be difficult to access outside Iceland, though you may find used copies at online retailers.

Nonfiction

Bringing Down the Banking System (Guðrún Johnsen, 2013). A finance scholar and banking regulator explains Iceland's colossal 2008 bank failure in layman's terms.

Does Anyone Actually Eat This? (Nanna Rögnvaldardóttir, 2014). Iceland's best-known food writer reviews the country's food traditions.

The History of Iceland (Gunnar Karlsson, 2000). This well-written general history of the country also comes in a condensed version, called *A Brief History of Iceland.*

The Indian (Jón Gnarr, 2015). Iceland's best-known comic actor—and recent mayor of Reykjavík—recalls his childhood, during which he was bullied and sent to a boarding school. Two sequels, *The Outlaw* and *The Pirate,* carry on his story.

Lake Mývatn: People and Places (Björg Árnadóttir, 2015). This is a friendly introduction to the popular Lake Mývatn region.

The Little Book of the Icelanders (Alda Sigmundsdóttir, 2012). An Icelander returns home after living in America and explains Icelandic culture with a critical and sometimes cynical eye.

Names for the Sea (Sarah Moss, 2013). A British academic writes about the year she spent in Iceland with her husband and kids.

The Ring of Seasons (Terry Lacy, 2000). An American and long-term Iceland resident describes an idealized year in the life of an Icelandic family.

Ripples from Iceland (Amalia Líndal, 1962). In 1949, a young woman from Boston marries an Icelandic student, moves to Reykjavík, and starts a family.

Viking Age Iceland (Jesse Byock, 2001). Byock provides a good introduction to the society and politics of Iceland in its earliest years, from settlement through the 13th century.

Wasteland with Words: A Social History of Iceland (Sigurður Gylfi Magnússon, 2010). This book focuses on the period from 1870 to 1940, when Iceland grew from a shivering, impov-

APPENDIX

erished colony to a land on the brink of prosperity and independence.

The Windows of Brimnes (Bill Holm, 2007). Minnesotan writer and poet Bill Holm, who spent several summers in a cottage in Skagafjörður near the home of his ancestors, reflects on the differences between Iceland and the US.

Fiction

Angels of the Universe (Einar Már Guðmundsson, 1993). An intelligent young man's descent into mental illness in 1960s Reykjavík is the focus of this gripping, award-winning novel.

The Blue Fox (Sjón, 2003). In this short, poetically written fable a 19th-century Lutheran pastor hunts an arctic fox.

Burial Rites (Hannah Kent, 2013). Kent writes a fictionalized account of the final months of Agnes Magnúsdóttir, whose 1830 beheading (for taking part in a murder) was the last time the death penalty was used in Iceland.

Frozen Assets (Quentin Bates, 2011). This book is one in a series of gripping crime novels starring Gunnhildur "Gunna" Gísladóttir—a shrewd policewoman who, in the course of a murder investigation, uncovers corruption at the highest levels.

Independent People (Halldór Laxness, 1934). Nobel Prize-winning Laxness' best novel tells the story of Bjartur, a farm laborer, who jumps at the rare chance to have his own farm. In his single-minded quest to take charge of his destiny, he destroys everyone around him.

Jar City (Arnaldur Indriðason, 2005). An older man is murdered in a basement apartment in downtown Reykjavík. A troubled police detective follows a trail of clues back many years, and ends up solving a medical mystery. *Silence of the Grave,* another crime novel by the same author, is also good.

The Sagas of the Icelanders (edited by Robert Kellogg, 2001). These classic stories, still fresh after 800 years, are set appealingly amidst the Icelandic landscape.

Someone to Watch Over Me (Yrsa Sigurðardóttir, 2013). Police detective Thora Guðmundsdóttir tries to prove that a young man with Down syndrome was innocent of arson. This book is part of another popular series of crime novels.

Film and TV

These films and shows are generally available for streaming in the US.

101 Reykjavík (2000). This comedy is set in downtown Reykjavík in the 1990s—before tourism took over—when it was still bohemian. Hlynur lives with his mother and is having problems committing to his girlfriend. He winds up involved with Lola, who is his mother's friend—in fact, more than her friend.

Devil's Island (1996). This film highlights the adventures of a lower-class Reykjavík family living in abandoned WWII barracks. It includes gangs, an Elvis soundtrack, and a main character aptly named Baddi.

Life in a Fishbowl (2014; Icelandic title: *Vonarstræti*). Three lives intersect during Iceland's financial collapse: an alcoholic writer, a young unmarried mother who has turned to prostitution, and a morally compromised banking executive.

No Such Thing (2001). This bizarre American-Icelandic indie film, with its *Beauty and the Beast* theme, stars Sarah Polley as a journalist who tries to tame the beast—who incidentally killed her fiancé.

Nói the Albino (2003). Nói is a teenage boy in the remote West-fjords who hates school and lives with his grandmother and alcoholic father. He falls for a girl at the local gas station in this portrait of small-town adolescence.

The Seagull's Laughter (2001). In the 1950s, shapely Freyja returns to her hometown in Iceland from America, where she has been living with her soldier husband, and stirs up all kinds of trouble.

Trapped (2016; Icelandic title: *Ófærð*). As the car ferry from the Faroe Islands arrives one day, a body is found floating in the fjord. The pass is snowed in, so none of the passengers can leave town, and investigators from Reykjavík can't arrive. Whodunit?

The remaining films may be harder to find (check www. icelandiccinema.com).

Angels of the Universe (2000). Páll descends into mental illness after being dumped by his girlfriend. The movie (based on Einar Már Guðmundsson's book) is a masterpiece but also tragic.

Children of Nature (1991). A man and a woman, once childhood friends, meet again when they move into the same senior citizens home. They decide to escape together and go on a car trip into the countryside.

The Icelandic Dream (2000). Tóti tries everything he can to get ahead, but keeps messing up. This dark, realist, somewhat-amateurish comedy explores class differences in Reykjavík and the effects of the former American military presence.

Mr. Bjarnfreðarson (2009). This black comedy stars Jón Gnarr as a sadistic misfit, damaged for life by his mother's left-wing activism and trying to regroup after serving prison time for an "accidental" murder.

Remote Control (1992; Icelandic title: *Sódóma Reykjavík*). Axel goes in search of his mother's lost TV remote and gets mixed up with a gang of mobsters. This low-budget comedy with a hard-rock soundtrack has been called Iceland's equivalent of *The Big Lebowski*.

When the Raven Flies (1984). An Irish boy whose parents are killed by Vikings travels to Iceland to take revenge.

Conversions and Climate

NUMBERS AND STUMBLERS

- Europeans write a few of their numbers differently than we do. 1 = 1, 4 = 4, 7 = 7.
- In Europe, dates appear as day/month/year, so Christmas 2019 is 25/12/19.
- Commas are decimal points and decimals commas. A dollar and a half is $1,50, one thousand is 1.000, and there are 5.280 feet in a mile.
- When counting with fingers, start with your thumb. If you hold up your first finger to request one item, you'll probably get two.
- On escalators and moving sidewalks, Europeans keep the left "lane" open for passing. Keep to the right.

METRIC CONVERSIONS

A **kilogram** equals 1,000 grams (about 2.2 pounds). One hundred **grams** (a common unit at markets) is about a quarter-pound. One **liter** is about a quart, or almost four to a gallon.

A **kilometer** is six-tenths of a mile. To convert kilometers to miles, cut the kilometers in half and add back 10 percent of the original (120 km: 60 + 12 = 72 miles). One **meter** is 39 inches—just over a yard.

1 foot = 0.3 meter	1 square yard = 0.8 square meter
1 yard = 0.9 meter	1 square mile = 2.6 square kilometers
1 mile = 1.6 kilometers	1 ounce = 28 grams
1 centimeter = 0.4 inch	1 quart = 0.95 liter
1 meter = 39.4 inches	1 kilogram = 2.2 pounds
1 kilometer = 0.62 mile	32°F = 0°C

ICELAND'S CLIMATE

First line, average daily high; second line, average daily low; third line, average days without rain. For more detailed weather statistics for destinations in this book, check Iceland's English-language website http://en.vedur.is, and for both Iceland and the rest of the world, www.wunderground.com.

J	F	M	A	M	J	J	A	S	O	N	D

Reykjavík

35°	37°	37°	41°	47°	52°	55°	54°	49°	44°	38°	36°
27°	29°	29°	33°	39°	44°	47°	46°	41°	36°	31°	28°
10	13	12	12	14	15	15	14	11	9	11	10

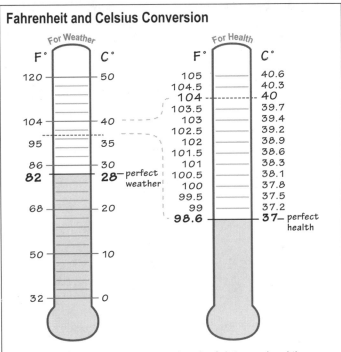

Fahrenheit and Celsius Conversion

Europe takes its temperature using the Celsius scale, while we opt for Fahrenheit. For a rough conversion from Celsius to Fahrenheit, double the number and add 30. For weather, remember that 28°C is 82°F—perfect. For health, 37°C is just right. At a launderette, 30°C is cold, 40°C is warm (usually the default setting), 60°C is hot, and 95°C is boiling. Your air-conditioner should be set at about 20°C.

APPENDIX

Pronunciation Guide for Place Names

For more help in pronouncing Icelandic words, see "The Icelandic Language" sidebar on page 402 and "Icelandic Survival Phrases" later in this chapter.

Akureyri	AH-kuh-RAY-ree
Baula (mountain)	BOY-la
Borgarfjörður (fjord)	BOR-gar-FYUR-thur
Borgarnes	BOHR-gahr-NESS
Dettifoss (waterfall)	DEH-tih-foss
Dimmuborgir (craters)	DIM-moo-BOR-geer
Djúpivogur	DYOOP-ih-VOE-ur
Dyrhólaey (promontory)	DEER-hoh-la-AY
Egilsstaðir	AY-ill-STAHTH-ear
Eldfell (volcano)	ELD-fehtl
Eyjafjallajökull (volcano)	EH-ya-FYAH-tla-YUR-kutl
Fjallsárlón (glacier lagoon)	FYATL-sour-lohn
Geysir (geyser)	GAY-sear
Glaumbær	GLOYM-bire
Gljúfrabúi (waterfall)	GLYOO-vrah-BOO-ee
Grábrók (crater)	GRAU-broke
Gullfoss (waterfall)	GUTL-foss
Hafnarfjall (mountain)	HAHP-nahr-FYAHTL
Hafnarfjörður	HAHP-nar-FYUR-thur
Heimaey	HAME-ah-AY
Höfn	HURP
Hofsós	HOFF-sose
Hólar	HOE-lar
Húsavík	HOOS-ah-VEEK
Hverfjall (crater)	HVER-fyahtl
Jökulsárlón (lagoon)	YUR-kurls-OUR-lohn
Keflavík	KEPP-la-VEEK
Kerið (crater)	KEH-rithe

Kirkjubæjarklaustur	KEERK-yoo-bay-yahr-KLOY-stur
Kleifarvatn (lake)	CLAY-vahr-VAHT
Krafla (geothermal valley)	KRAH-plah
Lagarfljót (lake)	LAH-gar-flyoht
Laugardalur	LÖY-gar-DA-lrr
Laugavegur	LÖY-ga-VEH-grr
Mjódd	MEE-ohd
Mývatn (lake and area)	MEE-vaht
Námafjall (thermal field)	NOW-mah-fyahtl
Nesjavallaleið (mountain pass)	NESS-ya-VAHT-la-laythe
Þingvellir	THING-vett-leer
Reykjadalur (thermal valley)	RAKE-yah-dah-lrr
Reykjahlíð	RAKE-ya-HLEETHE
Reykjanes	RAKE-ya-NESS
Reykjavík	RAKE-ya-VEEK
Reynisfjara (black sand beach)	RAY-nis-fyah-rah
Sauðárkrókur	SOY-thour-kroh-kur
Seljalandsfoss (waterfall)	SELL-yah-lahnds-foss
Seyðisfjörður	SAY-this-FYUR-thur
Siglufjörður	SIG-loo-FYUR-thur
Skaftafell (national park)	SKAFF-tah-fehtl
Skagafjörður	SKAH-gah-FYUR-thur
Skógafoss (waterfall)	SKOH-gah-foss
Skógar	SKOR-ar
Skútustaðir (pseudocraters)	SKOO-tu-STAH-theer
Sólheimajökull (glacier)	SOUL-HAY-ma-YUR-kutl
Þórsmörk (mountain ridge)	THORS-murk
Tröllaskagi	TREW-tlah-sky-ee
Varmahlíð	VAR-mah-HLEETHE
Vatnajökull (glacier)	VAHT-nah-YUR-kutl
Vestmannaeyjar	VEST-mah-nah-AY-ar
Víðgelmir (lava tube cave)	VEETHE-GHELL-meer

Iceland Packing Checklist

Whether you're traveling for five days or five weeks, you won't need more than this. Pack light to enjoy the sweet freedom of true mobility.

Clothing

- ☐ 5 shirts
- ☐ 2 pairs pants
- ☐ 5 pairs underwear & socks
- ☐ Waterproof shoes
- ☐ Sweater or warm layer
- ☐ Rainproof/windproof jacket with hood
- ☐ Fleece hat, gloves
- ☐ Swimsuit & swim accessories (eyeglass strap, bathing cap, or goggles; small towel)
- ☐ Sleepwear/loungewear

Money

- ☐ Debit card(s)
- ☐ Credit card(s)
- ☐ Hard cash ($100-200 in US dollars)
- ☐ Money belt

Documents

- ☐ Passport
- ☐ Tickets & confirmations: flights, hotels, car rental
- ☐ Driver's license
- ☐ Student ID, hostel card, etc.
- ☐ Photocopies of important documents
- ☐ Insurance details
- ☐ Guidebooks & maps
- ☐ Notepad & pen
- ☐ Journal

Toiletries Kit

- ☐ Basics: soap, shampoo, toothbrush, toothpaste, floss, deodorant, sunscreen, brush/comb, etc.
- ☐ Medicines & vitamins
- ☐ First-aid kit

- ☐ Glasses/contacts
- ☐ Sunglasses (esp. if driving)
- ☐ Sewing kit
- ☐ Packet of tissues (for WC)
- ☐ Eye mask (for sleeping)
- ☐ Earplugs

Electronics

- ☐ Mobile phone
- ☐ Camera & related gear
- ☐ Tablet/ebook reader
- ☐ Headphones
- ☐ Chargers & batteries
- ☐ Phone car charger & mount (or GPS device)
- ☐ Plug adapters

Miscellaneous

- ☐ Daypack
- ☐ Sealable plastic baggies
- ☐ Laundry supplies: soap, laundry bag, clothesline
- ☐ Small umbrella
- ☐ Travel alarm/watch

Optional Extras

- ☐ Second pair of shoes
- ☐ Travel hairdryer
- ☐ Picnic supplies
- ☐ Water bottle
- ☐ Fold-up tote bag
- ☐ Small flashlight
- ☐ Mini binoculars
- ☐ Inflatable pillow/neck rest
- ☐ Tiny lock
- ☐ Insect head net (if visiting Mývatn area)
- ☐ Strap-on ice cleats (winter only)

Icelandic Survival Phrases

Icelandic has some unique letters, most notably ð (the voiced "th" sound in "breathe," represented by "th") and Þ (the unvoiced "th" sound in "breath," also represented by "th"). The letter á sounds like "ow" (rhymes with "now"). The long i in "light" is represented by "ī."

English	Icelandic	Pronunciation
Hello (formal)	Góðan daginn	GOH-thahn DĪ-ihn
Hi / Bye (informal)	Hæ / Bæ	Hī / bī (as in English)
Do you speak English?.	Talarðu ensku?	TAHL-ar-thoo EHN-skoo?
Yes. / No.	Já / Nei.	yow / nay
I (don't) understand.	Ég skil (ekki).	yehkh skeel (EH-kee)
Please. / Thank you.	Vinsamlegast. / Takk.	VIN-sahm-lay-gahst / tahk
Excuse me.	Fyrirgefðu.	FIH-ree-GEHV-thoo
No problem.	Ekkert mál.	EHK-kert mowl
Super	Fínt	feent
OK	Allt í lagi	ahlt ee LAH-yee
Goodbye (more formal)	Bless	bless
one / two	einn / tveir	AY-teh / tvayr
three / four	þrír / fjórir	three-r / FYOH-rir
five / six	fimm / sex	fim / sex
seven / eight	sjö / átta	syur / OWT-tah
nine / ten	níu / tíu	NEE-oo / TEE-oo
hundred	hundrað	HOON-drahth
thousand	þúsund	THOO-sund
How much is it?	Hvað kostar þetta?	kvahth KOHS-tar THEHT-tah?
Is it free?	Er þetta ókeypis?	ayr THEHT-tah OH-kay-pis?
Is it included?	Er þetta innifalið?	ayr THEHT-tah EEN-nee-fah-lith?
(Icelandic) crowns	(íslenskar) krónur	(EE-slehn-skar) KROH-nur
Where is...?	Hvar er...?	kvar ayr...?
...the toilet	....klósettið	...KLOH-seht-tith
men	karlar	KAHT-lar
women	konur	KOH-noor
left / right	vinstri / hægri	VIN-stree / HĪ-grih
straight	beint	baynt
opening hours	opnunartími	OHP-noo-nar-tee-mih
At what time?	Hvenær?	KVER-nī
Just a moment.	Augnablik.	OOG-nah-bleek
now / soon / later	núna / bráðum / seinna	NOO-nah / BROW-thoom / SAYT-nah
today / tomorrow	í dag / á morgun	ee dahkh / ow MOR-goon
Cheers!	skál	skahl

INDEX

INDEX

MAP INDEX

Our website enhances this book and turns

Explore Europe

At ricksteves.com you can browse through thousands of articles, videos, photos and radio interviews, plus find a wealth of money-saving travel tips for planning your dream trip. And with our mobile-friendly website, you can easily access all this great travel information anywhere you go.

TV Shows

Preview the places you'll visit by watching entire half-hour episodes of Rick Steves' Europe (choose from all 100 shows) on-demand, for free.

your travel dreams into affordable reality

Radio Interviews

Enjoy ready access to Rick's vast library of radio interviews covering travel

tips and cultural insights that relate specifically to your Europe travel plans.

Travel Forums

Learn, ask, share! Our online community of savvy travelers is a great resource

for first-time travelers to Europe, as well as seasoned pros. You'll find forums on each country, plus travel tips and restaurant/hotel reviews. You can even ask one of our well-traveled staff to chime in with an opinion.

Travel News

Subscribe to our free Travel News e-newsletter, and get monthly updates from Rick on what's happening in Europe.

Audio Europe™

Pack Light and Right

Gear up for your next adventure at ricksteves.com

Light Luggage

Pack light and right with Rick Steves' affordable, custom-designed rolling carry-on bags, backpacks, day packs and shoulder bags.

Accessories

From packing cubes to moneybelts and beyond, Rick has personally selected the travel goodies that will help your trip go smoother.

Experience maximum Europe

Save time and energy

This guidebook is your independent-travel toolkit. But for all it delivers, it's still up to you to devote the time and energy it takes to manage the preparation and logistics that are essential for a happy trip. If that's a hassle, there's a solution.

Rick Steves Tours

A Rick Steves tour takes you to Europe's most interesting places with great

great tours, too!

with minimum stress

guides and small groups of 28 or less. We follow Rick's favorite itineraries, ride in comfy buses, stay in family-run hotels, and bring you intimately close to the Europe you've traveled so far to see. Most importantly, we take away the logistical headaches so you can focus on the fun.

travelers—nearly half of them repeat customers—along with us on four dozen different itineraries, from Ireland to Italy to Athens. Is a Rick Steves tour the right fit for your travel dreams? Find out at ricksteves.com, where you can also request Rick's latest tour catalog. Europe is best experienced with happy travel partners. We hope you can join us.

Join the fun

This year we'll take thousands of free-spirited

See our itineraries at ricksteves.com

A Guide for Every Trip

BEST OF GUIDES

Full color easy-to-scan format, focusing on Europe's most popular destinations and sights.

Best of England
Best of Europe
Best of France
Best of Germany
Best of Ireland
Best of Italy
Best of Spain

COMPREHENSIVE GUIDES

City, country, and regional guides with detailed coverage for a multi-week trip exploring the most iconic sights and venturing off the beaten track.

Amsterdam & the Netherlands
Barcelona
Belgium: Bruges, Brussels,
    Antwerp & Ghent
Berlin
Budapest
Croatia & Slovenia
Eastern Europe
England
Florence & Tuscany
France
Germany
Great Britain
Greece: Athens & the Peloponnese
Iceland
Ireland
Istanbul
Italy
London
Paris
Portugal
Prague & the Czech Republic
Provence & the French Riviera
Rome
Scandinavia
Scotland
Spain
Switzerland
Venice
Vienna, Salzburg & Tirol

Rick Steves guidebooks are published by Avalon Travel, an imprint of Perseus Books, a Hachette Book Group company.

POCKET GUIDES

Compact, full color city guides with the essentials for shorter trips.

Amsterdam
Athens
Barcelona
Florence
Italy's Cinque Terre
London
Munich & Salzburg
Paris
Prague
Rome
Venice
Vienna

SNAPSHOT GUIDES

Focused single-destination coverage.

Basque Country: Spain & France
Copenhagen & the Best of Denmark
Dublin
Dubrovnik
Edinburgh
Hill Towns of Central Italy
Krakow, Warsaw & Gdansk
Lisbon
Loire Valley
Madrid & Toledo
Milan & the Italian Lakes District
Naples & the Amalfi Coast
Normandy
Northern Ireland
Norway
Reykjavík
Sevilla, Granada & Southern Spain
St. Petersburg, Helsinki & Tallinn
Stockholm

CRUISE PORTS GUIDES

Reference for cruise ports of call.

Mediterranean Cruise Ports
Northern European Cruise Ports

Complete your library with...

TRAVEL SKILLS & CULTURE

Study up on travel skills and gain insight on history and culture.

Europe 101
Europe Through the Back Door
European Christmas
European Easter
European Festivals
Postcards from Europe
Travel as a Political Act

PHRASE BOOKS & DICTIONARIES

French
French, Italian & German
German
Italian
Portuguese
Spanish

PLANNING MAPS

Britain, Ireland & London
Europe
France & Paris
Germany, Austria & Switzerland
Ireland
Italy
Spain & Portugal

Acknowledgments

The authors wish to say *"Takk!"* to the following people for their travel savvy and expertise, which helped shape this first edition of *Rick Steves Iceland:* Angela Walk, Kevin Williams, Dave Hoerlein, Shawna Hewitt, Jens Ruminy, Kendra Willson, Austin Yuill, and Yorick Harker.

Avalon Travel
Hachette Book Group
1700 Fourth Street
Berkeley, CA 94710

Text © 2018 by Rick Steves' Europe, Inc. All rights reserved.
Maps © 2018 by Rick Steves' Europe, Inc. All rights reserved.

Printed in Canada by Friesens.
Second printing June 2018.

ISBN 978-1-63121-813-2

For the latest on Rick's lectures, guidebooks, tours, public television series, and public radio show, contact Rick Steves' Europe, 130 Fourth Avenue North, Edmonds, WA 98020, 425/771-8303, www.ricksteves.com, rick@ricksteves.com.

Rick Steves' Europe
Managing Editor: Jennifer Madison Davis
Special Publications Manager: Risa Laib
Assistant Managing Editor: Cathy Lu
Editors: Glenn Eriksen, Tom Griffin, Katherine Gustafson, Suzanne Kotz, Rosie Leutzinger, Carrie Shepherd
Editorial & Production Assistant: Jessica Shaw
Editorial Intern: Claire Connor
Graphic Content Director: Sandra Hundacker
Maps & Graphics: David C. Hoerlein, Lauren Mills, Mary Rostad

Avalon Travel
Senior Editor and Series Manager: Madhu Prasher
Editor: Jamie Andrade
Associate Editor: Sierra Machado
Copy Editor: Maggie Ryan
Proofreader: Kelly Lydick
Indexer: Stephen Callahan
Production & Typesetting: Jane Musser, Kit Anderson, Lisi Baldwin, Rue Flaherty
Cover Design: Kimberly Glyder Design
Maps & Graphics: Kat Bennett, Mike Morgenfeld

Photo Credits
Front Cover: ARTIC IMAGES/Alamy Stock
Title Page: Glacier lagoon at Jökulsárlón © Sumit Birla
Additional Photography: Sumit Birla, Paul Daniels, Trish Feaster, Cameron Hewitt, David C. Hoerlein, Sandra Hundacker, Rosie Leutzinger, Lauren Mills, Carrie Shepherd, Rick Steves, Ian Watson, Kevin Williams. Photos are used by permission and are the property of the original copyright owners.

Sun Voyager sculpture (pp. 2, 100): © Jón Gunnar Árnason/Myndstef

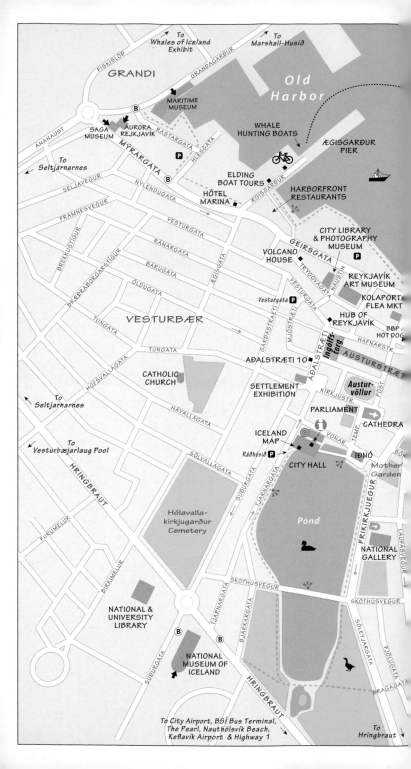

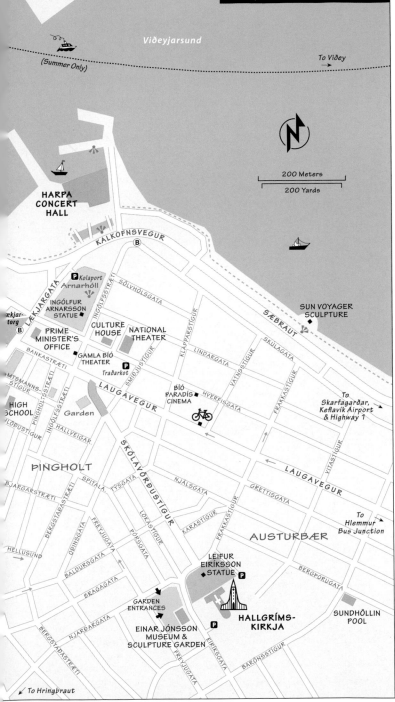

Reykjavík Center

Viðeyjarsund

(Summer Only)

To Viðey →

200 Meters

200 Yards

HARPA CONCERT HALL

KALKOFNSVEGUR

Kolaport

Arnarhóll

INGÓLFSSTRÆTI

SÖLVHÓLSGATA

SUN VOYAGER SCULPTURE

SÆBRAUT

INGÓLFUR ARNARSSON STATUE

Lækjar-torg

PRIME MINISTER'S OFFICE

CULTURE HOUSE

NATIONAL THEATER

KLAPPARSTÍGUR

LINDARGATA

SKÚLAGATA

BANKASTRÆTI

GAMLA BÍÓ THEATER

SMIÐJUSTÍGUR

Traðarkot

VATNSSTÍGUR

FRAKKASTÍGUR

AMTMANNS-STÍGUR

LAUGAVEGUR

BÍÓ PARADÍS CINEMA

HVERFISGATA

To Skarfagarðar, Keflavík Airport & Highway 1

HIGH SCHOOL

INGÓLFSSTRÆTI

PÍNGHOLTSSTRÆTI

HALLVEIGAR

Garden

ÞÓÐUSTÍGUR

SKÓLAVÖRÐUSTÍGUR

LAUGAVEGUR

ÞINGHOLT

SPITALA

TÝSGATA

NJÁLSGATA

GRETTISGATA

VITASTÍGUR

BJARGARSTRÆTI

BERGSTAÐASTRÆTI

ÓÐINSGATA

FREYJUGATA

LOKASTÍGUR

ÞÓRSGATA

KÁRASTÍGUR

FRAKKASTÍGUR

AUSTURBÆR

To Hlemmur Bus Junction

HELLUSUND

BALDURSGATA

BRAGAGATA

LEIFUR EIRÍKSSON STATUE

BERGÞÓRUGATA

NJARÐARGATA

BERGSTAÐASTRÆTI

GARDEN ENTRANCES

EINAR JÓNSSON MUSEUM & SCULPTURE GARDEN

EIRÍKSGATA

FREYJUGATA

HALLGRÍMS-KIRKJA

BARÓNSSTÍGUR

SUNDHÖLLIN POOL

To Hringbraut

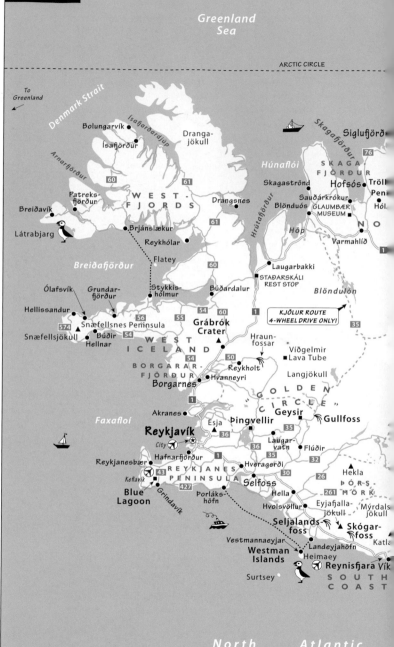

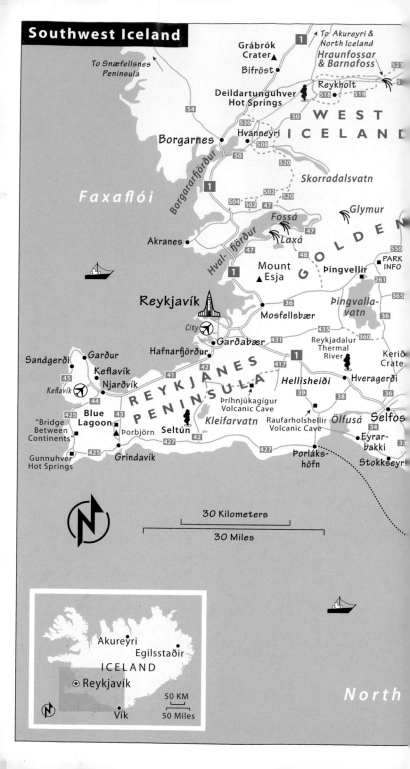

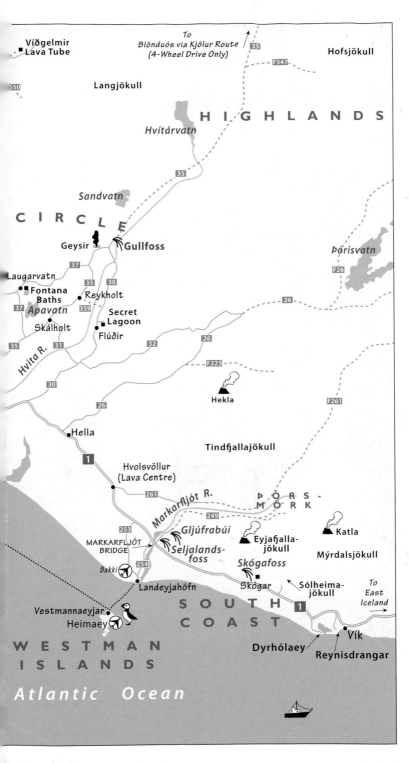

Víðgelmir
Lava Tube

To
Blönduós via Kjölur Route
(4-Wheel Drive Only)

Hofsjökull

Langjökull

HIGHLANDS

Hvítárvatn

Sandvatn

CIRCLE

Þórisvatn

Geysir · Gullfoss

Laugarvatn

Fontana
Baths

Apavatn

Reykholt

Secret
Lagoon

Skálholt

Flúðir

Hvíta R.

Hekla

Hella

Tindfjallajökull

Hvolsvöllur
(Lava Centre)

Markarfljót R.

ÞÓRS-
MÖRK

Katla

Gljúfrabúi

Eyjafjalla-
jökull

Mýrdalsjökull

MARKARFLJÓT
BRIDGE

Seljalands-
foss

Skógafoss

Bakki

Skógar

Sólheima-
jökull

To
East
Iceland

Landeyjahöfn

SOUTH

Vestmannaeyjar
Heimaey

COAST

Dyrhólaey

Vík

Reynisdrangar

WESTMAN

ISLANDS

Atlantic Ocean

Let's Keep on Travelin'

Your trip doesn't need to end.

Follow Rick on social media!